7/12 Wells

EARLY PRAISE FOR
ABBEY ROAD TO ZIGGY STARDUST

"Ken Scott's story takes you behind-the-scenes of legendary recording sessions. Unlike most hit producers/engineers, his career spans many decades, and the albums he recorded are often considered the artists' greatest work. Throughout the book, several of these artists chime in, adding perspective and credibility rarely found in autobiographies. A great read for music fans and studio types."
—**BRIAN KEHEW AND KEVIN RYAN**
authors of *Recording the Beatles*

"Fans will love this book, as I did, because of the never-before-told anecdotes while engineers will appreciate that Ken revealed some of his technological techniques. Simply, Abbey Road to Ziggy Stardust *is wonderful!"*
—**DEBBIE ROBINS, M.A.,**
producer of the film *Calendar Girl* and best-selling author of *Where Peace Lives*

"Ken Scott, fires on all cylinders with his new book Abbey Road to Ziggy Stardust. *It is an instant classic that felt like a period at the end of an incredible sentence."*
—**JW NAJARIAN,**
founder Metta Media Group & *On Purpose* magazine

"Scott's wonderful and revealing stories and anecdotes answer many questions which this *reader has often pondered, such as who actually played drums on 'Back in the USSR?' when Ringo took a sabbatical? Why the weird piano and phone ringing at the end of Bowie's 'Life on Mars?' Those and many wonderful insights litter the book, and I like the idea of listing the equipment and set-up details for the artists Scott worked with for those 'technos' for whom such details are of interest. I'm grateful to have been given the opportunity to read* Abbey Road to Ziggy Stardust—*this book has quenched some of my thirst for knowledge of the world of music and is fully recommended"*
—**PETE DICKS,**
host of Europe's longest running Beatles-themed show, *Beatles and Beyond*

ABBEY ROAD TO ZIGGY STARDUST

ABBEY ROAD NW 8 TO ZIGGY STARDUST W1

Off the Record with The Beatles, Bowie, Elton & So Much More

KEN SCOTT
AND BOBBY OWSINSKI

 Alfred Music Publishing
LEARN · TEACH · PLAY
LOS ANGELES

Contents

Acknowledgments

So many people have made this book a reality that it's hard to know where to begin to thank them all. I suppose at the beginning...

Mum and Dad for their belief and support.

Malcolm Addey, Norman Smith, Peter Bown, Stuart Eltham, Chris Parker, Neville Boyling, and Bob Gooch, without whose tutelage I wouldn't have become whatever it is I've become.

Ken Townsend, Dave Harries, Brian Gibson, Keith Slaughter, and all the other "amp room" guys who were always there to cover my rear end.

John, Paul, George, and Ringo for putting up with me.

George Martin, Gus Dudgeon, Tony Visconti, Ian Samwell, and all the other producers I worked alongside who taught me so much about the second part of my career.

Barry and Norman Sheffield for taking a relatively easy bet.

The Trident family. The whole was much greater than the sum of its parts. Well, maybe except for the Bechstein.

There are so many artists I am thankful to that if I began to list them all it would double the size of this book. I do, however, have to make special mention of Mr. Jones—David Bowie—for his instincts.

All of the studio owners, maintenance staffs, second engineers, and other studio and record-company staff that have helped or hindered, been nice or nasty, have had an effect on my life, for which (mostly) I am grateful.

Everyone at Alfred Music Publishing. I hate to single anyone out but... Ron (executive producer) Manus, Link Harnsberger, and the man who got this farce started Mike Lawson. All deserve special thanks. Oh, yes, and my copyeditor Sam Molineaux-Graham for keeping me a Brit.

Bobby Owsinski, thanks for all your help, hard work, and friendship.

My family, Kim, Laurie, Karen, Alex, Phil, Aislinn, and Peter. You are all in my heart even when you don't hear from me.

The fans. The record-buying public. You have from day one been the icing on the cake.

And Cheryl. My love, my wife, my friend, and my Queen Bitch. XXXXXXX

Ken Scott
February 2012

Thanks to all who provided additional background info and quotes, including (in no particular order) George Martin, Alan Parsons, Bill Spooner, Ed Thacker, Elliott Sears, John Smith, Klaus Voorman, Lee Sklar, Russell Bracher, Rupert Perry, Brian Kehew, Chris Thomas, Jackie DeShannon, Brian Gibson, Lester Smith, Tom Hartman, Stanley Clarke, Terry Bozzio, Phil Ehart, Mike Lindup, John Kurlander, Trevor Bolder, Woody Woodmansey, Ken Townsend, Roger Hodgson, Davey Johnstone, Bob Siebenberg, Warren Cuccurullo, Phil Gould, Cheryl Scott, Rod Morgenstein, Dennis MacKay, Dave Margereson, Bill Cobham, John McLaughlin, Olivia Harrison, and Wyn Davis.

Thanks to my homie Andy Ameden for the Trident pictures. What are the odds? And thanks to another homie, Bill Beatty, for being the biggest Ken Scott fan in the world. I remember you speaking about him in glowing terms (deservedly so) even way back when.

Thanks to the Alfred family, especially Ron Manus and Link Harnsberger. You guys do indeed make it feel like a family. And thanks to Ted Engelbart for being patient with us as we worked through the cover graphics.

Many thanks to Mike Lawson for putting this project together. Your vision has always been spot on, buddy.

And last but certainly not least, thank you Ken Scott for making this project so easy and enjoyable. May our relationship continue for a long time.

Bobby Owsinski
February 2012

Prologue

Ken Scott and I thought it important that you know a few things about this book before you begin reading since, in certain ways, it's not your typical biography. First of all, it doesn't always follow the exact chronological order of happenings in Ken's life. Instead we usually chose to group events under an artist or genre, like Bowie or jazz rock, because we felt this would actually add more continuity.

Back in the 1960s and early '70s, album projects were a lot shorter (sometimes only a matter of days), and Ken jumped from one to another so frequently that it would have been hard to follow along had we written everything in its exact order. Most albums even today have an on-again/off-again aspect to them, where the time between the beginning and end can be several months or even years, and the people involved often work on other projects in-between. As a result, we thought that if we eliminated some of this back and forth, it would be a much more enjoyable read.

Also, within each of these chapters you'll find subtopics of events or albums, which is unusual for a memoir. Sometimes the subtopic may contain a juicy tidbit that a fan of that particular artist might love, but in general, extraneous information is limited, often because nothing else stood out as exceptional to Ken (just try to remember what you did at work a year ago, for example).

That brings us to the second major point: Ken was a stickler for accuracy in *A to Z*. Unlike other biographies where the author writes what he *thought* happened, in this book whenever possible we attempted to cross-check the facts with other people who were there. This provided as much precision as can be possible in recounting events, some of which occurred as long as 50 years ago, and also resulted in some great side stories, which are included as quotes throughout the book.

Most people have trouble remembering what they had for breakfast a week ago let alone all the facts about something that occurred an entire generation ago. Frequently we interviewed multiple people on the same topic, where all remembered an event differently. When that occurred we kept on interviewing, usually to find out that everyone was right. Most people have a selective memory of an event, recalling only a piece of what occurred. Only when you put all the pieces together do you get the full picture.

The fast pace of the recording industry in the second half of the twentieth century does tend to render events a little blurry, as evidenced by a picture belonging to a friend of mine from my tiny home town of Minersville, Pennsylvania (population 4199) who just happened to be at Trident Studios in December of 1972 (imagine the odds of that). One of the pictures he took (which by chance happened to include Ken- (see Figure P1.1) clearly showed a 16-track tape machine in the control room, which was odd because the tape decks were normally housed in a machine room that wasn't even on the same floor. This caused a minor furor among Trident alumni, since no one could ever remember the machine being there. Finally, Trident engineer Malcolm Toft remembered that they did, in fact, have a tape machine in the control room for a brief period, but in his memory it was not paired with the console that was in the picture. Here we had physical proof with the picture, yet no one could remember what was clearly apparent.

My point is, whenever there was a question in Ken's mind about an event, we tried to corroborate his memory with someone else who was there. Yes, the mind plays tricks, but whenever possible we tried to get it right. (Thanks Ken, for insisting on that.)

Figure P1.1: The mysterious tape machine in the control room (that's Ken standing on the right shaking hands, and Roy Baker sitting on the left).

One additional thing: Ken didn't want this book to be overly technical, which is why all things tech are mostly included in sidebars, so readers who've never seen the inside of recording studio won't get bogged down by something they don't quite understand. We trust there's still enough techy stuff to satisfy the lust for gear detail that most recording engineers have.

This book was as enjoyable for me to co-write as hopefully it will be for you to read. It's been far and away the most fun of any book I've written to date. In talking to Ken and his associates, I vicariously lived some of his life. That in itself is pretty cool, but the fact that Ken and I have become great friends in the process is even better.

Bobby Owsinski

CHAPTER 1

The Early Years

The story begins on the 20th of April, 1947 at Charing Cross Hospital, Agar Street, WC2, London, where a baby boy was born to Margaret and Sydney Scott: one Kenneth Michael Scott—yours truly.

Tradition states that anyone born within the sound of the bells of the Church of St. Mary-le-Bow is considered a true Cockney, and that, proudly, includes me. Cockneys were working-class Londoners, often a lot of fun and very much looked down upon within the English class system. It was because of this that my mother always strove to be above the plebeians and why I don't speak with what is commonly accepted as a cockney accent like several other members of my family. It was during the 1960s that all that negativity changed with the popularity of local-born celebrities such as the actor Michael Caine, who blatantly refused to change the way they spoke.

Both my parents had a great work ethic, which became ingrained in me and which certainly came in handy later when having to work long and often intense hours. From my parents I also inherited a sense of teamwork to get things done. I was an only child, and while a very old and dear friend of mine insists that I was spoiled as a result, I don't see it that way. He has remarked that I always got whatever I wanted, which was true to a point, but my parents always made sure that I was an active participant as well. If I wanted a new bike, for example, I had to come up with half the money for it before they paid for the rest.

My father worked as a clerk at an insurance company and would have to work one Saturday morning every month. On occasion, I would go with him when there was no one else in the office. The office had a Dictaphone machine, which was one of the very first voice recorders used for business. I was very attracted to it for some reason, and would play with it the entire time I was there. While I didn't know it at the time, that was the start of my appreciation for recording.

I have come to learn, especially in writing this book, how strangely the memory works. I remember quite clearly taking piano lessons for a while and hating scales and having to practise exercises from a book by someone named Czerny. Yuk. Of course, at various times during my career I have wished that I had been at least a little into it.

I can't remember much about my earliest musical inclinations, but I do certainly remember my first record player, a wind-up gramophone and, yes, I would really have to physically turn a crank to make it work. I'm not sure at what age I got it, but I would spend hours in the spare bedroom upstairs listening to 78s by the likes of Elvis Presley, Buddy Holly, and Bill Haley (and yes, I do mean those big 78s that are even more ancient than vinyl records). That was the start of my music appreciation. What has always puzzled me is that I became so interested in music whilst none of the rest of my family were into music in the slightest.

I desperately needed to move on from the gramophone, and so for Christmas of 1959, at the ripe old age of 12, I received a present of a Grundig TK 25 tape recorder (see Figure 1.1) from my parents. I had requested a tape recorder rather than a new record player because I knew I could record the music I wanted off the radio and not have to buy anything other than tape (today that's called piracy). I loved recording things other than music as well. Several times friends would come over and we would record radio plays that we would later play in class. I had no idea how much fun playing with that recorder would be, and luckily for me, that fun is still the driving force in my life even to this day.

Figure 1.1: A Grundig TK 25 tape recorder.

It wasn't too much later that adolescence kicked in and I became enamoured with a young English singer by the name of Carol Deene (see Figure 1.2), who'd had a few records on the radio, all covers of American hit singles. There was a television series that I'd occasionally watch called *Here Come the Girls*, a half-hour weekly show centred around the popular female singers of the day. Of course they eventually featured the girl I had the hots for, and over a half-hour period my life would change forever.

The week that the show was based around hot, beautiful, sexy Carol, I placed myself as close to the TV as I could, completely in lust with Ms. Deene. At some point during the show the camera panned from the shot of her singing into a mic up to this large window overlooking her (see Figure 1.3). There was a man sitting behind a large desk of some kind, seemingly directing the operation. In that single instant, I knew what I was going to do with the rest of my life. I was going to become that man, someone they called a "recording engineer."

Figure 1.2: Carol Deene.

It was completely unbeknownst to me at the time that she was singing into a Neumann U 47 microphone, that the big room she was in was Number 2 studio at EMI Recording Studios, and that the man behind the desk was an amazing engineer named Malcolm Addey, who would one day become one of my teachers and mentors.

From that moment, everything in my life was geared towards getting that job. Not that I had much support in the endeavour though, at least from outside the family. If the subject was brought up at all at school, the usual reply would be along the lines of "Right, but why don't you think about a real job?" The thing was, no one knew anything about this mysterious process known as "recording" at the time. There had only been one famous record producer, and that was Phil Spector (who I'd later work with). As far as recording engineers … "What the hell is that?"

After doing a little research, everything pointed towards the fact that I'd have to go to university to qualify for any kind of an "engineering" position, which meant that I needed more schooling. Aargh! But I wanted that job badly, so if more education was required, that was something I was willing to at least try, as much as I disliked school. So instead of leaving school at age 15 (the age at which several of my friends left), I chose to stay on to pass the exams needed for entry into uni. Oh, how I hated it. The camaraderie was great, and I loved getting involved behind the scenes with the school drama society, but the education and exams ... especially the exams. Enough already!

Figure 1.3: EMI Number 2 studio. The control room window is on the top left.

On the evening of Friday the 17th of January, 1964, after an especially long day at school, I just knew I could not take one more exam, so I pulled out the phone book and wrote to every record label, television station, or radio station that I could find that might have recording engineers working for them. I probably sent out a total of ten letters, all posted the next day. On Tuesday, much to my surprise, I received a letter back from EMI Studios requesting an interview (this was when the British Post Office was very good at its job). I excitedly phoned them right up, made an appointment for the next day, and on Wednesday the 22nd arrived at the place that was to change everything for me—and for a whole lot of other people—forever (see Figure 1.4).

I remember very little about the interview other than at one point I was asked by Barry Waite, the assistant manager, who my favourite band was. Now Beatlemania was getting a firm grip on the country by then, and I was certainly a *huge* Beatles fan, but for some reason I answered, "The Dave Clark Five, sir." "Well, why? What makes them different?" asked Mr. Waite. "I think that the addition of the sax adds a lot and makes them sound different from everyone else," I blurted. (Where the hell did that come from?) Bingo!

Figure 1.4: The entrance to EMI Studios (later renamed Abbey Road Studios).

In my humble opinion, I nailed the interview then and there, but they didn't let me know it just yet. Instead, they took me for a long tour of the vast building, during which I got to see what appeared to be the most complex piece of electronic gear that I had ever seen in my life. Even the sci-fi movies I'd seen had nothing to compete with it. That piece of gear happened to be the REDD recording desk in Number 2 control room (see Figure 1.5), the one that was used for the majority of The Beatles' recordings, not to mention on hundreds of other artists that had the good fortune to climb the eight steps that led into what became the most famous studio complex in the world.

So with a smile on my face and a hope in my heart (I know, I know, cloying but true), off I trotted home. Hey, if nothing else, I'd got to see a recording studio in all its glory. At least it was a great story to tell at school.

Figure 1.5: The REDD recording desk in Number 2 control room.

When Friday rolled around and the post arrived, in amongst the bills was a type-written envelope addressed to me—an EMI Records envelope. Somehow amidst the excitement I managed to open the envelope and read the letter that offered me a job in the tape library at £5 a week. Was this for real? Was I asleep and still dreaming? It was too early in the morning to call them, so I took the train to school and called during the mid-morning break. It was only then that I knew the job offer wasn't at all a figment of my imagination. They really were offering me a job and, best of all, they wanted me to start the following Monday.

It was with the greatest of pleasure that I left school for good that Friday, the 24th of January. Only seven days after posting the letters, I'd be starting the job I dreamed of after watching Carol Deene on the telly. And for anyone interested, yes, I did get to actually work on some sessions with her, but it was never quite the same as the way I felt watching her that night on *Here Come the Girls*.

CHAPTER 2

Abbey Road

On Monday the 27th of January, 1964 I took the train, then the tube, to St. John's Wood station, from whence I walked the five or so minutes over to number 3 Abbey Road, NW8, the location of EMI Recording Studios, and the beginning of an amazing life.

THE TRAINING

My start was in the same place that most people began their EMI careers: the tape library. The reasoning was simple; it was the best point from which to learn all about the studio and how it runs.

The EMI training began simply with booking tapes into the library. Through this you learned how all of the information that might be needed during the life of that tape was notated. Things like the tape formats (mono, stereo, and 1-inch 4-track), and F/S or B/D (a "false start" which was a take that lasted no longer than a couple of bars, or a "breakdown," which was an incomplete take that lasted longer than a few seconds), and everything that might be needed by someone who may have to work with the tape at some time in the future. More important for the hopeful future assistant engineer, in the library you learned all the information you'd have to know to notate a tape box properly during a session.

The Studio Layout

EMI Recording Studios was and still is a rather large complex covering four floors. You would enter by ascending eight steps and as you walked through the front door, leaving Abbey Road behind you, you encountered a door on each side, each leading to a playback room, labelled Room 41 and Room 42. Continue through another glass door and to your left is the entrance to Number 3 control room (see Figure 2.1), and directly in front of you is a set of stairs leading up to management and payroll offices. Just to the right of the stairs is the security guard's desk, and after signing in, you may be asked to sit and wait in the reception alcove (see Figure 2.2) where Ringo supposedly learned to play chess during many long Beatles sessions when his talents weren't needed.

This is just the beginning, and so if you think you know enough about how number 3 Abbey Road used to be, I quite understand. But if you want to know more ... As you look to the right of this area there are another three offices: the producer's office, Vera Samwell's bookings office, and the large main office. Then directly in front of you is a long corridor running alongside Number 3 studio with various small rooms off to the right. Rooms such as the artists' green room, toilets, and the like.

Follow this and you come to the centre of the building. To your right is a staircase, the main artery to everything going on. To your left is what was the original control room for Number 3 (but is now primarily a store room) and the place where one of the first Moog synthesisers was set up for its use on an album that would eventually share its name with that of the complex.

Down the corridor are doors to the right leading to such places as Number 2 control room and Rooms 1A and 2A—the 8' x 15.5' rooms where the Telefunken 4-tracks (see Figure 2.3) were housed, 2A being where The Beatles set up to record "Yer Blues." Further down are maintenance rooms, copy rooms, more water closets, and finally the back staircase where Paul played a drum part on "Mother Nature's Son."

OK, back to the main stairway. Go down one flight and to your left is the canteen, not the cosiest of places back then. Take kind of a half left and you're taken to a secondary entrance to the building and directly in front of you is the Number 1 control room, and to the right, the entrance to the 55' x 93' studio that was first used on November 12th, 1931, for the last studio session that Glen Miller and his band would play together and the site of the historical worldwide broadcast of "All You Need Is Love." Walk past this and make a sharp right and you pass the mic storeroom and into the amazing Studio 2, the room where so many of The Beatles' and others' recordings were made.

Back to the stairs and up two flights. Stop and catch your breath, especially if you're a smoker like we all were back then. This floor holds the tape library, and to your right, the common room, where we all got to hang out when we had nothing else to do; in other words, an almost always empty room. This floor also contained the amp room, the hangout for all the techies of the day, and, if I remember, three cutting rooms. Up one more flight to the second floor (well, third if you're American) and there were four more cutting rooms and a copy room. This is also the floor that has a great view of the surrounding flats and houses. Nudge, nudge, wink, wink.

The studio formally changed its name from EMI Recording Studios to Abbey Road Studios in 1970 after the notoriety garnered from The Beatles' *Abbey Road* album.

Figure 2.1: Number 3 control room

Figure 2.2: The reception area.

Then there was learning how the studio worked. Simple things like the difference between a control room and a cutting room, or what kinds of things editors do. It's the kind of knowledge that's pretty much commonplace these days, but back then only a very, *very* small percentage of the population even knew what a recording studio was, let alone how it worked. This was all learned by the process of getting tapes to and from the different places they needed to be. Of course, when delivering tapes to the studios, cutting rooms, or wherever, you'd catch bits and pieces of what was going on since you tried to never just pick up, or deliver, the tapes and immediately leave, you'd hang out for a bit and watch. One of the most fascinating parts of hanging out was that as you got to know the "old-timers." They would regale you with stories of the studios and their history, and how records were made right at the beginning of what eventually became the record industry—stories unfortunately now lost to time.

Figure 2.3: A Telefunken 4-track tape machine.

The Library

By the time they were presented to the library, the tape boxes already had identification numbers since every control room stocked a number of labels with the numbers preprinted on them. As a reel of tape was used, the assistant engineer would stick a number on the spine of the box and one on the back. From then on, that number (which at this stage was a number with an "E" prefix, such as "E103") would live with the tape throughout its life. All tapes had the E number, a stereo always had a Z after the number, and 4-tracks had the E number followed by, you guessed it, "4-Track." When a master was made, it received an "AR" number (for example, "AR115"). The tapes were then filed away in the correct spot in the library.

There were three places where tapes were stored. A lot of the older tapes were stored down at the EMI Research building and Music Archive in Hayes, Middlesex and these were, and still are to this day, stored in metal cases called "tins." EMI also had taken over an old squash court located in a block of apartments across the street from the studios, which was the intermediate tape storage facility. The studio itself kept tapes from the last four to six months on the premises in the library, and if something wasn't used for about six months it would go across the street to the squash court storage facility. If it wasn't called out again or they began to run out of room, it was then shipped down to Hayes.

MEET THE BEATLES

Within three days of my arrival I had in my hands a 4-track master tape fresh from Paris. A&R manager (artist and repertoire) George Martin had wanted to release a Beatles single of the group singing in German and, as the band was performing several shows in Paris, he set up a day at EMI's Pathé Marconi Studios attended by an interpreter. They recorded the German versions very quickly, and as they had time left, it was decided to try something new. That something new turned out to be "Can't Buy Me Love" and here I was, a huge Beatles fan (one of millions), holding the master tape of what would turn out to be the next Beatles single. Just one thought raced through my mind: "Bloody hell!"

It was about a month later that The Beatles came in to record the songs for their film *A Hard Day's Night*. There I was carrying a tape up to the library from Number 3 control room when I noticed coming towards me the two Georges, Harrison and Martin. I freaked and almost screamed like one of the many girls outside, but managed to bite my tongue, a feat for which I would become extremely grateful, especially when considering my many future associations with the two of them.

It wasn't long before I met Norman Smith, the great engineer who worked on The Beatles' sessions from the first test recording through *Rubber Soul*, and I began to get friendly with him. I amazed myself by being very up front and asked him if there was any chance of me poking my head in the door so I could watch the band record for a bit. He hesitated for a second, then told me, "Yes, but keep to the back and don't let anyone notice you're there. They can be a bit touchy about new people, so just be a part of the furniture." Well, of course a cocky 16-year-old couldn't stop there. "Maybe I could take some pictures?" I asked, assuming I would never get this opportunity again. "Just be part of the furniture and don't make it obvious," Norman warned.

Come the day and I have this cheap old camera in hand, and whilst watching the session, I started to take some pictures. There were a number of people there having to do with the movie, including someone who was filming on an 8-millimetre camera (some of this footage has only recently come out on YouTube). After a while The Beatles decided they wanted to try some handclaps on a song and said to the room, "Come on. Everyone down to join in." I looked over at Norman and he looked over at me and sort of nodded his head to let me know it was OK to do it. "Blimey, I'm gonna go down and clap with The Beatles," I thought. Could it ever get any better than this?

There were eight or nine of us, including Ringo and Paul, gathered around the mic clapping along to "I Should Have Known Better." After the take, the two of them went upstairs while the rest of us stayed there looking up at the glass waiting for a decision, then someone came out to the top of the stairs and yelled, "It doesn't work so forget it. Just come back up here."

The moment I set foot in the control room, George Martin came up to me and politely asked, "Excuse me, but who are you?" Caught off guard, I sputtered, "Mr. Martin, sir, I just started up in the tape library a couple of weeks ago … " and George immediately stopped me mid-sentence and said rather sternly, "Get out!" I thought to myself, "Oh, hell. This is it. I'm going to get fired," but at least I'd had a chance to be in the studio with The Beatles. Did anything else really matter?

I heard nothing about being fired, and a couple of days later George Martin came up to the tape library and asked me, "So how did the pictures turn out?" Of course I showed him (see Insert Figures 2.4, 2.5, 2.6, 2.7), with much relief, now figuring my job was actually safe. Unfortunately this was just the first of many incidents at EMI where I thought my job was in jeopardy, all of them having to do with The Beatles.

I'M A BUTTON PUSHER

After working in the tape library for just over four months, I was promoted to "button pusher," or what today is generally known as an assistant engineer. The name "button pusher" arose because the principal job was to run the tape machines by hitting the Stop,

Play, Record, and Rewind buttons, or just, as the name implies, pushing buttons.

The training for that highly taxing job was to spend a week or two sitting there with another button pusher, then you were on your own. More often than not your tutor would let you take control after a short time, and if they saw you making a mistake, they'd immediately jump in and correct it. It was "watch and learn," then they'd give you enough rope with which to hang yourself, which as it turned out, was exactly what it was like all along the line at EMI: learning by watching, and learning even more by your inevitable mistakes.

We, the lowest-of-the-low button pushers, weren't allowed to touch mics, place them, or perform any duties that had to do with setting up the sessions. In fact, the engineers couldn't even put their own mics out. That was the job of the amp room guys (who all wore white lab coats so they wouldn't get their clothes dirty and, contrary to popular belief, were the only ones in the building to wear these coats), the technical and maintenance wizards from upstairs. The engineer could do the final placement, but the "white coats" had to put the mics out and set up the session, a feat accomplished by having the engineer fill out a setup sheet before every session. The engineer would map out where in the studio each instrument was to be placed and indicate which mics were wanted and generally where they were to be positioned (see Figures 2.8, 2.9). Also noted on the sheets would be the additional equipment (limiters, compressors, echo chamber, etc.) that would be required and what channels on the mixer these were all to be connected to, as well as any other session details.

While it may seem that button pushing is a rather benign occupation, there was one minor danger. The EMI ¼-inch tapes only had a flange (the metal retainer on a reel of tape) on one side of the reel and every now and again the tape would jump up and come off the centre hub. When that happened you had to have quick reflexes and slam your hands on both reels very quickly to stop the motion. There were people that really cut their hands up doing that, but that tape had to be protected at all costs.

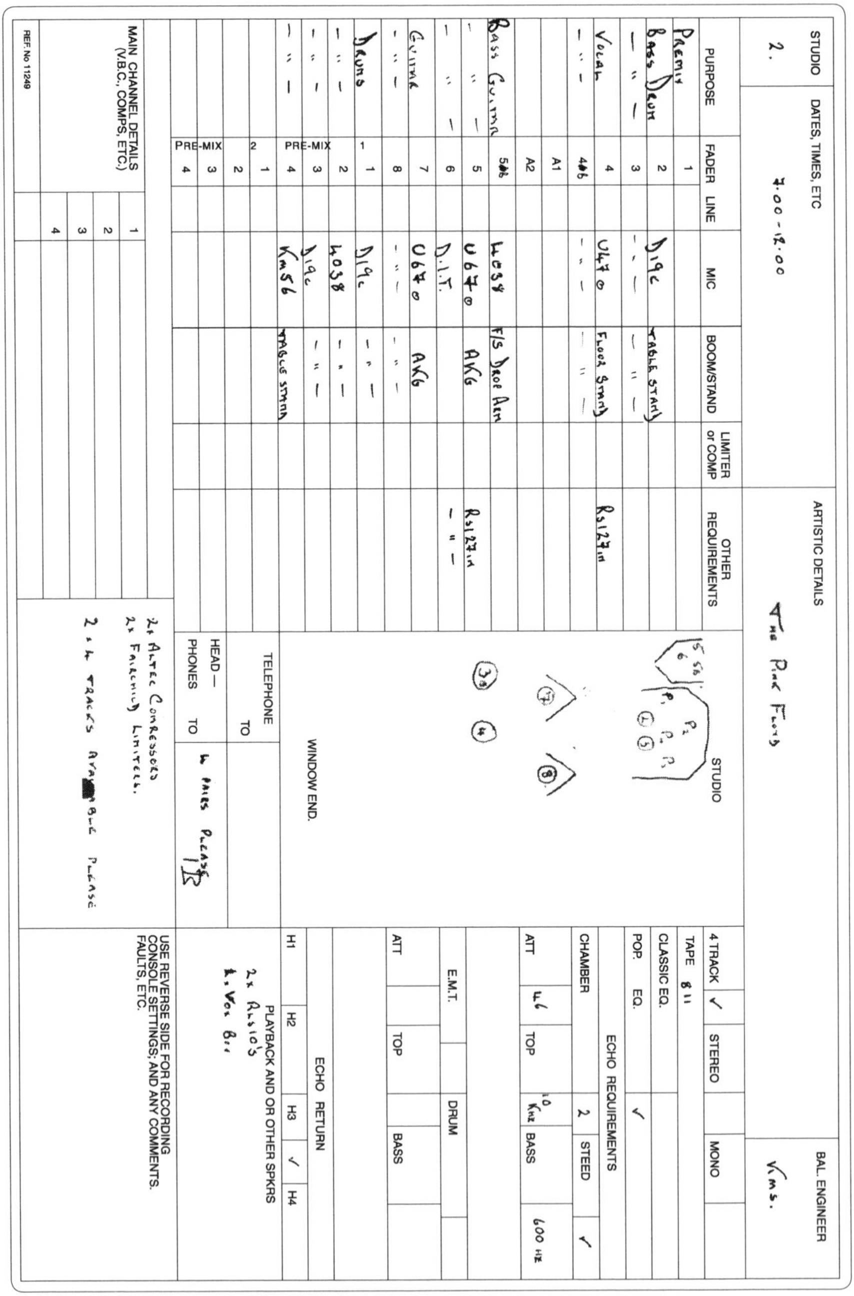

Figure 2.8: A setup sheet from one of my Pink Floyd sessions.

I should note that a button pusher didn't just have the complex job of looking after the tape machines—they also had to "band" album master tapes. This was one's first foray into editing, wherein we'd have to put exactly five seconds of leader tape (non-magnetic plastic or paper tape used for spacing or silence) between each song on the American albums received at the studio that EMI distributed in England. When you weren't on a session, you'd go into one of the side rooms in the facility and band albums.

Figure 2.9: Nick Mason's drum setup.

A lot of the American recordings came with the tape wrapped around only a centre hub without any flange whatsoever. I remember an occasion when one of the button pushers opened the box, took out the tape wrapped around the hub but with no flange, and as he was walking towards a tape machine the centre hub fell out and the entire tape unwound. He had to literally wind the entire tape on to a reel by hand. Ah, the good old days!

There was a rather unique initiation rite at EMI for new button pushers. When a new guy was being taught how to band, the teacher would say, "You don't even have to listen to the tape—you can just feel where the music is." Of course the new guy would look at the teacher with a "What the hell are you talking about?" expression, and the phenomenon would be immediately demonstrated. "You run the tape through your fingers until you feel where the sound is, then you mark it. When you turn the sound up you'll have it right." Then the tape is run and sure enough, the music is in the exact right spot. Of course the new guy believes that you can feel the music on the tape and starts to try, and try, and try again to feel the magic notes within. It doesn't take long for the poor guy to become so frustrated that he wants to cry because he just can't feel it. It's only then that the secret is revealed. There's a meter on the front of the tape machine, and if you watch it, the point of the deflection (the point where the needle jumps) is where the music starts. Of course you're not feeling anything. You're simply just watching for that meter to jump back and forth. The new guy feels completely stupid but is now initiated and can't wait for when it's his turn to teach the next victim.

We were taught only this basic form of editing because button pushers, and engineers for that matter, were not supposed to edit anything. EMI had dedicated editors housed in three rooms outside of the building, and their prime function was to do all editing other than banding, mostly for the classical department. When recording an orchestra, the producer would have the score in front of him and during a recording he would mark what he didn't like on the score, then they would go back and re-record just that part. Once the orchestra recorded it to his satisfaction, the tapes and score would go to the editors, who would perform the edits by cutting the tape pieces together at the appropriate places to achieve a perfect performance.

PLAYBACK FOR SIR MALCOLM

There was yet another job that a button pusher had, which was to run the playback sessions in the listening rooms. These rooms were at the front of the building (Rooms 41 and 42) and were used primarily by the classical producers, conductors, or soloists to listen to the edits of the completed piece. Usually they would approve what they heard, but sometimes on listening they would discover there was something still wrong and send it back to find another take that had a better part of the particular section in question.

One day I had to do a playback in Room 41 for a very famous English conductor named Sir Malcolm Sargent, oft know as Flash Harry, who was widely regarded as Britain's leading conductor of choral works. The session producer, Christopher Bishop, arrived before Sir Malcolm and rather interestingly requested, "Ken, when I scratch my head, I want you to start having a coughing fit." I said OK, wondering what I was getting myself into, and put on the tape and awaited the famous conductor.

About halfway through the playback, the producer scratched his head and I started coughing madly for about 15 seconds, at which time I profusely apologised, as the tape continued to roll on. When it came to the end of the tape, Sir Malcolm stood up and politely announced, "Yes, that's perfect. Thank you so much," and left. At that point I turned to Chris and said, "So what was that all about?" He sheepishly smiled and replied, "There was a bad note in there and I couldn't find anything to replace it with. I couldn't let him hear it at this stage. Thank you for covering it up for me." Leave it to the lowly assistant to bail out the producer in an uncomfortable situation, an activity that continues to this day. Or so I've heard.

My first day on my own as a button pusher was June 1, 1964 working primarily on side two of *A Hard Day's Night*, which were the songs that weren't used in the film. The first song recorded was Ringo singing a cover of Carl Perkins's "Matchbox," followed by "I'll Cry Instead," "Slow Down," and "I'll Be Back." None of them were hits, but it didn't matter. I was now officially working with The Beatles.

NEARLY FIRED TAKE 2

I have to say that at that time "working with The Beatles" wasn't all one hoped it to be. For a long time, the tape machines weren't even in the control room at EMI. They only had two Telefunken 4-tracks which were not only huge but also had to cover three studios. The machines were set in two rooms, 1A and 2A, which were by the side of Number 2 control room, and each machine could be patched through to any of the studios. The button pusher would sit in the room with the tape machine, and the only kind of communication with the control room came from this awful, distorted talkback system. You would get to go into the control room while the band were rehearsing, but other than that you were off in a separate room with only a big tape machine for company.

As a result, I got caught up in another "classic" situation towards the end of those *A Hard Day's Night* sessions. Norman had gone home early for some reason and George Martin was playing the recent recordings for some visitors in the control room, where he would come on the talkback to tell me what songs to play. This went on for a while until he finally comes on the talkback and I hear a bunch of people talking, but the only word I catch from George was "home." I thought to myself, "Ah, we're finished," and I put the tapes away, shut the machine off, got my coat, and was walking down the corridor when I see George standing at the door of Number 2 control room. He gave me a quizzical look and said, "So, is it up?" "I'm sorry?" I replied. "Do you have 'When I Get Home' up?" repeated George. "Oh, the tape's in the other room and I'm just going to go and get it," at which point I ran back and switched everything back on and cued up the song as fast as humanly possible. Dodged the bullet once again!

NEARLY FIRED YET ONE MORE TIME

Eventually EMI purchased some Studer 4-track machines. These were much smaller and so by the time we got to record *Help!* I was stationed in the control room seeing and hearing everything that goes on during the sessions. Being on so many Beatles sessions I got to know a lot of the people who surrounded the band, and I eventually became close with a number of people from Dick James Music, the group's music publisher. In fact, I was even offered a job working at their small studio, which I decided wasn't for me (but I did refer a friend of mine from school, who got the job), so I was well in with everyone there.

One day Steven James, Dick's son, and I were chatting and he began complaining, "Even though we're the publisher of The Beatles' songs, we never get a copy of their latest release until way past when we really need it. We have to do all of the sheet music and pull so much together, and getting everything that late is such a drag." Being the nice guy I am (and still oh so naïve at that point), I said, "That's OK, Steven. I can get you the tapes. I'll run off a copy for you." "Oh, that would be amazing. That would help us so much. Thank you so much," he went on. Of course, I did so the very next chance I had.

The following week an agitated George Martin came running up to me and proceeded to take me to task. "What the hell do you think you're doing giving out tapes of The Beatles!" he demanded. Now, there was a lot of money always being offered by radio stations for Beatles recordings before they were released, and as far as I know, no one at the studio ever succumbed to the temptation, but a tape prematurely coming out of the studio was a really bad thing. Not realising this, I confusedly asked George, "What do you mean?"

"Steven James is going around town playing all of The Beatles' songs that we just recorded," he shot back. "He said that you gave him the tape!"

"George, he was complaining about how they never got the tapes until it was too late. I thought it would be OK and he promised he wouldn't play it for anyone. I'm so terribly sorry!"

George simply turned around and walked off in a huff, and once again I was sure I was going to be fired. I was saved by the fact that he knew that Steven James could be somewhat of a manipulator, so he believed my story, and much to my surprise, he let me off the hook.

During my time as a button pusher, my work with The Beatles consisted of the second side of *A Hard Day's Night*, *Beatles for Sale* (called *Beatles '65* in the States, which only featured eight of the tracks off *Beatles for Sale*), *Help!*, and *Rubber Soul*. I also worked with just about every other major EMI artist as well, including Peter and Gordon, The Hollies, Manfred Mann ("Do Wah Diddy Diddy" was the first number 1 single I ever worked on), Johnny Mathis, Judy

Garland, Daniel Barenboim, the English cast recording of *Camelot* (which was amazing—I much preferred it to Richard Burton's version), Cliff Richard & the Shadows, Peter Sellers, Freddie and the Dreamers (a band that would moon everyone in the control room at every opportunity), and many more. Unfortunately, never realising that I might find it worthwhile to remember them over 40 years later, the sessions all blended together even then, and it's that much more of a blur now. As a result, I don't remember many specific sessions, although there is one that has always stuck in my brain, probably because of the person involved and his future project.

JACKIE AND JIMMY

One day, American singer Jackie DeShannon, who had had a fair amount of success as a songwriter in the U.K., came over to record at EMI. Her songs tended to be acoustic guitar oriented with a lot of 12-string and great guitar hooks. The track I remember her recording was no different in that it had a fairly strong hook, but the main guitarist on the session that day just couldn't seem to get it. We had to break the orchestra while she sat down and personally taught him the part over the next 20 minutes. The guitarist's name was Jimmy Page, who, as it turned out, wasn't the greatest music reader, but his playing abilities were so good that he was one of the top session guitarists at that time. Whilst recently chatting with Jimmy, he remembered the session very well and said that the problem was that when playing what was written on the paper, it felt very stiff, so Jackie wanted to teach him more how she heard it. I don't remember for sure, but it's more than likely that soon-to-be Led Zeppelin bass player John Paul Jones was on the session as well, since, like Jimmy, he was a first call session player.

> *I only did that one big session there [at EMI] where we did four or five sides. I was looking for a great guitarist because I was accustomed to working with the Wrecking Crew and had worked with Glen Campbell, James Burton, and a lot of great people in L.A. I asked around and they said that the one guy that would be best was in art school and his name was Jimmy Page. I said, "Get him over here," but we had to wait until he got out of school. My*

songs had special little riffs and a little different way that I would play. It's OK because George Harrison one day asked me how to play "When You Walk in the Room."
Jackie DeShannon

I'M A CUTTER

Following the completion of The Beatles' *Rubber Soul* on Monday the 15th of November, 1965, I was once again promoted. If you made it as a button pusher, then the next step up was to mastering (we were called "cutters" at the time), a most important part of training for the future recording engineer. The job consisted of transferring the audio from the recorded tapes onto the discs which would later be processed for pressing the vinyl records. It was called cutting because you were literally cutting the grooves in lacquer-covered metal discs. This was considered a major part of the training because there were inherent limitations as to how much and what kind of sound you could put on records, and those limitations did not exist with analogue tape. As a result, you had to be careful with the amount of bass on the lacquer (it would cause the record to skip if there was too much), and be aware of a phenomenon called phase (which could also cause the record to skip), along with a whole bunch of other problem areas. The EMI hierarchy therefore determined that an engineer should learn what would work for the final product before moving onto the easier medium of tape.

Once again you were taught by the last person who was promoted before you. I was trained by Geoff Emerick because he was hired before me and therefore in front of me for all of the time I was at EMI. I sat in a room and watched him do it for a while, then I did some as he watched over me, and then I was on my own after about a week.

The first thing you were allowed to cut were playback acetates. Since there was no such thing as CD-Rs or cassettes in those days, the only way for the artist, producer, and whomever else to hear what they recorded when at home was their own personal lacquer record. This was known as an acetate, which was a 7-inch 45 rpm vinyl disc that would last for maybe 10 plays before it would wear out. Since you had to cut as many as 12 of them for a single song so all the members of the session could have one, there were two Scully cutting lathes in the room so we could cut multiple discs at the same time (see Insert Figure 2.10).

One's start in cutting was always the same. You're suddenly in control with no one looking over your shoulder, so on the first tape that comes in it's always the same mind game, "I think this needs a little more high-end," and then you turn the treble at 10 kHz up full blast. "Oh, that's better, but now it's lacking a little low-end," so you pile on the bass. "Oh, it's almost there. It just needs some mids," and you pile on all of the mid-frequencies. It takes three or four days until you realise that what you got from the studio sounded pretty good already, and all it needed was maybe one notch at 10 kHz and it was perfect. No one stood there and said, "You don't need that much. You only need one notch," you'd teach yourself that. You realised that after you've piled on all of this EQ, you made it sound like shit, so it quickly began to dawn on you that less was actually more.

To this day, that's what I think a mastering engineer is supposed to do: stay as close as possible to what he's been given. You don't put it through a chain of compressors or use stems to alter the balance or change the sound in any other way. The engineer and the producer have a vision, they know what they want, and it's up to the cutter (the mastering engineer) to stay as close to what they provided as possible.

After cutting acetates, the next step up was to actually cut masters, which I did after about six months. Not only did I cut all the major EMI acts of the era at one time or another, but a number of American artists that EMI distributed as well. Since EMI distributed Motown in those days, I cut records sent over by every one of their big stars, such as The Four Tops, Smokey Robinson and the Miracles, The Supremes, and all of the others. I also cut several albums by John Coltrane, which was so out there and avant garde that I couldn't stand it. I knew the length of the album, and since each side was one song, I just put the head down on the lacquer, set it going, and I'd walk out of the room for however long the side was and basically let it cut itself. I couldn't stand listening to it then, and I don't know if I could now either, which is quite surprising given some of the great progressive jazz artists that I subsequently worked with.

One general conversation that all of us at the studio constantly had was how other labels, especially in America, managed to cut louder discs than we could. We experimented over and over and tried all kinds of things to no avail. Every now and again one or other of the EMI engineers would fly over to Capitol in Los Angeles to see what was happening on the American scene. Pete Bown did the trip once and when he came back he said that it was all down to the musicians. "They have a totally different sound in the studio, and because of that they manage to get records that appear louder," he reported. I don't know that this argument ever satisfied us though.

The Old Timers

Old-time engineers who couldn't engineer any longer, because of physical or hearing problems, always seemed to be found alternate positions. Since this was back in the day when you worked for a company for life, some were promoted to management, and others to tape copying and transfers, probably the last position they held before retiring.

There was one room at the end of the building where an old-time engineer named Edward Gadsby-Toni worked transferring old 78-rpm records to tape. One of the things that he had to do as part of this procedure was to de-click the copy, but since this was some 30 years before any effective digital de-clicking program existed, he did it all manually. The method of doing that was to take a ¼-inch square of ¼-inch splicing tape and place it on the magnetic oxide side of the tape wherever a click occurred. The small strip of tape caused a drop-out to occur, but it was so fast that you never noticed it audibly, but the attack of the click was eliminated.

I had to use this technique later with Procol Harum when we recorded a bass track where we'd get an electronic click whenever Dave Knight (Procol Harum's bass player) retouched the strings after having taken his fingers off. Since we were recording on multitrack tape, not only did I have to go through and eradicate the clicks, but I also had to make sure that I was doing it on the right track. Not too much fun, but effective nonetheless.

I remember one single that was particularly loud was a short-lived pop song called "Judy in Disguise (with Glasses)" by one-hit wonder John Fred and His Playboy Band. We tried and tried to get our records to sound like it and could never get close. The same goes for the bass sound that came out of Motown. We just never could duplicate it.

However, the grass is always greener. The Beatles would have given anything to sound like a Motown record, but EMI Studios received a telex from Motown congratulating them on the success of The Beatles that went on to say how much they wished they could duplicate the sound that we got. Go figure.

In the majority of cases with American records that we had to recut, we only got the vinyl records instead of tapes to cut from. We'd transfer the record to tape in one of the rooms, and cut from that. Even when we had the actual record, we could never cut it as loud as the original. Talk about frustrating!

I had now spent more time cutting than any other of my jobs at EMI, and I was itching to move up. One day in early September of 1967 I got a phone call to go see the management upstairs. "We want to move you up to engineering, if that's all right with you." Were they kidding? Of course it was all right. Finally, the chance to push some faders of my own.

CHAPTER 3

Engineering The Beatles

On Monday September 4th, 1967 my dream came true; I was promoted to engineer. The last person who had been promoted this way was Geoff Emerick, who, after six months on the job, had gone on to record the amazing *Revolver* and *Sgt. Pepper's*, so the bar had been set pretty damn high. No worries, I'd do it the normal way: some recording tests to get used to things and then onto some easy sessions. With Geoff firmly ensconced in his position with the Fab Four, I'd have a nice slow pace to my learning.

As was the way before I was handed a session of my own, I spent a couple of weeks training with various EMI engineers. Unlike the training for the other jobs at the studio, all an engineer-in-training did was watch, with very little actual hands-on experience. In fact, I never sat behind a console and pushed up even a single fader until the very first session on my own.

When it came time for that first session I was petrified because I really had no idea what I was doing. And who do you think it was with? The Beatles, of course. Why me? Why someone who had never raised a fader? What about "Ernie" (or "Emeroids," as Mr. Emerick was oft known)? The old-timers? Why me-e-e-e-e? Well, the way Geoff tells it, he had a holiday booked and so took off in the middle of recording *Magical Mystery Tour.* The old-timers hated to work with The Beatles, so that left only the new kid on the block.

It turned out that Paul wanted to change the arrangement of a song they had previously recorded called "Your Mother Should Know." Luckily for me, the arrangement idea didn't pan out, so the fact that I didn't know what the hell I was doing didn't seem so important. In retrospect it also seems to me that thanks to the amount of time I'd spent with them as a button pusher, they cut me a little slack as well. I can remember very little about the session except that I was almost paralysed with fear, which probably would have happened on just about any session I'd been given, but add on top of that that it was the biggest bloody band in the world and those long hours were an exercise in terror.

The next session I remember was my first orchestral date three days later and it happened to be for "I Am the Walrus," a song I would later mix as well. The basic track and vocal had already been recorded by Ernie, so the session I worked on added the orchestra, the choir, and maybe a few other things that I can't remember because, once again, I was thrown into the fire and scared to death.

As Geoff was the one I was following, I started off with the same setup and mics that he had used, just the same way he did when he followed Norman Smith or Malcolm Addey when he started. You saw how those before you had done it and just tried to replicate everything as best as you could. Slowly but surely you could start experimenting a little once you got a grasp of things, but this was way before I reached that point.

Surprisingly, I learned something from those sessions that later became invaluable to me as a producer. I discovered that the best way to work with an orchestra is to have the arranger over-write. The reason is that it's always easier to get rid of material than to put something in during a session. That's what George Martin used to do on his arrangements for Beatles songs, and that's what he did on "Walrus." The first hour of the session was John saying, "I don't like that bit. Keep this bit. Can you change that a little?" George made the changes and then we recorded it.

"FOOL ON THE HILL"

As already stated, my engineering debut with The Beatles was in the middle of *Magical Mystery Tour*, a strange project which seemed very disorganised in terms of material. It went from "Your Mother Should Know" to "Blue Jay Way" to "I Am the Walrus," each one so different from the next. There was no particular direction, but I only realised that later after I had settled into the job a bit. My memory is short on the specifics during this period since I spent most of my time trying oh-so-hard not to completely mess up, but one of the songs I remember very well is "Fool on the Hill," mostly because of the problems it caused us.

On "A Day in the Life" back on *Sgt. Pepper's*, Ken Townsend of the maintenance department had come up with a way to link two 4-track tape machines together, which was a revelation for the time. The way it was done was to record what's known as a pilot tone on a track of the main machine, then that tone would control the speed of the second 4-track. This worked great because the two machines ran together completely in sync to make up what was essentially a 7-track recorder (the pilot tone was on track 8). The trouble with the setup was that you couldn't get both machines to start exactly at the same time, so there was a lot of guessing involved.

Even though these sync problems were experienced on "A Day in the Life," it was suggested, by whom I know not, that we try it again for "Fool on the Hill," as by then everyone seemed to have forgotten the anguish the setup had previously caused. We recorded three tracks on to the first machine, then mixed it down to one track on the second 4-track, then overdubbed the rest of tracks from there. It wasn't until we came to the mix that we realised the machines weren't all that easy to sync together. The problem was that the music on the second 4-track didn't actually begin until about a quarter of the way into the song, so you could never tell whether it was in time or not until you were a quarter of the way through when you heard the music from the second 4-track. We'd start the mix, get a quarter of the way through, and then, "Oh, shit! It didn't start in time," and we'd have to go back and start again.

As a result, the final mix was more luck than judgement. We'd put a mark with a chinagraph marker on the tape and just try starting it from different places until we got lucky and they ran in sync. It was a real pain in the arse, but it worked out in the end, which is all that anyone ends up remembering.

As nice as they could be on the one hand, The Beatles could also be real arseholes on the other. I remember doing a session in Number 1 shortly after my promotion to engineer where I was still new to everything and didn't yet know the protocol for when one takes a break for dinner or anything like that. At that point, the studio canteen really didn't make food, it was more for tea. They had some biscuits, but not much else to eat, so you had to leave the studio or have food brought in when it came time for a dinner break.

We were recording the harmonicas for "Fool on the Hill" and the band had sent out for food. When it finally arrived, they just sat down in the studio eating by themselves and never offered myself or second engineer Richard Lush anything, and I was starving. Richard had already gone through all of this as he'd been the second engineer for the majority of *Sgt. Pepper's* and *Revolver*, so he knew what they were like during this period. I turned around to him and asked, "What the hell do we do?" Richard calmly replied, "It's easy. We get up and we go!" and leans over and pushes the talkback button and says, "OK, guys. We'll be back in an hour. We're just going to get something to eat. OK?" The band waved and cheerfully replied, "Yeah, OK." I was petrified because I'd never had to do that before and didn't quite yet know that it was perfectly fine to actually take a break from working with the greatest band in the world. But it was that easy; you just walk out on them. It was all part of my learning process, and also why I don't have as many memories of that period as I wish I had. I was just struggling to learn what I should be doing rather than taking mental notes of all the events at hand.

"I AM THE WALRUS"

Later when it was time to mix "I Am the Walrus" John decided that something else was needed for the ending of the song, so Ringo was dispatched to a corner of the control room with a radio tuner to scan around the dial to different stations. What was tricky was that since we didn't have any extra tracks to record it on, he had to perform the radio tuning live as the song was mixed. On one pass he hit on a performance of Shakespeare's *King Lear* on the BBC's Third Programme, which we all determined worked perfectly for the track. We kept the end of that take and decided to use another mix for the first part of the song.

I was asked to do an edit between takes to marry the good ending with a better front half of the song. Now, EMI engineers were not supposed to take a razor blade to the tape because, as explained previously, the studio employed a team of dedicated editors. But when you're working with The Beatles and they want to hear the first half of one mix and the second half of another, you can't wait until the next day for the editors to arrive. Even though I was used to banding, this was one of my first real actual edits, so once again I was gripped by fear. As I was rocking the tape backwards and forwards to try and find the edit point, everyone seemed to be talking at once at the top of their voices, and I couldn't hear a damned thing. At some point I lost it and screamed in a panic, "Please, shut up. I'm trying to do this!" Much to my surprise, everything immediately fell quiet, which might have been even worse because now the spotlight was directed squarely on me. "Can I cut this without spilling any of my own blood on a precious Beatles master?" I wondered. Luckily when I played it, all sounded fine and everyone was pleased, especially me. Dodged yet another bullet.

The mix of "Walrus" that we did that night was mono, and it wasn't until later that Geoff remixed it in stereo. If you listen to the end of the stereo mix where the radio comes in, it suddenly changes to fake stereo with the bass on one side and the treble on the other. This was because the part with the radio was done live as part of the mono mix and there was no other way to recreate it in stereo at the time.

Years later when it came time to do the *Love* soundtrack, it had been discovered exactly which broadcast it was that Ringo had tuned into, and the BBC made it available so it could finally be recreated in proper stereo and 5.1.

"LADY MADONNA"

"Lady Madonna" was recorded between *Magical Mystery Tour* and *The White Album*. The question I've always had was why I recorded the basic tracks instead of Geoff, since he had returned to work with the band by then. Geoff did finish up the overdubs and mixed it, but I never found out why it went that way.

Abbey Road (as the studio is now called) seems to think that an old upright that they have was used on the track, but it was actually the baby grand that was in Number 3. I have heard that they recently threw a big party to celebrate the installation of a new board in Number 2 and the upright had a large notice on it saying, "Lady Madonna Piano—Please Don't Put Drinks On It." It's possible that the piano part was doubled later with that piano, but it certainly doesn't sound doubled to me, and I know they didn't replace it because the piano was mixed with the drums on the basic track. There is something weird about the sound of that piano though, and in talking with John Kurlander, who was a second engineer at EMI at that point, he mentioned that he used to play it really hard and it would sound exactly like the record: slightly out of tune. Of course, Paul played it really hard. And as far as that sign goes, I just wish these people, who weren't around at the time, would maybe speak with those that were there to try and get the history correct.

"HEY JUDE"

We recorded "Hey Jude" at EMI over two nights. The first night was just sorting out the arrangement, while a film crew from the BBC walked around checking everything out to prepare for shooting a segment for a documentary called *Music* for the British Arts Council. Of course, the typical film thing happened where they say, "Don't worry, you won't even know we're here. We don't want to interfere with anything so just carry on as normal." Come the second night it's not like that at all. The crew was all over the studio and in everyone's way, so they managed to put everyone very much on edge. There was a huge argument between George (Harrison) and Paul as to what George should be playing, which ended up with George just hanging out in the control room for most of the takes. Of course, the film crew was shooting the entire time. The row between George and Paul was a filmmakers dream.

We eventually did get what turned out to be a master of the basic track consisting of Paul on piano, John on acoustic guitar, and Ringo on drums. However the next couple of days they were booked in at Trident Studios for the overdubs because they wanted to record on 8-track, and Trident was the first and only 8-track studio in London at that time. They ended up having problems transferring the 4-track master from EMI to the 8-track at Trident for some reason, so the band ended up recording another basic track and finishing the song at Trident. They also had to mix it there because, of course, Trident was the only studio in town with an 8-track tape machine.

I went over there to have a listen after the mix was completed and Barry Sheffield, who had engineered the Trident sessions, played it for me. The control room had these huge Lockwood cabinets with Tannoy speakers in them, which I had never seen nor heard before, and when they played me the mix I was just blown away. It was louder and clearer than anything I had ever heard. Everything sounded amazing.

A couple of days later the master tape came back to EMI and the playback acetates of the song were being cut. I went up to the cutting room to have another listen and this time it sounded as if there were curtains in front of the speaker. It was totally muffled, with absolutely no high-end on it whatsoever. This would obviously be a problem so I went down to the control room and awaited the arrival of George Martin and the band.

The first person to come in was George Martin, who immediately asked, "Have you heard it yet?" "Yeah, I heard it at Trident and it sounded absolutely amazing there," I replied. "Yeah, but have you heard it here?" the producer asked. I looked down at the floor and mumbled, "Yes, I have." "Well, how is it then?" "It sounds awful. There's no high-end on it," I told him.

At that point John walked in and George turned to him and said something like "Ken thinks it sounds like shit." Actually George was way too proper and too much of a gentleman to have used that kind of language, but in so many words, that's what he meant and that's what I heard.

As each one of The Beatles came in they were told my opinion, which turned the mood of the studio ice cold. They eventually all went down into the studio where a long discussion took place, which included the occasional glare up at the control room. I just wanted to crawl under a stone and die. All that raced through my mind was, "Oh God, it's another one of those. I'm going to get fired for sure this time."

Finally the five of them come stomping up into the control room where George (Martin) commanded, "OK, let's hear it. We'll see if you're right or not." I sent the assistant up to the cutting room to get the tape and sure enough, when we played it, they all agreed with me. It sounded awful. We then spent the next few hours EQing it to try to raise the high-end to a point that we felt was acceptable, and the result is what everyone's familiar with today.

We learned a hard lesson about the Trident playback system. The speakers were all hype. There was so much high-end coming out of those speakers that it sounded great there, but it sounded muddy anywhere else as a result. Later, when I went to work there, I already knew the problem so I compensated for it from that point on.

The whole thing about the monitoring at EMI, especially in Number 2, was that the speaker we monitored on (remember this was back in the mono days so we only listened on one) was an Altec 605 that sounded like crap. You really had to fight to get a good sound out of it. The saving grace was that once you got it sounding good you knew it would sound good anywhere. We really had to struggle, but I think that's why The Beatles' stuff still sounds as good as it does today. So many studios over time have had overhyped monitors so that the recording always sounded great there, but when you got it outside the sound fell apart.

Speaking of mono, I am old enough that I started mixing before stereo had taken over. That's one of the reasons I have always espoused that The Beatles' music needs to be listened to in mono, at least up to *The White Album*. The only mixes that the band heard and gave their seal of approval to were the mono mixes up to that point. When I first moved to stereo I found it really difficult, since I'd learned my art in a mono world and it was hard to change. Nowadays I couldn't do a decent mono mix for love or money.

Beatles Recording Notes

For drum mics we used either an STC 4038, a Neumann KM 56, or AKG D 19C over the top of the drums as an overhead mic. While Ringo's bass drum usually received an AKG D 20, it wasn't uncommon for a D 19C to be used for the same purpose. A Neumann KM 56 was used on snare, and a couple of other D 19s were placed over or under the toms. Bass guitar would have been recorded with a DI, with either a Neumann U 67 or an STC 4038 placed on the amp. The vocals would have all been recorded with Neumann U 47s.

When recording a string section, the cellos were miked with AKG C 12s, the violas and violins with U 47s, and any additional vocalists with U 47s.

The Beatles certainly used Vox amps exclusively in the beginning, but as they became more famous they were given/could afford many more different pieces of equipment. This led to a lot more experimentation by *The White Album*, with more Fenders appearing around that time. The miking generally consisted of Neumann U 67s placed a foot to two feet away. The good old standby mic, the AKG D 19C, was often used on acoustic guitar, as well as on the piano. We used various techniques for miking the piano, everything from the standard over-the-strings to setting it on the bottom of the soundboard.

Abbey Road had a few types of compressors and limiters but the ones used almost exclusively were Fairchild 660s and EMI modified Altec 436Bs. The Fairchilds would be used on drums, vocals, and sometimes piano. The Altecs were used on bass, sometimes guitars, and sometimes even across the entire mix. My best recollection is that the drums were never put through the Altec compressors, only a Fairchild.

We tended to hit the compressors fairly hard, but it varied with every session since we set them to sound right in any given situation with no hard and fast rules. Both compressors were used on the initial recording as well as during the mix. When you're working on 4-track, and later 8-track, you have to make decisions and commit to how things are going to sound right from the beginning. There was none of the more modern method of recording everything flat, then sorting it out later. Thankfully.

CHAPTER 4

Recording *The White Album*

The White Album sessions were just like the multitude of other sessions that occurred before The Beatles existed, and have continued ever since. The biggest difference is that no one's talking about any of those other, earlier sessions over 40 years later, not many of them anyway.

While recording *The White Album* there were long sessions and there were short sessions; the only problem was we never knew which it was going to be ahead of time. The session was always booked to start at 2:30 P.M., but quite often the band wouldn't arrive until much later, *if* they showed up at all. We would eventually know that they weren't going to turn up though, because the fans weren't outside. You could stick your head out the front door and you'd immediately know, "Oh, the girls aren't there. Looks like they're not coming in today, so we might as well go home." It was amazing, but those girls always knew way before we were officially told.

The thing that no one can quite comprehend is that The Beatles' sessions could often be boring. It could feel like absolutely nothing was happening for hour after hour and at times the band could be difficult to work with. In fact, most of the older studio staff did not want to work on Beatles projects. The sessions that were long could be long, long, long, and most of those older engineers preferred to work the standard three-hour sessions of 10 A.M. to 1 P.M., 2:30 P.M. to 5:30 P.M., or 7 P.M. to 10 P.M., strangely in sync with the pub hours of that time, which certainly didn't fit into the way The Beatles recorded at all.

The hours certainly helped us out in the wallet in that you didn't have to work more than the standard 40 hours to get overtime; overtime started at 5:30 P.M., and after midnight it would go into "golden time" where your pay doubled. Since Beatles sessions could go until 3 or 4 o'clock in the morning, most of that time would be overtime, so if you were working on those sessions you were not doing badly at all. It made up for the minimum salary that you'd make during normal working hours. Management tried to change the pay structure at one point but engineer Pete Mew wanted to organise a union, which stopped them in their tracks. He's still working there and still works Beatles hours, not coming in until 2 or 3 o'clock.

> *By 1969 all of the bands were unkempt and messy, and for some reason there was this backlash where we were all dressing up. Ken would walk in with a three-piece suit and a Samsonite attaché case. He would take his jacket off, undo his waistcoat, take off his gold cuff links along with a very impressive watch that he would place on the desk, roll up his sleeves, then proceed to do a punishing long day of 14 or 15 hours. At the end of it he'd put on his watch and cuff links and walk out like he'd only done, like, six hours. Fashion had changed but there must've been a subliminal mindset against all of that. Ken actually took the look to the extreme. It was definitely some kind of statement for sure* (see Insert Figure 4.1).
> John Kurlander, second engineer for many Beatles albums

Now let's be real: when you're in the studio five or six days a week and spend hours and hours with the same people, at times you're going to rub each other the wrong way. It's just natural.

That said, over the years there has been so much written about the animosity that supposedly pervaded the studio during the recording of *The White Album*, and it's all been blown way out of proportion. For sure, there were definitely times when things blew up, but it was *nowhere* near as bad as it's been reported over and over. There was a lot of pressure to finish the album, which put everyone on edge, but it just wasn't that bad.

Of course there was some strife, but there always is during any project, and what The Beatles experienced during the making of *The White Album* just wasn't that different from what I've experienced on most projects at some time or another.

Please let people know that we had such a lot of fun. It wasn't that bad. They were so funny and so much fun to be around.
Chris Thomas, George Martin's assistant

I don't ever remember any strife having Yoko there, or Linda for that matter. It certainly was never a big thing for me. This whole thing about the women breaking up the band certainly wasn't true from what I could see.
John Smith, second engineer for many Beatles albums

THE BASICS

For basic tracks on *The White Album*, all four Beatles normally played, which was a departure from their previous several albums, although there were a few exceptions. Whomever wrote the song would run through it with the rest of the band, they'd all work out the arrangement, then start to record.

They could take ages to get the basic track though. Remember, back then, we were recording mostly to 4-track and there was no, "OK, the drums are good, let's keep them and then redo the other things," like we do today. All of the instruments of the basic track were mixed together on one or two tracks for most of the record, so you had to get everyone playing well at the same time.

That could take a while, so there were a lot of takes, and there was really no rhyme nor reason as to what was kept and what wasn't. We didn't record everything, although it was common to do 50 takes or more on a song if it needed it, and occasionally we'd record over a take that everyone agreed was bad.

There were sessions where they kept on and on rehearsing a song in the studio and it kind of got very tedious and boring. It went on for days on end sometimes.
John Smith

Although there were periods that it seemed to take forever to get basic tracks recorded, there were also some periods where everything went extremely fast. During the two weeks when George Martin went on vacation (Figure 4.2), we recorded seven or eight titles. George was blown away at how much we'd done when he got back.

Figure 4.2, George Martin's postcard.

There was such a great vibe that we did seven songs in a couple of weeks. George Martin couldn't believe it. He phoned me up so excited and happy, which was a big thing for me because then I believed I earned a permanent job with George. That was the only thing I was really interested in. When George came back from holiday the whole thing gathered more and more momentum. We were working in different studios with different guys and it all became sort of a factory.

Chris Thomas

Once the basic was put down, the songwriter was the one that would be in charge for the rest of the recording, and the others might not even show up for days on end until the song was finished. If Paul had to come in to put a bass track on one of George's songs, Paul would come in that day, do his thing, and then leave. Every song was very much like that. The individual songwriter took control of the process.

WE POP OUT FOR A BIT

When the band was working out a new song, the tape would have to be rolling for a lot of the run-throughs and takes. It was decided after a while that there only ever needed to be one person in the control room at any given time to make sure that there was tape running. Sometimes it would be George Martin, while second engineer John Smith and I would go walkabout. Sometimes John (Smith) would be left there while George (Martin) and I went out, or I'd be there and George and John would disappear for maybe half an hour. The sound had been gotten at the beginning of the session and the levels were all set, so it was just a case of making sure that there was tape on the 4-track and it was rolling. The guys were just taping and taping and wouldn't bother to even listen to anything until the end of the session, at which point they'd come up and say, "OK, let's hear a few" just to hear how the arrangement was progressing over the course of the evening.

On this one occasion when George (Martin) was manning the control room, John (Smith) and I were walking out of the control room door when Len, the security guy, came up to us and said, "You've got to go upstairs and look out the window beside Harry Moss's room." "Well, why?" we asked. "Just do it. Go up there and take a look. Go on, hurry up," he urged.

So up we went, found the window, and peered out. We couldn't see what the hell he was talking about until suddenly a light in an apartment across the way caught our attention. As we now turned our focus on the window, plain as day we could see a number of girls exercising naked. Nude. Not a stitch on. Now, I was 21 and John was probably about 19 at the time, so our hormones were raging, and every time the two of us got to hang out together, we'd immediately go up there to catch a peek. Sometimes we'd get lucky and sometimes we wouldn't.

There was one really good night where the girls were putting on a splendid show when the hair on the back of my neck stood up as if there was someone watching us from behind. I turned around to find Paul and Ringo checking not only us out, but the girls as well. "So now we know what you're up to whenever you leave the control room," laughed Paul. John and I never went up there again, but the next day Ringo came to the session with the biggest pair of binoculars I'd ever seen in my life.

> *We were discovered by either Paul or Ringo, and the next day they turned up with binoculars. I think it was 99% imagination and about 1% reality since the women were quite a distance away. That cut it down to 95% imagination. Who knows what we were looking at across the way. We thought it was girls, but it could've been guys with long hair for all we really knew, but it kind of passed the time.*
>
> John Smith

"GLASS ONION"

One of the things that has always fascinated me is the way people read things into records that weren't necessarily there. You know, everything from "Paul Is Dead" to backwards masking of prayers to Satan. Another great example is in the song "Glass Onion." There's a snare drum part that goes blat blat at the start and then happens three more times in the song. To make it sound a bit bigger, we tracked several other snare drum hits onto a separate track. Later into the session, we had to record Paul and Chris Thomas playing recorders, but there were no empty tracks left. There was, however, an empty space on the same track as the extra snares where we could record the overdub. I had a new second engineer that night and I wasn't quite prepared to let him make what seemed to me like a tight punch-in right after the last blat blat, so I said, "Don't worry, I'll do it," maybe a little over-confidently.

We did a couple of takes where the performances weren't acceptable, but where Mr. Bigmouth here got the punch exactly right. We decided to try one more take and wouldn't you know it, I pushed the record button early and, much to my horror and total embarrassment, accidentally erased the snare double-track. John thought for a bit and decided he liked the way it got smaller after the biggest part of the song and as a result, the song has the snare doubles in the first three times, but on the last section it only has the original single snare hits.

What's funny is the number of people who've since said, "Ah, it's so brilliant the way they took it from that big sound down to that small one at the end there. Only The Beatles could be that clever. What meaning did that have?" Clever? Meaning? It was just a mistake. I admit it, I fucked up. The brilliance of The Beatles was that they would take a mistake like that and run with it.

"HELTER SKELTER"

The sessions for "Helter Skelter" were a bit weird because George Martin had gone on vacation. He was having less and less to do with everything in the studio by that point, since each individual Beatle was so much in control, and he became less and less important to them as time went on. I think they actually reached the point where they didn't even need him for orchestral arrangements, since they would play what they wanted the string lines to sound like on a piano and George just scored what they played. He wasn't so much creating the arrangement as just transcribing it.

So off on vacation George went and he left his assistant, Chris Thomas, in charge in his stead. Chris had been hanging out for a bit previously, but he was always in the background, so this was the first track that he actually had to take over from George Martin and be classified as the "producer."

As he was sitting beside me for that first session, I know how intimidated he felt by the whole thing. How could he not be? I had experienced the same feeling a couple of times myself, so I knew exactly what he was going through.

To make it worse, the band was always going, "How was that one, Ken?" with Chris sitting next to me knowing that he should be weighing in with an opinion, but not getting much of their attention.

He really thought they hated him because when he finally did come up with something, their response to him had very much of a "who the fuck are you?" attitude.

The 8-Track

Up until this point, everything done at EMI by The Beatles was still done on 4-track, but they now had a taste of 8-track recording at Trident and they wanted more. One day George Harrison, with nothing better to do, began to wonder around the building. Lo and behold, he caught sight of a new 3M 8-track machine (see Figure 4.3).

It turns out that George Martin actually knew EMI had two 8-track machines but didn't want to use them as they couldn't do a lot of things that we were used to. There was no varispeed on them, and they weren't set up for ADT (Artificial/Automatic Double Tracking—see "The Beatles' ADT" sidebar in the next chapter), so he didn't want them in the studio until they did everything that we needed them to. The trouble was, he was on vacation.

Any new piece of gear that came into the studio had to be pulled apart and rebuilt so the maintenance boffins knew how it all worked, which as a result, meant that if something went wrong, they knew how to fix it instantly. One of the 8-track machines was along the corridor in one of the maintenance rooms in the process of being pulled apart for just this reason, whilst the second was a little further down the corridor in plain view. George passed it and came running into the control with, "Hey, there's an 8-track down there. We've got to use it." Well, others may disagree but in my mind you don't argue with the biggest band in the world, so we wheeled it in. And, here's the part you'll see several more times: Of course, we all got into trouble with management, but how do you say no to The Beatles?

It turned out to be quite a bitch using the 8-track, as George (Martin) had surmised. Aside from it not being set up the way we were used to, the biggest pain of all was the fact that the board was only configured to monitor four tracks at a time, and after jury-rigging things a bit, we could only ever listen to seven tracks until it was time to mix, since it was an 8-channel board and we needed one of the inputs for a microphone input. What we did was to monitor three tracks from the board the normal way, then use an outboard pre-mixer for the other four channels.

There was another by-product of using the 3M machine before its time. The great designers over at Studer set their machines up so that when you would rewind, the audio was muted so you didn't hear the audio burble as the tape wound back over the playback head. When we got the 3M 8-tracks, the audio became relatively quiet during rewind because of the tape being pulled away from the heads, but if the second engineer stopped the machine suddenly the tape would immediately jam against the heads and blast out in both the control room and headphones. This took a lot of getting used to by the second engineers because it became their responsibility to flip a mute switch to kill the signal and they would often forget to do it. It happened several times during Beatles sessions where the band got blasted like that, and it appears that they held me responsible. There's supposedly a comment in the unreleased *Let It Be* movie footage where Paul is talking to John and George and he mentions "Ken blasting us out in the headphones."

They were in the middle of a take when Chris heard a mistake. Now normally nothing would be said and they'd just keep on doing takes until they got a perfect one, but on this occasion Chris felt the need to point out the error of their ways, a possible suicide mission! They were out for blood as they all stomped up the stairs to listen to "The Mistake," but Chris's observation was completely right, and from that point onward, Chris was one of the boys. We did a lot of recording once he settled in and they became very fast-paced sessions.

Figure 4.3, The 3M 8-track

It was trial by fire when George Martin went on vacation. He just said, "Make yourself available to The Beatles," so I just thought I'd hang out with Mal Evans [Beatles roadie] and bring tea up from the canteen and stuff. The first one to arrive was Paul who said, "What are you doing here?" I said, "George asked me to carry on while he was away." At that he said, "Well if you want to produce us, then produce us," which made me feel absolutely catatonic.

The first afternoon they only addressed Ken. I knew if they ended up telling me to fuck off, then that was the end of my career with George Martin, and that's what I was really worried about.

To make matters worse, they [The Beatles] always had these meetings about hiring and firing the people at Apple, and during one of these meetings I overheard John say, "He's not really doing his bit." I immediately thought he was talking about me. That evening we were doing "Helter Skelter" and I remember interrupting them when they made a mistake and they all came up the stairs one by one to listen. I thought, "Oh, what happens if I've just imagined this." Fortunately I was right.

Chris Thomas

Paul wanted the song loud and raucous, so they all turned the volume up to make it loud and raucous. A lot of it was cut live, though there were a few overdubs done. Since we'd just moved to 8-track, everyone was still used to playing the basic track live at that point, so we mixed everything together to two tracks and didn't separate each individual instrument to its own track yet.

We did about three takes on that track, so it was one of the quicker songs on the album, although there was a previous session where we did three takes of the song as well, including a 26-minute jam. Unfortunately, I have no memory of that session at all, and if it wasn't for the Mark Lewisohn book *The Complete Beatles Recording Sessions*, I wouldn't even believe that it had happened.

During overdubs, we put extra guitars on with George and Paul playing lead together. In looking at notes of the session, apparently there is some trumpet and some sax that were recorded as well but never used, which I have absolutely no recollection of. Back then I was still learning my gig, and I was concentrating more on what I was doing than what they were doing. (Well, that and watching naked calisthenics.) And of course all the vocals were overdubbed.

One day when they were particularly late coming to the studio, Chris and I decided to do a mix that probably would have worked well on the radio today because we compressed the hell out of it. We loved it. The band, however, didn't share our passion.

I remember mixing it in stereo with panning everywhere. One
guitar riff would pan from left to right and the next one would
pan right to left. John arrived and I said, "John, listen to what
we've done." I sat him down in-between the speakers and
turned it up really loud and there were guitars whizzing around
his head. I thought he'd be really knocked out, but he just
went, "Thanks for the trip," and walked out. The song wasn't
even finished at that point. It was just the backing track. I just
wanted them to OK the idea of the guitars whizzing around,
which he never did.

Chris Thomas

"PIGGIES"

Ah yes, time for a row with the studio management thanks to The
Beatles. The band was working out the song in Number 2 when Chris
happened to spot a harpsichord set up in Number 1. Once he started
to play it he felt that it might be just the right sound for the song, so
he immediately found George Harrison and said, "Come and listen."
When George heard it, the track immediately crystallised in his head
and he had to have it on the song.

As they started to wheel the harpsichord out of the studio towards
Number 2 I learned what they were doing, rushed down and hit the
roof. Number 1 was set up for a big classical project that had already
started and was continuing the next day. All the mics were in place
and everything was set up as they left it, so you just couldn't change
anything like the harpsichord in the middle of it. Everything had to
match up with what they did the day before in case they had to make
any edits. My solution? We just moved the whole band into Number
1 and recorded the basic there using the harpsichord, acoustic guitar,
tambourine, and bass. We put up fresh mics instead of using the ones
that were already set up for the session, I took a note of all the EQ
settings so I could reset everything, and nothing in the studio ended
up being moved. One of the great things about EMI was that they
had so many bloody mics that you could double them up easily. We
reset everything as it was after we recorded what we needed and
moved back into Number 2.

As often seems to happen after situations like this, the management found out what had happened the next day, and I, as well as the maintenance engineer who helped us set things up, were severely chewed out. Hey, the buck stops here. It was my fault as I was in charge and I allowed it to happen, but come on, you can't argue with the biggest band in the world. The fact was that management never left their phone numbers so we could call them when those things cropped up. Just once I would have loved to phone them up and say, "Here, you talk to them and tell them they can't do it." Of course that was never allowed because The Beatles ultimately had more power than the management of the studio.

For some reason I was looking for something different for the song. I was wondering around and found a harpsichord in Number 1. George [Harrison] came in and played this song "Piggies," and said, "We can do this one now." Then he started to play "Something" and I said, "Let's do that one. It's a much better song." He said, "Do you really think so? We were about to give it to Jackie Lomax as a single." He was quite adamant about not doing "Something" so we did "Piggies" instead. He got me to start learning and playing it. Then I got hold of John Smith and we started to push the harpsichord into Number 2, at which point Ken came in and went absolutely berserk because the studio was already set up for a session and nothing could be moved because they were trying to seamlessly edit performances together. I was pushing the harpsichord in one direction and Ken was pushing it in another while going absolutely bananas at me. We ended up recording it all in Number 1.

Chris Thomas

"BACK IN THE U.S.S.R."

By the time "Back in the U.S.S.R." was recorded, Ringo had temporarily quit the band. It wasn't that he was in the studio and stormed out, it was more like he just didn't turn up one day. The sessions were undisciplined enough that whatever any of the others felt like doing at any given time is what they did, so he never knew if he was going to be playing or not. He didn't feel needed or wanted and he was tired of waiting around, so he just decided not to show up anymore.

I don't remember the incident being spoken about too much at the time, and the whole thing was treated just as a "Ringo's not here today" kind of thing, so we just carried on as usual. We recorded the basic track of "Back in the U.S.S.R." first with Paul playing drums, George on lead guitar, and John on bass, but there were parts of Paul's drum track that just weren't good enough, so we recorded a second drum track. This time the drums were played by both George and John at the same time on the same kit, one of them playing kick and snare while the other played the cymbals and toms, or something like that. Between the two tracks, we got one solid drum track, so we mixed them all together and that's the drum track that you hear on the record. I never got a chance to record Paul playing drums well, although I know he did do it on a few of the songs on the album that were recorded outside of EMI.

In the end, Ringo returned a week or so later, and George (Harrison) had the entire Number 2 studio decked out with flowers and a banner that said, "Welcome back, Ringo." He was happy to be back, and they were extremely happy to have him back.

"MOTHER NATURE'S SON"

The Beatles were open to everyone coming up with ideas and openly encouraged us to do so. In fact they were so into experimenting that there were times that the band would get involved technically with things like, "Let's go to the mic room and find a different microphone." If they found one that they liked the look of, we'd have to try it. Please note, "liked the look of" meant that the sound quality never entered their thoughts.

Sometimes the experiment could be rather mundane and other times it would be totally off the wall. One of the more sane requests came from John, who came in one day asking, "How come it's always so much easier sitting at home recording a track? I want to set it up just like it is at home."

"But John, you're in a studio. That's going to make it different," George (Martin) and I told him. John was insistent though. "No, I want to set it up just like home." "OK, then," we thought. It's John Lennon so you're not going to argue.

In the middle of Number 2 we set up an armchair and a lamp, and made it as close to a home type of environment as we could. John sat there with the acoustic guitar, we miked it up, and he did a couple of takes. He came up to the control room for a listen and at the end said, "It's no different. It's just as bad now as it was before."

"Yep, that's right. This is a studio. You hear all of the differences here," I replied. "OK, then. Let's go back to the normal way," came the reply. He had to go through the experience of trying it before he'd believe it.

An example of a wild experiment in trying to get a different sound came during the recording of "Mother Nature's Son." Paul decided that he wanted a distant sound on the drums. Right at the end of EMI there was a staircase that went from the basement all the way to the top of the building, so we set up some drums at the bottom, and I put a mic up at the same level as the control room to capture it. When Paul hit the bass drum, much to everyone's surprise it sounded like tympani, and that's what you hear on the record at 1:54.

A bit later while listening to a playback, Paul began tapping a pencil to the beat of the song on the cover of a book that he had on his lap, and decided that should be in the song as well. They never taught you how to get the best sound out of a book at EMI, but I carefully miked it as best I could, and you can hear it about a minute into the song. These were the kinds of things that we were always trying. Sometimes they worked, and sometimes they didn't.

We were doing orchestral overdubs for John and George and it was going to be a fairly early night by normal standards. Usually we would finish by 5 or 6 in the morning, but on this particular session we were finished by midnight, so both Ken and I were looking forward to getting home early. Suddenly Paul walked in completely out of the blue, since we weren't expecting him. We had packed things up pretty much, as the floor was clear of mics. He asked if we'd mind if he could put down a track. What are you going to do? It was Paul McCartney. He promised it wouldn't take long.

He sat down with an acoustic guitar and started singing, and before we knew what happened it was 7 or 8 in the morning. How are you going to walk away from a song like that? It was just so magical and spellbinding. It was really neat just the three of us working together, as opposed to the band, which had its own kind of atmosphere. It was a very intimate working relationship.

John Smith

One of the things I was impressed by was that they had a very playful way they approached a backing track. They'd try to incorporate anything that anyone could bang or make a funny noise with. Afterwards things would get a bit more serious, but they'd still have this childlike "let's see what we can get out of this" attitude. I've never worked with a band that was that open and had that sort of fun. It wasn't scientific at all.

Chris Thomas

The Beatles' Drum and Bass Sounds

While the majority of The Beatles' drum sound can be directly attributed to one Mr. Starkey, there were a number of additional factors as well. One was the use of tea towels across the top heads of the snare and toms, which were used as standard operating procedure on all tracking sessions (a tea towel is a thin dish towel). This was something that the group was doing on previous albums, and if you listen to the earlier recordings you can hear the sound was very dead as a result. I've tried to use the same technique a number of times since, but it just never sounded as good as with Ringo.

The other thing that was rather radical for the time was the front head of the bass drum was removed and the sound was deadened with towels, a practise that's become commonplace today. Once again that was something they were already doing by the time I became their engineer.

A third thing was changing the position of the snare drum mic. Geoff had used it below the snare, while I preferred the sound of miking the top head instead. Although I'd been engineering for a while by the time of *The White Album* and I was far more comfortable with what I was doing, I was still coming in behind Geoff, so I couldn't instantly jump in and change everything. It had to evolve from the way he had started it.

Another thing that occurred during my watch was that the 4-string bass was sometimes doubled by a 6-string bass on some songs. By this time Paul had acquired a Fender Jazz bass which he used in lieu of his Rickenbacker, and a Fender Bass VI was always around the studio. What possibly happened was that the band had heard German orchestra leader Bert Kaempfert double an upright acoustic bass with a 6-string bass when they were in Germany, and decided to give it a try with electrics. Although they might not have known at the time, the practise was also used in Nashville on a lot of country songs and even had a name: "Tic-toc bass." You can hear it on "Piggies," "While My Guitar Gently Weeps," "Glass Onion," and "Rocky Raccoon." The two parts were always played together and never overdubbed individually.

A few weeks later, Paul decided to record a brass section on the song. This was during one of the more tense times within the band so it was just him and the brass section in the studio that night. As the session was progressing, John and Ringo walked in wanting to check on things, and for a brief period you could cut the atmosphere with a knife. The additional personnel just added an edge to the session that wasn't there before. As soon as they left, it all went back to normal again.

"YER BLUES"

You may remember rooms 1A and 2A originally housed the two Telefunken 4-track tape machines, and they weren't all that large at 8 feet by 15 feet. 2A was right next door to the control room of Number 2, and at some point they had put a window in-between the two. We were doing a track of George's called "Not Guilty," which finished up not making the album. As was the norm, he was doing the vocal in the studio, but he just wasn't feeling it, so he wanted to try something different. Why not sing it in the control room instead? A typical Beatles off-the-wall idea.

One of the rules of EMI was that you had to monitor off tape so you could hear if there were any problems with the recording. If you listened to the signal right from the desk, it could sound fine but you'd never know if there was something wrong with the recording until you played the tape back later, so the desk was set up in such a way that you always listened off the tape. The problem with this setup is that there was a delay between the live sound and what was being recorded because of how the record head and the playback head were placed on the tape machine (see "The Beatles' ADT" sidebar in the next chapter for more detail). This normally wasn't a problem, until George wanted to sing in the control room. As a result, the delay between George singing and hearing the playback was very disconcerting, and that didn't help the vocal much.

At the end of one of the takes I stood up next to John and said jokingly, "God, the way you guys are going the next thing you'll want to do is record in there," as I pointed towards the relatively small Room 2A. He just sort of looked at me and didn't say a word. We then spent a bit more time trying to record the vocal on "Not Guilty," but eventually gave up.

"OK, new song. It's called 'Yer Blues,'" John then announced the next day, "and I want to record it in there," and pointed towards Room 2A. "Me and my big mouth," I thought to myself.

The good thing was that the room was empty, but it was so small that after the four of them were set up, none of them could move. If one of them turned and swung his guitar he'd hit someone else in the head it was so tight.

With the instruments that close together, there was so much leakage of all the instruments into all of the mics that it was just a question of doing the best you could to blend it all together to get the sound, because you couldn't pull up the drums without increasing the level of the guitars as well. That said, I loved the drum sound we got, and it was one of the best drum sounds on the album as far as I'm concerned.

What you end up hearing on the record is what we heard during the recording. The only thing we ended up recutting was just a little of the vocal. You'll notice if you listen to the track that the sound of the vocal completely changes about halfway through the song. Where it changes is where we recut the vocal. John said, "It's going to sound different anyway, so let's make it completely different." So we didn't worry about the fact that the sound changed. That was the way they were; it was, as I can't emphasise enough, all about trying anything.

GEORGE'S DEMOS

There were always a lot of things going on at the studio with The Beatles, and no one person ever had a handle on everything that was happening. As a result there were many recordings that were incompletely documented or documented incorrectly. A perfect example is a session attended only by George (Harrison)—it happened to be on his birthday—where he recorded demos of "Old Brown Shoe," "All Things Must Pass," and "Something," songs that would eventually show up on later Beatles or solo albums.

When Lewisohn's *The Complete Beatles Recording Sessions* book came out, he had me indicated as the engineer for the session. When I saw this I thought to myself, "I never did that session," and immediately thought, "If that's wrong, then this whole book must be rubbish." Years later when I was working for George and sorting out his tape library I came across the very same tape and surprise, surprise, it has the initials "KS" in the "Engineered by" box. As I read that I thought to myself, "Oh my God, I must have done the session after all!" and started to doubt my own mind regarding what I actually remembered from that period.

A few months afterwards I related the story to Brian Kehew, author of the wonderful *Recording The Beatles* book, and a few days after telling him the story, he came back to me with the fact that he had contacted Brian Gibson, one of the maintenance guys at EMI at the time. "Oh yeah, I remember that session. I did it," Brian Gibson told him. "What do you mean? It has Ken's initials on it," Brian Kehew asked. "The maintenance guys weren't allowed to do sessions, so if we did something we'd use the initials of an engineer so we wouldn't get into trouble. I knew that Ken was doing a lot of Beatles sessions, so I used his initials," came the reply.

So it turned out that everyone was right: I wasn't losing my mind and the book was accurate. I didn't do the session after all, but it sure looked like I did according to the documentation.

"LONG, LONG, LONG"

The working title for George Harrison's "Long, Long, Long" was "It's Been a Long, Long, Long Time," and it certainly was in the regard that recording the basics for the song took a full 67 takes before the band felt it had a keeper. For this basic, the band consisted of George on acoustic guitar and vocals, Ringo on drums, and Paul on the Hammond organ.

The recording went along rather normally until the very end of the song, where you hear a knocking sound that came as the result of a bottle of Liebfraumilch (a German white wine) that was on top of the

Leslie speaker cabinet that the organ used. As Paul played the organ louder, the bottle started to rattle against the top of the cabinet and you can hear it on the record.

There's also a scraping sound heard at the end of song. When everything started to go a little hectic at the end, George grabbed the mic I was using to capture the acoustic, an AKG D 19C, and started scraping it up and down the strings of the guitar, and that was part of the chaos you hear. The Beatles always liked to take advantage of accidents.

"BIRTHDAY"

The recording of "Birthday," began rather normally in the afternoon. Sometime during the session Paul casually mentioned that *The Girl Can't Help It*, one of the first rock 'n' roll movies, was going to be shown on television that night. Since Chris had never seen it, we decided to take a dinner break when the movie was going to be on so we could watch it. We all went over to Paul's house, watched the movie there, then went back to finish the song. Maybe it was the vibe of the movie that put everyone in a good mood, but it was one of the few songs that was actually completed in only a day.

All four of them played on the basic track, but it's difficult to remember exactly who played what since they frequently passed around different instruments to each other. If Paul was playing guitar or piano, either John or George might play bass, or it might be John on piano. I do remember that Yoko and Pattie Harrison contributed "Birthday" background vocals, while roadie Mal Evans and Ringo provided handclaps.

We did do something interesting with the sound of the piano though. A lot of people think that it went through a wah-wah pedal at a couple of points, but what we actually did was feed the sound back through one of the Vox guitar amps in the studio (a Conqueror) that had a function on it called MRB (for mid-range boost). It was like a stepped EQ in that it didn't gradually change like most tone controls, it changed in large steps from one frequency to the next. We were looking for a different sound in those parts so I suggested putting the piano through the amp and using that effect on it.

I went down to the studio and plugged it up to show them what I meant. When John heard it he immediately said, "Yeah, that's great. You do it," and made me stay down there for the whole song turning the knob in time with the beat. I was terrified looking up at the window and seeing them all staring down at me while hoping that my time was on. I guess it was, because the take was a keeper and that's what you hear on the record.

CHAPTER 5

The White Album Epilogue

The White Album was very different from what The Beatles had done before, and that led to it being much disliked when it came out. People were expecting *Sgt. Pepper's* part 2, but that was not the Beatles way, as in their world, everything needed to constantly change. People seemed shocked by this album. It was stark and much more basic rock 'n' roll compared to *Sgt. Pepper's*, but thankfully over time it's grown to become one of the most loved Beatles albums, even climbing to number 10 on *Rolling Stone* magazine's "500 Greatest Albums of All Time."

The White Album was also different from other Beatles albums in that it was specifically mixed for stereo, and The Beatles were actually there to approve the stereo mixes. They'd never been interested in stereo before as their working process had been to mix a song in mono as soon as it was finished, and then leave the stereo to be mixed a while later, almost as an afterthought. Stereo still hadn't really caught on in England at the time so no one, not even the Fab Four, particularly cared about it.

As in the past, the stereo mixes for *The White Album* tended to be put off until the last minute, even though they were now deemed to be important. The reason for the importance was not what one might expect though. Paul explained to me whilst mixing the stereo version of "Helter Skelter" that it had to sound different from the mono version. Apparently fans started to buy both the mono and stereo albums and wrote to them asking if they knew there were differences between the versions, so Paul and/or the band saw this as a great way to boost sales.

By this time I had mixed some other things in stereo, but there wasn't much that you could do artistically when the material was recorded on 4-track or even 8-track, so it just wasn't that fulfilling. Everything was recorded with mono mixes in mind, and in many cases, a number of instruments were mixed together on the same track during recording. Routinely there might be a couple of guitars together on the same track, or even different instruments such as drums, piano, and tambourine. Try making that work in stereo. Another problem was that the desks at that time had been designed before stereo reached the masses, and so stereo facilities on them were almost an afterthought. Not until we moved to more tracks, and the desks were designed accordingly, could we separate the instruments and pan them individually.

Stereo Challenge

What made stereo mixing even more difficult was the limitations of the boards at EMI at the time. The default panning of channels 1 and 7 were panned hard left while channels 2 and 8 were hard right, with channels 3 through 6 fitted with a primitive pan control. That's one of the explanations as to why some of the stereo mixes were so weird in the early days, with the bass and drums on one side and the vocals on the other.

Even during the stereo mixes we kept comparing them to the mono ones. There was a strong possibility that a fan would take the record over to a friend's place and play it on a system that was only mono, so you had to make sure it sounded good in both formats. As is common today, that was accomplished with a stereo-to-mono switch on the desk to compare the song in both formats.

MIXING "BLACKBIRD"

"Blackbird" was originally mixed in mono the night it was recorded, but Paul decided he would like it remixed in stereo with one final touch: the sound of an actual blackbird. Assistant engineer John

Smith was sent to the old tin closet that housed the sound effects library to look for the bird effects. He returned with a tape that had numerous birds, each separated by a few seconds of leader tape. He spooled through the reel of bird sounds and said, "OK, this is the blackbird," and we laid it down without giving it much thought. A little while later while we were deep into mixing the song with the sound effect, Ken Townsend walked in, gave a quick listen, and said, "The song's called 'Blackbird,' isn't it?" We all nodded that it was. "Well, why are you using a thrush then?" he asked.

By now the embarrassed John (Smith) was running for the effects reel to do some bird verification. After a quick look at the reel, he realised that he hadn't gone back far enough on the tape and the actual blackbird sound effect was the one after the one he'd chosen. While the mix we had sounded great, to achieve complete ornithological accuracy we had to do the entire thing again. Millions of Beatles fans would never know the difference, but for sure there would be a few bird lovers out there who would turn it into a big deal if it wasn't correct, and someone somewhere would probably find a way to make it a further clue to Paul being dead.

MIXING "BACK IN THE U.S.S.R."

Paul decided that he wanted the sound of a jet plane on the intro and end of the song. We copied the effect from a tape in the EMI sound effects library and made a loop so that it could be constantly playing and we could bring it into the mix at any time. If you listen to the song carefully, the sound of the jet at the end is totally different from what it sounds like in the beginning because the tape loop was so worn out by the end of the song that there was no high-end left. It also stretched a little, which made it warble a bit as well. I don't think we could've gotten another mix out of it.

It was part of the tape op functions to take care of the tape machines and sound effects and stuff like that. We had this jet plane effect on a loop going around a pencil that I was holding because it was going to be introduced throughout the song. For the mono mix everything came out OK, but the stereo mix took a long, long time and I was holding this pencil to keep the effects tape taut. I guess I must've been leaning back on it because on the mono mix it sounds like a jet plane but on the stereo it has a wobble sound because the tape was starting to get creased. The mono has this clear, clean, lovely jet sound while the stereo is an abomination of a jet sound. That's simply because I was leaning back while holding the pencil and started to stretch it, unaware by me and everyone else what was happening. When you compare the two it's like, "Oh, my God. What were we thinking?"

John Smith

SONGS FROM TRIDENT

The band recorded and mixed a number of songs for *The White Album* at Trident, once again because they had an 8-track tape machine before EMI. These songs included "Dear Prudence," "Martha My Dear," and "Honey Pie." While I had no direct connection with these songs, I did find it interesting that we never had any problems with the sound of them the way we did for "Hey Jude." I don't know what they did at Trident after "Hey Jude," but something definitely changed. The basic tracks of "Savoy Truffle" were also recorded at Trident, but finished up at EMI, where I mixed it with never a bit of a problem with the sound.

"WHILE MY GUITAR GENTLY WEEPS"

I'd really like to remember the "While My Guitar Gently Weeps" sessions since I've been repeatedly asked about them, especially the Eric Clapton overdub session, but the only recollection I have is of mixing the song. Eric had been reluctant to play on the record because "no one plays on Beatles records," but was convinced by his good friend George that the rest of the band would be OK with it. To his credit, he wanted to sound as far away from Eric Clapton as he could, so he insisted on not using any of his own gear and used The Beatles' gear already set up in the studio instead (I wish I could remember exactly what gear he used).

This wish to sound as un-Clapton-like as possible extended to mixing as well. To make it sound "more Beatley," the ADT setup (see sidebar) was used to get the warbling sound that's on the lead guitar and organ, since they were both on the same track. Chris Thomas was put in charge of manually turning the varispeed of the tape machine up and down during the mix to obtain the distinctive wobble.

I thought it was stupid because it was such a gimmick, but that's what they wanted because Eric didn't want it [to] sound like him. They wanted it really extreme so that's what I did. I did that for hours. It was so bloody boring.

Chris Thomas

The Beatles' ADT

The Beatles, especially John, loved the sound of double-tracked vocals. The problem was that as much as he liked the sound, he hated having to sing the parts twice, so EMI head of maintenance Ken Townsend developed a remarkable way of simulating the same thing with something he named Artificial (some say Automatic) Double Tracking, or ADT for short.

ADT required two tape machines; our regular Studer J 37 4-track and one of the EMI BTR ¼" machines. The thing that was different about the Studer J 37 that wasn't readily available on the later 3M 8-track was that you could listen to both the output of the record (sync) and playback head at the same time (most tape machines allow you to monitor only one or the other), and this was the key factor enabling ADT.

All multitrack tape machines use the record head to both record on some tracks while simultaneously playing back, with a slightly inferior sound, the others. Because the playback head is located after the record head on the tape path (see Figure 5.1), if the performer listened back off the playback head to a previously recorded track whilst recording a new one, there would be a time lag. So by only using the record head during the recording process, everything stays in sync and eliminates this problem. Boy, I'm glad that's out of the way.

When mixing, the output from the record head would be sent to a BTR, which had a varispeed on it, and then the BTR's playback head would be sent to the desk. The output of the playback head of the Studer would be sent to another channel on the desk. The varispeed on machine 2, the BTR, enabled you to change the timing of the slightly inferior sync head signal in comparison to the playback head signal. Almost there. Once we had got it sounding close to what we were looking for, the wow and flutter variations between the two machines, be it minimal, created a constant pitch and timing difference that made it much more like real double-tracking than just putting a very fast delay on it.

It was soon discovered that moving the signal from the BTR from ahead of the other signal to after it, if done slowly, would give us a phasing effect. John being John decided to go a little wild with the varispeed, liked the effect, and christened it "flanging." This is the effect you hear on Eric and the Hammond organ on "While My Guitar Gently Weeps." *Phew.*

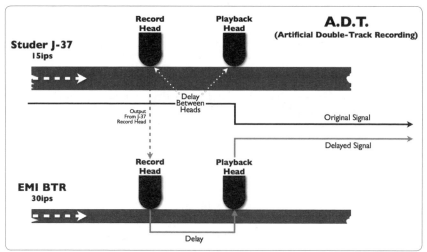

Figure 5.1: Artificial Double Tracking (A.D.T.).

THE COMPLETION

The last session I ever did with The Beatles as a band was a full 24-hour marathon to complete *The White Album*. Generally speaking, The Beatles never had a time schedule. They took as long as they wanted, and the project was done when they felt it was ready. This time was different though. It was the first time they were under the pressure of a deadline because the album was to be the first release on their new label, Apple Records.

We were always behind schedule, but the fact that it was a double album didn't help, nor did the fact that right towards the end John came in with a new song called "Julia." Luckily that was easy to record because it was just him and an acoustic guitar and a bit of double-tracking, but all of the recording just kept on going way past the time when we should have been mixing and cutting.

The release couldn't be delayed because there was a lot of promotion already set up and George (Harrison) was slated to fly out to Los Angeles with the masters for Capitol to master for the American market, so it had to be completed in time. We were far enough behind that as soon as everyone from the studio had gone home for the day, we took over the entire EMI facility, including all three studios and listening rooms. I was in one studio doing a mix with one member of the band, then I'd pop into another control room with someone else for another mix there. John Smith was in Room 41 with John (Lennon) and Chris listening to different running orders for the record. It was mayhem, but was also the beginning of a pattern that I became most familiar with as the years went on. It seemed that every time I was away from home on a project, the last 24 hours would be the same mad rush to finish it, then there'd be a mad dash straight to the airport to fly home. *The White Album* was just the first time it happened.

I was in Room 41 with John Lennon and John Smith making up running orders. Listening to so many different ones made us all a little nuts. By about 4 A.M. John [Smith] was up to about four foot of tape, cutting these bits out and then resplicing it. Ken came in about four in the morning and said, "Chris, can you help me? Paul wants to do another mix of 'Helter Skelter' but he's fallen asleep at the mixer." So I came in and we mixed it while he was still asleep, absolutely crashed out on the board.

Chris Thomas

John and Paul would sit down with a sheet of paper and make a running list on top of a copy of Sgt. Pepper's *on their lap in the first listening room. I'd then take the tapes into the second listening room and put it together while they were listening to a side that I had already edited in the first room. That took about 12 hours between all the re-edits of the four sides. Then they all went home and asked me if I could do the same thing with the stereo versions. I was probably up for 24 hours that day and working for at least 18. On many of the other days there was dope flying in and out of those studios, but on that night, everyone was stone cold sober.*

John Smith

The weirdest thing for me had nothing to do with the actual record. I was driving home during rush hour after everything was finally put to bed and I was absolutely exhausted. I came to a traffic light that was red and fell asleep while waiting for it to change. The next thing I know there was a car horn hooting at me. I looked in the rear-view mirror to find that there was my father in his car behind me, who then followed me all the way home to make sure I made it OK. The chances of that happening have to be at least a trillion to one, but like so much else in my life, it happened nonetheless.

CHAPTER 6

The Boys (and Girls) in and with the Band

I had a great time during my stint with the greatest and biggest band in the world (see Insert Figure 6.1). Believe me, I realise just how lucky I was for the amazing opportunity to work with them, and how much the association with The Beatles has helped me in my career since.

In the many years since then I've frequently been presented a pretty standard question when being asked about my time with them: "What was ____ like?" I've always been cautious in answering because it's sometimes difficult to gather all of one's impressions on the spot like that, and because I didn't want to say anything that might contradict the idea of what they think their favourite musical celebrity is really like. That said, it's time to put it all on record and answer the questions forever.

JOHN LENNON

John was everything you've ever heard about him. He could be sweet, he could be funny, or he could be the biggest arsehole you've ever met. You never quite knew which one you'd get, and he could sometimes become all of them within the same session.

65

John got bored very easily and as a result he liked things to move more quickly than everyone else, so he was always experimenting just to keep himself interested. That said, within his experimentation he still had very distinct ideas of what he wanted, like on "Walrus." The thing with "Everyone's got one. Everyone's got one" sung by the choir was all him, and he was the one who wanted Ringo to go through tuning to different radio stations during the mixing of "Walrus."

John always wanted to double-track his vocal, not because he thought he couldn't sing, but because he didn't like the sound of his voice. One of the more techie questions that I've been asked that illustrates this is, "Would John use pitch correction if he was recording today?" Yes, I can picture him using it. *Once*. And only then purely as an effect, and then he'd go on to something else.

We'll never know what music he may have come up with had he not departed, but maybe that's good. He was an amazing talent, but talent all too frequently diminishes and his reputation may stand stronger and longer because of his early demise.

GEORGE HARRISON

George, oh George. He was one of the nicest and most certainly one of the funniest people I have met in this business. He had his moments, we all do, but to portray him as sour or negative or untalented as some have is so far from anything that I ever saw during my time with him, both with The Beatles and afterwards. The other Beatles were funny, but I have to say that he most certainly was the funniest. He was the one that right in the beginning told George (Martin) that he didn't like his tie, and it just continued from there.

I think that George grew tired of the fame and adulation faster than the others. He was always kind and polite to people, but did his best to downplay who he was as much as possible. An example of this came one day when he and I stopped off to get a bite to eat during the installation of his studio at his Friar Park estate. A woman came up to him at the table and started with "You're him, aren't you?"

"I'm who?" George replied. "Him!" she said. "Who's him?" George countered. "You are. You're him."

Time plays tricks with regard to how long an actual event goes on, but it seemed to me that this continued for ages and not once did George back down. It became quite obvious that she recognised the face but couldn't put a name to it, and Mr. H. sure as hell wasn't going to help her.

I liked how he started to deal with that type of situation later in life. When someone would come up to him and say, "Aren't you George Harrison?" he would come back with "You know, I've been told I look like him by other people but I don't see it. I think I'm much better looking, don't you?" Very rarely did anyone pursue it further.

PAUL McCARTNEY

Paul the musician was amazing. From whence he started, he turned into one of the most melodic and influential bass players ever, which is astonishing especially when you consider that he wasn't even a bass player in the beginning of the band. He was brilliant as far as the lines he came up with, and the way he took to the piano was remarkable.

Writing-wise, Paul always went for commerciality, but John never wanted the boundaries that commerciality brought. Like John, Paul wanted to experiment, but that meant moving more into the classical arena, like using strings on songs like "Yesterday," and "Eleanor Rigby." If John was going to use an orchestra it would be very different, such as in "A Day in the Life." Even though Paul introduced him to avant garde music, John was the one who ended up using a lot of backwards loops and the like, which Paul never did.

Paul the person needs to be liked, but he's very specific as to whom he reciprocates. As an example, I felt that we'd grown close during the making of the Mary Hopkin album that I did with him. After I had left Abbey Road for Trident, I was upstairs in the mix room and saw that he had booked in with Wings, so at one point during the day I thought I'd go down and say hello. I popped into the control room with a "Hi Paul. How are you?" and all I got back was a brusque, "Fine," and he carried on with what he was doing. I thought, "I guess he's busy so I won't bother him any more," and just left. Sometime later he booked in again and I thought, "OK, let me give it another try," so I went down to the control room again. "Hi, Paul. How are you?" and this time he completely ignored me. At that point I just thought, "Fine. You've forgotten me. No biggie." It really didn't bother me because I knew that there were so many people in his life and I'd left that sphere of people around him.

Then he booked in one more time, and this time I wasn't about to go down to try to see him again. As it happened, I ran into Linda in the corridor. When she saw me she ran up to me put her arms around me and gave me a big kiss on the cheek. "Ken, Ken, how are you? You must come down to see Paul." So she dragged me down to see Paul and this time he was all over me like I was his long lost friend. "What's changed," I thought to myself. And then it suddenly hit me. That week I had the number one album as a producer with *Ziggy*. I was suddenly slightly more important. I did see him a couple more times at restaurants and he was always pleasant after that.

RINGO STARR

Ringo was and is a great drummer. His time was amazing. He wasn't technically brilliant, but that's what made him exceptional. That's what it was with all of them. They were street players, not schooled. Everything they did was unorthodox because that's how they learned it. They didn't know the rules and so had none of the boundaries that rules impart. That's the way it was with Ringo's fills. He would start off rather normally, then not know exactly how to get out of it, and end up with something unique as a result. Feel has absolutely nothing to do with playing in time. Ringo had both.

Ringo the person was quiet compared to the others, but he could be very funny and came out with some great lines from time to time. That said, you can't say he's a happy spirit. He's not a smiley or cuddly type of person, but he certainly seems a lot more comfortable with himself and his sobriety these days.

As heavy drinking has a way of doing, your less-than-perfect side can sometimes be amplified, and this unfortunately happened to Ringo sometimes. Later on in my career after Supertramp's *Crime of the Century* had done amazingly well worldwide (although not in the States), A&M threw a big party after the band's gig at the Hammersmith Odeon in London. We learned that Ringo was there and Bob Siebenberg, Supertramp's drummer, came to me and requested an introduction. We walked over and had an initial conversation that was quite pleasant until I asked "What did you think of the show?" "What show?" he replied. "The show with Supertramp." "Who?" "The band Supertramp. That's what this party is all about," I said. "Oh, I'm only here for the bar," came Ringo's reply.

Bob was so crestfallen and disheartened. His hero had pulled the ultimate dis in not only not acknowledging him, but not even being aware of his band. Of course, this was before Ringo cleaned his act up, but ...

Just to show you the difference between George and Ringo, later when the band and I were working on *Crisis? What Crisis?* in L.A. at the A&M studios, George came by several times to offer his encouragement. Of course, the guys always got a huge kick out of one of The Beatles stopping by and taking an interest in what they were doing.

YOKO ONO

Contrary to what I've read, I never felt that Yoko was ever in the way during the making of *The White Album*. Her presence obviously caused some problems but I didn't notice it as much as maybe the others actually felt. She was used on several of John's tracks and she was even one of the singers on Paul's "Birthday" along with Pattie Harrison and Maureen Starkey.

I never personally had any problems with her, and I never saw any specific problems with her and anyone else that I remember, but yes, she was always there with John. Once Yoko started to come to sessions, Linda did as well. It was that competitive thing between John and Paul, I suppose. If John could bring someone by, then Paul could too. Linda wasn't there anywhere near as much as Yoko, but she came by a lot more than Paul had had people come by before. Then again, Linda was taking pictures a lot of the time so it seemed like she was working rather than just hanging out.

I remember recording one of Yoko's songs one afternoon with only John in the studio. She came up to me and demanded, "Do you know how to record a scream?" "I think so. Yes," I replied, slightly taken back. "Good," was her only response.

She went down into the studio and that's what I had to record: just her screaming, which amounted to her entire vocal on this particular track. She didn't ask me very nicely, but I attribute that more to the cultural difference between us than anything else.

GEORGE MARTIN

My opinion of Sir George has changed over the years. As I've gotten older I appreciate him a lot more than I did when I initially worked with him. He was always good to me, because there were times that he could've fired me or gotten me kicked out of sessions, but he never did.

On the night we were finishing *The White Album* he did something that will endear him to me forever. At one point he pulled me out of the control room, took me along the corridor and said, "Ken, I have to be honest. I don't want you to feel bad about this and I don't want you to take this personally, but I don't think that this album is going to win a Grammy." He meant it in all kindness because The Beatles were expected to do something even greater than *Sgt. Pepper's* and keep on winning Grammys. It was obvious that this one wouldn't because it was such a different album from what they'd done previously. George was looking after me in a fatherly way. It was more, "Please don't feel bad when you don't get a Grammy as Geoff did" kind of thing. "It's no reflection on you," he gently explained. Just the fact that he made the effort blew me away.

Other than that occasion, there was one incident that really stands out. One day early in my tenure as a second engineer, we were waiting for the band to arrive. He and I were standing out on the steps of the studio when Beatles manager Brian Epstein drove up in his Rolls. Because of all the girls gathered around the studio, the gates were closed, so he had to honk his horn to get security to go out to open the gate to let him in. In the meantime all the girls wanted his autograph, so he got out of his car and began to sign. George just looked at me and said, "That should be me." I thought to myself, "Really? What an ego!" Yes, he had an ego, but I understand what he meant by that. He was the fifth Beatle, not Brian. He rightfully should have garnered more attention than Brian. In all honesty, I think Norman Smith should have gotten more attention than Brian too. They had more to do with the success of The Beatles than Brian did. As much as he had to do with them, once Brian got them their record deal he was riding their coattails just as much as a lot of other people, where George and Norman pushed the train.

NORMAN SMITH

I can't say enough about Norman. I really don't think Norm has received anywhere near the credit that he deserves for the early Beatles records that he worked on. He strove, within the strict precepts of EMI Studios, to change the sound on each one of The Beatles' albums. The changes are subtle but most certainly there, leading up to the amazing *Rubber Soul*. From our association with The Beatles, Geoff did well out of it, I've done amazingly well out of it, but Norman didn't. He started it all and most people don't even know his name.

All that being said, I don't know if the leaps made in *Revolver* and *Sgt. Pepper's* would have happened with Norman at the helm. Although one to always try to push the envelope, he may have been a little too steeped in the EMI way to be the facilitator of some of the off-the-wall practises used on those records. Still, he was such an innovator and made sure that the sound changed every album; he deserves a lot more recognition and appreciation than it seems he'll ever get.

71

REWARDED, BUT UN-AWARDED

The fact that Norman never received any of the accolades that he deserved brings up a sore point. Originally EMI wouldn't allow engineering credits on any of their albums. With Beatles records, the engineers never received any credit until the reissues. On *The White Album* they gave thanks to people where myself and Geoff are mentioned, but it didn't say who we were or what we'd done. In fact, the first credit I ever received was on the American version of The Jeff Beck Group's *Truth*, but not on the English one. Of course, over the years that's slowly changed to where engineers are fully credited, as they should be.

When it came to gold records, once again the only people who got them back in the day were the artists, and despite the massive Beatles sales worldwide, none of the engineers ever received one. It just wasn't done. Once again, the first gold record I ever received was from George Harrison's *All Things Must Pass*. One day a large package arrived for me at the studio that turned out to be the official gold record. I wasn't expecting it so I was quite blown away. George was always very good about those kinds of the things and always made sure that I received an award if I deserved it.

I understand about not receiving golds for the original Beatles releases because that's how it was in those days, but when you have releases like *One* where they compile the number one singles from all over the world, that's now a totally new record. In my estimation, if it's a new record, you should go by the new standards, which means the engineers should receive gold and platinum records. Apple still wouldn't allow it, however. Neil Aspinall, who took over Apple Corps in 1968 (and has since passed away), preferred to keep that part of the business working the old-school way, operating under the premise of, "Hey, we never used to give out gold records in the old days and we're not going to change now." It's kind of ironic because when you walk into Apple you see more gold, platinum, and diamond awards (sales of 10 million or more) than you'll ever see in one place for a single artist, yet they're perpetually reluctant to give us any awards, or even credits for that matter.

72

That never bothered me particularly until recently when things reached a peak in two ways. It started when I was invited to the opening night of the Cirque du Soleil *Love* show in Las Vegas, which was a huge opening with a very festive atmosphere. As soon as the music started I got this big shit-eating grin on my face just hearing the phenomenal job that Giles Martin (George's son) and Paul Hicks (an ex-Abbey Road engineer) had done. As the show went on I would glance through the program whenever there was a slow moment, until I noticed that everyone but everyone, almost to the point of including the pizza delivery boy, had gotten a credit except for the five engineers (Norman Smith, Geoff Emerick, myself, Glyn Johns, and Phil McDonald) who did the bulk of the original recordings. At that point I lost that grin really fast as my joy turned into anger. If the five engineers hadn't done a good job in the first place, it would never have sounded as good as it did. Giles Martin told me himself how amazing the original recordings sounded and how much of the time they never needed to change anything because the sound quality was so good. That was also the case on the recent remastered reissues. I know how little Abbey Road ended up doing to the original Beatles masters.

Immediately after the show at the big party I saw the head of EMI at the time and I was just about to lay into him when some friends pulled me away because they knew I was really going to lose it. Unfortunately I never did get to voice my opinion to him about the collective slap in the face that the five of us received.

Don't get me wrong; I've done very, very well from my association with The Beatles. Geoff has done amazingly well from his association with The Beatles. The one person that really didn't get much out of it, and he was probably *the* most important person with regard to the recordings, was Norman Smith. He was such an important part to their success, yet he got nothing.

The fact that he was never given a gold or platinum record, to show the smallest amount of gratitude for all that he did for them, just breaks my heart. When it was discovered that he was dying, a concerted effort was made by a number of people to make sure that he was recognised before he passed. Tragically and unfortunately nothing ever happened. EMI was supposedly getting something together and apparently even got to the point where they had decided what the award was going to say. But to this day, there's been nothing, and now it's too late.

The great American engineer Elliot Scheiner recently led an effort to petition Capitol/EMI to finally allow us to receive the awards, and they finally agreed, but, of course, you know it don't come easy. They had to pour some salt in the wound by asking us to pay for them. How the hell are you going to go to Norman's widow and say, "Look, we'd like to get you something that Norman deserved, but you have to pay for it"? They give them to everyone these days, the least they can do is give them to her. The cost is a drop in the bucket for them even if you only take into consideration the amount of money they made from the iTunes downloads, let alone the entire catalogue over a period of nearly 50 years (which is estimated to have brought EMI and Apple well over a £1 billion in profit). Every time there's a new reissue they make more and more money, yet they still won't pay for awards that are deserved. I generally don't carry a chip on my shoulder, but I suppose that this could be classified as one. It's only fair and right.

I did receive one gift from The Beatles: a set of gold cuff links, which I wore often while at EMI. They were a Christmas gift from The Beatles one year, the only year in fact. They supposedly came from Asprey, a very upscale jewellers in London with a heritage of luxury that dates back to 1781. Well, a few years ago I lost one of them, so on one of our trips to London, my wife Cheryl decided to try and get a replacement for me. She took the one remaining cuff link into Asprey and the person who was taking care of her, on seeing the cuff link, threw his nose up in the air, making her feel inches tall. He basically told her that they were definitely not from Asprey, as they would never sell anything that cheap, then suggested that she go to a jewellers in the arcade where she would stand a better chance of finding one. Whatever.

CHAPTER 7

Engineering Other EMI Artists

Although it seems like all of my time at EMI Studios was spent working with The Beatles, I also worked with a variety of other EMI artists in my time as an engineer. Unfortunately, many of them didn't make much of a dent in the music scene even then, so they're hardly remembered now.

For instance, I worked with a producer named Mark Wirtz on a production called *A Teenage Opera*, which was never finished because the record label pulled the plug after a few songs, and a producer named Paul Korda, who was a songwriter of some note but never made it big as an artist or producer. I did some stuff with a psychedelic band called Tomorrow, which featured soon-to-be Yes guitarist Steve Howe. Then there was the Third Ear Band, who were very much like Tyrannosaurus Rex before they became T.Rex, with a sort of acoustic love, peace, and happiness sort of vibe. And while there were a number of other projects that were instantly forgotten the moment the session was over, there were also some projects I worked on that garnered at least a small measure of fame as well.

I did a track for The Pretty Things' *S.F. Sorrow* concept album that former Beatles engineer Norman Smith, now in charge of Parlophone

Records, produced called "Bracelets of Fingers." The song was, to put it very bluntly, about wanking, male masturbation, but the theme was hidden enough that people didn't actually know it. Once you knew what was meant by bracelets of fingers, then suddenly it was, "Oh, shit. Now I get it." I never finished the album as I was pulled from the project to go back to work with The Beatles and the album was finished by Pete Mew.

A rather odd group that actually had a few hits was The Scaffold, which featured Paul McCartney's brother Mike McGear, poet Roger McGough, and comic John Gorman. I recorded what amounted to a live show with an audience in Number 2, and from that session came "Lily the Pink," which was then sweetened with some overdubs and issued as a single. Surprisingly, it went to number 1 in England.

Then there was *Lord Sitar*, which was the result of some bright spark at the record label having the brilliant idea of doing an album of contemporary hits using the sitar as the lead instrument. The sitar was popularised by George Harrison on "Norwegian Wood" and then "Love You To" on the *Revolver* album, which suddenly shone a spotlight on this ancient instrument to the world outside of India. They recruited Big Jim Sullivan, a much in-demand English session guitarist and mentor to Jimmy Page, who had learned to play the sitar for his session work. The album was centred around Big Jim playing the songs of the day with an orchestral backing. It earned quite a reputation because everyone just assumed it was George Harrison playing, since the album never specified exactly who Lord Sitar was.

Even though I spent a fair amount of time on projects that failed to make a lasting dent on the contemporary musical consciousness, I did work on a few that met with worldwide success.

THE JEFF BECK GROUP

Not too long after *Magical Mystery Tour*, I was assigned to do the first Jeff Beck Group album, *Truth*, which featured soon-to-be superstars Rod Stewart on vocals and soon-to-be Faces and Rolling Stones guitarist Ron Wood on bass. They weren't known at that point, but there was a great atmosphere and everything went rather smoothly, taking only about a week and a half, since most of it was recorded live (Figures 7.1, 7.2, 7.3).

Figure 7.1, Jeff Beck recording instructions.

I was blown away by Jeff, of course, and the majority of Rod Stewart's vocals were live and ended up on the master. He liked to use a handheld mic so we accommodated him by wrapping a KM 54 with a lot of sponge to reduce the handling noise. The song "Morning Dew" also marked the first time I ever recorded bagpipes. I had no idea how to mic them up and I still can't remember how I did it. I think I just listened around until I found where the sound came out and put the mic there.

| STUDIO 3. | DATES, TIMES, ETC 8·1·69 | | 4·00~12·0 | | | | ARTISTIC DETAILS JEFF BECK | | BAL. ENGINEER Kes |

PURPOSE	FADER	LINE	MIC	BOOM/STAND	LIMITER or COMP	OTHER REQUIREMENTS
Drums	1	1	Km56	AKG		
James Premix	2					
Bass Drum	3	4	D19c	AKG		
Piano	4	w	D19c	Mogus strings		
	4A			AKG		Rs124 in
Snare	A1	10	Km66	Mogus string		Rs124 in
	A2					Rs124 in
	5A					
Bass Guitar	5	5	U67	AKG		
Bass Guitar	6	6	D.I.T.	AKG		
Guitar	7	7	U67	AKG		
Vocal	8	11	Km54			Rs124 in
Vocal	1	1	Km54	AKG		
Drums	2	2	D19c	AKG		
Drums	3		D19c	AKG		

PRE-MIX	2	PRE-MIX	1
1	2	1	4
2	3	2	3

MAIN CHANNEL DETAILS (V.B.C., COMPS, ETC.)

| 1 | 2 | 3 | 4 |

REF No 11249

STUDIO

WINDOW END.

PHONES TO — be available please.

HEAD — TO

TELEPHONE TO

2 x Fairchild Limiters
2 x Altec Compressors.

4 TRACK	✓	TAPE 811	STEREO	MONO
CLASSIC EQ.		✓		
POP EQ.		✓		

ECHO REQUIREMENTS

| CHAMBER | | STEED | ✓ |
| ATT 46 | TOP | 10 KHz BASS | 600 HZ |

ECHO RETURN

| ATT | TOP | BASS |
| E.M.T. | DRUM | |

| H1 | H2 | H3 ✓ | H4 ✓ |

PLAYBACK AND OR OTHER SPKRS

2 x Rs 10's
1 x √on box

USE REVERSE SIDE FOR RECORDING CONSOLE SETTINGS, AND ANY COMMENTS, FAULTS, ETC.

Figure 7.2, Jeff Beck setup sheet.

During the first session when we were getting drum sounds, I remember thinking how good they sounded, only to discover after the fact that the drum mics had been moved from my standard positioning. And not just a little either. Someone moved the snare mic so that it was aiming at the shell instead of the head, which I never would have done. I have no idea if the mics were moved purposely or not, although I think they probably were since everything was placed a little too perfectly for it to be an accident. I left them placed where they were. It sounded fine, so why change a good thing?

One of the songs we recorded for the album was the show tune "Ol' Man River," which featured the infamous drummer from The Who, Keith Moon on timpani. Being ever so outrageous, Moonie had a Rolls Royce that was custom outfitted with a PA system, although I wasn't all too sure why when I first learned of it. It didn't take too long to find out. After the session as he was trying to pull out from the car park in front of the studio, this little old lady who was walking her lap dog stepped out in front of his car. Moonie immediately turned on the PA and began to lambast the poor woman with, "You fucking cow. What the fuck do you think you're bloody well doing stepping in front of my fucking car," and just laying into her something terrible. Again, this was not Moonie yelling at her face to face, it was blasting out of his PA.

Unfortunately the studio had never been liked by the neighbours to begin with, an animosity that grew steadily with the success of The Beatles. Whenever they were recording, there was always a pack of sometimes screaming girls loitering outside, which doesn't especially make for a quiet neighbourhood. As a result, there were always complaints coming in, but the little old lady episode happened at about 11 P.M. and was so loud that it woke up a lot of the neighbourhood residents. The next day came a mass of complaints, which was a much unneeded distraction for the studio management who already had their hands full. Moonie was *persona non grata* for quite a while after this incident, as EMI did its best to calm the neighbours with repeated promises for a more quiet egress from the studio by its more boisterous clients.

RECORDING SHEET

MONO/STEREO 4 TRACK
Sheet: 1 of: 1 Class: POP
Overall Title ....

Date of 16th May '68
Session ....
Job No :80,789

Ref. 9864

ARTISTIC INFORMATION

ARTIST(E)S AND/OR CAST: JEFF BECK

CONDUCTOR	
ORCHESTRA	
ACCOMPANIMENT	MR. PETER GRANT
ART. DEPT. REP.	

COSTING INFORMATION

MATERIALS USED	SESSION BOOKED TIME	SESSION ACTUAL	SET-UP/PLAYBACK
2 × 8"	7:00 — 10:00	6:00 — 11:00	— / — / 4

ORDER NUMBER	COMPANY	STUDIO/CONTROL ROOM	ENGINEERS
		3/3	K.S. / M.S.

TITLES and MATRIX Nos.	AUTHOR/COMPOSER/PUBLISHER	REEL NUMBERS	FALSE STARTS	TAKE No.	TAKE DETAILS FROM	TO	DUR. M	REMARKS
I AIN'T SUPERSTITIOUS		E 68610 4 TRACK (cont.)	5	5	COMPLETE		4.50 BEST	FROM TAKE 4
		10,11	13		—	—	4.16 BEST (FADE)	
			12		—	—	4.31 — GOOD END	
			8,9		—	—	4.45	
			7	B.D. COMPLETE			4.03	
OL' MAN RIVER		E 68702 4 TRACK	5	6	—		4.05	
			4	—			4.17	
			2,3	1	B.D. COMPLETE		4.43	
							4.26	
YOU SHOOK ME		E 68703 4 TRACK	5,6	7	COMPLETE		2.29 BEST	
		2	4	COMPLETE			2.28	
			3	COMPLETE			2.19	
			1	COMPLETE			2.22	

STUDIO INSTRUMENTS USED: KETTLE DRUMS, ORGAN

Figure 7.3, Jeff Beck recording sheet.

Truth was supposedly produced by Mickie Most, who had previously produced hits for The Animals, Donovan, Herman's Hermits, and Suzi Quatro, but in this case he only came along for the mixes. The person who was there for most of the recording was one Peter Grant, who was Mickie's assistant at the time. Peter later went on to become the high-powered manager of Led Zeppelin, but he didn't have much to say in the producer's role as he was there mostly to just look after the band. Many critics have gone on to say that the sound of Led Zeppelin was mainly derived from that particular Jeff Beck album, but it's debatable whether Peter actually had anything to do with it.

And speaking of the mixes, there's a lot of stereo imaging on that album that's pretty weird, although I can't remember exactly why. For instance, on "You Shook Me," the drums are hard panned to the left and bass to the right, but I have no idea why they're spread like that. Then on "Blues Deluxe," Mickie wanted to make it sound like a live concert recording, so we raided the EMI effects cabinet and found some audience sounds and generously sprinkled them in during the mix. In my opinion, that really didn't make it sound all that live, only like a bad recreation.

When we did *Truth*, everyone in the band was really down to earth and easy to work with, basically because they weren't "big" yet. After the album was finished, the band toured the States and became extremely successful, so when they came back to EMI to do the next album (*Beck-Ola*), they had egos the size of London. After the first day we knew that we weren't going to work well together again so they just cancelled the rest of the sessions and went somewhere else to record. It was a totally different atmosphere. As opposed to being the team effort that it was previously, suddenly it became more of a "you're the servant" kind of thing. I saw Jeff first as a regular guy, then with an oversized ego, then later when I worked with him again, I was to see yet another side of him.

I learned to stay calm under pressure from Ken. He was always unflappable, which is a trait that he passed on to me.
Alan Parsons, assistant engineer (later to become an engineer/producer and artist of note)

81

SACHA DISTEL

Sacha Distel was a very good-looking Frenchman with four claims to fame. One as an accomplished jazz guitarist, another in that he spurned French fashion model and starlet Brigitte Bardot's offer of marriage (he must have been mad), another being that he wrote the standard made famous by Tony Bennett, "The Good Life," and lastly because he was a crooner of some note, especially in France and Canada. The album I engineered, the name of which has long vanished from my memory, was produced by Tim Rice, who at the time was Columbia (not the American company) recording director Norrie Paramor's assistant, but later went on to write mega-shows such as *Jesus Christ Superstar* and *Evita*. The sessions consisted of Sacha singing some standards with an orchestra, which included, of course, his own "The Good Life,"(Figures 7.4, 7.5, 7.6) interspersed with some then current hits such as "This Guy's in Love with You" and "Raindrops Keep Falling on My Head." He actually has one other claim to fame as far as I'm concerned, and that is as photographer. It was he that photographed me, cigarette in hand, whilst mixing in Number 1 control room (see Insert Figure 4.1).

PINK FLOYD

A few more Norman Smith sessions I worked on were with Pink Floyd. This included my introduction to very long hours and my first 24-hour session. We were working on "Apples and Oranges" and "Paint Box," the last single recorded with Floyd's original leader and main songwriter, Syd Barrett. For any Hurricane Smith fans, "Paint Box" was probably his entry into singing on record, as he performed a very prominent backing vocal part. Later I also did a track with the new Floyd lineup that had guitarist David Gilmour. That song was "Corporal Clegg" and was the start of *A Saucerful of Secrets*. Once again Pete Mew finished the project due to my being assigned to work on *The White Album*.

MARY HOPKIN

I got a lot closer to Paul McCartney when we worked together on the Mary Hopkin *Postcard* album. I remember having the prettiest mic

Figure 7.4, Sacha Distel recording instructions.

Figure 7.5, Sacha Distel setup sheet.

Figure 7.6, Sacha Distel recording sheet.

setup I've ever seen on one of the sessions for that album. It was just Mary, Paul, and Donovan in Number 1 studio. The setup was just three C 12s placed in a triangle, one each for the two acoustic guitars and one for Mary's vocal. It sounded wonderful and just looked so aesthetically pleasing in an engineer-geek sort of way. Strange the things one remembers.

That was a particularly great session as Mary was very comfortable with the songs that day and we even had a special guest drop by to see Paul; Diana Ross, then of The Supremes. *Postcard* wasn't always the easiest of projects though. Although she loved singing the two Donovan songs, Mary had problems with some of the other material that Paul wanted her to do. Let's face it, "There's No Business Like Show Business" wasn't her kind of song at all. She was a lot more folky, but he had an idea of how he wanted the album to be and that's how it went. You didn't argue with Paul.

I remember one day we went around to Paul's for lunch, and since he had a place three or four blocks from the studio, we walked. Linda cooked us up some fish, as I remember. As we walked back there was a photographer and a reporter who spotted us. They began walking backwards the entire time taking pictures of the three of us, with the reporter just being as unsavory as a paparazzi can sometimes be. "Hey Paul. Is this a new girlfriend? Is this who you're seeing now? Are you going to marry her?" and on and on the entire time. That was the first time I learned first-hand how obnoxious fame can be. Up to that point I had only seen the more positive side of it with the Rolls Royces and adulation, but when you're just walking back from a nice lunch with a photographer and reporter in your face the entire time, no thank you. I don't think I could take it if it were handed to me.

GEORGE HARRISON

After the making of *Magical Mystery Tour*, George Harrison had signed on to create the soundtrack for a film called *Wonderwall*. It was during these sessions that George and I developed a friendship that would carry on for many years.

Much of the movie you could say was very psychedelic, so George made the music reflect that trippiness. George had gone into the EMI studios in India and recorded a bunch of Indian music in stereo, some of which he used for the film and some for other projects such as "The Inner Light," the B-side of the "Lady Madonna" single. Then there was a piece featuring Eric Clapton titled "Skiing." I didn't do the entire soundtrack, as initially it was split up among various engineers depending on everyone's schedule.

During the sessions George used to disappear for a half-hour to 45 minutes every day and it took us a little while to figure out where he went. There was a weird little room off to the side of Number 1 control room that housed an experimental artificial reverb called Ambiophony, an attempt to make the studio seem like it had a longer reverb decay time (see "Ambiophony" sidebar). It wasn't used very often and it wasn't successful by any stretch of the imagination, but the room was very quiet and George found it to be the perfect place to meditate amongst the turmoil of a busy studio.

Ambiophony

Even though Number 1 studio was one of the largest recording rooms in the world, it only had a relatively short reverb time; 2.4 seconds if you want to be precise. While this was plenty for most music recording, many classical producers preferred a longer reverb time like that of Kingsway Hall, a place in London where many classical recordings were being made by both EMI and Decca at the time. In an attempt to remedy the situation, EMI employed an experimental system known as Ambiophony.

The system was built around a new piece of technology known as a delay drum, a rotating metal drum with oxide on the outside that acted just like a piece of magnetic tape. The difference was that it doesn't take long for a tape loop to start to wear out, something the drum never did. A signal from the studio was sent to the drum, then multiple playback heads placed around the outside of it would pick off the signal and send it out to different speakers placed around the studio.

In the end, the Ambiophony system wasn't much of a success, since even though it may have been very clever for its time, it was extremely touchy to set up and suffered from feedback in the studio. It was, apparently, used by Geoff on one Beatles song, the incredible orchestral overdub on "A Day in the Life" from *Sgt. Pepper's*.

We finished *Wonderwall* fairly late one night and I had a Beatles session the next day to record the basics for what turned out to be "Lady Madonna." I had to get back into the studio by 2 P.M. to set up, never knowing if the band was going to come in by 2:30 or not. It turned out that everyone else came in on time that day except for George, who showed up much later. As soon as he got in, he went out of his way to make sure that I was all right since he'd kept me up so late the night before. As it ended up, I left the session early, officially due to "being sick," but it was really due to the long hours of the previous night. George was particularly sympathetic, and never let on to the others the real cause of my "illness."

PROCOL HARUM

Procol Harum's *A Salty Dog* was the last album I did at EMI. The album contained one track that they had completely recorded in the States and another that was started there, but the rest we cut in Number 2. It was done on 8-track, but this time it was easier than what we had experienced with The Beatles because of the new TG board (see "The EMI Consoles" sidebar), which was specifically designed for 8-track recording. It had a lot more inputs, and unlike the board it replaced, could handle all 8 tracks without having to do submixes.

With regard to actually recording *A Salty Dog*, I remember very little, although a session of orchestral overdubs does spring to mind. Piano player Gary Brooker had done an orchestral arrangement for "A Salty Dog" and organist Matthew Fisher did one for "Wreck of the Hesperus." This was still during a time when the orchestral studio musicians weren't into the whole pop thing, and they especially didn't like long-haired guys conducting them. That's what they got on those sessions because not only did Gary and Matthew do the arrangements, they conducted them as well and the orchestra was not happy in the slightest. It was almost a "fuck you" kind of attitude they had. Usually the orchestra was a lot friendlier and more eager to please with the regular arrangers that they were used to. If they found something wrong with long-hairs it was, "Well, of course there's something wrong. Look who's done it," as opposed to "Hey, you made a mistake here. Can you fix it?"

There was an incident that occurred when we were mixing that we didn't find very amusing at the time, but probably was very funny

88

looking back on it. We had just done a mix and Gary, myself, and Matthew were listening intently to a playback of it. Suddenly Matthew's girlfriend, who was sitting to the side of us, burst out into uncontrollable laughter for no reason that we could see. We were pissed. There we were paying all of this attention to every little detail and this woman just burst out laughing in the middle. We all sort of looked at her and said, "OK, so what is so damned funny?" Well, we three each had beards at that point in time, and apparently we were all sitting there with our right elbows on the board, and all three of us were stroking our beards in exact time to the music. This is what she found so very funny. I'm sure it was, but we certainly didn't feel it at the time.

The EMI Consoles

The sound of EMI studios came from a number of custom consoles designed in-house by EMI: the REDD.37 and REDD.51 "Stereosonic" 4-track mixer desks (see Figure 1.5), and later the TG12345. Although the very first Beatles album was recorded on the REDD.37, the REDD.51 was used to record about 85% of their songs, according to *Recording The Beatles*. Both consoles were nearly identical and were based around valve (vacuum tube) electronics. The consoles were what we'd consider very simple by today's standards, but were quite sophisticated for their time and very scary the first time I ever saw one as a 16-year-old kid. They each had 8 input channels that fed 4 output (subgroup/buss) faders, with 2 aux sends and 2 stereo returns. The console also had 2 auxiliary line inputs, but they were rarely used because of the lack of EQ on these channels.

Since the REDD series consoles were woefully inadequate for 8-track recording, a new console was eventually brought in. In 1968, EMI installed the solid state TG12345 in Number 2 control room (see Figure 7.7). It boasted 24 inputs and 8 subgroups/busses, 4 echo sends, 2 separate cue mixes, and a limiter/compressor on every channel.

I worked very little on the TG, using the one in Number 2 for a few tracks on the Mary Hopkin album *Postcard* and for the majority of *A Salty Dog* by Procol Harum, as far as I recall. I have to say that I'm a bad judge of the TGs though. The change from the old REDD desks to the more modern TG was a painful one for most of us at the studio, and I don't think any of us liked it. It had none of the warmth, both literally and physically, that the REDDs had. That being said, some great sounding records were made on it, but first impressions go a very long way.

When I think back to those sessions, one of the things I loved was working with drummer B.J. Wilson. He was one of the first really open drummers, leaving a lot of space in his playing. Ringo did it at times, but B.J. was fairly consistent and his playing matched the music perfectly. You could get really big tom sounds because of all the space he left. Nigel Olsson (Elton John's drummer) and Bob Siebenberg (drummer for Supertramp) played the same way, their tom fills being open and sort of loping.

Figure 7.7, The TG 12345 desk.

CHAPTER 8

I Finally Get Fired

During the recording of *The White Album*, the management of the recording studio changed. They normally brought up people from within the ranks, but this time they decided to bring in someone from the outside world named Alan Stagge. Now, Mr. Stagge was a classical engineer with a few credits, although his major claim to fame seemed to be recording the tapes used in the Mellotron, but he had several dislikes. Number one, he hated pop music and wanted nothing whatsoever to do with it. Number two, he hated other classical engineers, all of whom were never as good as he was, at least in his estimation. As a result, he basically wanted to get rid of almost everyone at Abbey Road from the day he started.

He came down hard on the classical engineers as well because he didn't think they were good enough. He also didn't understand pop at all, and that was his downfall.
Dave Harries, EMI maintenance engineer

He was OK as long as you were on the right side of him. If not, he just had it in for you.
Brian Gibson, EMI maintenance engineer

One evening he came into a Beatles session for a chat, which ended with the question, "What would you like to see changed here?"

They all instantly declared, "We'd like some coloured lights and better headphones, please." Stagge replied with a very reasonable, "OK, I'll see what we can do about that." After they'd all gone back downstairs into the studio, he turned to me and asked, "What do you think about the lights and headphones?" Considering that this was the middle of the psychedelic era and all the studio had for lighting were these hanging fixtures that had been there almost from the studio's beginning, and I think the headphones were only slightly newer, The Beatles were not out of line with their requests one bit, so I enthusiastically agreed. "I completely understand why they want that. It sounds like a great idea," I eagerly replied to our new studio manager.

> George Martin: *I remember all of you saying this is a sterile place, just white walls and ... bloody awful. Can't you do something to liven it up. And so they put in three fluorescent stands: red, blue, and white.*
>
> Paul McCartney: *No. Red and green.*
>
> George Martin: *That was to give you inspiration.*
>
> Paul McCartney: *And boy did it. [Both laugh.]*
> From a BBC documentary entitled *Produced By George Martin*

At that point the new studio manager ripped into me with a torrent of venom I never expected. "You do not side with the artist! You work for this studio and you side only with the studio! We can do no wrong! We don't bow down to them!" he screamed. I was totally caught off guard, but one thing I felt was that this was going to be the first of many such occasions and that I'd better watch out.

> *The only thing I remember is him [Stagge] coming in one night on a Beatles session and having a go at you [Ken] because you had taken your tie off. Everyone was smoking dope down in the studio, but you got completely shouted out for not wearing a tie! Even though the sessions started at 7 in the evening and went to 4, 5, or 6 in the morning, I remember that you had to show up at 9 A.M. in his office the next morning.*
> Chris Thomas

After *The White Album* was completed, I took two weeks vacation to recuperate. When I got back from holiday the first thing I discovered was that button pusher John Smith, my assistant for most of *The White Album*, had been fired, and Stagge wanted to see me. I went up to his office expecting to be immediately shown the door, but he surprised me with a rather normal question. "All right, Ken. What do you think we should look at to improve the product we put out?" Without thinking very much, the first thing blurted out of my mouth was, "We have never felt that we can cut singles and albums as well as the Americans, or some of the other British record companies, for that matter."

"OK, take two weeks and spend time in the cutting rooms and make some notes to show us what you mean. Let's see if we can figure this out," Stagge calmly replied. "Wow, this is great. I must have miscalculated the man," I thought to myself as I walked out the door.

I took the two weeks and collected records as examples and made all the notes I could. Finally at the end of the period there was a meeting in one of the playback rooms with Stagge, the head of cutting Horace Hack, two of the top honchos from the maintenance department, and me. Stagge started off with, "OK, let me hear one of your recordings." I thought to myself, "This is strange," and for whatever reason I played them a single I'd done by a band called The Locomotive. This was a band produced by Gus Dudgeon that was very reggae influenced, so Gus had wanted a lot of bass on it. Since he's the producer, I, of course, do what he wants.

Within ten seconds into the playback Stagge forcefully commanded, "Take that rubbish off!" As I took it off he started, "What is it with all of that bass? There's way too much low-end on that record." "But that's what the producer wanted," I replied as I tried to defend myself. "You are the engineer. You determine what the sound is going to be. You do not listen to the producer!" he shouted back. And then he did what I suspected he wanted to do all along: he fired me.

I have since found out that prior to this he went to Ken Townsend (head of the maintenance department) and asked him to come up with an electronics exam for me to take, an exam about all of the workings of the board and tape machines, because he didn't feel that I had enough knowledge to qualify as an engineer. Now part of EMI's training was that their engineers weren't supposed to know any of that stuff, and, in fact, no other engineer in the building knew any of it either. That's why we had the maintenance guys. We were supposed to learn sound, not electronics. Ken refused to do it, so Stagge found another way to set me up.

> *I was called up one day and he asked me to put a test together for Ken Scott. He said, "I don't think he's competent. He knows enough to operate the mixing console, but I want you to give him a technical test." I said, "I'm not going to go test Ken Scott. He's fine. The artists are real happy with him." It didn't become a nasty discussion but I said I'm not going to do it and end of story and it never went any further than that.*
> Ken Townsend, head of EMI maintenance department

So I'm fired. "He can't do this. This is insanity. It's ridiculous," I thought over and over as the rage grew inside me. After stewing for a bit I organised a meeting with the head of EMI Records to discuss my situation. I told him the story and he agreed that the firing was ridiculous. "You're reinstated. I will talk to Mr. Stagge," he assured me. Of course it helped that I had the number one record in the world at the time with *The White Album*. Soon I was back on the studio's payroll again, but I knew Stagge was out to get me. The realisation that I had won this battle but I certainly wouldn't win the war slowly began to dawn on me. I knew I'd have to be looking over my shoulder from that moment on, and I wasn't prepared to do that.

One day a few months after my reinstatement I found myself working with Gus Dudgeon and The Locomotive again on a second single. "It's time for me to leave. Any suggestions where I can go?" I asked him. Since Gus was an independent producer, he spent time in a lot of different studios, so I knew he'd have some ideas. "I work down at Trident quite a lot. Why don't you check that out?" he suggested. I had already been there and quite liked the place and its vibe, so I asked, "Could you set up a meeting for me with the guys in charge?" A short while later I went down to meet Barry and Norman Sheffield, who owned Trident, after which I gladly handed in my notice to EMI, and the next part of my life began.

CHAPTER 9

Trident—My New Home

Trident Studios was located at 17 St. Anne's Court, just off Wardour Street in the heart of the Soho district of London. It was originally constructed in 1967 by drummer Norman Sheffield and his brother Barry, who both managed the studio, although when it first opened Barry was also one of the only two engineers there. I was originally brought into the fold because Barry wanted to spend more time as the studio manager and get out of engineering and all the long hours that entailed, which as it turned out, didn't happen quite as soon as everyone had planned.

Figure 9.1: The Trident studio. The control room window is up to the right.

The facility was located in a large five-story building that had originally been a printing works and was supposedly on a burial site for the victims of the Great Plague of 1665. As you entered through the heavy glass and wood door you were confronted by stairs leading down to the studio (see Figure 9.1), and if you turned right you were in the reception area. Once in reception you couldn't help but notice another very heavy wood door that led into the control room (see Figure 9.2), not the most convenient arrangement for the musicians, as every time they wanted to hear something back they had to climb those stairs and hike through reception, only to be greeted by another three stairs to bring them in front of the mixing console. Now traipsing all that way up was just the beginning. If another take was needed the thing that happened all too frequently was that in the excitement of the moment the artist, me too on occasion, would jump down those three stairs and collide heavily with the door jamb. A severe headache quickly ensued, a not particularly good start to getting that perfect take.

The next floor up, reached by either stairs or lift, was a small lounge, the machine room where all the studio tape machines were housed, and, shortly after my arrival, the mix room (see Figure 9.3) and overdub booth. On the second floor (third for Americans) was a screening theatre. Wardour Street was home to many film companies at that time and rather than putting all their eggs in the record business basket, Barry and Norman thought that after coming to what was a particularly posh viewing room for the time, the film execs might be interested in using the studio to record the music for their films. It never actually happened that way, although it really didn't matter as the studio was constantly working around the clock anyway. On to the third floor, where maintenance and eventually cutting resided, then on the top floor was the kitchen. I use the term "kitchen" very loosely as it was geared more towards the making of tea and coffee and anything that could fit into a small toaster oven rather than a gourmet treat.

After having spent the better part of five years at EMI, the difference in culture could not be missed. EMI Studios had a certain coldness to it, and felt very much like a place where you went to "work." Certainly not the kind of place you'd want to go to if you weren't actually working, just ask Ringo. Trident however had this great feeling of camaraderie, everyone working together towards the same end, and it soon became a place to hang out. People would specifically come there even if they weren't recording. It was so much more laid back, and of course, you didn't have to wear suits and ties like everyone did at the very proper EMI.

Figure 9.2: The 20 input, 8 output Sound Techniques console.

There were a couple of work-related things for me that were different from EMI. The Beatles way of working seemed to have become the norm throughout the recording business, and so sessions were no longer booked in those union-dictated three hour time blocks. They generally started in the early afternoon and were open-ended. On occasion we'd have a brief morning session, but they tended to be more with session musicians than bands.

Another major difference for me was that there was only one maintenance guy there at any time, instead of the slew of them I was used to over at Abbey Road. That meant that from time to time we had to align our own tape machines and always had to set up our own sessions.

Figure 9.3: The Trident mix room.

The original engineers at Trident were Barry (Sheffield) and Malcolm Toft, who was also good with electronics and went on to design the studio's famous "A" Range consoles. Roy Baker came a little after me from Decca, where he'd been a tape op and engineer. No one can quite remember when Robin Cable came along, but soon it was the three of us who were doing the majority of the work. The people in charge of putting us on sessions learned pretty quickly that we each had our own genres that we did best in. Roy was put on more of the heavy and outrageous type of things such as Ginger Baker, Zappa, or John Entwistle but later went on to much success producing Queen and The Cars, to name a few. Robin was the more folky or orchestral type of things like early Genesis and Elton John, and I was somewhere in the middle.

"GIVE PEACE A CHANCE"

Even though I was now at a new studio, my connection to The Beatles still remained strong. I'm not sure what my first project at Trident was, but right after I started John Lennon brought in his first solo single, "Give Peace a Chance," for me to mix. The session was booked in by Apple, but whether it was because I was there, I have no idea.

"Give Peace a Chance" was a live four-track recording done by André Perry (who later built the excellent Le Studio in Quebec) in a hotel room in Montreal and who later bounced it to an 8-track machine and added four more tracks of vocals. There's a repeat echo on one of the tracks of someone hitting something, and as the song goes on, this repeat is pushed up higher and higher in the mix, which must have come from John saying, "More, more," which was typical of him. I had learned from my previous experience with "Hey Jude" about the sound of the monitors, so I strapped a couple of graphic equalizers across them and rolled off the high-end so the sound coming out of them was more realistic, and the result is the record that you're familiar with today.

ALL THINGS MUST PASS

George Harrison came by about a year after my start at Trident to do the overdubs on his first solo album, *All Things Must Pass* (see Insert Figures 9.4 and 9.5). The record was started at EMI (the name still wasn't changed to Abbey Road Studios at this time) on 8-track with Phil McDonald engineering. It was very quickly obvious that they needed more tracks so they moved to Trident because of our 16-track machine. Good old EMI, always late with the technology. The producers on the album were George and Phil Spector, even though Phil was never around for any of the overdubs. We were graced with his presence a little bit when we were mixing though.

By the time I got the project, there had been some overdubs recorded already, which is probably when they decided they needed more tracks. The basic track varied for each song but generally it was drums, bass, and all of the acoustic guitars, but there was also some pedal steel by the famous Nashville session player Pete Drake, and sometimes brass on a few of the songs. We recorded the vocals, electric guitars, additional brass, orchestra, and some keyboards at Trident.

I asked [Phil Spector], "What sound do you want?" and he said, "I don't care." My job was to play the arpeggio because everything got split into chords and arpeggios. I turned up early for the session and there were a few people milling around, and one by one all these people began to arrive very casually. It was Alan White on drums and Klaus [Voorman] on bass, one of the Badfinger guys on guitar, lots of people on percussion. Suddenly Ringo shows up and there's a second set of drums, then Eric Clapton on guitar, and the thing built up and up and up. After we put down the first track and had a listen, George asked to listen to what they'd done the night before, then asked to put Eric's guitar up a bit. Phil [Spector] said, "I can't," because everything had been mixed directly to two tracks live even though we were using an 8-track machine. There was a bit of a dust-up between George and Phil over that, but Phil said to him, "If you want me to produce it, this is what I do."
Chris Thomas (on playing Moog synthesiser on the basics of All Things Must Pass)

It's hard to know who played on which tracks on the album because it was never documented. Unfortunately, no one seems to remember much either. When we were doing the reissue of *All Things Must Pass* in 2001, George wanted to put extra material such as interviews on it, so one afternoon I went around to Ringo's L.A. home and after I set up a small recorder in the garden I was ready to ask him some questions. First question: "What do you remember about doing *All Things Must Pass?*" He looked at me blankly and said, "Did I play on it?" Unfortunately that seems to be an all-too-typical answer. George didn't remember who played on what song either.

We worked on *All Things Must Pass* for quite a while, having no sense of time, for I guess what amounted to about two months including mixing. George did so much himself. Virtually all of the backing vocals were George, like what you hear on "My Sweet Lord." We'd do four or six tracks of him singing a line and I'd bounce all of those down to one track. Then he'd do a harmony several times and I'd bounce those to another track. Then we'd bounce those two together at the same time as we were doing yet another backing vocal. It was painstaking, but it sounded amazing in the end.

When it was time to mix, normally George and I would begin at about 2:30 or 3 in the afternoon. We'd spend some time getting it to where we were both happy, then Phil would come by for maybe an hour. He'd pass his comments, we would mull them over, and usually make the changes he wanted. Then off he would go and we'd finish it off and come back the next day to start all over again.

THE NEIGHBOURS TAKE EXCEPTION

The mix room at Trident had windows along one wall which overlooked the backs of a bunch of old buildings, most of which had been turned into cheap apartments and bedsits, many for "ladies of the night." One evening one of the residents, or maybe a John, took umbrage with the amount of "noise" that was flowing out the closed windows and decided to let us know by throwing a bottle towards our building. He obviously didn't consider that if he'd actually achieved his goal of breaking the window it would have gotten even louder. Anyway, we were having a playback of the most recent mix and Phil was closest to the windows. Suddenly there was a loud crash and Phil freaked out. We quickly discovered what had happened by the expletives being shouted from across the way, but it took the rest of the night to calm Phil down. Both George and I expected to never see Phil back there again because he was, how should I put it, somewhat highly strung, but he came by the next night just as he'd done before and acted like nothing had happened.

THE "MY SWEET LORD" MIX

"My Sweet Lord" was the big hit from the triple album and as we got into the mix George decided he wanted a fairly slow fade at the end. Just a slight problem was that there wasn't enough of the song left to do it the way he wanted. Hey, he'd been a Beatle and they had all become used to minor miracles being made to happen by Ernie (Geoff Emerick) and Mr. Martin, so I had to come up with something. The conclusion was that I did a fade of the song that was about halfway finished when the song ended, then went back to the beginning of the ending section and continued the fade from the lower level to the end, finally editing the two together. I'd completely forgotten about that until it came time for the updated version for the remaster in 2001. When it came time to mix we were like, "Hang on. Why can't we make this work? Oh, I remember!" and we had to do the same thing again.

The Gear for *All Things* George

George used basically the same gear that he had used towards the end of his time with The Beatles, Fender amps and his Leslie cabinet. When using a Leslie cabinet, which he loved, the mics would have probably been a Neumann KM 54 or KM 56 on the top of the Leslie and a U 87 or U 67 on the bottom. As we were still working on 16 track, it was only a mono track, so we only miked one side of the cabinet."

The mics we used during overdubbing of *All Things Must Pass* would have been similar to what we used at EMI. Electric guitars would have been U 67s, and acoustic guitars would have been AKG C 414s and sometimes U 67s, as there were no D 19s at Trident. Vocals for George were all 67s. On orchestra, the violins and violas would have been 67s, the cellos would have been 414s, trumpets and trombones would have been STC 4038s, and the saxes would have been 67s.

All the mixing at Trident was done through a Sound Techniques console. There was a 20-in/8-out model in the studio from day one, and when that was later moved up to the brand new mix room, a 16-out version was brought in (see Figure 9.6). It was about 18 months later that the first Trident-built A Range was installed in the studio, but the mix room continued with the original Sound Techniques board.

At this point in time, both the studio and mix rooms used Tannoy speakers in Lockwood cabinets as monitors, but eventually the control room changed to JBLs (see Figure 9.7) and even later, the mix room changed to Cadacs.

For mixing we used an EMT plate reverb, and at times some tape delay, either with the reverb or single-repeat sort of tape echo on things, which would have come from one the Studer stereo tape machines that were there.

By the time we'd originally finished the album we *loved* the way it sounded as it was exactly what we were after, but as time progresses, people's tastes change. George came to hate all the reverb on it, and boy, would we have both loved to remix the whole thing before the remastering for the reissue. Unfortunately EMI wasn't keen on the idea and suggested/ordered us to put it out the way everyone was used to hearing it. I certainly don't regret it, but it would be nice to hear it not so "Spectorish."

Figure 9.6: The new 16 output Sound Techniques console.

Figure 9.7: The JBL monitors.

Just to illustrate George's sense of humour: whilst making *All Things Must Pass* George was constantly bumming cigarettes from me. How could it be that a member of the biggest band in the world never had his own? Well, he had quit smoking but somehow considered that not buying them was a very close equivalent to not smoking them, and so I became his main supplier. A couple of days after the completion of the album, a package arrived for me at Trident and in it were several cartons of Rothmans cigarettes and a small card on which George had written, "Smoking could be hazardous to your health" (see Figures 9.8 and 9.9). Funny, at the time, but very ironic when one considers he contracted lung cancer and ultimately succumbed to it.

9.8: The front of the card that George sent me.

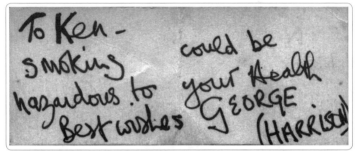

9.9: The rear of the card.

RADHA KRSNA TEMPLE

The Radha Krsna Temple was the headquarters of the International Society for Krishna Consciousness in London that was at the forefront of the movement in the late 1960s. George was really interested in this group because of his new-found religious beliefs, and a couple of the members used to come by from time to time during the making of *All Things Must Pass* to bring him vegetarian food. A short time after the completion of the album, he decided to do one with them as well.

The first song, "Hare Krishna Mantra," was done at Abbey Road with Geoff Emerick engineering and actually became a really big success in England as a single, so George decided to continue with an album. I did the next single, "Govinda," along with the rest of the album at Trident.

"Hare Krishna Mantra" and "Govinda" were the only two songs on the album done with a rock rhythm section, which for the latter, consisted of Alan White on drums and Klaus Voorman on bass, while the other songs were much more traditional as they used primarily Indian instruments. There would be one lead vocalist to mic, then a whole bunch of them doing answering vocals, so many that they couldn't be miked separately, so it ended up with just one or two mics on them as a group.

This was a strange album to do because there were all of these people with all of their bells just chanting away. It was totally disorganised, especially when it was just them without the rhythm section. You never knew how many of them would turn up.

I always had a good feeling being with them. Once you got used to the way they dressed and forgot about that shell, they were good people.
Klaus Voorman, bass player

"IT DON'T COME EASY"

After working on *All Things Music Pass* came Ringo's "It Don't Come Easy," which George produced. The tracking session for the song was very easy. Ringo on drums, Klaus Voorman on bass, and George on guitar. At one point Leon Russell came by and put keyboards on as an overdub and I've been told that Steven Stills did some overdubs as well but I don't remember him at all. It was before Crosby, Stills & Nash had hit and I wasn't aware of Buffalo Springfield at the time. Doris Troy, and Pete Ham & Tom Evans of Badfinger did the background vocals.

The [head]phones were so loud it blew your head off. In those days it wasn't like it is today where everybody can comfortably turn the knobs and make his own mix the way he needs it. Everything was full throttle in those days. After those sessions I remember driving home thinking, "What a nice quiet car." The car wasn't quiet—it was me who was still half-deaf. It's a miracle that we aren't all deaf by now.
Klaus Voorman

We used Tannoy reds and every speaker sounded different in the bass region. The Tannoy golds came a lot later, were more consistent in bass response but didn't sound as good. Barry Sheffield went out to one of the first AES Conventions and was so impressed with the JBLs that he ordered four pairs at the show and they were imported directly into the U.K. They had a much more consistent bass end and everyone was happy with them. They were also smaller and easier to mount in the studio. I'm not sure exactly when they were installed but I'd say around 1971.

Malcolm Toft, Trident engineer

Even though Ringo had written it (with George's help it turns out), he had a hard time singing the song's melody and just couldn't get it for some reason, so George sang a scratch vocal for Ringo to learn the phrasing at home. Since it wasn't meant to ever be part of the track, George had his vocal erased immediately thereafter because he knew what could happen if it got out. As it turns out, it did anyway and there's a bootleg version floating around, which is awful. After George and Ringo left it was time for some fun and games, so both Mal Evans (The Beatles' roadie) and I each had to give the vocal a try as well. I have no idea what ever happened to those mixes but I'm pretty sure no one will bootleg them, luckily for all. Oh, the things we used to get up to when we were young.

Ringo sessions were always great. He, like nobody else, needed the help from his friends. "It Don't Come Easy" was only half a song. He would play what he had to us and then he would look at us with his big blue eyes, which were crying out for help. So we all did what we could for our Ringo. What a sweet man. I love him!

Klaus Voorman

JUST A LITTLE CHANGE

Just before *All Things Must Pass* Phil Spector came in to do a session with his wife Ronnie, formerly the lead singer of The Ronettes. While he was downstairs teaching the session musicians the song, I was upstairs getting the sounds just as normal. I got it sounding the way I typically would when Phil came up and made some minor suggestions. It immediately changed from my sound to his. I have absolutely no idea whatsoever what those changes were, and I so wish I did, but they didn't seem all that much at the time. That's one of the things about engineering. It doesn't take much to change it from one sound to another.

I know there are a lot of engineers who are very secretive about how they get their sounds. At one point Robin Cable was like that with his string sounds. If he had a mix that was going over to the next day, he would cover over all of his equalization so that none of us could actually see what he did. For me, I have no problem whatsoever with anyone seeing what I'm doing because ultimately it's how you put it all together in the end that matters and that's not something you can teach.

Another example of this is when I did a John Entwistle session for Roy (Baker) when he had to go to the dentist. I got my typical sounds and when Roy came back he made a couple of minor changes and it immediately changed from my sound to his. It doesn't take much. Everyone can put the mics in exactly the same places, they can use exactly the same EQ, and it will still come out different in the end.

"COLD TURKEY"

"Cold Turkey" was a John Lennon single that I recorded and Phil McDonald mixed. Phil and I were going back and forth off each other quite a bit because The Beatles were constantly going back and forth between EMI and Trident. The song was recorded in a day with two guitars, bass, and drums. I'm not 100% sure but I think Alan White (who was later to join Yes) was the drummer, Klaus Voorman was on bass, and John and Eric Clapton played the guitars. The vocals were overdubbed and there may have been another guitar part added as well, although I don't remember whether it was John or Eric who played it.

It was aggressive and it was hardcore. I don't think I'd ever seen John quite like this. This was the period when he was going through his Primal Therapy and he wanted it on the edge. If I remember correctly, we recorded all the tracks in one day.

At Trident you had those big big speakers, which was a change after EMI with those silver Altec boxes. If something sounded good on those Altecs, then it sounded good everywhere. Now you had that big sound and we all were hanging there on that long lush sofa in front of the console digging what we just played coming out of those big big boxes saying, "Turn it up louder, Ken!" not knowing that the only place this was going to sound really good was right there in that studio. That frustrated John so much that he had EMI write on the record: "Play it loud!"

Klaus Voorman

Although it sounds like the guitar parts were doubled on an overdub, it was John and Eric simply playing the same part. This is something that we did with The Beatles when the 4- and 6-string basses were doubled as well. The double was always played live at the same time and never overdubbed. John was used to doubling lines like that so that's what we did on "Cold Turkey" as well.

You see Ken, you've been so subdued in the studio. You didn't say much like many other engineers, and that's a very important quality of a good engineer, but that makes it difficult for me because it means there isn't that much one has to say about you. We all were so involved in what we were hearing and what we were playing and what would do the best for the song. The engineer did his work. The only time you came in the picture was when somebody like a John Lennon bollocked you for not playing back the track from the right place or not answering quick enough. All the work you did wasn't appreciated. It was taken for granted. We weren't thinking of how you made that rattle disappear from the acoustic guitar, or how you managed to separate the drums from the piano, or how to make it possible that the guide vocal wasn't going to leak into the guitar. Not fair, my boy! Your work was underrated.

Klaus Voorman

RONNIE SPECTOR

"Try Some Buy Some" was a song that George had written and given to Ronnie Spector. The track was recorded at Island Studios down on Basing Street. George, Phil Spector, and Ronnie came into Trident one night to do the vocal and mix. Behind the mix room was a small overdub room where Ronnie was doing the vocal. At the end of the first take Phil began to tell George and I all of these great stories, while Ronnie waited patiently in the booth never saying a word. After about 20 minutes, Phil hit the talkback and said, "OK Ronnie, that was good but let's try it again." "Oh, yeah. OK, Phil," came Ronnie's reply.

We do another take and as soon as it's finished, Phil launches into his stories again, and once again Ronnie was left standing by the mic just waiting patiently, never saying a word. After another 20 minutes Phil hits the talkback again and says, "Ok, that was better. Now can you give the choruses a bit more feeling?" "Oh, yeah, OK, Phil," was the meek reply. This went on and on all night.

In retrospect it was obvious that she was terrified of Phil. She stood there the entire time and if he wasn't talking to her, she wasn't saying anything. Looking back on it now, it's very scary, although I only saw it as a bit strange at the time. Since we've learned a lot more about Phil, I see that night in a much different way.

NEARLY FIRED AGAIN?

Although this had nothing directly to do with The Beatles, I did run into a situation that was eerily similar to my near firings with them. Procol Harum followed me to Trident for exactly one session. It was a long session and we didn't accomplish anything because I think this was the beginning of the breakup of the band and organist Matthew Fisher. There was a lot of strife and we spent a lot of time getting nowhere. At the end of the session, the band's manager said to me, "This was an expensive waste of money. Is there anything we can do?" I told him that I would knock a couple of hours off the time, so on all of the recording sheets I put that the session had finished two hours earlier than it actually did.

I never thought about the tea boy however, who put in for overtime on the full number of hours. Of course, bright and early the next day Barry phoned me up with, "Can you explain to me how the tea boy finished up two hours later than you did?" "Oh, shit," I thought. I explained it to him and he said, "OK, but don't let it happen again."

Even though I had been found out, they never ended up billing the band for the extra two hours and the subject was dropped. I never did another session with the band after that as they went to AIR Studios with Chris Thomas, who eventually produced the album. It was another occasion when I thought I was going to get kicked out, but this was Trident and not EMI. You just can't underestimate the culture shift.

	PER HOUR
8 TRACK MIXING	£20.00
16 TRACK MIXING	£25.00
	PER REEL
¼" TAPE	£5.00
½" TAPE	£8.00
1" TAPE	£16.00
2" TAPE	£24.00
	PER HOUR
OVERTIME	£6.00

CANCELLATIONS:
If less than 4 clear days notice of cancellations is given, the client will be charged 50% of the total booking.

If less than 48 hours notice is given the client will be charged the full amount of the total booking.

Transport expenses will be charged for staff working after 11 p.m.

Figure 9.10: Trident's rate sheet.

GEORGE RECOMMENDS ME

American roots rockers The Band had recorded an album called *Stage Fright* that Todd Rundgren had produced. For some reason, they didn't want him to mix, so they began asking around for suggestions. They received a recommendation for Glyn Johns and they also asked George Harrison and he suggested me. Since they couldn't make up their mind between us, two sets of tapes were made and each of us were sent a set for a mix-off, which I was really looking forward to. A little friendly rivalry never hurts.

I had two weeks booked, which seemed like plenty of time. I put the first song on and was just about to get started when who walks in but the delightful Mr. Rundgren, who proceeded to make it very clear that he'd be mixing the album, thank you very much. Somehow he found out that I was doing it and was determined to do that mix no matter what. From that point on I was nothing but his personal tea boy for two weeks. He did it all himself and guess what? They used some of Glyn's mixes and had Mr. R remix the others again back in the States. I was pretty sure I could've done better mixes than those that Todd came up with if I would've had the chance. I must admit I have not been a fan of his since.

MY LAST SESSION WITH JOHN

Although this didn't happen at Trident, it did take place during the earlier days of my tenure at the studio. I was asked by John Lennon to come to his private studio at his house in Tittenhurst Park for what amounted to a one-off session. In the afternoon we recorded a Yoko track and everything went fairly smoothly, then we started one of John's songs, "I Don't Want to Be a Soldier," that was intended for what was eventually the *Imagine* album. He taught it to the musicians (Klaus Voorman on bass as usual, drummers Jim Keltner and Jim Gordon, and maybe one or two others that I can't recall) and sorted out the arrangement, and everything was sounding quite good. Even though there were two drummers there it started off with only Jim Gordon playing. The album credits Phil Spector as the producer, but I don't recall him being there for this particular session.

Before the first take, as unfortunately seemed to be the way at the time, someone put out a few lines of cocaine, they all snorted some, and went into the studio. Unfortunately the first take lost something from when they were learning the song and after listening to a playback, John said, "That wasn't very good. I know what will help," immediately putting out a few more lines of coke. Of course the next take was even worse. They came back in to listen and sure enough, "Nah, it's still not happening. We need a little more of this," and out comes even more blow.

After about three takes I could see where the session was going. It was pretty obvious that they weren't going to get anything that night and since it was a fairly long drive from John's estate to my home, I thought it was a good time to make my exit. I said, "Sorry guys. I gotta leave. I have an early session at Trident in the morning. Good luck and I'll see you soon," and just left. I never saw John again after that. Unfortunately.

That was a tough song and not easy for any of us. With Phil Spector at your side, you move even more into the background and are reduced to a gofer .
Klaus Voorman

When the news broke of John's murder in 1980 I had requests from all over the bloody place to speak about him, even from high profile shows such as *Good Morning America* and the like. But there was something about that last time of seeing him that I just didn't feel like talking about, so I turned down all of the interviews. Of course later on it all came out about his drug abuse, but at that time it was still fairly quiet and I didn't feel comfortable talking about it. Obviously there are a lot of other memories of John that I tend to regard far more highly.

CHAPTER 10

The Hits Keep Rolling, or Not

My time at Trident was filled with some amazing musical experiences that went far beyond The Beatles. In many ways, I had graduated from their training school and was now qualified to move onto much bigger and better things. A few of these new associations changed my life in a major way, but I also worked on a number of other great projects as well.

AMERICA

One of my early projects at Trident was a band called The Aynsley Dunbar Retaliation, the named leader being someone I'd work with again a few years later. The producer of this album was one Ian "Sammy" Samwell. Ian's initial claim to fame was that he was a member of Cliff Richard's original backing band, The Drifters, playing rhythm guitar and having written a song ("Move It") that became renowned as the start of U.K. rock 'n' roll. Shortly after Aynsley's album I worked with Ian again on an album with singer Linda Lewis (whom I would also work with again later), and so when he brought a new band in to record after that, we already had a bit of a history together.

He and a DJ named Jeff Dexter discovered these three American air force brats who used to perform at military bases in England. They brought them into Trident to record what ended up being their first album called *America*. It was interesting seeing the two producers working together, which is why I think I've never chosen to work with another producer since. Two producers can create too much indecision, as I saw then. Everything took a lot longer because they both had different ideas of how the project should go. It was like dealing with Labour and Conservatives or the Democrats and Republicans; they had to meet somewhere in the middle, but that wasn't always quick or easy. There were no major blowups or anything like that, but there were always compromises between the two of them.

The trio of Dewey Bunnell, Dan Peek, and Gerry Beckley didn't sing when we laid down the basic tracks, but since the album was built primarily around the sound of the acoustic guitars, the basics consisted mostly of acoustics and, on certain songs, drums. The bass was usually overdubbed later. I remember that they brought in a friend to play drums and I have a vague recollection that he wasn't much of a player, which could be one of the reasons they're not featured that strongly on the album.

The band had been gigging so their harmonies were already worked out, which was a plus. Generally all of the vocals were done at the same time, but I put them each on a separate mic as opposed to having them all around one mic and letting them get their own blend, which would have made the recording easier. I don't think they were quite at a point where they could do it that way yet. If I remember correctly, they each sang into a Neumann U 67. I know that later on in their existence as a band, they refused to sing more than one chorus, so the rest of them had to be flown in, which wasn't that easy back in the days of tape since it required a second tape machine that the part was recorded on, which was then recorded back onto the first machine. I have to state for the record that on this album they did sing every section.

Despite the push and pull of the two producers, the record finished up just fine, but Ian found it really hard to make up his mind on anything, an annoying trait that a number of producers have. He especially couldn't decide on a running order for an album, so he wanted to hear every possible combination before he would finally make a decision. This was before you could cut and paste so I had to physically edit every song together in different orders, which was incredibly tedious. He was a lovely guy and I liked him, but that almost pushed me to the limit at times.

The album was released and did nothing. Zilch. Died. It seems that the only problem with the album was that the record label didn't hear a single, so the band went into Morgan Studios in London and recorded "Horse with No Name," which turned out to be their first hit of many hits. I can only imagine what kind of problems it caused Ian with his many running orders of the album when he had to insert the newly recorded single into the re-release. The album finished up doing very well. We had a blast working together and the experience was really nice. When I first moved to L.A., one person I kept on running into just walking down the street was Gerry Beckley. For a couple of years, we just kept bumping into each other. It was strange.

THE COKE COMMERCIAL

I guess I was one of the lucky ones. You see it's quite normal for a young engineer to have to record the soundtracks for ads, and these can often become real pains in the ... you choose the spot. I only ever recorded two. One was an Asti Spumante ad with the band Spooky Tooth, and the other just happened to be "I'd Like to Teach the World to Sing," which became the centrepiece of one of the most successful campaigns that Coca Cola ever did. It was booked in as just a typical session with The New Seekers, who I'd never worked with. It was produced by Dave Mackay, who I had worked with at Abbey Road; it took a day for the tracking and another for the vocals and mixing. Roger Cook and Roger Greenaway, who wrote the song, were great guys and easy to work with as were the session musicians, so it just came together and worked right away.

Every commercial session always has someone there representing the ad agency, and in this case McCann-Erickson had a guy come by every day who was such an Anglophile that one day he came in

117

dressed in full English hunting gear. He was a little weird that way, but a nice guy and, by ad agency standards, pretty easy to work with. Not surprising actually, as I later discovered that his name was Billy Davis Jr., and he had been in the record business for years as a member of The 5th Dimension and later at Motown and then as head of A&R for Chess Records. We never received any abstract instructions from him, unlike the norm as the ad agency suits are notorious for, asking to make it sound "more purple" or something that no one can interpret, but he seemed happy with everything right from the beginning.

I don't think that anyone had an inkling that the song would end up being as big as it was. Soon enough, people began to call for a single, but the problem was that it was cut for a 60-second commercial and not a three-minute pop song. They ended up taking the track over to Morgan Studios, copied and edited it to make it longer, redid the vocals so it never said "Coke," and the song became a number one hit in England.

I was told that the commercial had upped Coke sales by 25%, which is a huge amount of money for a multinational company. It was so successful that it was awarded a Clio award, which Norman Sheffield got. I have never found out if it has my name on it or the studio's, as I never got a chance to see it.

CROSBY, STILLS, NASH & YOUNG

I'd fallen in love with the first Crosby, Stills & Nash album and I was blown away when I learned they'd booked about a week or so to do some recording, this time with the addition of Neil Young. I don't know if I was put on the session because I had worked with Graham Nash before at EMI, but he was very pleased to see me. Unfortunately he kept on telling the other guys, "This is the guy who recorded *Sgt. Pepper's.*" I was constantly going, "No, I didn't Graham. That wasn't me." It was embarrassing.

The band had already begun recording in the States so they brought the tapes with them, which immediately went upstairs to the machine room. I told the second engineer what we were going to start with and he began to play it back so I could get a quick balance. It was all going fine until the middle of the song when it went "ennn hue wooop" and then carried on playing normally again. "What the fuck was that?" I thought to myself. I didn't say anything to the band except to say, "I need to hear it again," and asked the second for another playback. He played it and right around the same place in the song once again it went, "bloooog, reh, naah, yaaaah," and then carried on again normally. Suddenly the second came on the talkback and coolly asked, "Ken, can you come upstairs for a second please?" "Uh, oh," I thought as I said to the band, "Excuse me guys, I've got to go check on something. I'll be back in a minute."

When I walked into the machine room, the second showed me the tape and it had, to say the least, stretched. What was once two inch wide tape was now down to about one and a half inches. Wondering what the hell was going on, we looked at the tape box to find that it was a kind of tape that we had never seen before. It was from 3M (one of the major tape suppliers at the time), but it was a type that was completely new to us. I called Barry Sheffield who immediately got on to the 3M rep who said, "Oh, yeah. That's the new tape that they're using in the States. It's much thinner. You need to completely change the alignment of the machine for that, but I have no idea how you do it because we haven't seen any of it over here yet."

I had to go downstairs and tell the band, "Sorry, mates. Your tape is ruined." Luckily it was a safety copy so all was not lost, but they cancelled the booking and walked out. Unfortunately, I never saw them again, which was a real drag as I was really looking forward to working with them. Eventually the 3M guy came in and showed us how to adjust the tension on the machine for that particular kind of tape, just in case we ever saw more of it, and all was well. I don't remember the formulation of the tape, but then I can't remember what tape I used yesterday either. Oh right, we don't use tape now do we. Bloody technology.

A KEITH MOON PRODUCTION

I worked with Keith Moon twice. Once during Jeff Beck's *Truth* album at EMI and again when he produced a song with Viv Stanshall, the eccentric lead singer from the deranged Bonzo Dog Doo-Dah Band. Someone had the bright idea of having Viv do a single by himself, and pushed the idea even further towards insanity by having Keith Moon produce it. I did the session and it was complete mayhem, with far more partying than recording going on, and on, and on.

At Trident, the desk in the control room was up two stairs and I remember at the end of the session walking off those steps right into a complete flood of booze. It was just everywhere. For the next couple of days the control room smelled like a club in the afternoon when you go in for sound check. I can't find any evidence that the single ever came out. They might have finished it somewhere else, but I think it was one of those things where the brilliant person that decided on this pairing in the first place realised what a mistake he'd made.

THE GHOST OF TRIDENT

One Sunday I was doing a session with Christine Perfect, later known as Christine McVie after joining Fleetwood Mac and marrying the bass player. This was just a quick, one-off thing (the session, not the marriage). For some reason they couldn't get any staff to work that day and we needed a second engineer and a tea boy. It finished up that Pete Booth, the maintenance guy, became the second and my wife Patience stood in for the tea boy. The session started in the late afternoon.

Apparently it got very boring for Pete and the Mrs. in the evening because they didn't have much to do, so she suggested setting up a Ouija board in the machine room. It turned out to be more than they bargained for. Pete told me on numerous occasions about how a cold breeze suddenly shot through the room and temperature dived like during a winter storm. He'd never believed in ghosts and gremlins, but at that point he had doubts about his doubts and began to think that there was really something to it all. I seem to remember being told that they had contacted the spirit of a sailor who communicated that he had found a place where he was comfortable (meaning the studio) and he was going to stick around for a while. From that point on, some strange things started to happen.

I don't remember how it started but we were upstairs in the machine room. There was this sudden cold draft and it was frightening. I never believed in any of that, but at one point that machine room got freezing cold and the glass [tumbler]on the [Ouija] board went nuts.
Pete Booth, Trident maintenance engineer

Roy was doing a Nazareth mix in the mix room sometime after and the band was sitting in front of the console having a listen. He felt someone tap him on the shoulder so he stopped the tape machine and turned around only to find that no one was there. It must've felt pretty real because it freaked him out a bit.

Another time Robin Cable went up to the kitchen about 3 o'clock in the morning to get a glass of milk. After he poured it, he turned around to get in the lift and something came up under his hand and knocked it all over him. That made him a believer too.

I can't say that anything like that ever happened to me at Trident, but I heard enough of the stories to believe that there was something extraordinary going on. Then again, most English studios have ghost stories for some reason, and even Abbey Road had a spectre in Number 1. There were various sightings of someone (the daughter of the original owners it was said, who had taken her own life after a failed romance) walking along the edge of the studio and then disappearing, and stories of doors swinging with no one around on the first floor. It's just part of the business, I guess.

THE GRATEFUL DEAD

The Grateful Dead were booked in and for whatever obscure reason I was put on the session. To me, that would have been something that Roy would have been better suited for, but for whatever reason, I was assigned.

There were a lot of "interesting" stories floating around about the Dead at the time, all of which made me a little uncomfortable about the thought of working with them. One was that the band had been in France and had managed to get a whole village tripping on LSD. It was later that I found out the full story. Apparently the band had been booked for an open-air festival and for whatever reason decided to go over early and stay at a French residential studio called Strawberry Studios, a place I came to eventually know very well. For some reason the gig was cancelled and, I suppose understandably, the band got kind of pissed off since they came all this way to play. They still wanted to make some music regardless of if it was at a festival or not, so they decided to put on a free open-air concert on the grounds of Strawberry Studios for the local villagers. Unbeknownst to the locals, someone in the Dead entourage spiked the free-flowing wine with acid and everyone in the village, including the police department, ended up tripping.

Now this was just a story at the time that no one was sure to be true, but it scared me enough that I gave explicit orders to the tea boy, "Under no circumstances do you put down my tea anywhere but in my hands. You don't let anyone anywhere near it." I didn't want to take the chance of someone spiking it and finding myself suddenly out of it in the middle of a session.

As it turned out, the sessions were cancelled so I didn't have to worry, but it was when I eventually went to Strawberry Studios (more commonly known as Château d'Hérouville) later with Elton that I heard the full, supposedly true story and that, as a result of this freebie concert, all the phones at the studio were tapped by the police, who then became very very careful about drugs coming anywhere near the studio.

SON OF SCHMILSSON

Robin Cable did Harry Nilsson's breakthrough album *Nilsson Schmilsson*, which met with great success, but soon afterwards he was in a serious car accident and nearly died. We all had to cover for him because he had sessions booked for some time ahead, so I ended up on Nilsson's follow-up, which became *Son of Schmilsson*. Once again, I recorded it but it was mixed at Abbey Road (EMI had by then been renamed) by Phil McDonald.

God, the drug use at that point, mostly blow, was over the top, with a lot of the imbibing coming from Harry and producer Richard Perry. I wouldn't join in, and while other people I worked with were pleased that I didn't partake, I think it worked against me here. I got the sneaking suspicion that they weren't enamoured of me because I didn't join in their fun, although Richard and I didn't get along that well anyway and that's probably why I didn't finish the album. You win some you lose some, but it still turned out very well and was nominated for a Grammy. It just was a very long drawn-out situation, and I don't know that it needed to have been that long and drawn out.

> *What can I say about Harry? I loved the man so much and played on every record he did if he wasn't using an orchestra. Even on this production, I was already frustrated because of his drinking habit.*
> Klaus Voorman

Harry was great fun to be around even without the blow. One day he had tanks of helium brought in and he tried to do a vocal with it. He'd take a deep breath of the gas and try to do a take, but it would always run out before he finished the phrase and he'd go back to his normal voice. There was a lot of craziness like that.

There was a song called "I'd Rather Be Dead" where Harry and Richard decided to bus in 20 or 30 old-age pensioners (retirees) to sing "I'd rather be dead, dead, dead, than wet my bed, bed, bed." They realised just before the pensioners arrived that perhaps these older folks might get offended by the lyric, so they brought a lot of booze in and got them all a little tipsy. It finished up with Harry dancing around the studio with various members of the pensioners group. It was absolutely hysterical. We had no idea what was going to happen with them, but it came out great. There's some great film of that somewhere that I think Richard Perry has.

Everyone you can think of played on the album: Ringo, George, Klaus Voorman, Pete Frampton, Ray Cooper, Nicky Hopkins on piano, so the music was great. One day we got into doing brass overdubs with Bobby Keys on sax and Jim Price on trumpet, who always played together. The one thing that I'll always be appreciative to Bobby for was while we were doing overdubs he asked, "Have you ever tried using two mics on the sax? You should try it. Put one up high by the mouthpiece and another at the bell." I tried it as he described and it worked so well that I've done it that way ever since. You get more of the air from the top mic and blend it with more of the note from the bell.

AN AMAZING ABILITY

Producer Richard Perry could really be a pain but the most amazing thing about him was that he had this incredible memory for takes. Richard had this thing about tracking that's quite true, to a point. When musicians first play a song, it's not perfect but there's an energy there. Then after a couple of takes that energy disappears as they now know what they're going to play and it becomes boring to them. If you keep them going long enough that boredom disappears and the feeling and excitement comes back. He always wanted to take the musicians through the first two stages into that last one.

There's a song on the album called "Take 54" where I think we actually went to about 80 takes, but there were always a multitude of takes and we had to keep every one of them. The amazing thing was that Richard could remember every take and he'd tell you at the end, "OK, we've got it. I want to take the intro from take 27, the first verse from take 13, the first chorus from take 2," and so on. You'd write them down and think, "There's no way this is going to work," but you'd go upstairs and edit the multitrack and find that he was always right. As an example, he gave me the list once and I did the edits, but when I played it back to him he said, "That's great except that the second chorus is from take 32 and I wanted take 33." "You're kidding," I said. "No, go up and check it." When

I checked it he was absolutely right. And that was after his doing a lot of drugs as well!

Richard was dictatorial and dare I say, the picture of what Brits considered a loudmouth Yank. He knew what he wanted and would kick ass to get it, but he didn't necessarily do it nicely. I can appreciate him as a producer but he's not the type of producer that I really like. I feel that my job as a producer is to take what the artist has and show that off in the best way possible. Richard is the type of producer who feels, "Fuck what the artist wants, I'm going to make it the way I want it." As an example, he did a successful album with Leo Sayer, who had some moderate hits in England but was completely unique and quirky. Richard turned him into something that was very ordinary, but a lot more successful. It's hard to say which is better. It's very similar to what happened with The Tubes and David Foster.

ROYAL ALBERT HALL

A number of ex-Abbey Road people who had left and gone our own ways—myself, Geoff Emerick, Malcolm Davis, and John Smith—would get together from time to time for a few drinks. As luck would have it, the Royal Albert Hall had a number of great artists performing this particular season, so we decided we would get a box for the shows to listen to some music while we all drank heavily. We went to see Chicago, Crosby, Stills & Nash, and Delaney and Bonnie, who were the band *du jour* in England at the time and would soon have both George Harrison and Eric Clapton playing with them as guests.

For whatever reason we got more wrecked than usual for Delaney and Bonnie and were very noisy up in the box. A couple of days later Malcolm Davis, who was working at Apple, ran into George H. Malcolm said, "Great concert the other night with Delaney and Bonnie," and George turned to him and said, "Yeah, but did you hear that bunch of yahoos up in that box making all that noise? What arseholes!" Of course he was referring to us. We never said a word and toned it down from then on.

THE CONSOLE BUSINESS

Trident was originally based around a Sound Techniques board that was used in the studio for about 18 months before being moved into a brand new mix room, at which point a new Sound Techniques was brought in for the studio. That lasted about 18 months before a prototype of the studio-built A Range console was installed (see Figure 10.1).

Figure 10.1: The Trident A Range desk.

The whole thing with the A Range was that the Sheffield brothers wanted to expand the studio business in every way they could. They wanted to get into management, video, and even console manufacturing. One of the staff engineers, Malcolm Toft, was an extremely technical guy, so they said, "Why don't you design a board and we'll build it and see what happens?" Malcolm came to the engineers—Roy, Robin, and myself—and said, "What would you like to see?" We gave him a list and every few weeks he'd come by with something for us to try out in the studio. We'd make our comments and he'd go away and do more work on it until we all liked what we heard.

The A Range turned out to be something that we all loved and is a console that I still seek out today for a project. To me all three boards were really good, with the major difference in the EQ, but there were progressively more options with each new one. The A Range EQ was basically what the three of us had requested and was far more flexible in what you could do with it. Bear in mind that everything that was mixed at Trident during that period was mixed using Trident's first Sound Techniques board, up in the mix room, and so that alone should give you an idea of how good that sounded.

The one thing that came from all this was that since then I have always hated the sound of Neve boards. You had these two competing sounds: either the Neve sound or the Trident. They sounded so completely different that you were in one of the two camps. Because I had some input as to how the A Range was going to sound and work, I suppose there was a certain bias and so I was more on that side. After leaving Trident, I tended to go to studios in England that had Cadac boards because they were closer to the Trident sound than a Neve, so I always liked them.

As far as A Range versus the original REDD desk at EMI, there really is no way to compare them. The EMI valve boards sounded so great and just happened to also have the best board distortion ever, something impossible to emulate with a solid state board. In fact, I can remember walking into Number 3 while The Beatles were recording "Revolution" and seeing John, Paul, and George all sitting in the control room, plugged directly into the board, which was unheard of at the time. That's the sound that you hear on the record.

By the time the A Range came into existence everyone was so used to the new modern solid state sound that it came across as a damn good desk. Unfortunately it took solid state to allow us to achieve the technical heights that we now have, but that meant losing a couple of sonically better things along the way. In fact, thinking about those "technical heights" and how they're used, and oft abused, today, maybe it would have been better to stick with valves/tubes.

We had UREI limiters that had china pencil marks for the settings. I used to get non-stop grief from a certain engineer [Ken] who used to call me up and say, "It's pumping." I'd go running down to the studio and listen and say, "Is it? I can't hear it." "Yes, it's definitely pumping," he'd say. I decided he was doing it just to make everyone aware that he was listening. For a few weeks I put up with this, and one day I went down to the studio, undid the knobs and turned them so the markings were in different places. He came in for a session that day and immediately called up and said, "These limiters aren't right," and he was right because I'd changed them. So I went down and turned them a bit to where they should've been and said, "Don't call me again about it," and he never did.

Pete Booth

RICK WAKEMAN

I did one track on Rick Wakeman's first solo album, *The Six Wives of Henry VIII*. We were going to work together for the entire album but it didn't happen, I guess because I must've gone off to do something else.

We were recording at Trident and it turned into an all-nighter. At about 7 in the morning Rick looked at his watch and ran out of the studio in a panic. None of us knew what was going on, but Rick sure was in the hurry. It turned out that he'd parked in a space on Wardour Street that had a parking meter. When he came in at 7 at night it was fine because the meter wasn't running, but at 7 in the morning they started up again. He ran out to put money in the meter, but got there just a little late. It turns out that Rick had one of the few American cars in the U.K. and it was huge by British standards. So big, in fact, that it took up almost two parking spaces on the street. The traffic warden was so pissed off he had a car that big that she gave him a ticket for each of the two parking spaces, so he wound up getting done twice. I didn't know American cars at that point, so I have no idea what model it was, but it sure was big. He was really proud that he had such a big car, but in this case it cost him.

Rick had a huge amount of gear, from Mellotrons to Hammond organs to a variety of synthesisers. It was a lot of stuff for the day, but by comparison with today it wasn't all that impressive. My, how times have changed.

JEFF BECK

One of the many times I worked with Jeff Beck was when he came into the studio to mix an album that he had recorded at the Motown studios with Cozy Powell on drums and the rest of the band made up of the regular Motown session players. At the time he was still supposedly produced by Mickie Most, but he wasn't happy with Mickie or RAK (Mickie's label), so I believe he was in the studio without Mickie's approval.

The sessions came to a rather abrupt halt and I later heard a bizarre story through the grapevine that Mickie had found out about the sessions and had the tapes stolen from a van as a way of stopping Jeff from doing anything further with them. I have no idea if that story is truth or gossip, but that album has never come out so it would make sense that something did indeed happen to those tapes. From what I remember it was really good and is another of those all-too-frequent instances when, had I known at the time that there would still be an interest in the recordings 40 years after the event, I would have kept notes and most certainly made a copy of the mixes we had done.

THE STONES

I recorded an orchestral date for The Rolling Stones one morning which consisted of two songs, "Sway" and "Moonlight Mile," that ended up on the *Sticky Fingers* album. Paul Buckmaster did the arrangements, and as was his way, he would invariably include some strange, little-known and seldom-used instrument. When I got the instrument lineup he had a bass crumhorn indicated, of which I had absolutely no idea what that was, so I just put out a mic and waited to see what showed up. It turns out that a crumhorn is a woodwind instrument that was popular during the Renaissance, but there are actually people around England who still play it. It finished up being not too hard to mic, thankfully.

It was strange to see Bucko with The Rolling Stones since he was more often working with Elton John or that kind of thing. To see him with The Stones didn't quite compute but it worked out well.

As far as I remember, the only member of the band who came to the session was Mick Jagger, who was very quiet and seemed quite sleepy, although I was not privy to whether the cause was because of an early morning or late night. I also did a brief stint on a Stones mixing session of a live concert that I took over for Roy, who I guess had another dentist visit, that I think must have been for the *Gimme Shelter* documentary, though I can't remember who attended.

MOTT THE HOOPLE

One day Ian Hunter, the lead singer from Mott the Hoople, came in for a quick fix to the "All the Young Dudes" hit single, written and produced by one David Jones (also known as David Bowie). It seems they were having a problem with some censorship issue at the BBC, but not for what you might think. David had a lyric about "Marks and Sparks," which is a nickname for the English department store Marks and Spencer. The BBC took that line as an advertisement so they refused to play the song as a result. We overdubbed two words from Ian, then I mixed only that section and edited it into a master specifically intended for the BBC. I had nothing to do with the recording other than that. I did, however, later record a much different version of the song with Bowie in New York during the making of *Aladdin Sane*. Good though it was, it didn't make it on the original album but did eventually come out as an additional track during subsequent releases.

I also did a quick mix especially for the BBC around that time for the one-hit-wonder Thunderclap Newman, who were produced by The Who's Pete Townsend. I have no idea how we changed it, although I suspect that it was a backing track without vocals for their appearance on *Top of the Pops*. What was strange was that The Who had their own studio by this time, so why Pete came to Trident to do it I haven't the faintest idea.

AL KOOPER

Former Blues Project and Blood, Sweat & Tears leader Al Kooper came into the studio to finish his *New York City (You're a Woman)* album. The album was partially recorded in the States, so I recorded only the second half and mixed it all. I do remember that Al played a lot of it himself. I didn't know what he was going to be like, but it turned out that he was a sweetheart and we got on very well.

Al was on a tight schedule so his label set up a number of press interviews during the time we were mixing. I'd get a mix set up, a reporter would come in, and Al would move to the front of the mix room and go through the interview while I just sat quietly behind the board waiting to get back to work. We'd get a little more done, then another reporter would show up, and it went just on like that.

We quickly realised that there were actually two categories of reporters and we soon began to be able to tell which questions they were going to ask by the cigarettes they would pull out before the interview. The arty ones always smoked these very evil-smelling French cigarettes, while the normal ones would smoke the typical English cigarettes like Players. By the time we finished, I realised that I probably could've done the interviews myself because every question was exactly the same and I knew the answers to them all by heart. Typical of reporters to never ask fresh questions.

LESSER-KNOWN ACTS

Just like at EMI, I recorded a number of artists that had little or no impact on the music scene. These included acts such as Hard Meat; Principal Edwards Magic Theatre (produced by DJ John Peel); Doris Troy (produced by George Harrison); ex-Blind Faith bassist Rick Grech; Dada, a jazz-fusion band featuring a young Robert Palmer; and The Iveys, who eventually became Badfinger, with Beatles roadie Mal Evans producing.

Interestingly enough, the producer for Hard Meat and Christine Perfect was Sandy Roberton, who later went on to become a very successful manager of producers in Los Angeles. Unfortunately he would never give me the time of day as far as managing me, so I suppose I didn't leave much of an impression.

I also did an album, *Fog on the Tyne*, with Lindisfarne, who actually did very well in England but never hit in the States. Their early stuff was produced by John Anthony, who eventually came into the Trident fold when they began managing producers. He also produced bands such as Van der Graaf Generator and he discovered Genesis and Queen.

Lindisfarne eventually went with producer Bob Johnston, who produced some of the early Dylan records and was fascinating to work with. He just sat there in the control room and hardly said anything at any point during the recording. He never told me what to do and left me on my own to get the sound and record it, but there was something about him that pulled out the best in you. Even though he wasn't saying anything, you wanted to please him and try as hard as possible. It was the same for the band since Lindisfarne never played or sang as well as they did on that record. I also think that was the first album I ever did where the producer wasn't at the mixing session. One of the things that I remember about Bob was getting a huge tip, a nice big cheque, from him after handing in the project, which was both unusual and very much welcomed. Two hits in England came from that session: "Fog on the Tyne" and "Meet Me on the Corner."

These sessions and many more that are much less memorable were mostly enjoyable and fruitful, but as I look back I can see that they were preparation for my association with three acts that would change my life and career in a major way.

CHAPTER 11

Enter David Bowie

Early into my time at Trident I was assigned to engineer an album with a young David Bowie and his American bass playing producer, Tony Visconti. My first impression of David was that he was rather flamboyant, with long blond hair and definitely inspired by the San Francisco "flower power" hippie movement that was at its peak in 1969. He was pleasant (and always is to this day), but neither he nor his music hit me as anything special. Please remember that I had been working with the biggest band in the world and had recently finished Procol Harum's *A Salty Dog*, and so after working with artists of that calibre, it made me very hard to please. A session with a little-known artist like David Bowie became just another gig.

David had already done a couple of singles and an album for Deram Records (a subsidiary of the well-established Decca Records) and had released such classic tracks as "The Laughing Gnome," a novelty record that many in the press interpreted as a children's record. At the time I met him, he had a real folky hippie kind of thing going, which was a little too rambling and wordy for me. Lucky for us all, Bowie, being Bowie, changed direction on every album, so the first one was folk, the second one leaned more towards metal, and onward with each record taking on strange mixtures of every musical genre.

The first Bowie album I worked on had various titles. *David Bowie* in England, *Man of Words/Man of Music* in America, and, several years later, after our success, it changed yet again. The single "Space Oddity" was quite successful, reaching number 5 on the English charts, but although it got David known, it really didn't help his career much. A great record, yes, but when push comes to shove it's not the kind of song to build a career on, just a novelty song (once again). "Space Oddity" was virtually forgotten after it left the charts, at least for a while, and everything else he came up with was so different that the album did virtually nothing. However after the later success, RCA decided to rename the album *Space Oddity* when they reissued it in 1972 and it eventually jumped as high as number 17 on the Billboard charts in the U.S., and when reissued again in the U.K. in 1975 the original single became David's first number 1.

Strangely, I didn't work on the recording of "Space Oddity." Tony (producer Tony Visconti) hated the song and refused to record it, so the role of producer was handed over to Gus Dudgeon who worked on the track with Trident co-owner Barry Sheffield engineering. Then it was up to me to record and mix the rest of the album along with Tony producing.

Man of Words/Man of Music (or *David Bowie* or *Space Oddity*) featured a variety of session musicians, from bassists Herbie Flowers and John Lodge (not to be confused with the bassist from The Moody Blues with the same name), guitarist Tim Renwick, drummer Terry Cox, keyboardist Rick Wakeman, cellist Paul Buckmaster, along with even Mr. Visconti playing the occasional bass part as well. Tony was definitely in control of the sessions and the arrangements, with David saying little after the players learned the song. Later during mixing, it was all Tony again, with David rarely around, a practise he would continue during all the albums I did with him.

The next album was *The Man Who Sold the World*, once again with Tony producing, but this time featuring a new band and a harder rock direction. David recruited guitarist Mick (Ronno) Ronson and drummer Michael (Woody) Woodmansey from an unknown band, The Rats, and convinced them to move from their native Hull to

London, while Tony became the one and only bass player. The project was started at Advision, another independent studio in London, and so I only became involved to do some overdubs and mix the album, and was unaware of much that went on during tracking.

> *For* The Man Who Sold the World, *it was the first time for us in a big, proper London studio. Before that we'd try to get all of our favourite licks in and David had to write above that, so there was not a lot of planning. It was done on the spot. Tony is a hands-on producer in that he played an instrument, so there'd be a lot of, "You play this, then I'll play that."*
> Woody Woodmansey, drummer with David Bowie

The album was released on Mercury Records in the U.S. in November of 1970 and the following April in the U.K., and although it met with generally good reviews, it failed to dent the charts. It was at that point that David, fed up with his lack of success, gave up and temporarily quit the music business.

WE MEET AGAIN

Our next meeting came one day in the spring of 1971 when I found myself scheduled on another session with David. He had booked time at Trident to produce a single with a friend of his, Freddi Burretti, who later became one of his clothing designers. Now Freddi was ... how shall I put it? ... very effeminate, and on this occasion he was wearing a very, *very*, tiny pair of hot pants and I, along with the rest of the Trident family, was extremely worried that he might suffer a major wardrobe malfunction, but thankfully the gods were with us on that day. I never did know if I was assigned to work on this session purely because David and I had previously worked together or whether he had asked for me, but as luck would have it, or those same gods, there we were together again.

There comes a time in many engineers' lives when they grow tired of coming up with ideas and having a producer take credit for them, and I had come to that time. Too often after my making a suggestion, the producer would accept all the accolades if it worked, or say, "Oh, it was only Ken's idea anyway," if it didn't. I didn't feel that was fair, and felt like I had a lot more to offer than currently being allowed, so I started to seriously think about giving production a try if the opportunity ever arose.

Robin, Roy, and I were sitting around talking at Trident one day and discovered we were all going through this same thing with various producers and all feeling the same way about moving on. We decided at the same time that we wanted to get into production so we could have more say. We went to Trident management and presented our idea, and they said that they'd begin to set up our own individual companies to look after us in that area.

So here I am working with David again when during a tea break I happened to mention to him that I wanted to start moving into the producing side of things. Much to my surprise he replied, "Well, I've just got a new management deal, and I'm about to start a new album. I was going to produce it myself but I don't know if I can. Will you produce it with me?" Of course, I wasn't going to say no. Just like that, I was a producer. Besides, I never really thought that David would amount to much at the rate he was going, so if I screwed up, no one would hear it anyway. Well surprise, surprise!

HUNKY DORY

After David and I had decided I would co-produce the album with him it was time to sort out the business details. Since I worked for Barry and Norman Sheffield, I of course told them about the upcoming production and they organised a meeting through Bowie's new management company, The Gem Toby Organisation, to work out the deal points. It was done at a local restaurant over lunch, but for whatever the reason (I think it was planned that way), I got there after the meal. Norman and Barry seemed happy enough and the management representative, one Tony Defries, was (what I came to learn later) his typical emotionless self. Little did I know what I was really getting myself into at the time.

Having decided that we were going to work together, David, his wife Angie, and his publisher Bob Grace came over to my house one evening and we started to go through the material David had written for the album.

As I've already said, my initial response to working with David was that it was an incredible opportunity. He was someone who was obviously talented, and whom I got on well with, but I didn't see him ever becoming a huge star. I looked at doing an album with him as more of an opportunity to learn my chops as a producer, and gauging from his past releases, it wasn't necessarily something that anyone was going to hear. If I screwed it up, no one would be the wiser. This was the complete opposite of the way it had been during my engineering career so far, since my progressions had all been under a microscope on Beatles records.

But as we were going through the material it suddenly hit me. "Hang on, this guy is really fucking good. He could be a lot bigger than I expected and this album might actually be something that a lot of people will listen to. Crap." Here it was again. Trial by fire.

That was it for preproduction. We worked out most of the songs that we were going to record, then it was a matter of just going into the studio. Some of the songs had been demoed and the band knew them already, and some of them they didn't so we started from scratch on those.

> *I'd have to say that there was more of a commitment from Bowie [on* Hunky Dory]. *Prior to going in to record he spent more time writing, where before on* The Man Who Sold the World *we went in with a lot of chord changes, sometimes even without lyrics. We didn't know what the song was about.*
> Woody Woodmansey

This was to be the first album with what would become the Spiders from Mars: Mick Ronson on guitar, Woody Woodmansey on drums, and the new bass player, Trevor Bolder. Rick Wakeman, one of the busiest session players in town and the one holdover from the "Space Oddity" recording, was recruited to play piano. Rick had become involved with David originally because he was the only guy in England that had a Mellotron at the time, and Gus Dudgeon, being keen to use it, had called him in.

Mick Ronson and Woody [Woodmansey] had played on The
Man Who Sold the World *album with David Bowie. They did
that album with him and then left—they didn't want to play
with Bowie anymore—so they came up to Hull, where I joined
them, and we played for about six months as a band. Then
Bowie rang up one day and asked if we'd go down and do this
John Peel [radio] show with him, because he needed a band. So
we said, "OK, we'll come down and do that." That's basically
how it all started.*
Trevor Bolder, bassist (from an interview on DMME.net in 2003)

Even though both Ronno and Woody had played on *The Man Who
Sold the World*, our dealings with each other were extremely limited
as I was only put on the session to do a few overdubs and mix. I have
a vague remembrance of Ronno coming by, but as far as any real
interaction ... nothing.

That being said, the team fitted together immediately. The band was
capable of playing exactly what Bowie needed, they were easy to get
sounds on, and they were very down-to-earth nice guys. Hey, even
David was down to earth at that time as he hadn't yet formed his
Ziggy persona.

We each had our own roles and we didn't have to talk about it—it
was instinctive. There were often moments where David would say
to Ronno, "OK, it's time to ... " and Ronno would cut him off and
say, "I know. I'll do the guitar at the end of the song." Before any
of us could say anything, he'd be in the studio playing the new part
brilliantly. He always knew exactly what was needed.

I guess you could say that we were in each other's heads right from
the start of our collaboration. We all knew our places, and I knew
when to shut up if David was sure of what he was doing. In fact, the
hardest thing for me during David's sessions was just making sure
I always had enough tracks. If he suddenly wanted to add another
vocal or a 120-piece orchestra, I had to be sure we could do it. It
was more of knowing when to be silent than knowing when to say
something, yet I knew that I always had complete freedom at the end
when it came to mixing.

On David's previous two records, Tony (Visconti) was the sometime bass player, often arranger, and always musical director, and I honestly think that's why David broke away from him. Tony had almost complete control and David wanted his own voice on his records, and that's the opportunity I gave him. Eventually, he referred to me in a radio interview as his "George Martin." It took me a little while to understand what he meant by that, but I think that George, through most of his tenure, had this thing with The Beatles where he allowed them to have their head, but knew just when to say, "OK, enough is enough." Several acts I've worked with since have used this side of me to their advantage, but more about that later.

So David had his freedom. He knew a lot of what he wanted, though not totally. The right team was there from the start, we all knew our places, and it all fitted together perfectly.

> *I presume it's [the reason why David split from Tony] because he went off and did Marc Bolan. Then Marc had a hit record and he [Tony] concentrated on him. He did Gentle Giant as well. Whether he was too busy or they had a falling out, I don't know.*
> Trevor Bolder

As was the norm at that time, tracking for *Hunky Dory* went very quickly. We generally worked Monday through Saturday, from about 2:00 P.M. until we finished, generally around midnight, not much later. We'd eat when we felt like there was a natural break, and drink tea. Lots and lots of tea. No drugs and the only alcohol use was that Ronno might have a couple of beers, but that's it.

With David, unlike on The Beatles sessions, it was very much him knowing what he wanted right from the get-go. That still, at times, led to a little experimentation as he might know what he wanted as the end result but not necessarily how to get it, but he knew most of the time what was going to happen. The only problem was he didn't always tell you until we got to that point, so you had to be ready. And it was very much trying to read his mind because he didn't always know how to put it across. You'd think that would hang up a session, but we'd figure it out quickly and the session would move on without any fuss.

Bowie Technical Bits

The setup I used for *Hunky Dory* was the same as for all the other Bowie albums.

Woody would always set up in the Trident drum booth. On occasion the drums were recorded in stereo, but not always. Sometimes they were all on one track with a separate kick track, and sometimes the snare was on a separate track, depending on the song. The drum mics were pretty much what I use today: ribbon mics for overheads (either STC 4038s or Beyer M 160s), an AKG D 20 on the bass drum, a Sony C-38 on snare (later I used a Neumann KM 54 or 56), and Neumann U 67s on the toms. I would often use the original Kepex gates on the drums because they were so simple and did the job adequately.

Trevor's Gibson EB-3 bass was usually DI'ed.

Ronno was a Marshall man through and through, and used a half stack (a Marshall Major 200 with a slanted 1960A cabinet) that was rarely turned up full. I would always use a Neumann U 67 or 87 just in front of the speaker cabinet and occasionally a distant mic, which would be any mic that happened to be handy at the time. Mick got his sounds via a Cry Baby wah-wah pedal that he'd move slowly through its travel until he hit on the right sound for the song, and then he wouldn't touch it again.

The acoustic guitar frequently played along with the electric rhythm guitar to give the sound of it a different feel. I usually miked it with a U 67 or C 12A and compressed it, sometimes quite heavily, with a UREI 1176 or LA-2A.

For piano I employed a three-microphone technique, with two U 67s on the bass and middle strings and a KM 56 on the high strings, all slightly limited with a couple of LA-2As if stereo was required. I placed the mics in parallel directly hovering over the strings left, centre, and right.

It depends on what was required and how the arrangement was written, but generally I used a mic on each section of the strings (Neumann U 67s or U 87s) and one C 12A, if possible, for every two celli. The one thing I seem to do as standard on the violins and violas is pull a little of the mids out, around 3.5 kHz or 4 kHz, and add a little at 10 kHz.

And last but not least was Mr. Jones himself on vocals. David was always exceptional with his vocals, and 99% of the time it was the first take, beginning to end, with no punches. I'd get the level and he'd sing the song down and that would be it. Sure made my job easy. You'd think there was a mistake when he was laying it down, but when we'd listen to the playback we'd find that what we thought sounded odd the first time through was intentional and worked perfectly.

What I quite often did while recording David's vocals was use an AKG C 12A and a U 67 and place them at a 90° angle to each other so he was singing in-between them. I came up with this method so I could instantly switch between the two to see which mic sounded better (and maybe even use both), instead of having him stand in front of one mic and sing a bit, then go in front of the other mic and sing a bit. It also had the added benefit of helping suppress any popping and sibilance as well. We didn't have many tracks at that time, so even if both mics were used, they were mixed together to a single track. Unlike many other recordings of the time, we never recorded the effects because David only did one take, so there was never any time to set them up.

The album, like the others that followed, was mixed on a 20-input Sound Techniques console, using moderate board EQ, a single EMT plate reverb, and just a little compression on the overall mix. Compression came from two UREI 1176s and two Teletronix LA-2As. The multitrack machines were an Ampex 8-track and later a 3M 16-track. Any delay came from a Studer C 37 stereo tape machine with a varispeed.

I don't think we ever did more than three takes on any Bowie song, and most of the time it was first or second take. When I listen now I wonder why I played some of the things I did, but mostly it was because we'd go for a take after about half an hour. The first take you were trying to keep the sections straight in your mind, and then we went for it, so we were always on the edge.

There's a newness the first time you're putting it down. It starts to lose something little bit by little bit the more takes you do. The first couple of takes pull out the right things because you're under pressure.

Woody Woodmansey

Though much of the recording of *Hunky Dory* is a blur, there were a few sessions that stood out for me. One is a track called "Quicksand" where David originally put down a single acoustic guitar and vocal, and for whatever reason, I had this thought of the acoustics getting bigger and smaller throughout the song. I asked him to double-track it, then I asked him to double-track it again, eventually recording the same guitar part six times. When it came time to mix, I had it set up in my mind that it would start with the single acoustic in the middle of the stereo soundfield, then it would open out to a guitar on either side, then finally open to all the acoustic parts at the biggest part of the song, then diminish back down to one. This was a way of making the song dynamic before any of the other instrumentation came in, and I think it worked.

We move on and start to record a song called "Andy Warhol." I, being the well-trained EMI engineer, slated the song and David corrects me on the pronunciation ("It's Andy War-hole, as in hole"). During the eventual playback I started to mess around and switch between sel-sync and playback on the tape machine so there were time jumps in the dialogue and everyone said, "That's cool. We've gotta keep it." Thus we kept that entire talking part in the beginning of the song, though that wasn't the take of the actual song that we ended up using. When it came time to mix, I programmed some stuff on Trident's ARP synthesiser (see Figure 11.1) and that was cross-faded from the track before ("Fill Your Heart") into the talking bit of "Andy Warhol" to make a seamless bridge.

Of all the songs on the album though, "Life on Mars?" was my favourite beyond any shadow of a doubt, but the outro of the song was a complete accident. One of the things about recording back then was we made decisions very quickly and very easily. If I didn't feel that what we recorded was the take, I'd record over it because we didn't want to have stacks and stacks of reels of tape with alternate takes laying about, so we just kept using the same reel until we got the take we wanted. When we recorded "Life on Mars?" it was just drums, piano, and bass on the basic track, but Ronno was down in the studio giving cues to Rick Wakeman, who was playing piano.

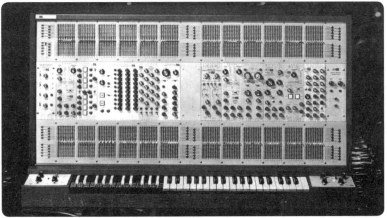

Figure 11.1: Trident's ARP 2500 synthesiser.

There was a bathroom attached to the studio that had a public phone in it. Its sole purpose was to allow session musicians to call out during breaks or after the session was finished and so wasn't meant for anyone to call in on. In fact, no one ever knew the number, so it never rang.

So we were coming to the end of this great take and the bathroom phone that never rang suddenly let out an annoyingly loud jingle that was, of course, picked up by the piano mics and made the take unusable, much to everyone's intense dismay. We all thought that we could get another take just as good, so the decision was made to tape over the one with the maddening ring on the end. Now, whether the band started to play the song sooner or played it slightly faster, I'm not sure, but it was some time later when we were doing the orchestra overdubs and they were holding their last note at the end of the song that the end part of the earlier take, that apparently hadn't been erased, blasted out of the monitors. Much to our surprise, it sounded great, so we decided that we had to use it. It's that earlier take that comes in at the end of the finished song and you hear the previous piano track with the phone ringing and much frustration voiced by Ronno in a very colourful way. Unfortunately we decided that I should fade that out fairly quickly though, so as not to cause offense. Censorship right from the beginning.

That was played almost live with Rick Wakeman on piano and Bowie singing. When we heard it going down we felt we captured what we were going for, but when we came in to hear it after Ken mixed it, for the first time I forgot that I was actually playing on it. It was like listening to someone else's music. The quality that had been put into it was awesome. I was concerned that we might've gone too far, but the quality of the song was a lot higher than what was around at that time.

Woody Woodmansey

David never particularly liked being in the studio recording and especially didn't like mixing sessions, so when it was time to mix *Hunky Dory*, I was on my own. Mixing in those days was sort of an "all hands on board" affair as there was no console automation, so whoever was in the room was conscripted into looking after a set of console controls and we all worked together until we got the mix. It was very much a performance wherein everyone had to get their parts right at the same time. But with *Hunky Dory*, there was only me and, for most of the time, an assistant. I heard a hundred changes in my head that needed to take place, but the only way I could do the mix without having a hundred hands to move the faders, change the EQ, and pan and adjust the reverb and delays at the appropriate time was to get one section right, then the next section, edit them together and listen to make sure that the edit worked, then on to the next section and continue from there. Not being completely dumb, I made sure to carefully make marks on the console with a china marker so that if the edit didn't work, for whatever reason, I could always go back to the settings for the section before and start again. That way I could make all the changes and get the mix sounding exactly as I wanted, and once all the sections were finally put together I had the complete song, love it or leave it. That's the way I worked for many years after that. The one drawback to this method of working is that if you don't like the finished mix you literally had to start from scratch. There was no "let's just try one more take." Over the years I have had it pointed out to me that if you listen on headphones you can hear some of those edits, but thankfully they're few and far between.

In the end, *Hunky Dory* took about two weeks to record and then two weeks to mix. Pretty fast compared to today's albums, but "back in the day" artists had to come out with an album every six months, there were limited tracks to use, and we made decisions as we went along instead of leaving everything for the mix. Elton was the same, as was Lou Reed and America. Two weeks recording and two weeks mixing.

Hunky Dory charted in April of 1972 and met with extremely limited success in both the U.K. and the States (its success would have to wait a while), but it set the stage for the Bowie's next album, the one that would change all of our lives forever.

CHAPTER 12

Elton John

As previously mentioned, one of the original reasons I was hired at Trident was to work with Gus Dudgeon but that never happened as planned. Shortly after Barry Sheffield finally gave up engineering, Robin Cable was put on Gus's sessions and they quickly developed a strong working relationship. He worked with Gus on the second and third albums of a very young singer/songwriter by the name of Reginald Dwight (known to the rest of the world as Elton John), both of which became fairly successful.

Robin had just finished recording the fifth Elton album, *Madman across the Water*, when he had his unfortunate car accident. Since the album still needed to be mixed, I was assigned the job, but I must admit that I felt I was being thrown in at the deep end a bit. That feeling seemed to ring a bell.

You have to remember that this was back in the day when the cast usually remained constant from beginning to end of the album. The same producer and engineer would start the record and take it through to completion because they had the vision of what it was going to sound like. You didn't have lots of remixes done by different mixers, or different tracks recorded by different engineers as you have today. To suddenly come in to mix someone else's vision was a little uncomfortable and I was slightly nervous, but it was a chance to finally work with Gus again.

Gus was originally an engineer himself, and one of his claims to fame during that period was engineering the John Mayall classic *Blues Breakers*, the album that catapulted Eric Clapton to fame (Roy Baker happened to be his assistant on the sessions). Gus was very funny, a little flamboyant, and he loved outrageous socks. He could also be a tightwad. When we used to order in pizzas he'd make sure to go around to everyone and say, "You've had two slices so you owe one pound six," and collect the money.

One of the things I learned from Gus as a producer was the benefit of keeping people happy. There are some producers who like everyone to be on edge or in bad moods in the studio because they believe they'll get a better performance. I learned from Gus that if everyone is in a good mood that comes across in the tracks and to the audience in the end.

> *He just made you feel relaxed and made the session enjoyable. He would do such a great job that you wanted to work with him.*
> Dennis MacKay, assistant engineer (on Gus Dudgeon)

The good thing was that we both thought along the same lines sonically. Since we both loved dynamics and knew instinctively how things had to happen during the mix, the transition from Robin to me went that much smoother as a result.

I had met Elton (we referred to him as Reg back then) back in my EMI days as well, although it took a bit of time for me to remember. At one point I worked with an artist named Katie Kissoon, and this very odd fellow walked in during the recording and was introduced to me as the songwriter. It was a long time until it suddenly clicked, "Hang on. That was Elton." He was one of the musicians always hanging around Trident so our paths crossed there too, but I guess I met him for real during the mixing of *Madman*.

Elton came by to listen to the final mixes, but he wasn't there that much while we were doing the actual mixes, a trend that would continue during my time working with him. That's the way it always was with artists back then. Once the recording was finished, you never really saw them. One has to bear in mind how quickly everything was churned out during that period. An artist was obligated to release two albums a year, so you had to record and mix them fairly fast, and the album could come out as soon as a month, maybe six weeks later, unlike the six- to nine-month wait that record labels now seem to demand. The artist would begin preparing for the next tour as soon as the album was mixed, so the time during mixing was the only time they had to hopefully relax a little.

What really stood out about *Madman* for me was how good the record was and how good Robin was. I hadn't really listened to the prior Elton records because I was always working and didn't have that much time to critique anyone else's work. I knew that they were good, but listening to the multitracks really brought that home.

> *You [Ken] called me down to the remix room. You were on one side of the console and Gus was on the other. You said, "Sit in the middle." I was a young kid and I felt really honoured. It was "Indian Sunset." I was so blown away over how great it sounded.*
> Dennis MacKay

HONKY CHÂTEAU

Since things had gone well with the mixing of *Madman* and Robin was still recovering, Gus asked me to do the next album, which was to be recorded in France. At the time there was a loophole within the English tax code whereby, to completely over-simplify it, if an album was recorded outside of the country, you didn't have to pay tax on its royalties back in England. As a result, Elton's money people decided it was a good idea to record the next album somewhere outside of the U.K. Elton was ready for a complete change and fed up with recording in London anyway, so Gus somehow found this studio in France that no one had heard of, and off I went with them for preproduction and recording.

The studio was located in a castle built in 1740 in Hérouville, in the Oise valley just outside Paris, and was supposedly once the home of Chopin. Film composer Michel Magne had purchased the estate in

1962, eventually installed a 16-track studio, and overnight the 230-year-old Château d'Hérouville became plain old Strawberry Studios. It was a working studio and various French acts had recorded there before, but I believe we might have been its first big international booking. It was both a delightful and a strange place, and like many studios on that side of the pond, seemed to be haunted. No one wanted to sleep in the producer's bedroom after Gus swore that he saw something in the middle of the night. The studio was in a separate building from the main living quarters, and there were times walking there that were just eerie. I never actually saw anything, but there were occasions where you could feel your skin crawl for no apparent reason.

PREPRODUCTION

Preproduction began about a week before we started recording, but it wasn't just preproduction; it was actually writing the material for the album as well. What happened was that Bernie Taupin, Elton's writing partner, would go up to his room at about 7 or 8 P.M. every night to write. In the morning he would come down to breakfast with a stack of lyrics that he would immediately give to Elton, who would go to his piano and sort through one piece of paper after another until something caught his eye. Elton certainly had the freedom to move things around a bit if he wanted to, but I don't know that he ever actually changed any lyrics. He did sometimes block some out to fit a song though. The third verse of "Daniel" being a classic example.

> *The final verse struck Elton as too American for a lad from Pinner in Middlesex to sing with real conviction.*
> Bernie Taupin, songwriter (on "Daniel")

The entire crew of about 12 people would all slowly emerge for breakfast around a huge table, and I remember him picking out this one set of lyrics one morning and exclaiming, "Oh, I quite like this." He was immediately over at the piano that was set up in the living room, and within ten minutes he wrote "Rocket Man." When we all finished eating, the band got behind their instruments, which were set up in the same room, and sorted out the arrangement. It was one of those amazing moments.

Preproduction seemed to move so damn fast. After a few days when all the arrangements were together, the gear was moved over to the studio and we started recording.

RECORDING AT THE CHÂTEAU

This was a time of huge change for Elton. Everything about the recording was different, but Gus and I knew that there was one thing we had to try and keep as close to his past recordings as possible: the piano sound. Trident had one of the best pianos ever for recording pop/rock music, a Bechstein grand that had the brightest sound I've ever heard from a piano. We realised how much a part of Elton the piano was so we had to try to make the piano at the Château match it as closely as possible.

We worked on matching it for a bit and did a quite good job, but then hit a small snag. The problem was that Trident had an enclosed drum booth, so you didn't have to worry too much about drum leakage into the piano mics. There was no such room at the Château, however, which meant that we had to set up the drums in the same room as the piano, and that gave us a huge leakage problem. As a result, we had to find a way to block off the sound.

How did we overcome this? Easy. Gus called in some carpenters to make this big plywood box that went over the entire piano after its lid was taken off. The height of the box went about 3 feet above the top of the piano, and there were a couple of holes in it so that I could poke the mics through. It ended up working out really well.

Another huge change: this was the first album recorded with Elton's touring band. They had individually played on tracks before, but up until this time he'd used mostly session musicians. Apart from recording in a different country and studio, Elton and Gus also wanted a different feel from the previous albums. They'd done the orchestral thing before, so now they wanted this record to sound more like a band and have more of a rock feel.

They couldn't have asked for three better musicians. Dee Murray was such a beautiful and melodic bass player, and very precise in his playing. We never needed many fixes after he recorded a part. He must've been a fan of McCartney because he played in that same very melodic style. It's only recently that I've come to appreciate how great he really was. He was a bit of a fiddler though, and was never satisfied with his amp settings. On more than one occasion Gus had to tell him, "OK, it's perfect. Stop!"

Every band has their own lingo that they use and you [Ken] made a comment back then that we use to this day. You said to Dee over the talkback about his sound, "It's a weeny bit woolly, Dee." We just fell about. Dee was like, "Give a chap a chance," because he was quite regal and proper when he wanted to be.
Davey Johnstone, Elton John Band guitarist

Guitarist Davey Johnstone had been in a band called Magna Carta that Gus had worked with, and was a bit nervous because this was his first time doing something of this scale and importance. Despite his inexperience, he fitted the bill perfectly and was always willing to try anything. He'd frequently move from acoustic guitar to electric guitar to mandolin to even banjo, and he was comfortable with each.

Nigel Olsson has always been an under-appreciated drummer. He played along the same lines as Procol Harum's B.J. Wilson in that his playing was almost more about the spaces that he left rather than the actual notes he played. I love that kind of drummer because it leaves more room for the sound to fill out. It's really one of those cases where less is definitely more.

As an added bonus, the vocal blend of Davey, Dee, and Nigel was amazing. To me, their voices blended the same as John, Paul, and George or the Hollies when Graham Nash was still with them. Elton was always very hands-off with the backing vocals and was never around whenever they worked them out or recorded them. It was all left up to Gus and the guys. Not to worry, the backing vocals always went so fast and easy.

Just to try something different, French violinist Jean-Luc Ponty was brought in to play on a couple of tracks. We recorded "Amy" first and it was wonderful and then went on to "Mellow." What he played was great, but it was sounding a little ordinary, so I suggested putting it through a Leslie. Jean-Luc was amazed, as he'd never tried anything like that before, and I think it really affected the way he played. When he first starts the solo it sounds just like an organ, but when he started to do all of these slides that you could never do on an organ you begin to realise, "This is a violin." He was blown away by it as was everyone else.

THE TAP DANCE SOLO

When we finished recording in France we went back to Trident for some overdubs with percussionist Ray Cooper, and to mix. On one song, "I Think I'm Going to Kill Myself," someone came up with the harebrained idea that it would be a perfect song to have some tap dancing on. Throughout recording there was much madcap humour, very Goons or Monty Pythonish, and so once that was suggested everyone became really gung-ho for the idea. Gus knew the exact person to call. He'd produced the Bonzo Dog Doo-Dah Band and who better for something as insane as this than "Legs" Larry Smith. I can't remember if he brought in his own floor or we just got some plywood for him to do it on, but we laid this hard surface down in the middle of the studio. I placed a U 67 (which I tended to use on everything back then) on each side of it and that was it. It wasn't complicated to record at all, just very, very strange.

Honky Château took about two uneventful weeks to mix, then I was off to another project. I wasn't sure if I'd work with Elton and Gus again, but I sure had fun on this one.

CHAPTER 13

Ziggy Stardust

A couple of weeks after the completion of *Hunky Dory*, I happened to run into David Bowie in the hallway at Trident. At some point during the conversation he casually mentioned "I'm going to be recording a new album." "You're kidding, right? *Hunky Dory* isn't even out yet," I replied. David went on to tell me that it was his management's idea to do another album, but he ominously added, "I don't think you're going to like this one. It's much more rock 'n' roll. More like … " I don't remember if he used Velvet Underground or Iggy and the Stooges as a reference to what he was going for, but as I hadn't heard of either one at the time it didn't really make much difference. "Well, we'll see," I cautiously told him.

David was no longer with Mercury after the lack of success of *The Man Who Sold the World* and had been without a record deal during the recording of *Hunky Dory*. In a huge show of faith in David, it was paid for by Gem Toby, his management company, part-owned by former accountant Laurence Myers and former lawyer and soon-to-become David's sole manager, Tony Defries. Defries used some of the *Hunky Dory* tracks as a demo to get record labels interested and David signed a record deal with RCA shortly thereafter. For reasons only known to himself, Defries (or "Deep Freeze" as he was occasionally, and not so affectionately, known) wanted another album ready to go after *Hunky Dory* was released. So into Trident we went again, and *Ziggy Stardust* was born.

As to whether Gem Toby also paid for *Ziggy* I'm not sure as my production contract had been, and continued to be, with Gem (for a little while longer anyway). In fact, I had no idea about any of the specifics of the budgets for any of David's albums. Unlike today, I never had to worry about going over budget as I was never given one. We just went in and did what we wanted to do and everything was paid for. It was a few years after my move to the States that all that changed and I started to have to put costs down on paper. Oh, unhappy day.

IN THE STUDIO

David had a few demos prepared for the album, but interestingly two of the songs that he decided to record were actually from that first day I reconnected with him (the day of the possible wardrobe malfunction nightmare) when he produced Freddi Burretti: "Moonage Daydream" and "Hang on to Yourself." Even though David had originally written these songs for Burretti and not for himself (they were eventually released under the name of Arnold Corns), David thought they might fit nicely on this record, and they did. One song that eventually made the record, "It Ain't Easy," had initially been considered for another album. It was a leftover from the *Hunky Dory* sessions and so was the only track on Ziggy that Rick Wakeman played on.

During the brief period in-between albums, Woody had complained to me that he wasn't overly happy with the drum sound on *Hunky Dory.* He felt it sounded too much like he was hitting "corn flake packets." For the first session when recording an album, I always ask the drummer to come to the studio a couple of hours early as drums always take longer to set up and it takes longer to get his sound than the rest of the band. The last thing you want is a bunch of bored musicians hanging around while you try and get the drum sound, as they quickly become as bad as kids in the car's back seat with their "Are we there yet? Are we there yet?" Even if the drums are already set up beforehand, every drummer will move them slightly, which affects the mic positioning, so it's not until he has the drums set up the way he wants them that I can set the mics up the way I want them and we can start getting the drum sounds. The sometimes interminable bang bang bang, boom boom boom is excruciatingly hard to listen to if you're not a part of it.

Since Woody had rather audaciously compared his drums to corn flake packets, I had the tea boy go out and buy as many different size packets of Kellogg's Corn Flakes as he could find. Then Peter Hunsley, the band's roadie, and I set up these packages on stands in place of the drums. When Woody walked in and saw the setup he fell about laughing at the absurdity of it all, yet understood very well that I had taken his point seriously. We quickly moved the real drums back in and got back to work, finishing about three hours later with a drum sound we both liked.

Speaking of the drums, because this album was going to have a different type of music, I knew instinctively that the drum sounds would have to be different to better fit the music. The dead sound that we used previously on *Hunky Dory* wouldn't work for this record. Although the tuning would probably be slightly different, it was more about using less damping than we used on *Hunky*. As I tended to do at that time, I used gaffer's tape and sometimes a small piece of sponge on the drum head to get rid of some of the ring of the drums. It was a subtle difference from the *Hunky* drum sound, but enough to make them fit with the harder rock 'n' roll sound of what would soon become *Ziggy*.

Each project I go into I think of slightly differently just because musically it's always different. The basic setup I use is always the same but it all comes down to the individual songs that determine how I go from there. Musically *Ziggy* was edgier than *Hunky Dory* and so it needed to be sonically edgier as well. A tame sound would not have meshed with how the band was playing. However, there's a major difference between something that you're going to piece together with overdubs versus, say, a Mahavishnu Orchestra, where it's almost completely live. Once again, the basic setup is the same, just bigger, and it's what happens once they start to play that will be the genesis of the sound more than anything else. I still think of each song and each piece of music as an individual entity and I still look to get the best out of each. For me there are no hard and fast rules, it's whatever works for the music.

As with *Hunky Dory*, what was to become *Ziggy* was recorded at Trident in about two weeks, with another two weeks for mixing. The sessions themselves weren't much different to any of the other Bowie sessions. The basics took about 4 or 5 days and were virtually the same for every track. It was only the nuances in each song that would vary. What's more, nothing was recorded 100% live. There were overdubs on every track, and as is usually the case, some more than others.

There were a lot of tracks recorded for *Ziggy* that didn't make the album (most of them I had forgotten about until I began mixing *Ziggy* for 5.1 release recently)—"Velvet Goldmine," "Bombers," "Holy Holy," and Jacques Brel's "Port of Amsterdam." If I remember correctly, we put a lot of work into "Velvet Goldmine" and so it was fairly finished, "Bombers" was only somewhat finished, "Port of Amsterdam" was David with just an acoustic guitar, and "Holy Holy" was only a basic track and I don't think we even got a good one. Originally one of the tracks intended for *Ziggy* was "Round and Round," the old Chuck Berry rock 'n' roll classic. That one had the least number of overdubs of all the songs that weren't strictly acoustic and was completely finished. It was actually supposed to be on the album until RCA decided they needed a single and that was the track that got kicked.

As I said before, David is an amazing singer, and 95% of his vocals on *Ziggy* and every other album I recorded with him were done in a single take. There was one completely calculated exception however. In the first part of the song "Rock 'n' Roll Suicide," David sings very quietly, and so in order to optimise the sound quality, I had to crank the level of the mic preamp. He eventually becomes a powerhouse and his vocal range was quite different for the latter part of the song, so I had to readjust the levels to compensate for that, hence the vocal for that song was recorded in two parts. Each part was a first take, of course. I learned not to expect anything different.

As with everything Bowie, there are lots of myths and misconceptions and the so-called "sax section" on "Suffragette City" is certainly one of them. The fact of the matter is that it's not a sax section at all, but a synthesiser. We thought we had finished the song but, as these things often go, it was lacking something. I'd been spending a lot of time messing with the ARP 2500 synthesiser (see Figure 11.1) that Trident had recently purchased and suggested we give it a try. I got the sound, and Ronno played the part that David came up with. We were not specifically going for a sax sound and to me it sounds nothing like saxes so it always surprises me when people tell me they thought it was a sax section. Then, of course, came the really big surprise when David told American DJ Redbeard during an interview that he played all the saxes in the song. Then again, lest we forget, we're talking about Mr. Bowie. One can never tell if he really didn't remember or he was just telling the interviewer what he wanted to hear.

Of course there's always a favourite track and on *Ziggy* it's "Moonage Daydream." All the songs work for me but that one just works a couple of percent more for some reason. David has said in interviews that he's always been like a chef. He takes ingredients from all of the music that he's heard, mixes it all together, and it comes out being his own. In this case, he took an idea from the B-side of the 1960 Hollywood Argyles number 1 hit "Alley Oop" called "Sho' Know a Lot about Love," where a baritone and flute play the same line together (well, a couple of octaves apart, but I think you know what I mean), and used that same concept for the solo of the song. The only difference on "Moonage" being that it was a recorder not a flute playing with the bari, both of which David played.

> He was incredible in that he'd see a trumpet or an accordion or some other instrument in the studio and say, "Let's find a way to put this on there." We were so into rock and roll and wanted to remain true and pure, and we'd think, "Oh, God [covers his eyes and hangs his head], he's not going to put that on it?" He'd do it and place it somewhere back in the mix and it would work. That amazed me.

The same with takes. We'd do the second take and feel, "Now I know the song," and he'd go, "That's the one." We'd all argue that we could do a better one but he'd say, "No, that's the one." After a while we'd begin to think, "We'd better get it by the second take."
Woody Woodmansey

I really enjoyed doing that album, but I remember it being a nightmare because Bowie would come in and just throw songs at us. We were used to it, but the unfortunate thing wasn't, "Here's a song. Let's rehearse it for an hour." It was "Here's a song. You got it? Let's go." You had one or two takes, and that was it. It still turned out great.
Trevor Bolder

One of the things that really made *Ziggy* (and all the albums I co-produced with David) that much better were the great orchestral arrangements that Ronno put together. They were even more brilliant when you consider the fact that he always had this habit of running out of time before they were finished. I have this remembrance of him rushing in about 10 minutes before the session was due to start, running up to the bathroom on the first floor, and locking himself in so he could find the privacy to finish writing. He'd come out about 20 minutes later (10 minutes after the session should have begun) with a huge grin on his face and a stack of charts. That happened almost every time.

Ronno's contribution to not only *Ziggy*, but every Bowie album I worked on was major, major and, did I mention, *major*. He was a great guitarist, a great arranger, and a great down-to-earth guy. He knew exactly what was needed at exactly the right time. Neither David or I would have achieved anywhere near the success we had without him.

The orchestra we used generally consisted of eight violins, four violas, and two cellos (or 8, 4, and 2 as we'd call it), with the violins divided into four first violins and four second violins. There were occasions Ronno would use a smaller string section but also times, as in "Rock 'n' Roll Suicide" when he'd add double basses. He actually went all out on that particular track and added a brass section comprising two trumpets, two trombones, two tenor saxes, and a baritone sax.

This was one of the few times that the saxes were session players as opposed to David playing them himself.

I've come to realise that an unusual thing about *Ziggy* is that there's acoustic guitar on every track, even the rock 'n' roll ones. It didn't seem unique at the time as I had started my rock 'n' roll listening to the likes of Presley and Bill Haley, both of whom used acoustics, so using them seemed quite natural and gave the songs a whole different feel. I wasn't into cymbals at that point (I have no idea why), so I used the high-end of the acoustic more as a percussive instrument, almost as a high-hat sort of thing. It wasn't something we consciously thought of or went for, but it's always there. The acoustic guitars were always compressed, sometimes heavily, most likely using a UREI 1176 or LA-2A, and miked with a U 67 or C 12A.

When the album was turned in to RCA they apparently didn't hear a single, so back in we went to cut "Starman" at the beginning of January 1972. The song turned around quickly, I think a day to record the basics and most of the overdubs, a day to finish overdubs, including the strings, and another to mix. The song finished up replacing "Round and Round" on the album (see Insert Figure 13.1).

There were some strange things going on with the Bowie recordings during that period that I didn't find out about until much later. There appears to be a second mix of "Starman" wherein the only difference is that the Morse code part on one mix is really loud and on the other really quiet. I have no idea which one I actually did or how or why the second one came about. After hearing both, it sounds to me like there was only one mix and that those sections were copied louder, or quieter, and had been edited in to make it different, but no one seems to have any recollection of it being done.

Another strange occurrence was with the song "John, I'm Only Dancing," which was recorded as a single to take advantage of Bowie's growing popularity after the release of *Ziggy*. The song was recorded at Trident in June of 1972 in much of the "wham, bam, thank you, ma'am" fashion of "Starman," meaning recording the basics and overdubs over two days, and mixing on another. I was never aware of it until doing the 5.1 mix, but there were actually two versions of the song. Apparently David and the band went over to Olympic and recut the song almost identically, directly after we had recorded it at Trident. To this day, I don't know why this was done and neither does anyone else, except maybe David, and the details of both sessions seem fuzzy to everyone involved.

The only one [version] I can remember is the one at Olympic, because we recorded it, then the Faces came through the door when we were recording backing claps in the hallway, and they all joined in. It was in the daytime. We might have done it at Trident, but I always remember putting it together at Olympic. Maybe we just did the backing track there and finished it at Trident. We never mixed it at Olympic.

Trevor Bolder

ZIGGY AS A CONCEPT

There's always been this whole thing about *Ziggy* being a concept album, but it really wasn't. There are only two rock albums that I would 100% consider concept albums: *Tommy* and *Quadrophenia* by The Who, and that's because they were written as a complete piece, whereas *Ziggy* was just a patchwork of songs. Yes, they fit together very well and one can weave a story from some of them, but when you consider that "Round and Round" was originally there in place of "Starman," it doesn't make much sense as a concept. How does "Round and Round" ever fit into the Ziggy story? It's a classic Chuck Berry song. How does "It Ain't Easy" fit in with the Ziggy concept? That was taken from the *Hunky Dory* sessions. All this about Ziggy being Starman is bullshit. It was a song that was just put in as a single at the last minute at the record label's insistence. So while it's true that there were a few songs that fitted the "concept," the rest were just songs that all worked well together as they would in any good album.

Even David didn't take the Ziggy concept too seriously at first (that would come later). He has told various stories of how the character came into existence. Supposedly, in one tale, the name

Ziggy came from a London tailor shop (Ziggy's) which David had seen from the train, and in a later version he told *Rolling Stone* that Ziggy "was one of the few Christian names I could find beginning with the letter Z." David has also been quoted in many interviews stating that the character Ziggy Stardust was based on the Elvis impersonator Vince Taylor, an eccentric leather-clad Brit who achieved a level of stardom in England in the late '50s before having a very public mental breakdown and winding up in a psychiatric institution. And just as an aside, many, including The Clash's illustrious Joe Strummer, even considered the bizarre Mr. Taylor to be the beginning of British rock 'n' roll.

> *I met [Vince Taylor] a few times in the mid-'60s and I went to a few parties with him. He was out of his gourd. Totally flipped. The guy was not playing with a full deck at all. He used to carry maps of Europe around with him, and I remember him opening a map outside Charing Cross tube station, putting it on the pavement, and kneeling down with a magnifying glass. He pointed out all the sites where UFOs were going to land.*
> David Bowie, from *Golden Years: The David Bowie Story* on BBC Radio 2, 18 March, 2000

But as David and the band hit the stage after the album was complete, David began to become the Ziggy character and the public ate it up.

ZIGGY HITS THE CHARTS

There's a conversation I've had twice with the acts I was working with. Once when we were close to the end of *Ziggy* and the other was during the recording of Supertramp's *Crime of the Century*. Basically we thought both of those albums would be successful in America but not as much in England. What gave us the opinion they were more U.S.-oriented I have no idea, but that's the way we felt. On both occasions it turned out to be the complete opposite. For both acts it took five years to happen in America, and in the meantime they had number 1s throughout the world.

Hunky Dory came out on December the 17th, 1971 in the U.K., almost immediately after we finished recording *Ziggy*, and didn't make a huge splash. It did give David more notoriety and allowed him to begin to build a following through touring, but everything changed with the release of *Ziggy Stardust* on the 6th of June, 1972.

The record blew up in the U.K. immediately, eventually reaching number 5 on the U.K. charts, but only number 75 on the Billboard 200 a full year later. The single, "Starman," reached number 10 in the U.K., but again, only number 65 in the U.S. The second single off the record, "Rock 'n' Roll Suicide," reached number 22 in 1974. David had now become a full-fledged cultural phenomenon in England and other parts of the world, as Ziggy, with the Spiders from Mars, played to sold-out concerts in the U.K., Japan, and a few parts of the U.S.

One of the by-products of a hit record is that it lifts the sales of the entire catalogue, and Bowie was no exception, as *Hunky Dory* entered the charts in September, two months after Ziggy was released. Eventually the album would hit number 3 and have a chart run for over a year. "Life on Mars" was released as a single and also soared to number 3. "Changes" was released three years later and reached number 1. Still, both albums only slightly dented the U.S. charts, even with pockets of success in the larger cities of the north and west, but five years later, America finally got Bowie fever. There were small areas where *Ziggy* did really well, but it was mostly underground in the rest of the country. Of course, David's whole androgynous image was way too much for many people to handle, especially in the deep South, and I seem to remember a story about them having to run for their lives at a roadside cafe when they were touring down there.

So how did I hear about David's success? I was sitting in the reception area at Trident reading the paper when Gus Dudgeon walked in and congratulated me. Surprised, I asked, "What for?" "Ziggy entered the charts this week at number 7!" he exclaimed. That was how I learned it was a hit. My feeling, although I have no direct evidence, is that the record was bought into the charts because that's the kind of thing that David's manager, Defries, would do, and at that particular time in England it wasn't that difficult to do, or that unusual. In fact, there was a story that the whole Virgin chain was built around a company's ability to buy records in. Supposedly Richard Branson set up just enough stores in key places so you only had to go to his stores to buy a record into the charts. Management or labels would give students the money to go buy the record from Virgin stores which created just enough sales around the country to register it as a hit. If the story is true I can say nothing other than … "Brilliant!"

> *I actually always thought it was because we did* The Old Grey Whistle Test. *We did a TV show up in Manchester in which we did "Starman" on that, which reached a lot of the kids. Then we did* The Old Grey Whistle Test *which reached a lot of the hippie crowd, and it took off after that. We played a club and Defries was all excited because he managed to get Mike Moran down from* Top of the Pops *to come and see us. And it worked. I think we played* Top of the Pops *even before "Starman" had charted.*
> Trevor Bolder

Although success seems to be a wonderful thing, it frequently doesn't play out the way you'd think. Right after Ziggy became a success, all kinds of unfortunate legal things around David started to transpire— everything from Trident not having their bills paid to me not receiving any royalties. At that point it became common knowledge that Defries had split from Gem Toby, set up his own company (MainMan) and took Bowie, and others, with him. From then on, there were lots of lawsuits all around that wouldn't stop for many, many years.

I have to pass comment on how amazed I am that 40 years after we recorded *Ziggy* we're still bloody talking about it. It was never meant that way when we originally did it because back then we thought that an album would have a six-month life span. We had no idea that all these years down the line people would still be interested. Rock 'n' roll wasn't even that old at that point, so how could anyone know?

CHAPTER 14

Bowie Post-*Ziggy*

As the gigs got larger around the U.K., David and the Spiders received more and more press attention, pushed along gladly by the English rags with stories about David's androgynous appearance and supposed bisexuality. Live appearances on both radio and TV also started to prime the ever increasingly bored youth for what was yet to come. Shows such as *Sounds of the Seventies*, *The Old Grey Whistle Test*, and finally *Top of the Pops* started to break down the barriers and build the buzz.

In the meantime, David began his metamorphosis into the character of Ziggy, pulling the band along, sometimes kicking and screaming, into the alternate reality that was the Spiders from Mars.

In the north of England no one ever dressed in bright colours, but when I first met David he had hair down to his chest, red corduroy trousers, blue shoes with red stars painted on, and a rainbow-coloured shirt. I'd never seen clothes like that before.

That was pretty new even for London then. We were just in jeans and T-shirts and we never changed to go on stage. But with him it was all geared to be more of a show. We used to go to see theatre shows to see what theatre lights could really do, because no one was really doing anything [theatrical lighting] for bands at the time. There was no finesse, whereas he took theatre lighting

and put that onto rock and roll, and that was a big part of the
atmosphere, plus the costumes and moves. It was very different.
Woody Woodmansey

By this time Tony Defries had established his own management company, MainMan, and had taken David with him. As seemed to happen a lot around Deep Freeze, a number of legal battles ensued that extended to everyone around him and never seemed to stop. Defries, a lover of huge cigars, was certainly an interesting man in many ways, not least of which was his sense of fashion. No matter what the weather was, he could always be seen wearing this huge fur coat, but strangely enough I never once saw him sweat. I guess that helped lead to his nickname.

Nonetheless, David was beginning to break both critically and commercially, and everyone knew it was only a matter of time until he became a star. But despite David's notoriety, Trident wasn't getting paid and neither was I. A by-product of the Defries transition from Gem Toby to MainMan, perhaps?

As the guys were getting their kicks from the growing audiences, I got my little ego boost one day walking around Christchurch, Dorset. I was there to visit someone in the hospital and had parked a couple of streets away. Enjoying the brisk walk, I suddenly noticed sound wafting from someone's upstairs window. What a kick I got hearing someone following the instructions on the album sleeve to "play it loud." The "it" this time being "Suffragette City."

LOU REED'S *TRANSFORMER*
Bowie was a big Velvet Underground fan and had taken to playing a few of singer/songwriter Lou Reed's songs ("White Light/White Heat," "Waiting for the Man," and "Sweet Jane") in his shows, so it was no surprise when David announced that he was going to produce Lou's second solo album in August of 1972.

Although the record took the typical two weeks to record (again at Trident), it was different in that it was all done during the day because David and Ronno would run off to rehearsals for a big

Rainbow Theatre show (one that would prove to be a critical career turning point) during the evenings. It was also different because we used all session musicians, except for Ronno. Lou would teach Ronno the song, then Ronno would teach the session musicians, then we would carry on as if it were a Bowie record until it was time to do Lou's vocals.

The album would become *Transformer* and was particularly noted for Lou's signature track "Walk on the Wild Side," which was special from recording right through mixing in terms of creative inspiration. For instance, when Ronno was teaching the band the song, the drummer, Ritchie Dharma, who was in the drum booth, was initially playing it with sticks. As I was listening upstairs in the control room, I knew immediately that the sticks were too heavy for the song and wouldn't work so I dashed down and asked him to try brushes, which we finished up using all the way through.

The classic double bass line by Herbie Flowers was another inspiration, although not for the reason you may think. It didn't take very long to put down the basic track, and after we were finished, Herbie came up to the control room and asked me if he could add another bass part using an electric bass. After he explained what he had in mind, we all said, "Sure. Let's have it," and it was magic. What we didn't know (as Herbie's gone on to explain in a variety of interviews over the years) was that he was mostly concerned with getting paid double for playing the additional instrument under Musician's Union rules. A bit mercenary, but the line he came up with ended up making the record, let alone becoming one of the most copied and/or sampled bass parts ever.

Lou and David got on like the world on fire. Those were two that found each other. Their discussions were witty, funny, and cheeky. Very camp, it was. Lou had his fingernails painted black. He played a fantastic rhythm guitar. I love the bass Herbie Flowers played on that record.
Klaus Voorman, bass player

After the track was finished, there was still something missing, and David asked, "Do you know any backing vocalists that we can use?" I called up this group that I used to work with called Thunderthighs (consisting of Dari Lalou, Karen Friedman, and Casey Synge), who came in and sang it. While the line of the song goes, "And the coloured girls say … " it's more like, "And the Jewish girls say … " since they were all white and a couple of them were Jewish, but they got the effect that everyone was looking for and certainly painted the necessary picture.

Finally when it came to mixing, thanks to his fear of flying, David was on his way to America via the QE2 for his introductory U.S. tour. Ronno came by for one mix that we didn't get very far with, and Lou was there physically but not mentally, so it was just me mixing all by myself once again. By the time it came to mixing "Wild Side," I was so sick of hearing the "doo doos" so many bloody times that I had to do something just to relieve the boredom of it. I had this idea of them coming from way back in the distance and walking forward finally singing it right in your face. I started off with just the reverb signal which I kept at the same level during the mix, but I had the source background vocal level come up and up until you hardly hear the reverb at all and they're almost dry and in your face. It's amazing what comes out of boredom sometimes.

Other than that one song, *Transformer* was rather uneventful. While I've heard and read many claim that it's a classic rock album, I really don't see it that way. "Walk on the Wild Side" yes, I think is amazing. It's a classic track. But a single classic track does not a classic album make.

As I said, Lou was there in body for the sessions, but that's about it. A couple of weeks after we finished the album, I saw Lou again in a Chinese restaurant in Wardour Street and he had no idea who I was. It just didn't register. Then recently I was asked to do an English TV show that's based around classic rock albums, where they interview everyone they can get who's connected with it to tell the story of the album. I went there and did my bit in the morning, then it was going to be Lou's time, then I was going to do a bit more. So Lou comes in and they introduced me, and once again he had no clue, "Oh, you're Ken Scott." It was the strangest thing to go through "Who is this guy?" all over again.

For *Transformer* I was only credited as an engineer, but it was exactly the same teamwork as all of David's albums, so why were the credits different? It wasn't like the Arnold Corns/Freddi Burretti stuff where I was put on just because I had worked with David before. Never could figure that one out.

ALADDIN SANE

In September of 1972 Bowie and the band, now firmly established in the Ziggy and the Spiders persona, set off on their first American tour, which was originally planned for only eight concerts but met with such great success initially that it was extended for a full eight weeks. The tour started in the great rock 'n' roll town of Cleveland (where American jazz pianist Mike Garson joined the lineup), then moved to Memphis, Boston, a triumphant Carnegie Hall concert, and eventually ended with a now-legendary show that was captured on a live FM radio broadcast at the Santa Monica Civic Center. While many of the initial dates were indeed successful, Bowie mania had not taken hold in all parts of the country, as dates in Houston and Oklahoma City were cancelled due to lack of sales and a concert in St Louis had attendance so small (only 180 in an 11,000-seat hall) that David gave what amounted to a private show, but as the tour progressed, so did the buzz. By the second time back in cities such as Philadelphia and Cleveland, he was selling out 10,000-seat venues.

Since Bowie was gaining some traction in at least some parts of the country, RCA was hungry for another single, so the band rushed into RCA studios in New York to record "The Jean Genie," which came from what was essentially an impromptu jam on the tour bus. Although I wasn't there for it, the song was recorded very quickly, they did a mono mix, and that's what came out as the single. It was different from what we'd done before, but that was more because of David's mood so it didn't bother me, especially when I got to put my touch on it later when I mixed it in stereo for *Aladdin Sane* back at Trident.

Since the tour was extended and David and the band wouldn't be back in the U.K. for some time, it was decided that I should come over to the States to begin recording their next album. We started recording tracks, some of which would eventually become part of *Aladdin Sane*, in New York City at RCA studios, such as a version of "All the Young Dudes" that was never used until various releases a lot later, "Drive-in Saturday," "The Prettiest Star," and another that we started but didn't get very far with. Everything else on the album ended up being done back at Trident. The only change in the band was the addition of Mike Garson on piano.

For the tracks that we did in New York, I had to act literally as a real producer and not as the engineer/producer that I usually was because RCA was heavily unionised, and not being a union member, I wasn't allowed to touch the board. This became unexpectedly problematic at one point after we'd finished putting down a basic track for one of the songs. It was dinner time so we decided to eat before moving on to the next number. The band and I had some food brought in, but engineer Mike Moran and the second engineer decided to go out to eat instead. We finished eating before they got back and everyone was anxious to start running through the next song, so being unaware of the ferocity of New York style union contracts, I hit the one button on the desk so that they could hear themselves in the headphones. When Mike returned and found out what I had done, he hit the roof. "Do you realise what you've done? The entire studio could have come to a halt if they caught you doing that," he admonished me on and on. Hard to imagine that a simple button push could bring down a mighty New York recording studio, but there you go. A heavy moment that soon was forgotten as we carried on creating.

Another interesting but slightly embarrassing situation came up while working with Mike. I had always hated it when someone would come up to me and ask, "What was it like working with The Beatles?" or "What was it like working with Elton?" because it's a loaded question that always gets the same sort of non-answer: "They were fine. It was great. I had a good time." In the middle of recording in New York I found out that Mike had worked with Elvis, and I had been a huge Presley fan growing up. Of course, the first question out of my mouth, much to my surprise, was, "So what was it like working with Elvis?" I never minded that question being asked of me again. I guess we all fall foul of things like that from time to time.

Besides the fact that we were in a different country, city, studio, and I couldn't touch the board, the general feel of the sessions in New York was a bit strange as well. For whatever reasons, it happens frequently that some of the members of English bands touring the States for the first time get involved in cults or religions. On this particular occasion, Mike Garson was deeply into Scientology and was preaching to whoever would listen, and had got Woody and Trevor involved. As a result, the dynamics of the band changed slightly; not in a bad way, but they were different, and you could feel it. Some time later, Trevor eventually left Scientology, but Woody is still involved to this day.

BACK AT TRIDENT

When the band came back to England in January of 1973, we got back to work on *Aladdin Sane*. David was starting to experiment more, which was one of the reasons for his liking Mike Garson so much and having him join the band. Garson was an experimental player from that peculiar avant-garde Cecil Taylor atonal school of jazz. David especially had him get into that mindset on the track "Aladdin Sane," and that piano part is phenomenal. The interesting thing for me is that Rick Wakeman's piano on "Life on Mars" is so amazingly beautiful and so classically oriented, but equally as good in a totally different way is the piano on "Aladdin Sane." It was incredible and still sends shivers down my back.

Thanks to Mike Garson, one of the more interesting differences between British and American music that I came to learn of during the making of this album was how much written music differed in both countries at the time. In the States, musical note timings are indicated in whole-notes, half-notes, quarter-notes, eighth-notes, and the like. In England it's semibreves, minims, crotchets, and quavers. As a result, there were times when Ronno was trying to teach something to Garson, who was a well-trained musician, where he was saying things like, "You should be playing a semiquaver there," and Garson would have absolutely no idea what the hell he was talking about. Over the years, with Brits coming over here and Americans going over there, this may well have changed, as it seems to happen with a lot of things, but at that time, music was talked about in a completely different way and it was quite funny watching the two of them trying to communicate. It was as if one was talking French and the other English.

Other songs that stand out from those sessions include "Cracked Actor," where David wanted to try harmonica on it. Ronno had been particularly loud and distorted on that track and the harmonica sounded smaller than everything else, so I gave him a different mic and plugged it directly into Ronno's Marshall. It worked. It was both very nasty and very lovely, if not unusual for the time.

I also loved "Drive-in Saturday." It feels more American to me than anything else on the album, probably as a result of David's time in States. That whole American thing must have rubbed off not only on David and his writing but also in the way I heard things too, at least on that track.

In the end, *Aladdin Sane* took a bit more time than previous Bowie records, but not that much. All told, we recorded in NYC every day for about a week, then another two weeks at Trident. The mixes then took about the normal one day each.

In all my time with Bowie, record label involvement was very minimal to say the least. They never came to the studio, although they were welcome, and never questioned a mix, except once. When it came time to mix "Watch That Man" I felt it worked better to have the vocal really low in the mix to keep it more like one of the instruments. It just seemed to have more power that way and so that's the way I mixed it. After handing in the album to David's management company, they got back to me and asked if I could try another mix with the vocal up. I told them my concern, but they said, "Do one more and let's see," so I did one with the lead vocal up. They listened and said, "You know what, you were right. We're going with the original." About two weeks later RCA called me up and said, "That track 'Watch That Man,' can you try one more mix on it with more vocals?" I said, "Yes sure, but I've already done that once and MainMan said they preferred the original." Again they said, "Can you go in and do another mix with the vocal up for us?" So I did it again, they heard it and said, "Yeah, you were right. Let's go with the original." Hearing it today I feel that I went overboard and I wish that vocal was louder, but at that time, that's the way it seemed to work. But that was the only time there was ever a problem with a mix.

The other mix that was different on this album was "Lady Grinning Soul," a love song. For whatever reason, it must've really meant something special to David because it was the first time he ever came in for a mix and had a very strong feeling about how he wanted it. Although not specifically the way I had initially heard it, we leant more in his direction and I have to say I love the way it finished up. The vocal is phased all the way through and that was a very specific request of his. I have no idea who he wrote it for, but it was obviously very important to him.

THE CRACKS BEGIN TO SHOW

After another short run of gigs in the U.K., the band headed back to the U.S. for another tour, starting in New York City—this time for a sold-out Radio City Music Hall concert with a very eclectic array of personalities in attendance. People including Salvador Dali, Andy Warhol, Truman Capote, Johnny Winter, and Todd Rundgren all joined the throngs wishing to pay homage to the alien, Ziggy. The band then left for a series of five sold-out shows at the Tower Theater in Philadelphia, then on to Nashville, Memphis, Detroit, and Chicago before finishing up at the Long Beach Arena outside of Los Angeles.

While Bowie was experiencing ever greater acclaim, all was not well within the band, as Woodmansey and Bolder, still on their original modest payment schedule, began to feel more and more disrespected whilst David enjoyed all the affectations of stardom. They were getting paid peanuts, but everything looked as though David was raking it in. Little did any of them know that Defries was the only one getting rich. Finally, the blowup came in New York when they refused to go on stage until a new payment arrangement was made.

It wasn't just that the Spiders weren't being paid much by Bowie/ MainMan, but they were being courted with other opportunities to make their own money that Defries would effectively squash.

A lot of it stemmed from when we went on strike in New York because we weren't being paid any money. Mike Garson was getting a thousand dollars a week and we were getting 30 quid, and all we wanted was a fair deal. Then CBS offered us a huge record deal, and Defries crushed it. He [Defries] took Ronson on the side and said, "You go solo, and we'll get rid of these two." Ronson was played along. He got the, "I'm going to make you a star just the way I did with David," treatment.

Trevor Bolder

With the money row sorted out, at least temporarily, the band then left for a month-long tour of Japan. Once completed they returned home for a series of non-stop dates in May and June, with the prospect of yet another much larger American tour after that. Or so they thought.

The other thing is that we were promised we'd get 500 quid and have family for a week on the next tour, but we wouldn't get it until we got to America. So Ronson gets his solo deal and me and Woody don't know where we stand, so we have a meeting in Japan with Defries. So he calls us into his room and says, "About this money. RCA has agreed to pay you the 500 pounds a week, but I don't think that you're worth a penny of it. In fact, I'd rather give the money to the road crew because they're worth more than you." So Woody stood up and said, "Well if that's the case, you can stuff this tour and everything else," and he walked out of the room.

Defries was quite happy for him to do that because that's what he wanted, but not right at that time. We went back to England and Ronson had to beg Woody to come back.

Trevor Bolder

With stardom comes money, but that's usually when the hard feelings begin as well, regardless of the success or how close everyone is. Ziggy and the Spiders were no exception. Their end was near, and it would end up affecting me as well.

ABBEY ROAD TO ZIGGY STARDUST

INSERT FIGURES

Figure 2.4: A picture I took during a session for A Hard Day's Night
(I still worked in the tape library at the time).

Figure 2.5: Another picture I took during the same session.

Figure 2.6: Yet another one from the same session.

Figure 2.10: That's me cutting an acetate.

Figure 2.7: And yet another one. That's Norman Smith at the console.

Figure 4.1: My fashion statement.

Figure 6.1: In the studio with the biggest band in the world.

Photograph by Richard DiLello

Figure 9.4: George Harrison and me in the Trident control room.

Photograph by Richard DiLello

Figure 9.5: Another one of George Harrison and me at Trident.

AB 0248029

TRIDENT HOUSE, ST.ANNES COURT,
WARDOUR STREET, LONDON, W1.
TEL. 01·734·9901/4

Side 1

APRS-6819 **TRIDENT** STUDIOS

DATE 9·2·72   CLIENT   GEM PRODUCTIONS.

JOB NO.   PROGRAMME DAVID BOWIE.

DOLBY

	Title	Time	
1	"FIVE YEARS"	4·42	8
2	"SOUL LOVE"	3·34	9 RECORDED AT +4 'O' V.U. UNDOLBIED. TONES AT FRONT OF TAPE.
3	"MOONAGE DAYDREAM".	4·40	10 # 1KHZ — : 1? # 15KHZ — : 18 # 10KHZ — : 26
4	Starman ✓	4·13	11 # 60HZ. — : 12
5	~~Round~~	2·34	12
6	"IT AINT EASY".	2·58	
		20·10	13
7			14

Remarks   Round 'N Round APC6 689 239 to be sent by reel Not part of the album

Prod	KEN SCOTT + DAVID BOWIE.	~~MONO~~	MASTER	REEL ONE.
Eng	KEN SCOTT.	STEREO	~~COPY~~	OF TWO.
Op		15 IPS NARTB 7 IPS	~~CCIR~~	NO.

Figure 13.1: *Ziggy* tape box. Concept album?

Figure 15.1: Me, David Bowie and Mick Ronson.

Figure 18.1: Bill Cobham and Ken in the control room of Scorpio Studios

Figure 21.1: Supertramp's "gold" presentation. Designed by Freddi Burretti?

Figure 24.1: Ed Thacker (left) and me (3rd from the right) with Happy The Man.

Figure 26.1: Missing Persons with lots of Capitol people, Steve Brooks, and me.

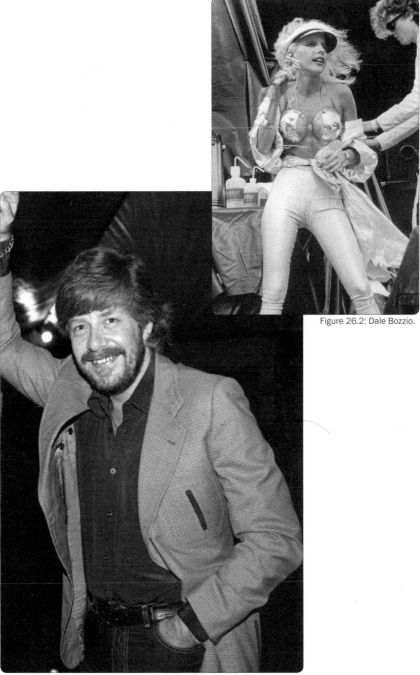

Figure 26.2: Dale Bozzio.

Figure 25.2: My managerial look, circa 1982.

Figure 27.1: From Warren's Playgirl spread

Figure 28.2: Phil Gould, me & Mark King.

PHOTO GALLERY

ABBEY ROAD TO ZIGGY STARDUST

ADDITIONAL IMAGES

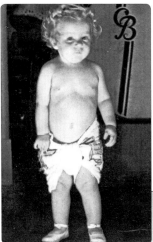

Figure A:(left) Yours truly, ironically standing in front of a bass drum.

Figure C: (below) Paul McCartney, George Martin and me.

Figure B: Me and John Lennon. That's the infamous Magic Alex in the background.

Figure D: Me and Paul McCartney.

Figure E: Me, George Harrison, and Ringo Starr.

Figure F: Me, Chris Thomas and George Martin at the 2011 APRS Sound Fellowship awards luncheon.

Figure H: With David Bowie at Château d'Hérouville during a *Pinups* session.

Figure I: Me with Patrick Swayze, Larry Gatlin, and Jackie Krost in 1989.

Figure G:(left) In the studio, 1972.

Figure J:(below) Back where it all started in Studio 2.

CHAPTER 15

The End of the Bowie Team

Bowie and the band began an eight-week tour of the U.K. with a massive stadium event at Earls Court in London on the 12th of May, 1973 that was attended by 18,000 adoring fans. As the tour progressed, demand was such that they began to play two shows a night in some venues as Bowie's popularity soared. Meanwhile, plans were being made for a triumphant return to the United States for what was to be the biggest tour yet. Prior to that, though, at the end of the tour there were two dates at London's Hammersmith Odeon, the second to be filmed by D.A. Pennebaker as a concert film with an accompanying double album soundtrack. Jeff Beck, who was Ronno's hero, would be a guest star and would play three songs.

The first night was strictly used as a run-through and since they weren't filming, the film people decided there was no need to record it. However, knowing the importance of the event, I decided to bring in fellow Trident engineer Roy Baker, to help me record the second night in the RCA mobile.

The show went without incident until prior to the last encore, when David stepped to the mic and announced:

Everybody ... this has been one of the greatest tours of our lives. I would like to thank the band. I would like to thank our road crew. I would like to thank our lighting people. Of all of the shows on this tour, this particular show will remain with us the longest [cheers from the audience] because not only is it ... not only is it the last show of the tour, but it's the last show that we'll ever do. Thank you.

We were gobsmacked. The whole thing about David's departure from touring came as a complete shock to everyone. My later understanding from band members was that Ronno knew about it, but Woody and Trevor didn't. My general feeling was that David actually believed it was his last ever gig, knowing how much under Defries thumb he was by then. Later there was some backpedalling, and came the explanation that "it was only Ziggy's last ever gig," which wasn't exactly the case either as he went on to do Ziggy for *The 1980 Floor Show* television show.

Defries wanted to be Colonel Tom Parker (Elvis's manager), and so many of his moves were based on the type of thing that Tom Parker did. Elvis quit playing live and was just selling records, as happened with The Beatles. Defries wanted David to do that, or at least that's the way he must've put it to him.

Because of the character that he [Bowie] is, there were always things of that nature thrown around, so we weren't sure that it wasn't just a publicity stunt.
Woody Woodmansey

If Woody had found out before the show, he would've never played it because he already knew he was leaving. He already told Defries in Japan. We had just done the biggest tour that any band ever did, with two shows a night every night. We were doing a 6 o'clock and an 8 o'clock show every night. We finished up at Hammersmith where we were thinking, "Next week we're going to America for this huge tour because he's now breaking there." Then it gets to the end of the tour and he says, "This is our last show together." Me and Woody looked at each other like, "What is going on?" Then we went out to a club and were told that the American tour was cancelled.

The worst thing for me and Woody is that Bowie and Jagger were there, Jeff Beck was there, Aynsley Dunbar was there, Lou Reed and a bunch of other people were there sitting at a big table having a jolly good time, and me and Woody were ignored like we weren't even in the band. You couldn't get a proper answer out of anybody as to what was going on, except, "That's it. That's the end of it."
Trevor Bolder

While that might've been the end of that phase of David's career, it seemed like that was the end of the film of the show as well. First of all, Jeff Beck said that he didn't like his guitar solos and wanted to re-record them, but after a while it came out that he was unaware that the show was being filmed, hated what he was wearing, and also wanted to be paid for his participation. Then there were some questions as to who actually owned the film in the first place. By the time the film, titled *Ziggy Stardust and the Spiders from Mars*, was mixed for the first time ten years later in 1983, David was back working with Tony Visconti again. It was remixed again by Visconti and Rich Tozzoli for the 30th Anniversary DVD edition in 2003. To be quite honest, I'm not a fan of either mix.

PINUPS

Pinups, a tribute record of '60s cover songs, was started a few weeks after the "retirement" concert and it was strange right from the start. I met with David a couple of days after the show at a hotel in Kensington to see if we could sort out any of the legal stuff that was starting to boil up. The lawsuits hadn't started at that point but the threat of them had been very serious, so I was trying to find a middle ground with David, although it's more than likely he had no idea of what was going on anyway. I had been advised not to do the record because MainMan weren't paying us, but I really enjoyed working with him, and let's face it, David was huge at that point. So even though the royalties were proving hard to get, it would have been silly to say no, and, to reiterate, I really wanted to do it.

What became *Pinups* was originally going to be the complete opposite of David's other albums. Each of his previous albums consisted of all of his own songs except for one cover, so *Pinups* was going to be all covers except for one song that would be David's, but it didn't end up that way. I remember David saying he wanted to do songs that weren't known as well in the States as they were in England, so there was a certain "they won't realise it's a cover" aspect to it, but I don't really think the choices worked within that concept.

David had decided that he wanted to record in France at Château d'Hérouville instead of at Trident, just like Elton and for exactly the same reason, to avoid paying British tax on royalties. I'd already done the two albums over there, *Honky Château* and *Don't Shoot Me I'm Only the Piano Player*, so I knew the place and was very comfortable with it.

Thanks to David's "retirement," the band for this record would change, although not as drastically as originally planned. Aynsley Dunbar, who I knew from working on his *The Aynsley Dunbar Retaliation* album, was on drums instead of Woody and the bass player was supposed to be Jack Bruce, but he pulled out at the last minute for unknown reasons (money?), so David called Trevor again. This made for a certain amount of weirdness, since he was there basically for the money and he obviously knew he wouldn't be around much longer having already been fired once. All around, it was fairly obvious that it was the end of that great team. Since David had already dumped two members of the band, and even though I went on to work a little more with him after this project, it was, in hindsight, obvious my days were also numbered. My managers were doing everything they could to get the money that was owed, and Deep Freeze never liked anyone other than himself adding to their bank balance, and so, much like the Spiders, he wanted me out.

Pinups certainly didn't have as friendly an atmosphere as we'd been used to previously and was, to say the least, a little bit tense. Not just for the people involved with the recording either. I remember a day when Angie, David's wife, arrived unexpectedly and, even with all the stories about how they had a completely open relationship, hit the roof on finding him in bed with another young lady.

It was a magic marriage of all those people together for that brief period. The sad part was that when we started out, he [David] didn't have anything and we didn't have anything, and it grew and it grew until it got really big. But it finished off as he was the star and we were the employees, which was sad to finish that way.

All I remember is walking into his hotel suite and Ronson was there. He brought me in to listen to the songs he wanted to do for Pinups. I was really annoyed about Woody, and Ronson grabbed hold of me and pulled me into another room and said, "Don't say anything. You're jeopardising your job here." I think at that point it was about if I was going to do it or not, but if you're going to change one, you might as well change it all.

Trevor Bolder

Unbeknownst to me, David was set to produce a version of "The Man Who Sold the World" for pop singer Lulu and had asked her to come and stay at the Château for a couple of days while we were recording. I called Jack Nelson, who was looking after me and all the other producers for Barry and Norman Sheffield, and he told me not to work on the Lulu sessions under any circumstances. "OK, fine," I said, but it was a really ridiculous situation where we'd put down a track for *Pinups* (see Insert Figure 15.1), I'd have all the sounds together, then Lulu would walk in and I would walk out. Everything was already set and they didn't have to do anything except press the record button, but that's what I was instructed to do. Because of all the legal wrangling going on, I had to follow instructions. Nearly every time Lulu came in over the next couple of days, I had to go.

All told, we were in France for about three weeks (see Figure 15.2). I came back to England for a couple of days in the middle as my wife gave birth to twins. I caught a flight back from France the night before it was supposed to happen and, of course, in typical rock 'n' roll style, I still got to the hospital late the next day. While I was away, they may have done a bit of Lulu recording but nothing on *Pinups*.

Eventually we did a few overdubs back at Trident and mixed it there as usual. Even though we recorded in France partly for tax reasons, you could still mix it back in England as long as most of the album was recorded elsewhere.

179

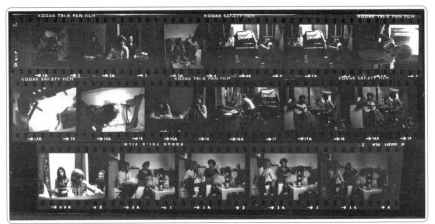

Figures 15.2: The Pinups sessions.

My favourite song on the album turned out to be "Sorrow." It just worked so well. We overdubbed strings in France and Ronno once again did the arrangement, but had an interesting time trying to communicate with French string players whose English wasn't very good, somehow reminiscent of the earlier Mike Garson situation.

The drum sound on "I Can't Explain" is interesting in that we originally recorded it at a faster tempo that was close to the original record, but after a while decided it wasn't working. When we came back to Trident, we tried slowing it down and loved the tempo but also loved the sound of the drums, so we redid all the instruments in the original key.

ONE MORE TIME

Following *Pinups*, I worked with David again on a track titled "Dodo/1984," two songs that were linked together for David's next album that eventually turned into *Diamond Dogs*. With all the legal wranglings still swirling about, communication had broken down a lot, and generally the session felt very strange, but we carried on regardless and eventually finished the track.

When it was time to mix, most unusually David chose to be there, and was obviously now very influenced by American music, as he kept playing me Barry White songs and saying, "I want it to sound like that." The mix went all night long.

It wasn't long after that we, the Trident mob, heard through the grapevine that David had booked time at Olympic, very obviously without me. I know I was pissed off, but more because I was never told anything by David in relation to not actually doing the album. It was obvious in France that his original relationships were falling apart, but ... in the end, my version of "Dodo/1984" failed to make the cut for *Diamond Dogs*. It did, however, eventually appear on one of the many compilations down the road.

THE 1980 FLOOR SHOW

The last thing I recorded with David was in October of 1973, a little something called *The 1980 Floor Show*. It was a show specifically put together for the U.S. concert television series *Midnight Special*, which wanted to do something different one summer so everything was shot outside of the U.S. An entire show was dedicated to David where he was given almost free rein, even to the point of picking the artists appearing with him. He did songs from *Pinups*, *Aladdin Sane*, and *Ziggy*, and chose Marianne Faithfull, a Tony Visconti-produced Spanish group called Carmen, and The Troggs as guests. It was shot at the Marquee Club, which was just down the road from Trident and happened to have a recording studio attached. The filming was all done in the club whilst the studio was used as a dressing room and for makeup and the control room was where I recorded it all.

David had also chosen a lady to do the introductions who at the time called herself Dooshenka, but later became Amanda Lear. She eventually became quite a success in Europe as a disco queen, girlfriend of rock stars, and mistress and confidante of Salvador Dali. They chose to shoot all of her introductions one after the other, which led to her changing costumes frequently and quickly. At one point David and I were sitting behind the board and she comes into the studio right in front of the window and completely strips off. My jaw drops and I'm just gawking when David says to me, "She's not bad, is she?" with a sly smirk. "Are you bloody kidding, no!" I replied. Then nonchalantly he dropped the bombshell. "Yer, especially considering that six months ago she was a guy." At that point, I almost lost it. I was never sure if the story was the truth or if it was just a case of David being David, but I can't say I ever looked at her in quite the same way again.

American censors were all over this bloody show and David didn't disappoint them one little bit. At one point, he came out in an outfit that had three mannequin hands: one on either breast, and another coming up from between his legs. Of course, as soon as the producers saw that they began screaming, "You can't wear that," so he had to have the costume quickly changed in order to take the hand holding his crotch away.

Later the band was performing "The Jean Genie" and the normal way the song went during a performance was that during the guitar solo, Bowie went down on his knees in front of Ronno in such a way that it looked like he was giving Ronno head. On an early take that's what happened and musically, it was absolutely superb. The producers, being more into the visuals than the music, didn't agree however, and once again started in on David, "You can't be that sexual on American TV! You'll have to do it again." This time the band played it as badly as they could and David did nothing in the solo in order to make the take totally unusable. What finally aired was so ridiculously edited to try to make it work that it was really quite funny. They basically cut to people who weren't really doing anything just to get rid of the "naughty" parts. This from the country that when playing "Time" from the *Aladdin Sane* album would beep out the word "Quaaludes" but leave in "falls wanking to the floor." You've gotta love censorship.

The 1980 Floor Show was broadcast on NBC on the 16th of November, 1973 and since then has shamefully only been available through very poor quality bootlegs. It was a memorable event as it was not only the last time I worked directly with David, but also the last time that Ronno and Trevor performed with him. Truly the end of an era.

THE FIGHT FOR ROYALTIES

Unfortunately the Bowie saga doesn't end there. As the deal was set up prior to David having a record deal, my contract was with his management company. Despite working on numerous excellent selling albums and singles, I still wasn't getting paid by MainMan, run by, guess who, one Mr. Anthony Defries.

There were a couple of royalty statements that came regarding my work with Bowie early on, but the numbers never made sense. Since our original deal had been with Gem Toby, there were many questions as to who was responsible for paying us after Tony split from Gem and started MainMan. Right after the very first meeting with Defries I formed a company with Trident called Nereus, and we unfortunately finished up having to sue both Gem Toby and MainMan in an attempt to obtain the monies owed (see Figure 15.3).

RECORDING COMPANIES

Top independent production teams work as part of the Trident organization. Ken Scott's Nereus Productions Ltd, and Neptune Productions Ltd. with Roy Baker, Robin Cable and John Anthony are continuing to notch up recording successes. Trident staff engineers too are on hand on a full production footing.

DESIGNED & PRODUCED BY VERNON OAKLEY DESIGN ASSOCIATES · PHOTOGRAPHER FRANK UNWIN

Trident. Trident House, St. Anne's Court, Wardour St. London W1V 3AW · 01-734 9901/4

Figures 15.3: Trident production companies.

To start off, it was just a threat with letters from our attorney and that sort of perfunctory legal intimidation, but finally, after a long time trying, the lawsuit was brought and scheduled to begin. In all too typical fashion there was a deal done at the last moment in Switzerland (where Defries had moved to) where a little of the money was paid, and it looked like everything was going to get sorted out.

In the meantime, Bowie sued Defries to get out of his contract, which was a very Elvis/Col. Parker-type 50/50 split. Even worse, Defries received 50% of gross revenue, and David had to pay all the expenses from his 50%. That's why David made virtually nothing from his early tours. They were so expensive and that all came out of his part of revenues, especially when he started to break in America during the big-production *Young Americans* tour. With all of the touring that he'd done, he made virtually no money for himself. It was all for Defries.

In fact, the first tour David did after splitting with Defries, the only stage lighting he used was fluorescent tubes on stage because they were dirt cheap. While the industry was appalled at the obvious skimpy production values (although many critics saw it as a brilliant artistic move), that would be the first tour he would actually make some money from.

We stayed at all the best hotels and flew first class. But it would've made a lot more sense if all the costs were taken off the top instead of David paying all the expenses. I totally understand why he became so hypersensitive about money.

We did one more tour as the Spiders after that with everything cut right down in order to pay for the last one. We were selling out big places, but it all had to be paid back.
Trevor Bolder

In the end, David was able to get out of his contract with Defries, but anything prior to that point (including all my work with him) he still had to do the 50/50 split with him. Suddenly it wasn't just Defries that we were going after to get paid, but David as well, since he was personally responsible for his half of my royalties. The response we got back from Bowie's people was, "David is perfectly willing to pay his 50%, but are you getting paid from Defries?" The answer, of course, was, "No, we're not." To which they replied, "David will start paying his 50% as soon as Defries starts paying his," which Defries never did.

This back and forth actually carried on for a long, long time and only got sorted out (to a point) when finally Bowie issued his "Bowie Bonds" in 1997. The Bowie Bonds were asset-based securities using all future earnings from David's 25 albums and 287 song catalogue to secure what amounted to a purported $55 million advance. The bonds paid an interest rate of 7.9% and had a life span of ten years, and were immediately bought by the Prudential Insurance Company and never offered to the public. The proceeds were used to finally buy Defries out of the deal. After that transpired, David became totally honourable and the payments have been regular ever since.

In the end, Defries never paid, and although some of it was made up by Bowie, we never saw everything that was owed to us, especially when you consider the amount that was spent on attorneys over the time.

I always saw it as David was a puppet and Defries was the puppet-master. He was playing him. There's a part of me that has the utmost respect for him because in certain ways he was absolutely brilliant, but he was brilliant for himself and not for his artists, or anyone else for that matter. He was an arsehole, but he was a brilliant arsehole.

One more story illustrates the point particularly well. David came around to the house one day and I happened to be reading *Stranger in a Strange Land* by Robert Heinlein, which, if you know the book, was the perfect vehicle for Bowie to begin his movie career. He sees it laying around and says, "Who's reading this? I'm going to be starring in the movie version." It seemed so perfect and he was so happy about doing it as he also saw it as the perfect foray into acting. So we start to see these newspaper articles about how he was starring in it, but there never seemed to be any actual plans to make the movie. It turned out that Defries, instead of calling up film studios and saying, "I handle a rock 'n' roll star who wants to become an actor," found a book that would be a great vehicle and just started to send the word around that David was going to star in the film version. What immediately happened was that all of these scripts started to pour in for David to star in, and Defries never had to make a single phone call. It was brilliant.

Some time after that he was in a movie called *The Man Who Fell to Earth* instead, just a cheap imitation of *Stranger in a Strange Land*. I could be totally wrong, but based on how happy David was when talking about the role, my feeling was and still is, along with others I have spoken with over the years, that David never knew the truth. He actually believed that he was going to be starring in the movie version of Heinlein's book. The control that Defries had over Bowie at one time was amazing. I'm pleased he got out from under him. I would bet a penny to a pound he was even more so.

POSTSCRIPT: DAVID IN SURROUND

My past was certainly coming and biting me in the arse. It was 2003 and I was approached about mixing *Ziggy* in 5.1. Apparently when asked by EMI about doing surround mixes of some of his earlier records David stated that he'd only allow it if the original producers/ engineers worked on them, which is exactly the way it should be as far as I'm concerned. I, of course, promptly agreed.

For the mix, as it was for EMI anyway, I went back to Studio 3 at Abbey Road, and because it was a whole new format for me and a new studio—well, kind of a new studio—I thought I should work with someone familiar with both the format and the room. I chose Paul Hicks, who was one of the engineers on all of The Beatles' recent releases and someone I had worked with, briefly, at Friar Park on the re-release of George's *All Things Must Pass*. He really knows Pro Tools inside and out and I, as an old-timer and very much a Pro Tools novice, needed someone like that. The project proved to be both an education, in many ways, and an absolute joy.

David had the original multitracks copied to Pro Tools for me, as he apparently had many problems acquiring them in the first place and would not allow them out of his storage facility. Apart from them possibly going missing, older tapes are prone to all kinds of damage. Not a pleasant thought for the masters of a "classic album."

One of the learning experiences that I went through during the mix was in regard to the whole analogue versus digital controversy. As it was one of the first things I had to mix from Pro Tools that I had originally recorded to tape, I got to really hear the difference. I'd pull up a track, do some EQ to match it up to the original mix, and since the frequencies I work at have never really changed, the task was relatively simple. That being said, there was a weird thing where individual tracks would sound identical to the original tracks, but as I added more and more of them together, there was a harshness to the mix that I couldn't get rid of. The more tracks I added, the more it built up and up. If you listen to only a couple of tracks it sounds fine, but there's something about the digital format, in my humble opinion, that the more you bring in and combine, the more harsh it becomes.

One of the big comments from many reviewers about the final 5.1 mix is that it's thin sounding. Before doing the mix, I asked EMI if they wanted it to sound true to the original or be new and relevant sounding (David was disconnected from the process, as always, so he wasn't available to ask). They told me that they'd love both, but as time was a factor, they'd prefer it as close to the original as possible. Back then we didn't use as much low-end as we do now, so that's the way I made it. As a result, there wasn't all that much being sent to the subwoofer so that the final result was as close to the way people have heard it through the years. After all, that's the sound that made *Ziggy* a "classic."

It was interesting rediscovering things from way back when. For instance, orchestras in England at that time refused to use headphones, so when we were overdubbing them, we had to feed them the audio through speakers set up in the studio. Obviously if it was loud enough for them to hear it then it would also be picked up loud and clear on the mics. That was one of those things back then that we were used to and dealt with as part of daily recording sessions. But having completely forgotten about that, I was fascinated to go back and listen to all of these orchestral tracks with the basic track blasting out of the speakers. It still sounded great. Beyond that, I would love to know how I got some of the sounds that were on the multitracks. For whatever reason, there was a warmth to everything that you don't seem to get these days, even when working completely analogue.

Thanks to Paul, another major learning experience was about English comedy. During meal breaks he organised that we watch episodes of *The Office*, way before the U.S. version, and Alan Partridge. Since I'd been living in Los Angeles for many years, I hadn't realised quite how much I missed the best of Brit TV.

I know I've already said it once but think it bears repeating: I truly believe that David did it the right way by reverting back to the people who did albums originally. We are the ones that know the product best and know what was going on back then, and ultimately, how it was meant to sound.

CHAPTER 16

Elton Take 2: *Don't Shoot Me*

When it was time for Elton to record his follow-up to *Honky Château*, Robin was still recovering, so once again Gus asked if I'd do it. And of course I was more than willing after the previous fun experience. For the album that became known as *Don't Shoot Me I'm Only the Piano Player*, we were back in France again at Château d'Hérouville. The tax loophole still existed, and since we were all comfortable there, it was a logical choice. Once again we were there for a few weeks of preproduction, writing, and recording.

When I think about it, I'm surprised at just how much got done so quickly.
Davey Johnstone, guitarist

On this record they wanted to keep it as French as possible, so the search was on for a French string arranger. The one person that kept on being suggested was the famous composer and conductor Michel Colombier, who one day came down to the studio to check things out. It all seemed to be going quite well until Elton took a close look at his dog, who was gorgeous and very, very well disciplined. Elton suddenly noticed that the dog had a spiked collar, but the spikes were on the inside pointing into his neck, which is why he was so damned obedient. Just one little twitch on that lead and the dog did whatever was wanted. As soon as Elton saw that he decided, "There's no way we're going to use this guy." We finished up using the tried and true Paul Buckmaster for all the arrangements.

On both *Honky* and *Don't Shoot Me*, all the brass sections were played by local French players. Gus fancied himself as a horn arranger, but he couldn't physically write the arrangement out because he wasn't a musician, so he would literally sing the parts to them. The problem was that he wasn't a particularly good singer, and the players had a hard time understanding exactly what he wanted. This would have been amusing enough with English-speaking horn players, but these guys would start to question him in French and he would have no idea what they were saying. He would then try to answer them and they'd have no idea what he was saying. This would go back and forth and back and forth, much to the amusement of everyone else in the studio. Once they got the line, it worked out really well, but getting there wasn't always easy.

IN THE CLOSET

I saw the nastier side of Elton on two occasions. Elton was still in the closet at that point but everyone around him knew that he was gay because he and his manager, John Reid, were a couple. There was one occasion when John apparently had a quick fling with another man in Paris. Like a lot of gay relationships, theirs was seemingly open, but Elton lost it completely when John told him about it. It wasn't so much that John had the fling, it was more that Elton couldn't do the same thing because he was too well known. The jealousy came not so much from someone sleeping with his partner, but because he didn't have the same freedom. Ah, the price of fame and fortune.

The other occasion where he totally lost it was when the band was going to Italy to do a gig and one of the flights got screwed up, an occurrence very common with Alitalia Airlines, which is renowned for its incompetence. This resulted in a histrionic screaming tantrum similar to what you see in *Tantrums and Tiaras*, the documentary on Elton that David Furnish made. The rest of the time Elton was a total sweetheart, and nothing even close to that ever happened while we were recording.

PORT AND A CONTACT HIGH

We worked continuously and didn't really get much of a break during this period, and since we were all living together, it got tense every now and again. One night Elton decided we all needed a break, so we took the evening off.

Although Elton never touched it (neither did I), the band loved their weed, but they were forced to go up to someone's bedroom to smoke because the management of the studio was very anti-drug after the Grateful Dead experience. On this particular night, the band went upstairs for their usual "high-level meeting," and when they came back down they were indeed flying high.

As I understand it, a contact high is what happens when an otherwise sober person comes into contact with someone who is high, and somehow that high is transferred psychically. While I wouldn't have thought it possible, that's exactly what happened to me. Within five minutes I was just as wasted and was giggling just as much as they were. It wasn't from any residual odour because I never smelt anything; it was totally psychological. It was absolutely bizarre. I've never known anything like it. Without ever breathing any of it in, I was as high as they were. Funny how that group psychology thing works.

As it happened, John Reid had been to Paris and had bought Elton this ridiculously old and very expensive bottle of port, and Elton decided it was a fine night to break it open. He downed the whole thing and by 2 o'clock in the morning he began to make obscene phone calls to friends in England. He would wake them up, and with a Bela Legosi type voice, say something like, "I vant to suck your body," then he'd just hang up. He kept on doing it all night and we were all in utter hysterics. All the tensions fell away and the next day we went back to recording and it was great. Boy, was he wasted that night. How was he the next day? Fine, amazingly enough.

THE FOOSBALL TOURNAMENT

Elton was very competitive and hated to lose at anything. I remember one time when he was playing Monopoly and losing, he smashed his hand into the board and pieces flew everywhere so the game could never actually finish. He hated to lose that much, so you can image how anyone felt when playing him at anything.

It so happened that the studio had a foosball table that we all got into in a big way. In fact, it became so competitive that we actually had a doubles tournament. I was terrible playing it, and because of this, I was paired with one of the roadies who was as bad as I was. As it turned out, quite surprisingly, we made a great team and we started to beat everyone. Eventually we made it to the finals where we faced Gus and Elton. Elton himself has said many times in books and interviews about how much he hates to lose, especially back then, so we were terrified before we even started. What the hell do we do? Do we just let them win? Hell, no! We just couldn't.

There we were, set to begin a best-of-three final. We won the first game, and Gus and Elton were like, "Hang on, we can't let this happen," and they won the second one. So now comes the third game and everyone is gathered around the table watching. This was the biggie: palms sweating, knees wobbly ... and we did it. The underdogs were victorious! Suddenly both Elton and Gus declared, "Oh, it's best of five." We come to game four and they won. Here we go again. The tension was unbelievable in that room ... and we won again! They were so pissed. It was an incredible feeling because no one had expected us to get past the first round as we were so bad, but for whatever reason, every bloody shot went flying past their players into the goal. It was amazing, and we weren't even fired for showing up the boss.

"CROCODILE ROCK"

"Crocodile Rock" took a long time to mix because it required all three of us—myself, Gus and second engineer Dennis MacKay—to make all the moves (remember, this was way before the days of automated mixes). At about 11 P.M. we finally got what I thought was the one, but Gus said, "No we can do better." "Come on. That one was perfect. It's got everything we want," I exclaimed. "No, we can do better," said Gus, sure that we had a better one in us. "OK, but I'm going to cut that one out and put it to one side just in case," I said, knowing deep down that this take was hard to beat. "Oh, that's a waste of time. We won't need it," Gus still insisted.

We kept going until about 4 in the morning, when finally Gus announced, "Now that's the one!" Now it was my turn. "Gus, it's nowhere near as good as the other one," I said. "We'll put both of them together, come in tomorrow, and listen and make a decision then," said Gus, although he seemed to have his mind already made up.

Just to be sure that he wasn't biased towards "his" mix, which he thought would be played second, I asked Dennis to reverse the order of the two songs on the reel so the one I liked came up second. Well wouldn't you know it, it just so happened that Elton and the guys walked in for a listen the next day and Gus said, "Let's let them decide."

So we played the first one and he said, "That's the one that Ken likes." When the second one played everyone immediately said, "Oh, that one is so much better." Gus was like, "See, Ken. I told you so."

There was something in his attitude, as if he was trying to show me up, that got to me in a way I'm not proud of. I had to tell him, "Sorry Gus, I played them in the reverse order." I wouldn't have said a word even to Gus, it would have been Dennis and my secret, but he made such a point of it that I just had to do it.

A PREVIEW OF THINGS TO COME

When we had dinner at night we all sat down at the same table as breakfast and Elton or Gus would always put on some music in the background. They would very often put on this one record that they absolutely loved called *The Inner Mounting Flame* by a group called the Mahavishnu Orchestra. Now when you've got 10 or 12 people sitting around a dining table talking, you don't hear much of what's going on with the music, so I just caught snippets of it and didn't understand it at all. I thought, "What a load of crap. It sounded like bunch of druggies all in different rooms playing whatever they want to play at any given time." I couldn't understand what they liked about it.

Later while mixing the album back at Trident, I got a call from one of the A&R guys at CBS who said, "John McLaughlin and the Mahavishnu Orchestra are coming over to the U.K. to do a television show and want to meet you about doing their next album." At that point it clicked, "Hang on, that was the band they were raving about in France. Maybe I should listen to it properly." So I asked the A&R guy to send me a copy of the album. After it arrived I put it on at home, sat back for a listen, and was absolutely floored. It was like nothing I had heard before. It was the beginning of a whole excursion into jazz-rock fusion that became like a second career for me, and it all started with Elton and Gus over in France.

YELLOW BRICK ROAD

The "in" studio at the time was Dynamic Sound in Jamaica. The Stones had just recorded *Goats Head Soup* there and Elton wanted a change from the Château, so we headed to Kingston to record. One small problem: no one bothered to check if the studio would be the right studio for an Elton album before we got there.

The studio was part of a record company that also manufactured and distributed the records all from this one facility that was located in the middle of an industrial complex. An American union was there trying to get the workers to join, which the owners of the company weren't liking at all, so they locked them out. On our first trip to the studio, these lines of workers began rocking our mini-bus with the intent of trying to push it over. It was very hairy for a bit and we were all terrified, and almost cancelled the session then and there.

Finally we got to the studio, set everything up, and I started getting the drum sound. Nigel was playing away but I couldn't get any depth out of the drums at all. It was very rinky-dink sounding with no power. I couldn't understand it. I had Nigel going for ages while I tried all the tricks I could think of, but I just couldn't get any balls out of his drums. Nigel began to get a bit uptight about how long it was all taking, so I said, "I'll tell you what, Nige. Let's just record a bit, then you can come and hear what my problem is." So we put a bit down on tape, and when I played it back it sounded even worse. It was obvious that the tape machine was completely out of alignment, so I asked Nigel to relax for a bit while I sent for a test tape.

I aligned 1 kHz and 10 kHz, and then came to the low-end. I started on 100 Hz and all I heard was tape hiss. "What the hell?" I thought. I could see the meters move so I knew 100 Hz was there, but we just weren't hearing it. I continued on down to 50 Hz and still nothing. It then dawned on me that the problem was the monitors had absolutely no low-end on them whatsoever and that was why I was having such a problem getting the drum sounds. It suddenly clicked that reggae records were renowned for having a lot of low-end to them. The general perception was that it was put on purposely, but that was probably totally wrong. No one could ever hear the low-end to begin with. That's why they added so much of it!

At that time "Jean Genie" was number one in Britain. We'd all been going around singing it, so we decided to play a bit of a thing on you [Ken] when you arrived. So me, Dee, and Nigel and I think Elton were all hiding behind a hedge at the hotel, and when you walked by we all leapt out and sang "Jean Genie." Unfortunately it all fell flat because you looked at us like, "What's wrong with you?" It wasn't funny at all.

Davey Johnstone

It finished up that there was no way we could work there, so we cancelled the remaining time and hung out another couple of days as a short vacation. Everyone was depressed because we were all set to record, there were a lot of great new songs, so we all just wanted to get back to England and regroup.

Even though this was a pretty down time I did get one of those "moments." Elton played me some of the songs that he had planned for the new album. I have had more than my fair share of these "moments" and often finish up wondering "Why me?" Paul played "Let It Be" ... just for me. And then Elton played songs including "Candle in the Wind" ... all just for me. Unbelievable.

A short while after we got back I received a phone call from John Reid, who said, "Ken, we're not messing around anymore. We're going back to the Château to record the album. We'd love you to do it, but that trip to Jamaica was fairly costly. Can you drop the charges for your time in Jamaica?" I wasn't sure that I heard him right. "I'm sorry?" I said. "Can you drop the charges for Jamaica, because it was so expensive?"

I was stunned. "That's not up to me. It's up to the management of Trident. They're the ones that bill you. I'm paid by them," I replied. "Oh, yeah, but you can talk to them. If you can't drop the charges, then we can't afford you to record the album in France," was John's comeback. "You've got to be joking," I said in disbelief. "Oh no, we really can't afford it," he insisted.

Here was one of the biggest acts in the world, one that already had four albums that sold over a million and three huge hit singles (including a number 1 in the U.S. with "Crocodile Rock" and a number 2 with "Daniel"), and they claimed they couldn't afford to pay £75 a day (about $120US) for a week due to the poor studio choice that they had made. Elton John could not afford that?

I went to Barry Sheffield who said in a not too nice way that, "No, we will be charging them!" As it turned out, it was a win-win situation for Trident and myself. Although I didn't go over to France to do what would become *Yellow Brick Road*, Dave Hentschel, who was by this time another Trident staff engineer, did. Trident made their money no matter what. Although I didn't know it at the time, I'd have my own share of "wins" about to come in the not-too-distant future.

Recording Elton

Château d'Hérouville had a 16-track MCI tape machine with Dolby A noise reduction, and a board that was custom made. We rented in some Kepex gates since I used them all the time on drums.

On the piano I used a KM 56 on the high-end and a U 67 on the low-end, and it was recorded in stereo. On "Elderberry Wine," we felt that the piano needed to be beefed up a bit, so I resorted to a trick I'd used before. We double-tracked the piano with the tape speed slightly faster to put it slightly out of tune. It just really fills out the sound, but we only used it for certain parts of the song.

I remember thinking, "My God. What is that?" We'd never heard anything like it before. That's still Elton's favourite piano sound to this day. He uses it all the time.

Davey Johnstone

All the vocals would have been overdubbed using either a Neumann U 67 or an AKG C 12A. I don't think we even would have done rough vocals during tracking since it was so open that it would have been picked up on the drum mics. Elton wasn't quite a Bowie where it was first take every time, but he was pretty damn quick. When it came to harmonies, he would almost always get it on the first take since he felt harmony instinctively. There was no going over to the piano to work out parts. If he knew he wanted to do the harmonies himself, he knew what they were immediately and nailed them fast.

> *I love the mix on "Daniel." In fact the recording too. I remember that you [Ken] got him out of bed to sing when his voice was a little bit scratchy. I think it was a first take as well.*
>
> Davey Johnstone

My approach to recording Nigel was slightly different from other drummers because he used concert toms which didn't have a bottom head. It's a strange sounding kit for me, and although a lot of people love what we did, these days it leaves me a little cold. We put mics up inside each tom, and knowing the way I was, it was probably pretty close to the head. I've been asked if I flipped the phase on the mics, but we never bothered with phase back then. That's a new thing that's only come about with people looking at meters and displays. Back then, if it sounded fine, that's what we went with.

That's the whole thing for me. I read on various blogs online that you have to do this, and if that happens, you have to do that. It's such bullshit. If it sounds right, then do it. That's all it comes down to. People that buy records don't care if you flipped the phase on that thing; if it sounds good, fine. That's why I've seen too many engineers that I don't think are particularly good because they know too much technically and they won't do things that might make it sound better because it might overload something or violate a "rule." If it sounds good, go with it.

On overheads I probably used Beyer M 160s. The snare would have been Neumann KM 56, KM 54, or KM 84. Bass drum would have been an AKG D 20. Unfortunately, I don't know what I finished up using on toms.

I thought Dee Murray's bass was all DI, but listening to the multitracks recently I've discovered that it's a mix of DI and his amp. We did the blend to a single track at the time of recording because we had a limited number of tracks to work with. We made the decision as we were recording and that's what we lived with. The amp probably would have been miked with a U 67.

On electric guitars I would have used a Neumann U 67 or a U 87. Remember that back then, these mics were the norm; it's only now that they've become expensive and collectable. On acoustic guitar, it would have been either an AKG C 12A or a C 414.

The mix was done with many hands on the board. Gus always liked to take control of the drums, because he always liked to push them up for the fills. I would tend to take care of the piano, lead guitar overdubs, and vocals. Any other little changes needed would be done by the second engineer, who would lean over the two of us. As for the reverb, at Trident we would have used one EMT plate. Sometimes we'd put delay on it, sometimes we wouldn't, but everything was going through the same reverb.

> *Gus Dudgeon knew about dynamics. Every tom fill he'd push up, every guitar lick you [Ken] would ride, pushing up the rhythms in the chorus.*
>
> Dennis MacKay, second engineer

We had an ARP 2500 synthesiser at Trident. David Hentschel, who was a second engineer at the time, and myself spent a lot of time experimenting with it. While I was in the middle of mixing "Daniel," Gus decided Davey's mandolin solo didn't pop, so I actually doubled the part on synthesiser. On "Rocket Man," the sound of the "rocket" taking off and bursting in and out of the atmosphere was the ARP 2500 put on by Dave Hentschel.

I was playing Caleb Quaye [who has also played guitar with Elton off and on] "Hercules" from Honky Château shortly after we came back to England and he said to me, "Ken Scott is doing this?" I said, "Yeah." He said, "I can tell from the ADT on the guitar solo. That's one of Ken's tricks."

Davey Johnstone

CHAPTER 17

Jazz Fusion

As mentioned earlier, my first exposure to Mahavishnu Orchestra was with Elton in France when he played their album during dinner. Having received the phone call from CBS about working with the band, I went to a TV studio where they were doing a live performance for a meeting with them. We all got along great so the project was a go, and it wasn't long before we were in the studio together working on a project that would eventually lead me to do many more records in the jazz-fusion genre.

> *We were there [at the television studio] for a sound check. A couple of guys came out in white smocks with sound meters. They said to John [McLaughlin, the guitarist], "I just want you to know that we will stop this program if you play over 90 dB." John just smiled politely. The guy turned to us again and said, "Does everyone understand?" There was just silence from the band. The first chord we played was 130 dB. The cameraman in front of us actually fell over, and they stopped us right away. After that we agreed to not play at 130, we just played at 115. It was intense. Once it got started there was no stopping us.*
> Billy Cobham, drummer with Mahavishnu Orchestra

The big question that I've always had, which has never been fully explained, is "Why me?" I had no previous experience or credits in that type of music, and to even be considered by a band like this has always baffled me. I have asked everyone in the band, and have yet to receive a suitable answer, but no matter what that reason might be, I'm certainly thankful for the opportunity and all it led to.

> *It's possible that when we were ready to record and we knew we were going to be in London, [Columbia Records label head] Clive Davis said, "There's this great studio with this incredible engineer. Why don't you check them out?" Or it could have come from Nat Weiss, who was the band's manager and a partner with Brian Epstein for The Beatles in the U.S.A. He had a very close relationship with George Harrison, who would stay at his apartment when he came to New York. Since Ken had recorded All Things Must Pass, the suggestion could have come from George. I don't think that John [McLaughlin] was listening to Elton John or David Bowie and said, "Get me Ken Scott."*
> Elliott Sears, Mahavishnu Orchestra road manager

> *As far as you [Ken] recording "Birds of Fire," the answer is pretty simple: I wanted to record at the "world famous" Trident studios, and you were the man. I believe I was the lucky one in this deal!*
> John McLaughlin, guitarist with Mahavishnu Orchestra

BIRDS OF FIRE

Time was booked at Trident to record the Mahavishnu album that would become *Birds of Fire*. What was extremely amusing was how many members of the staff came by the control room just to take a look down at the setup. The main reason for that was Bill Cobham's drum kit. Up until that time, the drum kits brought into Trident had a maximum of four toms, and even that many was rare, so a kit that size was always small enough to be tucked away inside the Trident drum booth under the control room. The Fibes drum kit that Bill had was huge and there wasn't a hope in hell of him fitting in there, so I had to set him up in the studio, which everyone found absolutely fascinating.

> *I didn't know who Ken Scott really was. Anything that the band did I never questioned anyway, but in this case, Ken just fit right in. The drum sound was an educational experience for me. Prior to that*

I'd recorded with a lot of people, but I never got a sound like that. I thought to myself, "I need to just shut up and watch and enjoy the moment." It was such a smooth transition that I felt Ken had always been there.

Billy Cobham

On a technical level, I looked at his drum kit the same way that I looked at any other drum kit, it was just bigger. I miked it exactly the same way as I always did, I just had to use more of the same old mics (U 67s or 87s) on the toms, plus he used two bass drums as opposed to the more usual single one. We put lots of screens (small moveable walls that help contain the sound) around him to cut down on as much bleed as possible, but having seen and heard the band play, I knew this was going to be mostly a live recording in the studio so I wasn't that concerned about leakage. That was one of the great things about my EMI training; I'd worked during the time of 4-track tape recorders where most everyone played live, so I knew just what to expect.

When we first went into Trident we set up Billy Cobham's drum kit, which had two 24-inch bass drums, four rack toms and three floor toms, and nine cymbals. Ken stood over kit and flicked each drum with his finger to hear the sound and just looked up with a grin and said, "This is going to be very interesting." I think he was not only in awe of the size of the kit, but the way they were tuned. We're talking about a different animal with Billy Cobham.

Elliott Sears

The sound you got on the drums in particular really shaped what a lot of guys did after that. Amazing drum sounds. The other [jazz] records in those days sounded as if you just put up two mics and recorded it live. Some were nice sounding, but on your records you heard a lot of detail and subtleties. The drum sound was unique for the time. I think that the sound actually helped a lot of listeners get into the music. It was powerful, even when it was quiet.

Stanley Clarke, bassist

After the very first take of the first song, the band came up into the control room to have a listen. After the playback was over, keyboardist Jan Hammer turned to me and said, "You're a bad motherfucker!" My heart immediately sank. I hadn't a clue as to what I'd done wrong. I had no idea that in the American vernacular at that point, "bad" actually meant "good," and put together with "motherfucker," it meant "amazing." I was really disheartened for a while until someone explained, "No, no. Don't worry. He means it's good." That slang term hadn't hit our side of the Atlantic yet. Go figure.

> *"Badass motherfucker" is more of an American slang term whereas "bad motherfucker" is more Czech. You have to understand that Jan is from the ghetto in Prague [laughs].*
> Billy Cobham

Besides the genre of music, something else new to me were the complicated time signatures that they played in. On one song I tried to count and just couldn't get it, so I asked Bill, "I have tried to count this out but can't seem to come up with it. What is it?" He said, "It depends on who you speak to." Apparently each band member counted it differently, yet they all finished up in the same place. Amazing!

We got a lot done at Trident but didn't have enough time to complete the recording of the album, so time was booked in Miami at Criteria Recording, which was riding high at the time thanks to their association with the Bee Gees. This was to be my first trip to the States and, boy, I was excited. We had a week booked at Criteria to finish recording, then we were going to go to Electric Lady Studios in New York to mix. Because I thought this might be my one and only trip to the States, I, of course, brought the Mrs. and our daughter with me.

WE GO TO MIAMI

When we got to Miami it was a huge culture shock. I couldn't believe the heat and humidity, which was about as far away from English weather as you can get. John McLaughlin met us at the airport and once in the car I immediately opened a window to get some air. John quickly instructed me to close it telling me that the car had air-conditioning and that it would soon cool down. A/C in a car? You *must* be joking. It didn't take long before that became my accepted norm. I also couldn't believe seeing the police brandishing their guns as police at that time didn't carry weapons in England. One time, I think in New York, we walked up to a patrol officer to ask directions and I suppose we surprised him as his hand went immediately to his gun. And of course, I expected to see how big the cars were, but seeing only those behemoths on the road with hardly any of the smaller cars that we were used to in England was impressive, I have to say. Everything was just so completely different, a huge culture shock.

After a couple of days of just settling into the environment, the band and I finally headed into the studio. After we were set up, John turned on his 100-watt Marshall and began to play for a bit, but it seemed like there was hardly any volume coming out of it. The sound was really small, more like a Pignose amp (for anyone who remembers those) than a Marshall. Now John liked to crank, and there were times when we recorded where it was just a little too distorted for my tastes, but that's the way he liked it, so it was especially unusual for his sound to be so small. He turned it up some more, but it didn't sound much different, then turned up again. Finally the amp blew up. We all thought it was just a bad amp, so he changed over to another one, and exactly the same thing happened. What the hell is going on? This wasn't good, so we sent out for some more amps and I left John and the roadies to sort it out.

In the meantime, it was time to get a drum sound with Bill. As I normally do, I started with the bass drum. It sounded dead. I figured that Bill had already put some damping in, so I went outside to adjust it. "Bill, we need a little less damping," I said to him. Much to my surprise he replied with, "I haven't put anything in yet!" Both bass drums were completely open with zero damping, yet the sound was still too dead. It was at that point that it struck me that Criteria was *the* studio for disco at the time, and disco records revolved around a dead studio sound. I decided to check out the rest of the studio and, sure enough, everywhere I listened was completely devoid of reflections. That's not the type of studio that works well for a band like Mahavishnu. The studio just sucked up all the life from their sound.

It was decided by all of us that the studio wouldn't work and so we had to cancel all of the time that we had booked there. We stayed down in Miami for the rest of the week, then went to New York. Since we hadn't finished recording, there was nothing to mix, so the New York time became a vacation as well.

> *Criteria was the happening studio at the time. It was so dead, too dead for a band like Mahavishnu. We tried all sorts of different things to try to deal with it, but in the end we just bailed.*
> Elliott Sears

Cancelling Criteria caused a bit of nastiness for me since Mack Emmerman, the owner of Criteria, was close with the owners of the studio in Jamaica where we booked time to record with Elton that we ended up cancelling because of the problems with the monitors. I had now pulled out of both studios, so Mack started to go around saying, "Ken Scott makes his living by going to studios and cancelling after a few days in order to get a free vacation. He did it in Jamaica and now he's done it here." Luckily, that never turned into much of an issue as the studios I did work at subsequently welcomed the business I brought them.

> *I think that's the reason why I was really belligerent to someone who called me up about recording with Joe Cocker in that studio [Criteria]. I told him, "Get somebody else," but to this day I regret it. It was an opportunity lost.*
> Billy Cobham

MIXING IN NEW YORK

A bit later I flew back to New York to complete the recording of the album at Electric Lady, then mixed it there. Once again, not being used to America, a couple of things happened that initiated me to the New York scene. On the first day in the studio, one of the roadies said he was going to the deli and asked if I wanted him to bring me back a sandwich. I immediately replied, "Yeah, get me a couple of roast beef sandwiches." He looked at me kind of funny and said, "A couple? Are you sure?" I replied, "Yeah, I'm quite hungry," so he smiled and nodded his head and off he went. Of course I was used to the typical English sandwiches of two pieces of white bread with maybe two slices of roast beef in the middle. Two of those would have been perfect. Instead he returned with two New York deli-style sandwiches that each stood at least six inches tall. I was blown away. Half of one was all I could eat. I had absolutely no idea what I was letting myself in for when I asked for two sandwiches, but at least the band and all the Electric Lady staff got a good laugh out of it.

The other thing that I didn't realise about working in New York was how steeped in unionism New York record companies were at the time. I was astounded, and even offended, to find that on the first day at Electric Lady a CBS engineer was sitting there waiting when we walked in. I angrily thought, "I'm supposed to be doing this. What's he doing here?" Then I found out that all we had to do was sign off that he was there and he then disappeared for the rest of the day. He was paid for the entire time that we were working as per union rules, but we were doing the work, not him. The thing was that CBS wanted their artists to record at the CBS studio facility, but they realised from past experience that position was a thorn in the side of some of their acts, so they allowed them the freedom to go to other studios as long as they had a CBS engineer with them. The CBS engineers didn't want to be there any more than we wanted them there, so they would just turn up at the beginning of the session and go, "OK, I'm here. OK, I'm gone." They'd come in at the beginning of the next session and ask, "OK, what time did we go to last night? One o'clock in the morning? OK, see you tomorrow." It should also be noted that the cost for the CBS engineer to be at an outside studio for all those long hours was always tagged on to the recording costs that had to be recouped by the artist. That was my primer on "the union way," one that reached its peak when later recording in the city with Bowie.

The Electric Lady recordings were always kept a secret. None of the albums ever mentioned the studio. The reason being that there was a deal between CBS and the engineers' union that stated that a CBS act had to use the CBS studios.

Elliott Sears

As far as recording, the band had been playing a lot of the material live before entering the studio and so everyone knew it thoroughly. That, of course, made it all go very smoothly and very few takes were needed for any of the numbers. If I remember correctly, there were very few overdubs, if any at all. We recorded at Trident for two or three days, then did the same thing at Electric Lady. We mixed the album pretty easily, and when it came out, my understanding was that it sold very well, even considering the type of music it was.

The band had only allotted five days for recording but they couldn't finish it because of touring commitments. The rest of the album was done at Electric Lady Studios in New York with the sole exception of the acoustic tune, "Thousand Island Park," which was recorded at CBS Studios. The reason why it was done there was that Electric Lady was a rock 'n' roll studio and the piano there wasn't to Jan's liking for what he termed "a serious piece of music." We went into Studio B at CBS, which was the same studio that they used to record Leonard Bernstein, and it had a massive Steinway. The record says, "Engineered by Jim Green" because Ken wasn't a member of the local New York union so they wouldn't even let him in the control room. That was the first time I ever heard John McLaughlin swear, since he was normally so spiritual.

Elliott Sears

There was an incident tied to mixing that did come back to haunt me a bit and even changed the way I worked in the future. In Mahavishnu there were three soloists—Jan Hammer on keyboards, Jerry Goodman on violin, and John on guitar—and they all would trade off solos. The way I had it set up in stereo was to pan them left, centre, and right, with the guitar panned to one of the sides. I heard some time after the record came out that the band was doing a press event in Europe to push the album and whoever set up the stereo system only took one side of the stereo album and played it back through both speakers. It just so happened that he took the side that didn't contain John's guitar, so when it played back John couldn't hear any of his playing whatsoever and hit the roof. From that point on, I always put the solo in the centre and on most pop recordings I will invariably double-track almost every guitar I do and have them panned to either side so nothing like that can go wrong again. No matter what anyone does, it's going to come through. It might be down in level, but it will always come through.

Mo' Drums

Bill Cobham's drums were treated in exactly the same way as I recorded every other drummer, I just used more mics: Neumann U 67s on toms, D 20s or RE20s (at Electric Lady) on the bass drums, Neumann KM 54 or 56 on snare, and either STC 4038s or Beyer M 160s ribbon mics for overheads. One other thing: in order to dampen the snare, Bill just laid his wallet on the top head.

SPECTRUM

After *Birds of Fire*, Bill Cobham was scheduled to do a solo album and he asked me to do it with him. On May the 14th to the 16th, 1973, we recorded *Spectrum* at Electric Lady. This was a remarkable album because in my mind, it was truly the first record where rock and jazz truly melded.

Why *Spectrum* and not a Mahavishnu record? You have to understand that John McLaughlin started off as a session guitarist in England. Whether I ever worked with him in that capacity, I have no idea and he doesn't either, as neither of us seem to remember. When he moved over to the States he immediately got very into the jazz scene, working with Miles Davis and Tony Williams Lifetime. Even though he played loud electric guitar, his roots were still very much in jazz. For *Spectrum*, Bill took it in a slightly different direction for several of the tracks. He still used Jan Hammer on keyboards, and he picked a session bass player, Lee Sklar, to play bass, which was slightly unusual. The big thing was that he picked a true rock guitarist in Tommy Bolin, and that was an absolutely inspired idea. Tommy was an incredible player and brought a real rock energy to those sessions. The fact that he could play that kind of complicated music with all its strange time signatures floored everyone, but he really did bring a rock element to the album that someone with a jazz background could not. As a result, I don't think there's ever been an album quite like it.

> Spectrum *is such a benchmark for so many people. There was a*
> *sort of fire in it. It was new ground and it wasn't very analytical.*
> *It was more flying by the seat of your pants. That's where great*
> *accidents happens, which seems impossible these days. We never*
> *did more than a couple of takes on any of it. It was more or less a*
> *two-day record. It went by so fast.*
> Leland Sklar, bass player on *Spectrum* and noted L.A. session player

To me, Mahavishnu was always considered fusion, but the fusion came from a loud distorted guitar, as opposed to a mellow electric jazz guitar, that still came from a jazz background. On the other hand, *Spectrum* was the closest to the fusion of rock with jazz that, at least for me, has ever occurred. Bill brought in jazzers Ron Carter to play upright bass and Joe Farrell on sax for a couple of tracks so the album had different feels, but the thing that everyone picks up on is the stuff that Tommy plays on.

Unfortunately Tommy Bolin, who was a great talent, died far too young at the age of 25, but as far as I'm concerned, he died the way he wanted to. Tommy was born to be a rock star in every way, shape, and form, and if that meant dying from an overdose as well, so be it. Alas, he went the way he wanted to.

> *This guy was like he was from another planet. He couldn't have*
> *been more than 20 but he played like he was 50. He knew how to*
> *make all the notes the right ones, and many times it was about the*
> *spaces and not the notes.*
> Billy Cobham

I can certainly say that I had a blast making *Spectrum* and I fully believe everyone else did too. Interestingly, getting a sound on Bill's kit was easy. Firstly, I already knew what to expect as I'd already recorded him on *Birds of Fire*. Luckily he was still carrying the same wallet we used to dampen the snare. And of course, Bill's a true pro, and that helps so-o-o-o much. If I'm not mistaken, we took three days to record it, and almost everything, if not all, was live. That always speeds things up and is also why the songs on the album feel so great. It was all the musicians getting off on one another—no egos, just great playing.

Electric Lady Gear

Working at Electric Lady, I had to move from using an AKG D 20 on bass drum to using an EV RE20 because they didn't have AKGs in the States yet. For overheads, I still used ribbon mics, but they were Beyer M 160s because STCs weren't found there yet either. Apart from that, I still used U 67s all over the place because they were plentiful.

This was the first time I ever used Pultec equalizers as well. I hadn't even heard of them until I came over to the States. The console was a 24-input DataMix (see Figure 17.1), which was a big brand around New York City at that time (Record Plant had them too). The tape machine was a 24-track Ampex MM-1000.

One of the other things that amazed me was the age of the second engineer working with me. He was maybe a year or two younger than me, and there he was still working as second. I'd come from the background where you left school by 15 or 16, and those are the years you were a second. To see one in his twenties seemed very strange.

Figure 17.1: Electric Lady's DataMix console

I just loved New York at that point. It was vibrant, a word I hate to use, but that seems to describe it best. England was on its downward spiral by this time. The '60s were over, and even though I was enjoying the success of Bowie, you could tell that England was on the way down musically, culturally, every way. People just didn't seem interested in anything. You'd be driving down the street and you'd look around and get the feeling that people would walk in front of you and not care if they were run over. There was this apathy pervading everything. Politically it was very bad too, and all of this certainly helped to ease the decision when the possibility of moving reared its head.

THE LOST TRIDENT SESSIONS

Birds of Fire did well, Mahavishnu was riding high, and so the decision was made to record the next record again at Trident. Unfortunately it turned out to be one of the hardest projects that I ever worked on both mentally and spiritually because it came during the breakup of the band. It was not pleasant at all, and to just illustrate the typical insanity that prevailed, there was one time Jerry Goodman became so angry that he tried to put his fist through the studio door, a door that, due to soundproofing, was at least six inches thick. How he didn't break anything on his person I have no idea. That was the typical mood and it was just nasty.

> *I remember thinking to myself, "I can't be here," and leaving to take a walk. [Bassist] Rick [Laird] walked out behind me shaking his head, so I said, "What's wrong, Rick?" He said, "BVIS." I said, "What?" He said, "Bad vibes in studio."*
> Elliott Sears

The whole thing was over the fact that John insisted that he do all of the writing for the band, where Jan, Jerry, and bass player Rick Laird wanted to write as well. Bill had gotten that out of his system by writing all the material for his solo album, but that wasn't the case with the other guys, and they were desperate to contribute.

One of the main bones of contention was a cut on *Birds of Fire*. The band had arranged to play a joke on me at Electric Lady. Typically, just before getting into serious recording, I would always say, "Let me just hear a bit," just to make sure that everything was blending together well and the sounds were what I expected. The band secretly arranged that the next time they heard that phrase they would all go musically nuts for about 30 seconds. Much to everyone's surprise, this random mayhem actually sounded pretty good and luckily it was recorded, but John went on to classify the "song" as something that he'd written. As you can imagine, the rest of the band was very pissed, and this was the catalyst that started the whole "we want to write as well" movement within the band. Begrudgingly, John finally went along and did some of their material, but to make matters worse, they never felt that John was giving his best for their material as he was for his own. They thought he was almost phoning it in.

It was all between Jerry, Jan, and John. Rick and I were the bookends on the outside going, "What's going on here?" The crazy thing was that they loved McLaughlin so much that everything they wrote sounded like he wrote it. They were so oblivious of it, and just wanted to get their stuff out. At first I was that way too, so I asked John if we could collaborate. The first time he didn't respond so I asked him again, and when he didn't respond again I took it to mean "No." That's when I decided to put something together for myself, because I could see that at some point I was going to be out there on my own.

Billy Cobham

This was a very contentious time for the band. When the band first got together though, they recorded all of John's songs, but Jan contributed a lot to those tunes and never got any credit. Nobody gave it a thought at the time because in the jazz world, that's how it worked. What really pissed off the band the most was when we were at Electric Lady the first day of recording Birds of Fire *there. Everyone started making a lot of bizarre noise but the tape was rolling. It ended up on the record as "Sapphire Bullets of Pure Love," but John took credit for it. Whether a song was 35 seconds or 5 minutes long, the mechanical royalty rate was the same. If you take a million units sold worldwide, it was a pretty good amount of money that went only to John instead of being split five ways. That rubbed the guys wrong.*

Elliott Sears

When recording for the third album was complete, John and I mixed it, but it never came out. Once they all got back to New York, everything became very political and it was decided to re-record the majority of the material live in Central Park. The album was released as *Between Nothingness and Eternity*, but I had nothing to do with it. It should be said that John was always very nice to me. There were obviously some ego problems, hence the breakup of the band, but none ever headed in my direction.

Sometime later someone had the bright idea to finally release the album recorded at Trident. There was just one tiny problem: no one could find the master tapes. I got phone calls for years asking for copies, outtakes, or anything I could find, but I didn't have anything, and apparently the original tapes were nowhere to be found. Finally someone did come up with them (I have no idea where they found them), but by this time the project had taken on a life of its own in fusion circles, and it became sort of a holy grail album. Because of the story behind it, they called the album *The Lost Trident Sessions*.

When I left Trident, I had outtakes of some of the things we did on ¼-inch tape. I put it away and never even listened to it because of the frustration from all this craziness. That material became secondary to me and very obscure. I can't even remember playing on some of the stuff. We never really did much with it after that. By the time the live record came out, the band was finished.
Billy Cobham

The Lost Trident Sessions *became unlost because of me. I had a copy of that record on both cassette and a 7½-ips reel-to-reel [tape] from the day we left England. I don't know why I even had it. It's always baffled me why so many years had lapsed before it was ever released.*
Elliott Sears

MAHAVISHNU LIVE

Although I never recorded the band live, there were two gigs that Mahavishnu played that I remember all too well. One of them was just after recording *Birds of Fire* at Crystal Palace in London, an open-air gig that happened to occur during the Olympics. For those that don't know, Crystal Palace is in a suburb south of London and within its area there are two very large transmitters used by the BBC to broadcast radio and television throughout London, so they were quite powerful; powerful enough that for some reason every now and again a broadcast would break through on John's amp. The band was playing up a storm and the audience was really into it, even though not that many were familiar with the music. Then came one of those Spinal Tap moments. John was coming up to the peak of a solo when suddenly, "And Mark Spitz wins yet another gold medal!" came blasting out of his amp. Of course everyone just broke up. Even the normally stoic Mr. McLaughlin had to laugh.

Another time they played at The Rainbow Theatre right after recording *The Lost Trident Sessions* and for some reason, someone had plugged all of the gear, including the PA, into the same electrical circuit. Of course, once again as John was reaching the peak of a solo, all the power went out: the PA, the amps, the works. The only thing that could be heard were the drums acoustically from the stage. Bill, always the consummate professional, not only kept playing, but took the song over as a drum solo, brought it up to a peak, then brought it down to an ending. It was absolutely phenomenal. Almost by the time he finished the fuse was replaced, everything was fixed and the band continued, but for sheer professionalism, that blew me away.

> *To this day, everyone in the band thinks that Ken is a genius. They all speak of Ken in glowing terms.*
> Elliott Sears

> *Ken's ears and his thoughts and his ideas were so pioneering, so revolutionary and so spot-on that everything he did then holds up today still better than anything else.*
> Jan Hammer, keyboard player with Mahavishnu Orchestra *(from Power, Passion & Beauty: The Story of the Legendary Mahavishnu Orchestra* by Walter Kolosky)

JAN AND JERRY

Shortly after *The Lost Trident Sessions*, I did an album with Jan Hammer and Jerry Goodman that was basically re-recording a lot of the material from that album, only with them playing all the instruments. It was interesting, but not one of the favourite albums that I've worked on. We recorded *Like Children* at Caribou Ranch in the mountains of Colorado, which was certainly a nice place to spend some time.

Jan was always a frustrated drummer so he played drums. Unusually for this style of music he wanted a Ringo sound and had all the drums damped down with towels à la Ringo. Unfortunately, Caribou didn't have Fairchild limiters, so it didn't sound the same since that's the only way to truly get that effect due to the unit's unique sound. I finished up never being completely happy with the drum sound since it sounded more or less half-arsed to me as a result.

Jerry played violin and the guitar. On one song a string quartet was needed and so we built it up with Jerry playing everything except the cello. Instead he played an odd instrument called a violow for the low-end of the section, which was a custom viola fitted with cello strings. The bass was all done on a keyboard, which I think was another contributing factor as to why the sound of the album never totally did it for me.

Jerry had a viola that he outfitted with cello strings. We didn't know what to call it, so we just called it a "violow." It was a term that Jerry made up. It really did sound like cello. It was incredible.
Elliott Sears

And I have to admit, neither did the singing. Jan and Jerry are just not singers, a point that they more or less agreed with me on. When we went back to Trident to mix, we hadn't tried recording the vocals yet. We were in the mix room and set up for vocals in the adjoining overdub booth, but after we got the sound, I was told in no uncertain terms, "You have to leave." "What?" I replied, incredulous that the thought was even being brought up. "You have to leave. We're doing this with the second engineer," they said. "Fuck you," was my reply. "You're leaving." "No, I'm not!" After much back and forth, finally I relented and left.

After they had finished the vocals, they told me their reasoning behind asking me to leave. As they knew they weren't singers, they were totally embarrassed to do it in front of me. They felt that there might be too many occasions where I would burst out laughing and they wouldn't be able to say anything to me about it. If the second engineer burst out laughing, they could at least scream at him, but they couldn't bear to have me in there for it. Not much of a consolation though. Maybe, a huge maybe, I could've helped.

CHAPTER 18

All That Jazz

I loved doing jazz, jazz fusion, fusion, or whatever you damn well want to call it. It stopped me from getting bored. I can't conceive of being one of those people who does the same thing day in and day out. Much as I am a creature of habit and will do things the same every time I record, I need other things to stimulate me. The same goes with albums. I know that I can only do four albums *at the most* with an artist because after that neither of us will be learning from each other. The whole idea is to constantly learn something new with every situation, so the opportunity to move from doing a project with someone like Bowie to something in a completely different genre was perfect for me.

CROSSWINDS

Bill Cobham's next album, *Crosswinds*, was another recorded at Electric Lady, although we mixed it at Trident. This album was much more jazz oriented and less fusion than his previous album, thanks to the presence of John Abercrombie on guitar and the great Randy and Michael Brecker.

Sax player Mike Brecker I thought was astounding, but trumpeter Randy, who is actually a great player too, left me a little lacking because he liked to use effects on his horn way too much for my taste. Mike was an incredible soloist and Bill knew him very well, which turned out to be a very fortuitous thing. The first time we recorded a solo, Bill said, "Make sure you take the first one." I did and sure enough, it was great, but Mike said, "No, no. That was no good. I can do better." He did another one and it wasn't quite as good as the first, and he immediately said again, "No, no. That was no good. I can do better." The same thing kept on happening for some time—doing takes, each one getting a little worse, and every time wanting to do one more. He never did get anything better than that first one. I'm so glad we kept that first solo, and that I'd learned how to work with him from then on.

My favourite track on the album is called "Heather" and Mike Brecker just plays an amazing sax. I've mentioned the learning part of the work, and one of the things that was great about recording him was that I was able to take what I had learned from Bobby Keys about using two mics on the sax and teach it to Mike. That breathiness from the top one and the tone from the bottom one became a sound we both loved.

While making the record one night we were graced by the presence of Mr. Rolling Stone himself, Sir Michael Jagger. Drunk as a skunk, Mick got quite upset with me because I hadn't heard the latest Miles Davis record. He simply couldn't understand how I could possibly be recording Bill's music without listening to Miles first, and was actually angry at the prospect. Funny what sticks in one's mind.

> *Jagger came by and started bouncing up and down in front of me. I thought to myself, "What is this idiot doing?" I was sort of measuring him thinking, "Who let this crazy guy in," when I looked at his face and thought, "No, it can't be." Then it was more like, "Where'd you come from?" He just seemed to appear out of nowhere, and then zip, he was gone.*
> Billy Cobhamm

VISIONS OF THE EMERALD BEYOND

Visions of the Emerald Beyond was a record with the second version of Mahavishnu Orchestra, with only John McLaughlin remaining from the original lineup. The new band consisted of Ralphe Armstrong on bass, Narada Michael Walden on drums, Jean-Luc Ponty on violin, and Gayle Moran on keyboards, but with a typical left turn, there was also a string quartet.

This was a very pleasant project to work on and a totally different atmosphere than with the original Mahavishnu lineup, but the fire just wasn't there. With Michael Walden on drums and Ralphe Armstrong on bass it was funkier, so that obviously made it different, but with the vocals and string quartet it was taken even further away from the sound of the original band.

Michael Walden was an incredible drummer, but he did have this one annoying habit. Every time we stopped recording after a take, he'd pull out a pitch pipe, give a whistle, and tune his drums. That's OK except he always played the pitch pipe really loud, so we had to remember to pull down the monitor volume as soon as we finished a take. Even if it was just a breakdown, he'd pull out those damned pipes and immediately give a toot.

The other thing about the album for me was reconnecting with Jean-Luc Ponty, who I'd met when he played with Elton John at the Château in France. It was fascinating because it was another one of those circles that kept coming around. I first heard about Mahavishnu through Elton, and I first met Jean-Luc through Elton. Then a few years later I meet up with Jean-Luc again and he's with Mahavishnu, be it the second version.

Since the lineup for this album was so different it meant there were a lot more overdubs than the original, primarily because of the vocals and the string quartet, which would have been difficult to record at the same time as John playing. Once again it was recorded at Electric Lady, between December 4th and December 14th in 1974, and mixed back at Trident a few days later.

TOTAL ECLIPSE

Bill Cobham's *Total Eclipse* was again recorded in New York, but this time at Atlantic Studios. I kind of put my foot in it when I initially listened to their monitors and declared them to be out of phase. I passed a comment to one of the studio techs about how they had to do something about it, and heard nothing but disgruntlement in return. They finally agreed to check them and reluctantly concurred with my assessment that they were indeed miswired. Unfortunately, instead of, "Wow, thanks for pointing that out. We don't know how we could have missed that," there was more of a, "Who the hell does this Limey think he is coming in here telling us what's wrong" attitude, and as a result, everyone seemed very pissed. To me this was a strange reaction; I thought they would be thankful that I found a flaw that would make the studio sound better when it was fixed, but oh no. Bill claims that the event actually turned Atlantic against him for some time, but all I wanted to do was to get the studio sounding as good as possible. That said, I really loved it there and we ended up having some great sessions.

Boy, did I catch hell when we walked in to do Total Eclipse *and Ken said, "The speakers are out of phase." They could not physically abuse me in public, but I was never friends with those guys anymore after that.*

Ken tended to wreak havoc in studios, but everything in that studio was a little odd, despite its history. The faders on the board were wired backwards where as when you brought them down, the sound would get louder.
Billy Cobham

By this time George Duke was on keyboards, bringing a certain funk thing and a lot of fun with him. Always the happy camper, he would constantly be cracking jokes. This album showed another side of Bill's versatility within the jazz genre. All of Mahavishnu and some of *Spectrum* was very heavily into the rock side of things, then on *Crosswinds* it was more into straight jazz, but on *Total Eclipse* he was much more into funk.

There was always a lot of activity around the Atlantic building and the studio. I remember that the Average White Band had a party in one of the studios after they had just become successful with *Pick Up the Pieces*, which, if I remember correctly, turned into a bit of a food fight and a lot of fun. The amazing Atlantic producer Arif Mardin was always around too. I remember them all coming into our session and hanging out a bit.

On one occasion, drummer Bernard Purdie (who's had quite the reputation as a result of playing with James Brown, Aretha Franklin, and, if you listen to his stories, The Beatles) came by to one of the sessions. During the course of tracking, Bill called out from the studio, "Can someone get me some water, please?" The second was going to fetch the requested liquid, but Bernard insisted that he'd get it instead, which raised a few eyebrows. Why would he be so anxious to do an assistant's job? As he took it out to Bill, the esteemed Mr. Purdie just happened to trip over a mic cable and there went an entire glass of water all over Bill. I can't 100% say that it was on purpose, but no one else was tripping over any cables, and everyone in the studio kind of looked at each other with the same idea in mind. Bernard's an interesting guy, let's leave it at that.

On yet another occasion, after a session we were leaving the building and Atlantic's other famed producer, Jerry Wexler (who had produced so many of Atlantic's hit R&B acts such as Wilson Pickett, Aretha Franklin, and Ray Charles), was leaving at the same time, and he was kind enough to give us a lift in his limo. It was only a short trip back to the hotel, but all I could think was, "Fuck me, I'm in a limo with Jerry Wexler!" That was the entire ride for me. I don't think I even said anything the whole time we were in the car. I left that to Bill since he and Jerry knew each other a little and were talking about things and people that I had no idea of. I would have loved to get into a discussion about the early days of Atlantic with him, but it was neither the time nor the place. Unfortunately, that time never did occur.

Arif Mardin and Jerry Wexler ... I can only liken it to the first time I saw the two Georges walking along the corridor at Abbey Road. This time I didn't want to scream like one of the girls, but I was in the same kind of awe. These really were people that were important to musical history, and I was getting to mingle with them.

Total Eclipse was another quick album. We mixed it at Scorpio (see Insert Figure 18.1) back in the U.K. since I had parted ways with Trident by this time.

SHABAZZ

Another Cobham solo album, *Shabazz*, was recorded live at the Montreux Jazz Festival, and once again we mixed at Scorpio. That was a real learning experience for me in regards to strange time signatures. Most of the numbers were very long and so they had to be edited down to fit on the album (remember you only have about 24 minutes a side on a vinyl record). One day I got to the studio before Bill did and I decided that I would edit the piece we had mixed the night before. The first thing I did before I started to edit was to sit down and count the whole thing out to be sure that I knew what I was doing. I thought to myself, "I know where one is. I've got this down." I edited out a huge chunk of the song, thinking that I cut on the downbeat on both ends of the edit.

When Bill came in I very proudly stated, "Oh, you've got to listen to this edit I did." Bill listened to it, and when it was done he turned around with a slight grin on his face and said something like, "You know, that edit is really good, but you were counting in seven, when it was really in eleven." "Oh, shit, I guess I can't count this stuff," I thought. I had to put the edited piece back together again and re-edit it with him telling me where the downbeats were. It kinda made sense, but I can recall all of that song 'til the cows come home and enjoy every bit of it, and I still can't count it.

STANLEY CLARK

Bassist Stanley Clark loved the sound on Bill Cobham's record, so he contacted me about doing a record with him. We turned out to be a great combination.

I called Billy and I said "How the fuck did you get that drum sound? That doesn't sound like a jazz drum sound where you go in and the whole album is done in 3 hours and you spend like 5

minutes on the drums." And he says, "No Stanley. It's this guy
Ken Scott and this is what we do and he uses these kind of mics."
And I go, "Yeah, that sounds great. Perfect. Where is he?" So that
was really Billy talking to me, because I was fascinated with the
drum sound. The music just had a certain sophistication sonically
that the other jazz records didn't. The other records in those days
still sounded like you put up two microphones, and some of them
were nice, but on Ken's things you heard little subtleties. You heard
everything, a lot of detail, you know. Man that was great, so I said,
"I gotta have that."

Stanley Clarke

On a technical level, he played an Alembic bass, and although he used
an amp, it didn't matter much because the Alembic had a stereo output
which separated the low- and high-end of the instrument. This gave me
complete control when I took him direct, which was needed because of
his style of playing. He would slap a lot, so the sound could sometimes
get very thin, but because I had the ability to play around with the low-
and high-end, I could keep everything a lot more consistent.

Everything I ever knew about recording basically started when I
worked with you [Ken]. Many a bass player has asked me how we
got those sounds. The only thing I tell them is, "I know he used
Fairchild limiters." I actually went and bought some.

Stanley Clarke

During the course of making *Stanley Clarke*, I introduced Stan to
half-speed recording. He played some really fast licks that he was able
to execute, but because they were so fast there wasn't much clarity
to them. I said, "OK, I want to double that at half-speed." He said,
"What the hell are you talking about?" I told him, "You're going to
hear the tape and it's going to be at half the speed. You'll play in the
same octave, but when we play it back it will be an octave higher
and you'll get more clarity." We finished up using this technique on
all the albums that we did together. That's the kind of thing I love
about studio recording over live. Because of the excitement of live,
you don't miss that clarity, which I feel you really need when making
a record. What is the point of a great musician playing great parts if
you can't hear them properly? I try my best to allow everything to be
heard, even if it's not noticed until after many listens.

This was also the album that I worked on with drummer Tony Williams where I came up with an interesting and unique bass drum miking technique that I've used on occasion ever since. We had done a couple of songs with Tony playing and his performance was OK, not great. When we came to the third number and it just wasn't happening, I went out to the studio and asked, "Tony, tell me what's wrong?" He proceeded to tell me that he was used to playing with both heads on the kick drum, and needed to feel the rebound of the kick drum pedal the way that you only get from having both a front and back head. You just can't get that with a single head because the sound projects out into the studio instead of rebounding back to the beater head. I said, "OK, take a break and give me some time to figure something out so we can both get what we want." In that time I came up with the idea of suspending a mic inside the drum with some wire while keeping both heads on. We then cut off the connector from the end of the mic cable, snaked it through the bass drum's air hole, then soldered it back on once it was inside. With a little damping placed inside, now we were both happy, so we went back and recut the original two titles because Tony was feeling it so much better.

The things that all of us musicians always loved was that your playbacks were like records. I tell engineers today, "When you're playing something back, don't just let it go. Fix it and make it sound good."

Stanley Clarke

On the last day of the project at Electric Lady, engineer Eddie Kramer, who was managing the studio at the time, brought in a bottle of champagne. Neither Stan or I wanted any because we still had to record Stan's acoustic bass on a track called "Spanish Phases," but Eddie insisted. During an orchestral overdub session where we put strings on some of the other titles, Stan had them record three separate and isolated parts for this piece. The original concept was that it would be like a single piece with three separate movements. The strings were to play by themselves, then Stan would come in playing upright bass, he'd stop and that would be the first movement.

After a short break the strings would come in again by themselves, then Stan would play by himself, another break, then the strings, and then Stan again. So we had the string parts, but we needed to record Stan's bass parts. Stan had no specific part, he was just jamming, and we really didn't know how long he'd play after each string section, so I told the second just to put in a blank piece of tape of an arbitrary length between sections. We didn't need to count the beats or anything because it wasn't supposed to be that type of piece. He would follow the strings and that was it. The second asked, "How much tape is enough?" "A minute or a minute and a half. He's not going to play that much," I replied.

So there's Eddie pushing the champagne. We had a glass or two and then it was finally time for Stan to do it. I got the sound, we began to record the first part, and unbelievably, it was as if he knew exactly when the next set of strings were coming in. He would stop and instantly the strings would come in for the next section. There was absolutely no logical way of his knowing when they'd come back in, but … it finished up being one complete piece, something it was never meant to be. That must have been some really good champagne that Eddie gave us!

I was worried how I was going to structure it ["Spanish Phases for Strings and Bass"]. You put something together, I don't know how, but it felt really right, so I just started playing. That was amazing. I thought it would be a lot of effort. I thought we'd have to go back and piece it together, but it was one take.
Stanley Clarke

We mixed that album in Chicago at a studio called Paragon. I have no idea why, since I had no reason to go there, so there must have been some reason for Stan to pick it. One of the cool things about the place was that they had a little radio transmitter where you could do a mix, transmit it, then listen to it on the radio in the office or out in your car. It was never quite the same as the real thing because it didn't have the compressors that real radio stations use, but you got a good idea of what it would sound like on the radio. That didn't really cause me to mix any differently, but there were occasions when

I brought something in the mix up just a little louder because it was getting lost. I never took it to the point where I would completely change a mix after I heard it on the radio though. It was just a nice little double-check that everything was coming through.

A mix will sound different on every speaker you listen on, and there are going to be things that aren't quite loud enough on certain speakers while other things will be too loud. The idea is to get it sounding great on the speakers you like, and then try to get the other little problem areas minimised on the other speakers as much as possible without spoiling it. Having your own private radio transmitter helped, at least in those days.

CHAPTER 19

Supertramp

So Bowie and I had parted ways, I'd been doing well within the jazz-fusion arena, but what was around the corner was another of those strange twists. I received a call from A&M Records about the possibility of mixing a track called "Land Ho" by a band called Supertramp—a strange name, but what the hell. I had them send a rough mix, liked what I heard, and agreed to give it a try. It seems the record company liked what I did, but the band was iffy about it, to say the least, and I don't think it was ever actually released. Well, not for many years.

A&M didn't forget me though, and some time later sent some demos from the band, wondering if I'd be interested in producing their next album. All well and good, but the only problem, a fairly big problem, was that the demo was utter crap. It was all over the place, with a verse of one song, then a chorus of another, then some jamming, then 5 seconds of a chorus and then the ending of another song. It seemed completely random, and as a result, I wasn't the slightest bit interested.

Jack Nelson, an American that Trident had brought in to manage its producers, said to me, "A&M are really into this band. You should do it because it could be very good for you." "It's crap, no way," I replied. This carried on for a while and then came an invitation to go to a showcase to hear the band play live. Jack told me with some finality, "Let's go along and see them play and then give the final yes or no." We went down to have a listen and what happened was a complete turnaround. After a few songs Jack leaned over to me and said, "I see what you mean. You were absolutely right. They're crap." My reply? "Are you fucking kidding? They're great, I've got to do this record." That inner feeling, an indefinable gut reaction hit, and I *had* to do that album.

I tend to think that the band had recorded the tape that I heard only for themselves, maybe to work out song arrangements and parts, but they were so much better than those demos. It was probably put together by the record company who thought, "We've got to send him something. Let's send him these bits and pieces."

We'd had one experience with you [Ken] on the single and we also wanted you for the album, but it was hard work getting you interested. Very hard work. I had to keep sending and sending …
Dave Margereson, A&M Records A&R, later Supertramp manager

Our soundman Russell Pope was a big fan of Ken's because he really liked Ziggy Stardust. He kept on saying, "You gotta get this guy." What did we know? So we went after this guy through the record company, where it eventually worked out.
Bob Siebenberg, Supertramp drummer

THE TRIP

After seeing the band, things became very organised and started moving quickly, and after the typical "my people speaking with their people," a deal was quickly settled. A&M had put them up in a farm way out in the countryside to work on material for the album. I decided to go down there by train for preproduction, since it was quite a way from where I lived, by English standards anyway.

I found this place, a farm called Southcombe in Somerset, and rented it from a chap that was in the fleet air arm, Wing Commander Peppy. He used to fly over occasionally, distinctively low. That was a really good time then, and when the demos started to come together, it felt like a concept album.
Dave Margereson

The record company put us in a farmhouse out in the country, with all the wives and kids and cats, to take the pressure off us while we made this record. We were in the middle of no place.
Bob Siebenberg

The night before I was about to leave for the countryside to see the band, some friends came over to the house for a visit and we had a good old time together. After they left, my wife Patience and I went up to the bedroom to get ready for bed when I suddenly got this very strange feeling that something was going to happen tomorrow and maybe I shouldn't go. Mmmm. An omen or silliness? Go or stay home? I told myself, "Scott, you're being fucking stupid," and carried on getting ready for bed. When I got into bed Patience suddenly turned over and said to me, "You know, I've just had this very strange feeling that something's going to happen tomorrow. Maybe you should think about not going." "That's weird. So did I," I replied. "Nah, don't worry. No problem," I thought, trying to talk myself out of the feeling.

I laid down to go to sleep and about 15 minutes later, the phone rang. It was one of the friends that had been over who had just arrived back home. "Thank you for a great evening, but I just have to say this," he said. "As I was driving home I suddenly got this very strange feeling that something is going to happen tomorrow and perhaps it's a good idea if you don't go."

That was it. Maybe with Patience I said something that she subconsciously picked up on, but when it involved a third person who wasn't even in the house when this strange feeling came over us, that made me think a little more seriously about it. The first thing the next morning I had Patience phone up the band to very apologetically let them know I wouldn't be down because I had contracted mumps, measles, black plague, or some other highly contagious disease. As it turned out, nothing happened that day. We watched the news very carefully for train accidents, hurricanes, terrorist attacks, tropical storms, and anything that might have confirmed that feeling of dread, but there was nothing. Who knows? Maybe if I had gone I would've fallen in front of the train or something. Luckily I'll never know.

I did finally make it down to the farm for preproduction a few days later, after I'd fully recovered from the "German measles," but I decided to drive instead of taking the train. Much bloody safer.

THE MAKING OF *CRIME OF THE CENTURY*

We soon began recording the album, of course at Trident. The first job, as always, was to get the drum sound. Something was different on this album though, as on and on and on the drum sounds went. I guess I had something in my mind at the time about getting a very particular sound, since it took over a day and a half to get it to where I was satisfied—an insane amount of time for those days, and something I hadn't done before.

I had worked with Bob Siebenberg, 'Tramp's drummer, once before whilst producing an RCA act named Jonathan Kelly. He had done a session for an album, but probably due to the lack of success of the project, neither of us actually remembered each other at the time. His kit had been fine that first time and so I don't think it would have sounded bad enough that we had to spend all that time on it under normal conditions, so I can only conclude that I must've had it in the back of my mind that this record was going to be special and we had to treat the recording that way right from the beginning.

I thought that I was going to throw the drums up and blitz through this album, but Ken completely transformed the sound of my drum kit. He transformed the whole sound of the band. He took this pretty roadworthy drum kit and put it under a microscope. I had never come across the process of working like this before, so it was a real eye-opener to work with Ken like this because of how he went about recording these things.
Bob Siebenberg

That seemed to take weeks. Dear me, bang, bang, bang. I'd come back a day later and it's bang, bang, only slightly higher. But I remember you [Ken] were a real stickler and it was Rothman [cigarettes] city in there, wasn't it?
Dave Margereson

We would record the basic tracks with either acoustic piano or Wurlitzer electric piano, bass, and drums. Any guitar was always recorded as an overdub. Rick Davies was solely a keyboard player, while Roger Hodgson went between keyboards and guitar, but only played keyboards on the basics when it was one of his songs. Then it was on to overdubs. Many, many overdubs. It was a slow process that at one point got us all very worried about taking so much time.

About two weeks into the project we heard from Dave Margereson (our A&M A&R man who later became the band's manager) that Jerry Moss, the "M" of A&M, was in town and wanted to come hear what we'd so far done. "B-b-b-b-but we've only got very little on the tracks," we said. "No problem," is what we heard back. All of the basic tracks were recorded at this point, but we hadn't gotten very far with the overdubs. There were some rough vocals, piano, bass, and drums and maybe a few guitar overdubs recorded, but that was it.

Now, this was my first time as a producer dealing with the label execs coming down to the studio for a listen—oh, the joy of yesterday's freedoms. I really didn't know what to expect and we were all pretty terrified. Jerry came in, and we sat him down in the prime listening spot and began a playback. After a few songs he got up and said only, "Very nice. Thank you," and in his always amiable manner, bade us farewell. That was it.

At that point we all thought, "Oh, crap! That's it. It's all over." How could someone from a label have the foresight to see where we were heading with this? Oh well, we had fun whilst it lasted. We then ended the session there because it seemed pointless to go on, since he was just going to say, "Forget it," anyway. Is it worth even coming back the next day and continuing to work on this dismal failure of ours?

We all downheartedly decided that we should continue until the plug was pulled, but when we all convened the next day there came an unexpected surprise. Dave called with the word that Jerry was actually quite blown away. *What?!* "Yes, Jerry loved it and said that you can have as long as you need and do whatever it takes to bring this album to fruition," our A&R man informed us, much to our utter amazement. Boy, was that a good day.

Once Jerry opened up his chequebook, then we knew we'd get it right. We *had* to get it right. What I'd learned from The Beatles to the nth degree, and Bowie as well, was try everything and quickly decide if it stands a chance of working. That became our mantra for the rest of the record.

DIFFERENT SOUNDS

One way of looking at how I approached *Crime* was that it started as Google Earth. I knew the overall shape of it, and as we went along it became more like the "street view" as we slowly saw every nook and cranny. The fact was that I was actually bored with recording. I'd recorded drums, guitars, tambourines, and everything else you can imagine so many bloody times and it was always the same. Since we were going all out on this record, I decided that we should try to make it as different as we could. I threw that concept at the band, and they just ran with the idea.

Like with the sound effects: most times when sound effects were used on records back then, the engineer would go to the closet that had the sound effects records or tapes, and that's what he'd use. Everyone used the same ones. I insisted, "If we're going to do it, we're going to do it properly and record our own, exactly like a movie," so we rented a stereo Nagra portable recorder and recorded all of our own sound effects. For example, for the song "School," I went down to a friend's house that was two doors down from where my three daughters were going to school, just in time for the lunch break because I knew the kids would be out in the yard playing. I recorded for a half hour, then went off to the studio. Roger would then listen on headphones to try to find bits that might actually work in the song, and we'd go through it and finalise what we were going to use.

Another example was for "Rudy," where it was decided that we needed some train effects. I think it was Roger and saxophonist

John Helliwell who went down to one of the train stations in London, set up the Nagra, and recorded some of the effects. When they'd packed up and were walking out, there was a busker playing a violin just outside the door. They immediately thought, "This is too good. We've got to get this," so they set it all up again and recorded this violinist. That's what you hear between the main part of "Rudy" and the end section, which is just orchestra. I'm sure that most people think that the violin part that's in there was actually written for the song, but it was just the busker who was playing that part, and it happened to work so bloody perfectly. That also happened with the station master's announcement in the middle of the song, something that wasn't noticed until they were back in the studio. When listening for what parts would work in the song it became evident that the announcement they recorded referred to the train stopping at Didcot, where Roger was from, and Swindon, Rick's stomping ground.

For percussion we tried to use different things that weren't typical percussion instruments. On "Dreamer" there's a part that under normal circumstances would have been a tambourine, but that would've made it so ordinary. In trying to get something different, I had the idea of getting Rick to shake a pair of drum brushes. He started off doing it rather heavily, but all you could hear was a whistle from them. We got him to slow it down a bit and do it with more wrist than arm action and suddenly we got the effect that we wanted. There's a kind of whistle there at the same time as the brushes go through the air, which makes it sound totally different than anything you'd expect but still fills the rhythmic need.

Some of the sounds that we got would be done on a synth these days, but synths weren't around so much back then and we made a conscious effort not to use them if possible. We only used a Minimoog and an Elka String Ensemble occasionally. For "Dreamer" I had this idea for two sustaining notes, so we decided that I should play it on wine glasses. We got a couple of wine glasses, poured the right amount of water into them to tune them up, then I played them. We recorded the first note, then went back and got the second. By playing wine glasses I mean that I was rubbing my fingers around the top edge, just like those damn annoying kids in restaurants. Everything has its use eventually.

On "Hide in Your Shell" I had an idea for a melodic line. Now I can't say that these type of ideas spew forth from me all the time and that might be a blessing in disguise, as it's often hard for me to get them across as I'm not a musician. On this occasion I finally managed to get this line idea across to Roger, who worked it out and played it on a keyboard, but it sounded too ordinary. We tried it a couple of other ways and finally we brought in a guy to play it on a musical saw, which is what you hear on the record. What an amazing sound. It was so cool that we asked the musical sawist to jam a bit, which we of course recorded as well. Unfortunately I have no idea whatever became of the tape of the jam, but his part on the song worked perfectly.

Probably one of the best examples of teamwork was when recording some tom overdubs, also on "Hide in Your Shell." We wanted to get a change in pitch on each tom hit, so every time Bob hit a tom I changed the varispeed, speeding the tape up and then bringing it back to normal. When played back this makes the tom's pitch go down and then as it tails off it goes back up to normal. Bob had to hit the tom on beat with the tempo going all over the place, a feat he accomplished admirably as can be heard on the final product.

Everything but the kitchen sink went into this recording. Actually we got pretty close to a kitchen sink as well. The session percussionist extraordinaire and all around nice guy Ray Cooper had once told me of something which apparently was used a lot in horror movies: a water gong. You take a gong, hit it, and then gradually lower it into water. This creates a strange, eerie effect because as the gong is immersed the water makes its pitch change. We were working on the ending of "Crime of the Century" and, for those that don't know, "Crime" is in two parts. There's the song and then it goes into a seemingly endless piano part during which it builds and builds with different instruments and lines coming and going throughout. We were at the point where the drums came in and we needed something to point out that something big was about to happen. Enter the water gong.

Now that name is slightly incorrect because it ended up that we didn't actually use a gong; we used a piece of sheet metal instead, but it worked just as well. We rented a large fish tank and filled it with water and, at the appropriate time, Bob struck it and lowered it into the water, and it sounded amazing. What's great is that if you hear it on its own with no other instruments and without any reverb, you actually hear the water bubbling. So cool. That effect actually became a pet thing for me as I used it in one form or another on a number of future albums as well. A word of warning, however. The filling of the fish tank is slow but fairly easy to accomplish, one bucket of water at a time. But, once you've finished the recording you're left with one hell of a heavy fish tank to empty and so you have to have a fair number of pretty hefty guys to get it to the kitchen or bathroom sink to empty it.

We were always looking for different things that could be used for percussion. If we saw a cardboard box or a pillow, we'd be hitting it all over to see what it sounded like. It was that kind of thing. I remember walking into the studio very early on in the recording process and I just went all across their wooden floor on my hands and knees with this block of wood, hitting it on the floor in various places to see how the sound changed. I finally found the right spot, which we then recorded. That's the way we were.

For the instruments, we used the varispeed out-of-tune piano trick that I used with Elton on occasion. We put things through Leslies. On "Hide in Your Shell," for instance, we played a bass note on the Minimoog through the Leslie so it doesn't sound like a synth. Anything and everything we could come up with, but the big thing was that we made decisions, quickly and without hesitation. After all, we only had 16 tracks to work with.

We had to have exactly the right sound for exactly the right section. A lot of people might say we went over the top, especially when you consider that on any given song there could be as many as 30 different guitar sounds. Another example: the drum sound that we had for the first half of "Crime" started to sound wrong. We were at Scorpio by this time and we just decided to re-record the drums for the first half of the number. To me, it's another one of those situations where a unique sound was achieved purely by accident. There was a certain amount of drum leakage into the piano on the original track, and as Bob is a human and not a machine, he didn't play the part exactly the same way on the overdub, which you can hear. As a result, there is a double-track effect, but as the original kit was in the Trident drum booth and is only picked up through the piano mics, it lacks any kind of presence and gives this almost "am I really hearing a double or is it my imagination" effect.

We had a lot of fun making the album and wanted to pass along some of the silliness to the listener, hence things like at the end of "Asylum," where we put in a cuckoo clock. Being the last track on the side meant that this happened to occur in the lead-out groove of the record. As it turned out, most people missed it because on automatic record players the tone arm would lift up before it got to it.

We went completely overboard on everything, which is why the album took close to six months, a very long time for an album back then. Once we were given that crucial go-ahead from the label, we had no real choice but to strive for perfection.

THE VACUUM CLEANER

At some point we moved upstairs to Trident's mix room. I remember one late night/early morning we were trying to do a mix of one of the first completed tracks. One of the great things about 'Tramp for me was the two completely different sounding vocalists, along the lines of John and Paul, with songs often set up in such a way as to have one answering the other. On the track we were mixing I wanted to get a completely different placement on Roger's vocals as opposed to Rick's, so I was sending Roger through a speaker into the studio, two floors down, and using a mic some distance away so the sound was not as present. There we were having the time of our lives and suddenly there's this awful noise blasting out of the speakers, which I, of course, had pretty loud, as usual. My immediate reaction was to pull all the faders down, suspecting something wrong with the gear. It didn't take long to discover that no gear was at fault however. Everything was working perfectly; it was the sound of a vacuum cleaner. The cleaners had no idea that we were using the studio and so were doing exactly what they were supposed to do, much to our chagrin.

CHAPTER 20

Completing 'Tramp's *Crime of the Century*

It was during this time that it became very awkward working at Trident as I was going through a major battle with my management, who, of course, also owned the studio. The disagreement was over the typical things: money, the feeling of abandonment as they got bigger, and, of course, money.

I had formed a company with Norman and Barry Sheffield called Nereus Productions before my first Bowie production. Since Trident was a sea god, Nereus was another sea god, just to keep the names along the same lines. Bowie was the first project to go through the company, as Supertramp did later. Once Bowie had become successful, it was decided that I wasn't going to engineer anymore except on my own productions, so my salary moved from being paid by Trident to being paid by Nereus. Unfortunately, management began to take out expenses that I didn't know about and, of course, we eventually got into an argument about them. The underlying problem was that the Bowie money wasn't coming in the way we all had expected, thanks to his manager Tony Defries. Had the money for Bowie come through, getting paid by Nereus wouldn't have been a problem, but as it didn't and I still had to make a living, Trident paid me by loaning Nereus money. It turned out that when collecting on the loan they were also throwing other expenses in, which I disputed. We started to fall out over it and eventually I found someone else I wanted to manage me. Things got nasty, and I just decided it was best to leave the Trident fold.

My last time in the Trident offices was, in my mind at least, one of those classic moments that live with you for a lifetime. I'd already left Trident and we were trying to sort out my contract. It started off with myself and my future manager, Ian Farrell, arriving for a meeting with Norman Sheffield to discuss the situation. We were sitting in reception and waiting and waiting, getting madder and madder. Half an hour goes by and nothing. An hour goes by and still nothing, at which time our patience finally gave out. Now it just so happened that the first gold record I was ever given was for *All Things Must Pass*, which I loaned to Trident, as I thought it would do both me and them more good hanging at the place of business rather than in my living room.

Once we had reached that point where we could wait no longer, I stormed up the corridor, took down my gold record, and Ian and I left. I had parked on the side street by the offices, and as I put my gold record in the car, a head popped out of a second floor window. There was Norman screaming the classic line at me, "I'll make sure you never work in this town again!" He was there the entire time, knew the meeting was going to be adversarial, so he kept us waiting to try and show who was boss. The classic side to this is that the window was in the ladies bathroom and the only way he could have got up high enough to look out was by standing on the toilet. Oh, for a video of that scene.

Even with all the fun and games of that last non-meeting we still continued working together and do to this day. Nereus held the contracts for all of the productions I had done up to that point and so all too often we had to join forces to try and keep record companies and artists paying what was owed, not always an easy task.

Having just mentioned my parting of ways with Trident, I do feel the need to mention something here that has often bothered me. There have been many times that Barry and Norman (Norman especially) have really raised my ire and I've felt one way or another ripped off, but I do feel that in many instances they have been given a bad rap over the years. In the end, the Sheffields contributed much to the British recording industry and gave many talented engineers and a few artists the start they needed, and for that I really have to give them their due.

OFF TO RAMPORT

Back to 'Tramp. Since we could no longer work at Trident, we went to Ramport, The Who's studio, to do the rest of the overdubs. Having gone through the "Hey Jude" fiasco due to bad monitoring, I was acutely aware that I had to get the monitors at Ramport to my liking. As soon as I started to listen to some music I brought with me, I knew that they weren't what I was used to. I asked if I could change their alignment but was informed that they had been perfectly aligned the day before and I was not to touch anything. I listened some more and knew that if they couldn't be changed, we'd have to go somewhere else. The studio hierarchy finally relented and said I could adjust them only if I marked exactly where everything was currently set so they could put it back when the sessions were finished. Slowly but surely, by a minor adjustment here and a slight change there, I got the monitors to my satisfaction and work on the album began again.

When we came back into work the following day the second engineer immediately told me, "The tech came by this morning to check the speakers again." I hit the bloody roof. "You mean to tell me that I have to go through all that again?" "No, he didn't change it at all. He said it was perfect," replied the second. The thing was, my settings were still in and so there should have been a major difference between each of the readings. Acoustics is purported to be a science. It was at that point I realised that sometimes it's more luck than judgement and there are people making a science, and a whole load of money, out of rubbish.

WE MOVE AGAIN

On and on we worked. Out of time at Ramport, we moved to Scorpio Sound, which although having a rather staid design, had a great Cadac board (see Figure 20.1), great monitors (also Cadac), and a really good and friendly staff. This became my home away from home for several projects. I remember those speakers so well because they were fucking amazing. They were seven feet tall and weighed half a ton each and had so many bloody speakers that I have no idea how they could ever get it all sounding so good. You could get them incredibly loud, yet they were always clean. I've tried to find some information about them for this book, but even Cadac doesn't seem to remember—a shame, as they were astounding.

Figure 20.1: The Cadac board.

Every mix took five pairs of hands, even doing it in sections. The boards weren't as huge as they are now because we were only working on 16-track at the time, so they may have had 24 channels but some of those had to be used as echo returns. You couldn't bring up the five different things that you might have had all on the same track on five different faders so you could EQ each one perfectly like you can now with the megaconsoles that have become commonplace. You had to manually change everything as it was going. You had to manually change the EQ, panning, and effects from one part to the other whilst you were mixing. Those were the days. Each mix was a true performance!

> *I would reach over the front of the desk, do my switch and then get out of the way because I was in front of the left-hand speaker. So I'd kinda sit there on the floor with the bottom end going "woo woo woo" and then, "OK here it comes," and I'd stand up again. It was a great way to make records. There was a communal energy to it.*
>
> Dennis Weinreich, Scorpio engineer

WE MAKE A MISTAKE

With *Crime* I continued the way of mixing I had become used to since the Bowie mixes, doing only a short section at a time. It took about a day and half for each of the mixes, although there was one track that made me slightly wonder about the amount of time we were spending on each. During the mixing of Rick's song "Asylum," Rick wasn't able to stay into the night as he had a prior engagement that he couldn't get out of. The song was one hell of a setup. There were effects on this, and effects on that. It took us forever to get it together. We eventually started to put things down on tape. We'd get one section and I'd edit. Get another, and I'd edit. We were far enough along with it that Rick felt comfortable leaving us to complete the rest as he left to deal with his commitment. By 2 or 3 o'clock in the morning the song was finished. We sat back and turned the monitors even louder than they already were, and marvelled at how fucking amazing it sounded. I then cleared the board and set up for the next mix.

The next day we came in after too little sleep, and when Rick arrived he asked to hear the mix of his song. Boy, we were feeling so proud of ourselves. So I turn up the volume and away we go. The closing notes come and go and we all look at Rick and notice the puzzled look on his face. "It's great but why did you leave out the _____ section?" he asked. "*What?*" we seemed to all say at once. "The _____ section. It's not in there." We played the mix again, then played the multitrack. A collective "Oh shit!" went up. At the end of the song there is a repeating theme as Rick's vocal becomes more manic and we had indeed left out one of the more manic sections of the song. As I had been editing, I evidently didn't put it in.

This became one of those situations that really shows how much you can sometimes fake yourself out in the recording studio. It had taken us hours upon hours to set up the day before, with each minuscule detail that had to be dealt with. For the missing section, it took about half an hour to set up, and we edited it in, and no one could tell the difference between the two. I can't wait to hear where everyone thinks it is.

I remember that one of the things that impressed me most about you [Ken] was your skill at editing. It was watching the craftsman at work. And you never spilt [cigarette] ash on anything. I could never work it out, you know. You were never one to spill your ash.

Dave Margereson

SELLING *CRIME*

Crime of the Century was released in September of 1974 and it was amazing how fast the album took off. Miraculously, by January 1975 *Crime* was a big hit. It always seems to come down to one DJ that starts the ball rolling, and the one in England that really helped was a guy called Alan Freeman ("Fluff" to his friends). He loved the album and started to play it regularly, and once he started, then other DJs followed.

The funny thing was that the band and I had a conversation that was eerily like one I had had with Bowie a few years earlier in that we thought this was the kind of record that could never be a hit in England, but would be huge in the States. Of course, we were wrong on both counts: it took five years for each of them to break the *big* market. *Crime* became number 1 in England and most of the world, but did absolutely nothing in America initially. You have to admire Jerry Moss's guts though. A&M took out a full-page ad in Billboard announcing that it had gone platinum on a date six months in advance. When that date arrived, it was nowhere close. In fact, I don't think it even got to 100,000 sold at that point. It did end up being nominated for a "Best Engineered" Grammy, but it lost to McCartney and Wings' *Band on the Run*, which was engineered by my old buddy, Geoffrey "Emeroids" Emerick.

With *Crime of the Century*, we knew on several levels what we'd achieved. One of the things was how good we actually managed to get it on vinyl. A&M was distributed by CBS in Europe at the time, and we talked the label into putting the release through its classical division, which had much better vinyl and took greater care in manufacturing. As a result, the first pressing run of *Crime of the Century* was absolutely phenomenal. The problem was that as it became successful, they couldn't continue to keep pressing it through that classical division because of the expense, so it then went through the pop department and boom, immediately a lot of the quality was lost.

One of the more amusing instances occurred following 'Tramp's first gig after the release of the album. A&M decided to throw a party for the band at a restaurant in the Chelsea area of London. All of the A&M brass, even Jerry Moss, were there, and it was a rather big deal. Everyone was having a grand old time when for some obscure reason, the place was raided. There were cops running everywhere, handcuffing the guests, and being very policeman-like, but everyone thought it was a joke because, of course, the record was called "*Crime of the Century*," so no one took the raid seriously. As a result, some of the guests began to tell the cops to piss off and generally become very indignant and disorderly in the face of what they believed to be fake police, before we all finally realised that this was a real raid! Eventually we understood the cops, and they understood us, and they determined that we were no great threat to society and let us go. That didn't do much for the party though, as an imminent threat to one's freedom tends to put a damper on things.

It was great. It was the after-gig party for our very first show after we made the album. The gig was for all the record company execs from America. We went to this club down on Kings Road and we were having our party and I don't know what time it was, but 25 or 30 cops all come piling through the door. Everybody thought that it was a stunt because the name of the album was "Crime of the Century." It was because there was alcohol being served way past time and somebody had tipped them off, so here they came and they were prepared to arrest everybody until they sussed what it was. They really did have Jerry Moss by the arm. They got it and were cool and left and everyone dwindled out after that.

Bob Siebenberg

THE SHOW

Once we had recorded the album and the quality of it became obvious, the band knew that somehow their live act had to come up to the same standard and they could no longer just do a gig the way they'd done it before. Supertramp didn't have a "star" who could capture the audience with his charisma, so the choice was made to capture the sound of the recording as closely as possible at the live gig.

Supertramp's sound guy, Russel Pope, was amazing in that capacity. He worked his arse off to get the best possible live sound and get it as close to the record as possible. Eventually the band and the road crew formed their own PA company because they couldn't find anything that was actually good enough to put everything across as they wanted it. The company was called Delicate Productions and Russ was the brains behind it.

After a couple of gigs the band realised, "Hang on, we're actually quite boring to watch," even with the great sound, so they started to come up with all sorts of staging to complement the music. They utilised a famous piece of old movie from the BBC of a train ride from London to Brighton that starts off at normal speed where you see the train pulling out of the station, then it goes really fast for the entire trip, then slows down as the train pulls into the station and then stops. The band got the rights to use this, then had it projected behind them at the end of "Rudy." You go on this train ride, which is perfect for "Rudy," working along with all of those train effects on the record.

The movie was originally four minutes long but it was edited down to fit the ending of the song. They actually accomplished an incredible feat as every time the band performed the song they managed to come to the end of it just as the train came to a stop in the movie, and this was way before things could be synced up by click tracks and time code; it was all done manually. Whoever started the film every time had it down.

Then at the end of "Crime," they'd project a starry sky and you'd be moving amongst the stars, and gradually these bars with two hands started coming towards you and get bigger and bigger until you realise that it's the cover of the album. The band was quickly learning how to put on a show as opposed to just a performance, and soon became a huge concert draw as a result.

CHAPTER 21

Supertramp Take 2:
Crisis? What Crisis?

With *Crime* now a bona fide success, Supertramp completed a tour of America and liked it so much they decided to hang out in the States for a while afterwards (see Insert Figure 21.1). The band especially loved the West Coast and landed in L.A., and thanks to the whole A&M family atmosphere (the label was based in Los Angeles on the old Charlie Chaplin film studio lot), the decision was made to make their next record there. Fine by me. I'd never been to L.A. and certainly didn't mind coming over for two or three months to soak up the sun while doing some recording. It sounded like heaven.

Unfortunately, that plan was briefly put on hold when Roger and one of the roadies went out in the woods for some recreational boys' fun (please don't misunderstand that) and broke his wrist jumping on a log (and no I don't mean log in the way your mind is thinking). That totally messed up the recording schedule for a while, but the band still decided to hang out in L.A. during his recovery period. As a result, they got the lay of the land (and you can take that any way you wish) well before I arrived. In fact, Bob was an L.A. lad, born and raised in Glendale, so of course he already knew the place.

Eventually Roger's wrist healed and he was ready to start recording, so off I trotted, family in tow, to the land of sun and fun. When I arrived, the first thing we did was go around to look at possible studios to record in. I didn't really know any of the studios in town, so I was more or less led around to different places since the band had already been there for a while. The only one that I remember for sure was The Beach Boys' studio, primarily because it was my first time driving along the beach on the famous and breathtaking Pacific Coast Highway—Southern California at its most beautiful!

For some reason we never looked into some of the bigger and more famous facilities such as Record Plant or Sunset Sound, and in the end we decided that Studio D on the A&M lot, which was right in the middle of Hollywood, would work the best.

Studio D was a really good studio for us, but the best part of working at the record company's HQ, normally an absolute no-no, was the whole atmosphere of the A&M lot, which was absolutely astounding. I had never dealt with a label like that before nor have I since. Even though it was a big record company that had experienced a great deal of success, it still really had a family atmosphere. Whenever you'd go "on the lot," you'd see someone walking by and you probably knew them and hung out with them personally, everything was so tight-knit. And then walking up the steps to the studio you'd see Charlie Chaplin's small footprints in the concrete, so you really felt you were in a special place and that could only help to inspire you. Unfortunately, the family feeling eventually started to fade when Jerry and Herb both got divorced. It had been basically a two-person business for a long time, but apparently with the divorces it suddenly became four people running it, and that ultimately changed the atmosphere forever. Fortunately, that didn't happen until way after we completed the album.

Here's something from an American perspective. Here's this English group and big-time English producer coming to A&M studios and they're asking to do things differently. There was a little resistance from the maintenance staff. One thing that Ken wanted to do was retune the speakers, which they really didn't

want to do. Ken did it anyway, so right away they were put off.
Ed Thacker, second engineer at A&M Studios

Because the facility had four studios, there were always a lot of other artists recording in the building as well. We'd be walking down the corridor and there would be stars like Karen Carpenter or Joni Mitchell walking towards us, but because we hadn't yet made it in the U.S., we still felt somehow inferior to them and other big American acts. There was always this feeling of gratitude when we'd pass by the aforementioned Ms. Carpenter in the hallway though, because we felt that she, as one of A&M's biggest-selling artists, was somehow funding our recording. How naïve we were, since we were actually making plenty of money for the label ourselves thanks to more-than-brisk worldwide sales.

The one thing about that record that was really different, at least to the people at the studio, was that it was a big project that was going to take a lot of time. We were going to basically move into the studio, which people didn't do in those days. You did 10 to 6 or 7 to midnight. We moved in for 24 hours a day for many months, and worked 7 days a week. We left everything set up, and that was new.
Ed Thacker

RECORDING IN L.A.

Crisis? What Crisis? was a hell of an album to try to do. We had put so much into *Crime*, and it had been so successful as a result, that trying to match up to that success and quality was really bloody hard in every respect, from the writing to the recording to the performances. You could tell that things would be a bit different right from the beginning because, unlike *Crime*, there was no real preproduction for this album. Even though we had plenty of time before we began recording, a lot of it was sorted out in the studio.

There were a lot of aspects about recording *Crisis* that were the same as *Crime*, but a lot that wasn't too. For instance, we didn't go quite as far out with percussion instruments as on *Crime*, and tended to stick a little more to the norm, but only a little. I did try some drum things where I had poor Bob doing some unusual playing. On "The

Meaning" and "A Soapbox Opera" there were some tom fills that I wanted to sound bigger, almost tympani-like. I knew exactly how to get the effect, which was by putting them through Fairchild limiters, à la Ringo, but that meant we had to isolate the toms from the rest of the kit so the limiting would only occur on the tom fills. In order for this to happen, Bob had to play normally, then when the tom fills occur he had to stop playing and then start up again as naturally as possible. Not an easy thing to do, in fact impossible, and so we finished up putting pillows on the toms and Bob played through the track as he normally would, then played the pillows when it came to his fills. Once we got the take of the drums that we liked, he had to go back and play it again to get just the fills, but this time everything else had a pillow on it except for the toms. That's the kind of ridiculous things we did. It got a little silly at times, but it gave us the effects we—or was it I?—were after.

Ken would have me do odd things like put pads on the toms, then he'd have me play the whole song with just bass drum, snare, and cymbals. I'd play the fills but they wouldn't get recorded. After we were happy with all of that, then I'd have to go back and put towels on everything else and play only the tom fills with the tape speed cranked up so the drums would sound heavier, so the drum track is actually two performances put together at different speeds with different mic setups.
Bob Siebenberg

A Fairchild was a piece of junk until Ken resurrected it. When we started using those, nobody knew what they were. Ken's problem with the 670s that we had at A&M was that they didn't link properly in stereo. He was used to using the mono 660s in England.
Ed Thacker

In another case I wanted a room sound on a couple of the drums tracks and didn't want to do it with reverb, which meant using some distant mics to achieve the effect. The problem was that the studio wasn't large enough to get what we needed, so we had to find some other place to put the mics. As it turned out, the facility's rather large maintenance room was right behind the Studio D drum booth, and so we waited until the evening for all the maintenance guys to clear out (except the one working the session, who promised to remain quiet), before doing a couple of the basics. We put one mic there and another out in the corridor and left the doors of the studio open to get the distant sounds we were looking for. Unorthodox, but it worked.

> *We actually put mics everywhere we could. Just the fact that we were doing that was unheard of. Room sound on the drums? That was the era of dead drum sounds, so we were pushing the limits of what they were used to.*
>
> Ed Thacker

Then for "Two of Us" we wanted to record a real pipe organ, so A&M managed to get us into Royce Hall on the UCLA campus, which had a world-renowned instrument. Roger tried playing it, but the thing about pipe organs that none of us realised until that moment is that there's a delay on everything you play as it takes some time for the sound to come out of the pipes after the key is struck. It's just like the delay you often get on the phone where it's so disconcerting that you can't carry on a conversation. You … start … to … talk … ve…ry … slow…ly. The part wasn't Roger's norm with a lot of eighth notes, but it was coming back with such a delay on it that it was impossible for Roger to play anything in time. We knew fairly quickly the idea wasn't going to work, so we ended up using his harmonium, back in Blighty, for the part instead.

One off-night a few of us went to a jazz club in the Valley to see Supersax, a Charlie Parker tribute band that harmonised his music with a full horn section. They sounded amazing and that set our brains going. What if John could do the same thing on a solo? We realised that if John knew what we had planned he could do a simplified solo to make the harmony parts easy to work out, so we recorded a sax solo on "Another Man's Woman" as normal, and once he'd got one down that satisfied us all we told him, "Now we want you to harmonise it exactly the same way as Supersax!" He was obviously doubtful about it, but being the trouper that he is, he went away with a rough mix and came back a couple of days later with everything written out to complete the solo. At times he goes into unison because it just wouldn't work any other way, but the final product is great. I *love* that solo.

Once again we did a lot of guitar overdubs for *Crisis* as we'd done on *Crime*, because once you show someone what can be done, they tend to want to keep with it. Roger had been used to doing a single guitar track all the way through a song on the albums prior to *Crime* and that was fine, but once he saw what a difference that different guitar tones can make in different parts of a song, there was no stopping him. Exactly the same thing also happened with Steve Morse later on when I worked with Dixie Dregs. Once we started down that road, the guitar parts took on a whole new life.

> *The attention to detail and the absolute insistence that it be absolutely right [was remarkable]. I'd been on other projects and I'd seen other records being made, and I'd seen some go down where maybe it wasn't what everybody wanted. This was a record where every sound and every performance had to be the best it could be no matter what. It was great to work on that kind of project.*
>
> Ed Thacker

THE TROUBLE WITH WIVES

Doing the record in a totally new place had several pros but also a couple of cons that threw us off our stride. As this was a three-month stint, everyone brought out their family to L.A., which eventually caused some problems. When the wives were at home in England, they had their family's lives to take care of so they stayed out of the business of the band for the most part, but in L.A. it just became a long vacation where all they did was hang out. Part of that hanging out was coming down to the studio and meeting up with the other wives, and they'd start talking. I have to say that my wife was well in there with them as well. There was a lot of "I don't feel that my husband is getting all that he deserves" kind of talk that did nothing but stir up shit. It was exactly the way that people thought Yoko and Linda affected The Beatles, which never actually happened in their case, but certainly happened here. So much of it was like in the movie *Spinal Tap* where the girlfriend suddenly turns up on the scene and starts to take over.

> *When we made* Crisis *we had some weirdness with wives and vibe and stuff like that a couple of times, but we all got over it. It was more girls and booze that was causing it. We never had any blowups in the studio at all.*
>
> Bob Siebenberg

I remember at one point it began affecting me as well. One day Dave Margereson, who by now had become 'Tramp's manager, dropped into the studio and made a very innocent comment about having to use earplugs, because I was monitoring loudly (nothing new there). For some reason, I thought the comment was a personal slight and took absolute offense, then stormed out of the studio with a, "I'm not going to work here ever again if that man is allowed in the control room." We had reached the point where we were all on edge and it didn't take much to set any one of us off. I was called in to see Kip Cohen, who was the head of A&R at the label, and he calmed me down and patched things up. The funny thing was that as soon as we went back to England, everything was fine. There was just something about the close proximity in L.A. and the women getting together and stirring things up, my spouse included, that just created tension between us.

WE RETURN TO ENGLAND

After a few months we ran out of studio time at A&M, so we decided to return to England to finish up the record. We had accomplished quite a lot in L.A. as all of the basics and a lot of the overdubs were complete, but we still had much to record and then mix. This was unlike the making of *Crime* though, because this time we had constraints put on us. For *Crime*, no one knew what to expect and so there was no release date and no tour set until the album was completed. But that was then, and for the follow-up to a huge success, everything had to be arranged way in advance. We had no choice but to plough on in any way possible to meet the deadline.

When we got back to the U.K., just like with *Crime*, we started out at Ramport for some of the overdubs, then went back to our old stomping ground Scorpio. The only thing I specifically remember recording at Ramport was on "Easy Does It," where the song starts out with whistling in the street. To record that part we put a couple of U 87s out in the street outside of the studio, then John walked down the street whistling. We wanted a car horn to start the song, so I was in my car waiting for a signal to hit the horn as John gradually walked closer to the mics. There's not much else to the story, except it's the only thing I remember about the studio during this album.

Back to Scorpio and, of course, we ran out of time there as well. Carl Palmer, of Emerson, Lake & Palmer fame, had time booked for a solo project right after us, so it was arranged that we would turn up at the studio around midnight, and when he finally finished we would start up again and finish our session, usually just as he walked in the door to start his new day. Of course, this was in the days before there was such a thing as a studio lockout, where you bought the studio for the entire 24-hour period and could leave everything set up at the end of your session. If that would have been the norm, we'd have been off to another studio to finish things up as Carl would have probably locked us out.

There were a couple of habits that we got into during this period. One was that we'd always bring food in and cook the most amazing English breakfasts, because Scorpio had a fairly reasonable kitchen. Roger the vegetarian would have his muesli and the rest of us would take great joy in cooking typically English fry-ups of eggs, bacon, tomatoes, sausages, mushrooms, baked beans, and, of course, fried bread. The smell of that sure beat the hell out of any of the incense that had been burning earlier. The other habit was a board game called Mastermind, a code-breaking game that was centuries old, but had just been released in a modern version. Much like it was with foosball during the Elton days, so it was with us and this game. We eventually even had championship series, again like with Elton. As this was pre-video games, we were totally into it during our breaks. Good times.

THE ORCHESTRA AND CHOIRBOYS

When we decided that we were going to use an orchestra on *Crime of the Century*, I got in touch with a person that I first met through The Beatles called Richard Hewson, who did several arrangements for

Mary Hopkin's *Postcard* album. He had done such amazing work for us on the first album that we, of course, got him to do the arrangements for *Crisis*. We did the strings at Abbey Road Number 2 with my old second John Kurlander engineering. I love doing orchestral sessions but at the same time I hate doing orchestral sessions. I hate them because of the pressure you feel from having a studio full of people who are getting paid by the session, so if anything goes wrong, the last thing you want to do is go into overtime because of the costs involved. There will always be some musician within the orchestra who will make a noise on the last take just before you go into overtime, so you want to make sure that your keeper is before that last one if you can. I didn't want that pressure for this particular string session, and since the other studios where too dead for strings, we came back to my favourite studio on earth, Number 2 in Abbey Road.

We used Richard again on "A Soapbox Opera," a song that's basically anti-organised religion. Roger wrote it when the band was on tour in the States and he heard various Southern preachers on the radio. He made up a tape of bits and pieces of these preachers, which is used in the beginning of the song. In the English mind, what's synonymous with organised religion? Choirboys, of course, so that's who we had to have sing on it. We asked Richard to do the arrangement and find a suitable boys choir.

The interesting thing about using choirboys is that you don't have to pay them because they're not professionals—you just make a donation to their church. What was really funny about it was that we had all of these little kids in their school uniforms come in, and they were absolute angels as they were about to perform. As soon as you'd say, "OK, we're going to listen back," they immediately turned into demons, screaming and running everywhere and having a blast. It was quite the opposite of the old-age pensioners on Nilsson's "I'd Rather Be Dead."

ANOTHER MIX SAVED

Mixing was exactly the same as for *Crime*. All hands on deck to move faders and parameter settings, and the Cadac speakers blasting. There was one track we mixed where after a few days of living with it, we decided that the vocal wasn't quite loud enough in the verses. Everything was so good on "Ain't Nobody But Me" that we really didn't want to mix it again though. I decided to try something that was a pain in the arse to pull off, but ended up not only working but providing a great vocal effect as well.

What I did was play the mix off of one stereo machine and by trial and error, sync it up to the 16-track with only the vocal soloed. Of course, there was no timecode back then to keep both machines locked together, so we'd finish a section and put that to one side, then finish another bit, then edit them together. The whole thing is that when you have two tape machines that are running unlocked like that, due to wow and flutter of the motors, they will never run exactly together, but as it turned out, that finished up as almost an ADT effect. Every now and again the additional vocal would go slightly ahead of the mix vocal, then it would start to slow down slightly and you'd get this slight phasing effect, which wound up being the perfect addition to the final vocal. It took us a couple of hours to do, but was well worth it.

FINALLY FINISHED

When it came time to mix we managed to get some extra time at Scorpio so we didn't have to work late-night after-session hours again, but we were once again running out of time. As a result, the last day of mixing was one of those 36-hour almost non-stop marathons. On that last day we mixed the final song, then had to put all of the songs on the album in a running order. After that task was complete, I quickly drove home and had a bath (we didn't have showers in England at that point), then blasted out again to mastering. That was cutting it close and I was knackered (exhausted) to say the least. In the end, the album ended up taking about the same amount of time as *Crime*—between five and six months, but we had finished on time.

At the end of the day, we felt pretty good about *Crisis*, but not quite in the same way as with *Crime*, and that feeling goes on until today for me. There are a couple of tracks on *Crisis* that I feel are better than anything on *Crime*, but as an album I don't think it stands together as well as *Crime* does. *Crime* to me was timeless. I don't think there's a sound on it that you can pin to any particular era, like with certain synth and drum sounds on some songs where you just know they came from the '80s. On *Crisis* we used things like vocoder and electric sitar, and somehow those dated the record for me, and it's not as timeless as a result.

THE NEXT RECORD

Crisis was a success, and although not quite as big as *Crime*, the sales were still nothing to sneeze at. We'd all come to enjoy L.A whilst we were there, so it didn't take long for everyone to move over. I started to do a lot more work for A&M because of all the success I had as the producer of *Crime* and *Crisis*, so we came to a family decision that maybe California really was the place to be.

So there we were about to start our new life in the City of Angels, or the land of fruits and nuts depending on your point of view: Los Angeles. After a couple of weeks of hotel living and after much looking around, we ended up renting a house up in the Hollywood Hills. Where else? I was still in the throes of trying to finish mixing an album and was working bankers' hours. We had only one car at that point and the gas and electricity were due to be turned on at the new home, but I had to go into the studio, so I dropped the family off at the house early in the morning and disappeared into the darkness of A&M's Studio D.

When we were finished mixing at the really early time of 6:00 P.M. (early for me anyway), it was back to the family and our new abode. When I got there, however, I came upon a dark, empty house with no visible trace of life. Strange, they haven't got a car, so they couldn't have gone anywhere unless they'd called a cab, yet they hadn't called or left a note. I still had no key for the house so I just sat in the car waiting for a sign from above as to what the hell was going on and getting a little madder with each passing minute.

After about a half-hour there was a knock on the car window and there stood my eldest daughter and another girl. "Oh, I guess they've made some friends. I suppose that's good," I thought as I tried to remain calm. "Daddy, this is Moon," she said. I thought to myself,

259

"OK, I don't think there are too many girls named 'Moon.' " Next question she asked was, "Do you know a guy called Frank Zappa? We're at his house across the street." Amazingly, we had moved into the house directly opposite Frank's. Suddenly all the animosity that had built up whilst sitting in the car was forgotten, and off I trotted with the girls to meet our new friends. Welcome to Hollywood.

Soon it came time to discuss the next Supertramp album. Everyone came to my house one night and we had a very productive meeting, then once business was completed, it was time to party. Wow, did we ever! Bob ended up getting busted for drunk driving and spent what was left of the night in the local lock-up. Dougie Thomson, the band's bass player, passed out cuddling a teddy bear belonging to one of my daughters. Unfortunately, in the midst of all the revelry my wife said something to Roger that he didn't take very well at all, although I honestly can't remember exactly what. I remember being defensive about it at the time by saying, "Yeah, but at least you always know where you stand with her." Whatever it was, it seemed like such a small incident at the time, and everything seemed good for the next album. That was the last time I spoke to the band for a very long time.

I always looked at Ken and thought, "Wow, this is such a great experience doing this with him." In hindsight, over all the years, I still feel the same way.
Bob Siebenberg

By this time I was managed by Barry Krost Management, or BKM. Barry managed both recording artists and actors and had offices in both L.A. and London. I had met Barry and his brother Jackie in L.A. during the recording of *Crisis* when the label approached me about producing an act that happened to be managed by BKM. When I decided to finally move to L.A., I asked them to manage me, since they were British and had the same sensibilities as I had. This went well, and I was primarily looked after by Jackie.

After we had the meeting with the band, everything seemed ready to go, so I told Jackie the next day to go ahead and make the deal ... but nothing happened. Jackie reached out to the band's representatives, but didn't hear anything back from them. This went on for quite a while until it dawned on us, "I'm not going to be doing the next album!" No one actually said that to me, but so much time had gone by that it became obvious that something was going on, and it didn't include me.

The big question has always been, "Why?" and there are various stories. The first one I heard was about a year after they had finally made the album *Even in the Quietest Moments*. A friend that was very close to the band came over to the house one evening, and during our conversation I finally asked, "What exactly happened?" He said, "The way I heard it, the band was told that you had doubled everything you had asked for on the prior albums," meaning the advance and royalty points. I admit that we were asking more for an advance, but it wasn't outrageous (especially after two hit albums) and we knew that at the rate the band was selling they'd earn that money back very quickly. We didn't think that part was a problem, but the funny part was, the number of points we asked for hadn't changed. I was perfectly happy with the points I was getting, so where the story that we had doubled it came from, we had no idea.

Much later I heard a story that Roger wanted more of an American sound, but what doesn't make sense is that if he wanted that kind of a sound, why did they go with Pete Henderson as producer, who was English? There was also the possibility that the night of our drunken meeting/party that whatever my wife said to Roger scared him so much that it had some sway over the matter. There had been other occasions before where that occurred and I had been asked, "Your wife won't be there, will she?" In fact, with Elton, I was given explicit instructions not to bring her to the Château for the recording of *Don't Shoot Me*. She had a habit of pissing people off, and I, of course, was very defensive at the time. To this day I still don't know exactly what happened.

I was obviously very pissed off. I would have felt a lot better about the situation if they told me that they wanted to move on or if they, like Bowie, had radically changed their sound. Neither occurred. It didn't help when much later the *Paris* live album was mixed in the studio

I had been working in for the last two years (Chateau Recorders), which made me feel as if they were riding on my coattails. When *Paris* finally came out using sound effects recorded specifically for *Crime and Crisis*, I got in touch with my attorney. This led to a cash buyout which made me feel a little better, but ...

> *I remember all of us having thoughts about moving on. I know that Roger especially didn't like to work in the same location or with the same people at that time, Pete Henderson ending up being the exception. It seemed like the whole thing was shifting in another direction. It wasn't so English for one thing since we were now living in America and Ken represented* Crime *and* Crisis *and a real English vibe. Now we were in America and everybody's world had exploded a little bit. We knew more people and we had moved a couple of pegs up. There were more things being presented to us, I think.*

> *I remember one of the things about working with Ken is that it always seemed kind of laborious. It always took a long time to do things. Part of that was our fault as we were inexperienced and not the players that we became, but it took us a while to get things done and it was wearing on us. It's really not a reflection on Ken, but I think we were looking for a situation where things just happened quicker. I don't think that anyone could have been unhappy with what Ken had done for us. It wasn't a professional thing, it was just that we needed a change. Especially Roger was inserting this into the band because he wanted to go off and record someplace else.*
> Bob Siebenberg

> *My understanding of why he [Ken] did not do* Quietest Moments *was it was a financial decision. He asked for more points or more money or something, and we ultimately decided "no" and maybe it was time to try someone else. Personally, I know even though it's my favourite album today, at the time I was very disappointed with the way* Crisis? What Crisis? *came out and obviously elated by the way* Crime of the Century *came out and enjoyed working with him on that. But* Crisis? What Crisis? *was another animal altogether. So it just felt to me that it was time to try a different combination. Sometimes doing the same combination to try and capture the same magic doesn't work and that is what I felt with* Crisis? What Crisis?
> Roger Hodgson, Supertramp guitarist/keyboard player

CHAPTER 22

Los Angeles

Despite not doing the next Supertramp record, so many great opportunities came my way after I decided to permanently move to L.A. There was always something new, cutting edge, unusual, or just plain weird presenting itself, but hey, can you expect anything less from Hollywood? Not everything I did during this period came to pass or was a hit, but that doesn't mean the experiences weren't memorable.

DAVID BATTEAU

Whilst in L.A. doing *Crisis? What Crisis?* with 'Tramp, I was approached by A&M to work with a singer/songwriter named David Batteau. He was managed by Barry Krost along with his brother Jackie Krost, who also eventually became my managers. David had previously done an album on CBS with his brother Robin that I thought was just amazing, so I was very gung-ho to do a record with him.

We started off at A&M Studio D with the great Jeff Porcaro on drums and David Paich on keyboards (both of them would later go on to form the band Toto). On the first day of recording, Jeff set up his drums and they were dead as hell, almost like Ringo's drums. This was at a time when the "L.A. sound" was very dead, but in England, we'd already moved on from there. I said to him, "Jeff, you're going to have to take off all of that damping." He looked downheartedly at me and said, "You've got to be joking. I've spent ages getting it just right. Everyone loves it." "Yeah, ummm, sorry. It won't do," I politely replied.

Being the pro that he was, he pulled everything off and we went from there. I did my normal thing with the drums, and he just freaked after the first playback. He loved the sound we got so much that I was told that from then on he went into every studio going, "I'm not putting any damping on, and you're going to use U 87s and Kepexes on my drums," which of course was the gear I initially used. Jeff was the ultimate professional. I requested the damping off, so it was off. There was no argument. What a sweetheart of a guy, and no slouch as a drummer.

That [the David Batteau record] was a lot different from Supertramp because it was a single artist with studio musicians. The thing that was amazing on that session was that the band far outweighed the artist. It was basically Toto backing him up. They had a similar fascination about working with Ken because he had sort of an aura and a mystique about him.
Ed Thacker, second engineer at A&M

This was my first experience with L.A. session musicians, and I normally don't like to work with session musicians. Most often I would prefer to work with a simple club band because I like people to play to their limit, and hopefully extend their limit, as opposed to these guys who could come in and with no problems play anything that's put in front of them. I just think that when they're struggling to play something there's more feeling than when you get someone who's so good that he can play it straight off. But that's just me; I know a lot of my peers disagree. That said, I really enjoyed working with Porcaro and Paich.

It was also incredible to work with someone like percussionist Milt Holland. Something I didn't know at the time was that Milt had been a part of the legendary group of studio musicians known as the Wrecking Crew that played on virtually every hit, television show, movie, and commercial that came out of the city from the

'60s to the '80s. Milt lived a great life. He worked six months a year, took three months of vacation, then spent the other three months visiting some of the more remote places the world has to offer. It could mean living with Pygmies somewhere in the depths of the Amazon or a tent with Bedouins in the desert, where he'd learn all about their instruments and come back with new rhythms and techniques he could use on sessions. Jeff Porcaro used to make me laugh because he would always call him "Uncle Miltie."

Roger Birnbaum was David Batteau's A&R guy at A&M, and over Thanksgiving, a holiday I knew nothing of, he insisted that I come to a party with him. I had intended just to hang out in my hotel room (this was before I brought my family over and we rented our house) since we weren't working over the holiday, but Roger wasn't hearing it. He and his wife took me to a true Hollywood party. The guest of honour was The Fonz himself, Henry Winkler, of the hit television show of the moment *Happy Days*. The only problem was that I had never seen or heard of the show, so I had absolutely no idea who this Fonz/Winkler character was. He was sitting there holding court and telling all of these stories, and I just couldn't see why everyone seemed so enraptured by the guy. It was fascinating to watch everyone fawn over a TV star, especially when you don't know that he's a star. It sort of puts the whole celebrity thing into perspective.

The David Batteau album *Happy in Hollywood* never did anything, although one of the tracks, "Walk in Love," was eventually covered by Manhattan Transfer and turned out to be a big hit for them in Europe. David has gone on to do quite well for himself as writer, writing songs for Trisha Yearwood, Michael Sembello, and Shawn Colvin

We would mix 8 bars at a time, put them together and that was it. There was no such thing as "Let's do another pass and see how it turns out." The degree of detail could only happen by doing it this way given the technology we had. There was so much detail involved in just those 8 bars, that there's no way you could do it any other way. This was also new and different.
Ed Thacker

THE TUBES

Whilst I was in L.A. doing *Crisis*, one evening off we went to hear a band that A&M was really keen on us seeing. We weren't too enthused about going, but decided to do the politically correct thing and attend the show. It turned out to be nothing like I expected. The band was called The Tubes and they were astounding and hysterical, with the kind of show that I had never, ever seen before or since. I loved it. When I was approached to do their second album, I jumped at it.

One of the things about The Tubes was they really didn't have an identity in terms of their musical direction. With most acts you have to try to stay within their unique musical identity, but with The Tubes it was all over the place already. This gave us the opportunity to explore each track for what it was and take it to its limit. There was one track on *Young and Rich* that we did that was early Presley-style rock 'n' roll ("Proud to Be an American"), so we got in these old-time singers à la The Jordanaires to sing background parts. Then there was what ended up being the single, "Don't Touch Me There," which was very Phil Spectorish, and we took it so far as to get in Jack Nitzsche (who was Spector's arranger) to do the arrangement. Then there was a disco thing ("Slipped My Disco") which we pushed as far in that direction as we could. It was a fascinating thing for a change. We could take the music to any extreme that we wanted to.

WHATEVER IT TAKES

I learned more about drugs on that album, not from usage but as a spectator, than I every thought I needed, or wanted, to know. The drug deals were going on in the vocal overdub booth in Studio D as we were recording and I even began to know all the local dealers. I love it when people know their limits though, and especially how to get the most out of themselves.

He was very sober and calm, just the opposite of us. We were very frenetic and crazy all the time. We were fueled by various chemicals and really fried, but Ken put up with that. It was a delicate balance in those days.
Bill "Sputnik" Spooner, guitarist, singer, and songwriter of The Tubes

*That's where we all learned about drugs. The one thing about The
Tubes was that there was a whole entourage with the band; about
25 of them. We did a lot of all-nighters. They exposed us to the
white powder. There'd be a salad bowl full of the stuff sitting on the
console every night.*

Ed Thacker

We needed to do a vocal on "Pimp" and Bill Spooner, who was one
of the guitarists and the vocalist on this particular song, and I were
talking about it up front. He said, "The verses need to be raspy and
the choruses need to be smooth, and I know exactly how to do that,
but you're going to have to take control." "What are you going to
do?" I asked cautiously, not knowing what to expect. "Don't worry.
Just give me a couple of minutes while I get it together," he said.

Bill came back into the studio about 5 minutes later with a fifth of
Jack Daniels. "OK, let's start going for the smooth parts," and he
downed some of the Jack and started to sing. By the time we got
all of the choruses done he had just about finished the bottle. "OK,
we got those. Now let's get the verses, which need to be rough," he
announced. "Do you know how you're going to do that?" I asked.
"Oh, yeah," he replied. "All right then. Go ahead."

He then took out a bag of cocaine and laid out a bunch of lines, and
took a big sniff. "Alright. We're going for the first verse." We got to
the next verse, and he did a couple more lines, and began to sing. By
the time we finished he could hardly stand, but he got exactly what
was needed for the song. The vocal was amazing. I don't totally agree
with the methods he used, but it worked perfectly. The interesting
thing was that sitting beside me getting just as high as Spooner was
Boz Scaggs. David Paich was also coming by a lot to hang out, since
they were all partying together.

*When you listen to the song "Young and Rich," you can hear
Spooner singing his vocal at about 6 A.M. He had a music stand laid
out flat in front of him with a pile of blow on it. He could hardly get
it in his nose, it was so clogged up by then. You could hear his nose
whistling during the vocal. It was perfect for that song.*

Ed Thacker

The label executives were coming to hear the album after we'd been recording for about a month, so we had to stay up for almost three days straight to get it finished enough for it to be presentable. The morning of the day they were coming, Ken said, "Let's clean this place up so it looks nice." I said, "No, let's go across the street to the trash bin from the bar and get like hundreds of empty booze bottles and spread them all over the place." Ken said, "Are you sure?" and of course I was. It turned out to be a very bad idea. We did a lot of drinking but nothing like what it seemed. Everywhere you tried to sit was a bunch of bottles. At that point the execs pretty much made their mind up that we were crazy and at that point they were probably right, but Ken went along with it. You have to give him points for his tolerance to stupidity.

Bill Spooner

The song "Don't Touch Me There" is a boy-girl call-and-answer duet. When the band played live they had a huge troupe of people around them. One of them, Kenny Ortega, has gone on to great fame as a choreographer and movie director (he directed Michael Jackson's *This Is It*), and was the band's choreographer at the time. They had girl dancers, jugglers, acrobats, actors, and lots of people around that were part of their show, but for whatever reason, the band decided that the lead dancer, Re Styles, would do the girl lead vocal. The problem was that she'd never sung before, and she was really nervous. It was so hard to get a vocal performance out of her that we had to try virtually every trick in the book. We eventually did it, but the ad libs at the end we had to do wild without the track, then we had to pick the ones that worked and fly them in at the appropriate places. Once again, you do what you have to do.

We'd play some of the songs 30, 40, or 50 times and really think we finally nailed it. Ken would say, "Well, it wasn't perfect," which was the top praise that you could get out of him.

Bill Spooner

One of the things besides the layering is the reverbs. First of all, Ken would turn all the reverbs as long as they would go, so on all those old EMT plates, the decay is on 9. That was for everything. For "Don't Touch Me There," everything got one straight plate and one tape-delayed plate to thicken the sound without it being too in

your face. The other thing is that people just used either a 15- or
30-ips slap, but not Ken. The tape delay was VSOed to time it to
the track. That was another really different thing. Tape flanging was
also something we hadn't done over here. Ken showed me how they
got that sound on "While My Guitar Gently Weeps." All of those
organic tape-based things that they had to invent in the early days
was much more of a European thing, at least early on.

Ed Thacker

A BIT OVER BUDGET

As we were coming towards the end of the album, one day Jerry
Moss came up to me and said, "Ken, we're going way over budget.
You've got to do something about this." I was keeping track of the
studio time, so I said to him, "Jerry, I don't think we're even close."
"You want to come and have a look?" he asked/commanded. When
I looked at the ledger I was shocked. It turned out that the band's
managers had been putting in for union session fees for each of the
band members the entire time we were in the studio. The normal
union way is that each player gets paid for one session per title,
and one person would get double for being the leader, which was
arranged to rotate among the players. Here they were filing session
fees for every day they were in the studio. No wonder we were going
over budget. I had no idea because no one ever told me.

One of the things the band didn't spend much on was artwork, since
both synthesist Michael Cotten and drummer Prairie Prince were
incredible artists. While we were mixing, they were on the A&M
soundstage silk-screening the T-shirts that were used on the backside
of the album. Their artwork is amazing, and Michael has gone on
to be a top production designer for everything from the Super Bowl
to the Olympics. (Prairie has since been an in-demand session and
touring drummer when he's not with the band.) They also painted
a beautiful mural on the wall of the A&M lot. I wonder if Jerry got
them to do it for free because they were over budget.

THE LINER NOTES

As we were coming towards the end of recording, the band came
to me and asked, "We'd like you to do some liner notes about the

recording process." "Oh, you gotta be kidding. I can't do that kind of thing," I said, trying to dismiss it. "No, we really want you to," they replied. I put it off for as long as I could, but they finally demanded, "You've got to do it."

Finally, one evening, I sat down and wrote some liner notes that were 100% true. Then I read it and came to the conclusion that it was the most boring heap of shit I'd ever seen and tossed it away. Then I started to think about what The Tubes were all about, and I thought maybe I could do something that might be quite amusing to the people who catch on to it. After all, that's the essence of the band, right? So I began to write another set of liner notes of which about a third is completely true, one third you could try but you'd blow up some mics, and the last third complete make-believe.

As an example, at the close of the band's stage act, they'd bring on this English glam-rocker called Quay Lewd, who's really singer Fee Waybill dressed up with a big wig and these giant, almost two-foot high platform shoes. He comes out for the finale during which he is "killed" by all of these amplifiers on stage falling on top of him. The amps of course are all fake. If anyone cared to look carefully they'd see that the name on the plummeting amps is "Kill" amplifiers, in a Fender logo kind of script. I put in these liner notes that some of the sounds are the result of these Kincade Instrument Low Level amplifiers, or "Kill" amplifiers. I made up more and more stuff, and when I showed it to the band, they loved it.

I also put in something that I stole from engineer/producer Glyn Johns. He had done some things on a Stones video where he had put STC 4038 ribbon mics right up against the bass drum head. This mic is very fragile because the ribbon inside can get destroyed from a sudden air blast, especially something as severe as what comes from a bass drum. Glyn had placed the mic there obviously as a joke, or maybe to throw people off what his technique really was, I don't know. Either way, I thought that was something that I should borrow for the liner notes.

A lot of people took those notes very seriously, and, from what I heard, Standard Telephones and Cable, the maker of the STC 4038 (today it's made by Coles), reported that they had more returns for blown ribbons than they'd ever had in their history. They obviously didn't see the funny side to what I wrote, and neither did the people who used the mics in that way.

After the album came out, I later heard from A&M that they were getting calls from people asking where they could find Kincade amps and mics that I had made up. Sometimes people will believe anything that's written down.

Young and Rich Liner Notes
Technical Notes
From Producer Ken Scott

When recording the album *Young and Rich*, one of the primary concerns was for complete separation between instruments, allowing absolute control over everything when mixing. The first step to achieving this was to lay down only the bass and drums as the basic track. The bass was always taken direct and the sound was always obtained from the guitar as opposed to using excessive equalization on the desk. The mixing of the drums consisted of eight Vanguard PK20s on toms, a Neumann KM 84 on snare, two STC 4038s specially suspended inside the bass drums, and three RCA 44s for cymbals. Due to the extremely flat response of the PK20s, no equalization was needed on the toms. To obtain the snare sound, two Pultec Equalizers were used to boost the low and high mid-range, and an Albatronics Parametric Equalizer for the extreme high frequencies.

Having laid down the basics, we then overdubbed guitars. The electric guitars went through The Tubes' specially built Kincade Instruments Low Level amplifiers, a very versatile amplifier being capable of giving both ultra-clean and also very heavily distorted guitar sounds with none of the problems found with most other amps. These were mixed using a Neumann U 87 on the front, an STC 4038 on the back, and usually a PK20 as far away as possible. The acoustic guitars were recorded via a Vanguard SK 150 contact mic attached to the back of the guitar. The only equalization required was through the Albatronics slightly boosting at approximately 350 Hertz on a very narrow bandwidth and 14 kHz on a very wide bandwidth.

The keyboards were then recorded whenever possible direct. The acoustic piano was always mixed using a U 87 for the bass end, an RCA 44 for the top end, and an SK 150 attached to the sounding board, giving an additional ambience. The limiting was via two Teletronics LA3As linked for stereo or via two Albatronics SN 750 Compressors for heavy compression.

Due to the difference in characteristics of each singer's voice, different techniques had to be used. For Fee Waybill, a combination of one PK 20 and an AKG lavalier mic was always used. As Roger Steen's movements are somewhat unpredictable, it was decided to use a handheld KM 54 covered in sponges to prevent rumble. And for Bill Spooner, an RCA 44 was found to be the most consistent. An SN 750 was used for all vocals.

While The Tubes were never huge in the U.S., they were very influential in Europe and I got several jobs because I worked with them. I was asked to do their next album, but they wanted to do it up in San Francisco where they were based. I did consider it, and even went up and looked at San Francisco's Record Plant. I was shown this one studio where the wall covering had this most unusual paisley pattern. The guy showing me around said, "Yeah, we did that because Stevie Wonder likes it." I think he must have confused the esteemed Mr. Wonder with someone else. In the end, I really didn't want to spend the time in San Francisco away from family, so I didn't do their next record.

> One time a short Mexican-looking guy and a couple of Japanese guys walked into the back door of the tracking room. I hit the talkback button and yelled, "What the fuck are you doing? Get the hell out of there." It turned out it was Herb Alpert and two Japanese affiliates. Ken immediately pointed out to me that yelling at them was probably not a good idea.
> Bill Spooner

A&M didn't know how to market The Tubes and ended up letting them go, and they immediately signed with Capitol. I've always believed that my job as producer was to put across the act as best as possible in the way the band wants to be thought of. I don't give a shit what the record company wants; I'm there for the band. When The Tubes signed with Capitol they went with the complete opposite of that, producer David Foster, who didn't even use the band for several of the tracks except for the vocals. They had their biggest success ever but it resulted in the breakup of the band. Was having a hit worth it? Capitol thought so but I'm not sure.

The Tubes were, in their own unique way, exceedingly professional, as strange as it may seem. It's that typical thing where you see their stage persona and you think they've got to be lunatics, but you get them in the studio and they're perfectly straight. Well, that's not actually true. They were professional though. They were very good at everything they did. All I know is that album was a lot of fun to do and I enjoyed it immensely.

The record actually sold quite well, but I'm waiting to see my first dime. I get royalty statements all the time, but we still haven't recouped the recording costs after all these years, thanks to those damn session fees. We're getting close though, and I can't wait for that day because suddenly my royalty reverts back to record one, which would be a nice little windfall.

CAT STEVENS

Among the other artists that Barry Krost managed was Cat Stevens, so it was very easy and convenient for him to put two of his clients together for a project. It was late 1976 or early '77 and I was looking for my next project. After I agreed to do the album, Steve (none of his friends knew him as "Cat") and I travelled around the world looking for the right studio. We went to New York, Vermont, Rome, England, and finally we wound up in Holland. How we came up with these places I have no bloody idea, but we got a list together of studios to check out. It was one of those things where I needed to find the technically agreeable studio for me, and Steve needed the right vibe. He needed to feel well beyond what we'd normally term "comfortable," so if he tripped over a matchstick on the way in, the studio was eliminated.

We got on like a house on fire. In New York we went to see the Mel Brooks movie *Blazing Saddles* together. In Rome we went to see the Sistine Chapel. I almost wanted to give up everything at that point. "How could I ever do anything to compete with that?" That lasted for a couple of hours.

On leaving Rome to fly to Amsterdam, we made the mistake of flying that poor excuse for an airline Alitalia. We were given our boarding passes and took our seats on the plane when suddenly these two very official-looking gentlemen came up to us and asked to see our boarding passes. We handed them over and they proceeded to put them in their back pocket and said, "We're sorry, but you're going to have to get off. This flight is overbooked." They made us get off, even though we were in our seats waiting to take off. We had to wait for the next flight. Having heard Elton rant about Alitalia many years before, I now had my own taste of their "service." As you can imagine, I haven't been found on the airline since.

Eventually we found a studio in Amsterdam that we both liked, and after some preproduction, we finally made it into the studio to start the album with his normal band of drums, bass, acoustic guitar, and keyboards. Unfortunately, there was something wrong with the tape machine. Now, it doesn't happen very often, but the one problem for me wearing the hats of both the engineer and the producer is that every now and again when there's a fault in the control room, you have to become just the engineer and forget the producer role, and that's exactly what happened here. I had to remain in the control room to deal with fault, since I had to explain it to the maintenance guy, and being in a foreign country, the language barrier made it that much more difficult. Even though they speak some English, once you start to get into technicalities, it can get a little shaky since it's not your everyday English that we're speaking.

As a result, I had to stay in the control room to make sure that everything was being taken care of technically. The problem was that Steve liked to be, shall we say, babied. He wanted me in the studio taking care of him, and I couldn't at the time, so he started to lose his temper, which made me lose my temper, and we ended up screaming at each other. Before you knew it, the whole album was called off. I didn't work with him ever again.

It was funny because just travelling around, we got on so well, but I should have seen that we were obviously looking for totally different things in the studio; he to be pampered, whilst I needed everything to be up to my high technical standards.

DEVO

It is now 1979 and I have started to use a studio in North Hollywood named Chateau Recorders. The second engineer at Chateau Recorders, a guy called Chris Gregg, was from the Midwest and was always raving about this band from Ohio who thought that the whole world was falling apart and believed in something called "de-evolution." As a result, they called their band Devo. He brought in some of their garage tapes and I must say, I did not get it at all. "That sounds atrocious," I remember telling him after a quick listen. A short time after that, their first album came out and they happened to be appearing on Saturday Night Live on an evening when I was off. I thought, "OK, this is the band that Chris was telling me about. Let me check them out." When I saw them, I suddenly got it. I loved them.

A while later I received a phone call from Devo's management company about meeting with me and talking about doing their next album. My understanding is that they liked what I'd done with Bowie, and that's what brought us together. My wife and I flew up to San Francisco to see the band perform, then had breakfast with them the next morning to talk to them about doing the album. Patience had never been to a first meeting with a band, so she wasn't familiar with the bit of territorialism, so the speak, that pervades the proceedings. Everyone there will try to see who's in control of the situation, and no one is quite sure how it's going to work at that first meeting. During the give and take that naturally goes on, my wife decided to get very protective of me for some reason, which I appreciated but certainly didn't need.

When we got back to Los Angeles, I got a call from the band's manager, who said, "Ken, they want to work with you, but they wanted to check one thing first." "Sure. What's that?" I replied. "They want to make sure that your wife doesn't come to sessions. Does she?" "No, don't worry. They won't see her again," I told them.

Let's see. That's Elton she wasn't allowed around, she managed to piss off Supertramp, and ... Right.

RECORDING DEVO

In the studio Devo was totally professional but a little stand-offish. There was none of the insanity of their stage performance. It was exactly like The Tubes. You're in the studio to do a job and you're on stage to do a job, and it's not necessarily the same one, so those stage characters they have aren't needed to make music in the studio. The only time that mindset changed was when one of the owners of Chateau came to me during a session and asked if he could show someone around who wanted to book some studio time. I asked the guys first and they were OK with it. As soon as the owner and the prospective client entered, singer Mark Mothersbaugh went nuts, reverting back to his stage character, running around screaming and generally acting very strangely. The person who was looking around left very quickly looking a little scared, and then it was, "OK guys. Back to work," and they were perfectly normal again.

Duty Now for the Future took about three or four weeks to record because they didn't mind trying a lot of different things. There's a solo on "Secret Agent Man" where they were looking for a *little* guitar sound. We couldn't get the sound through any of the amps in the studio, or even going directly into the board and overloading the input. On a solid-state board that never worked anyway. The one time I know that it worked was on the REDD desk at Abbey Road on The Beatles' "Revolution."

Finally someone in the band came up with the idea of taping a pair of headphones to a mic to get the exact sound they were looking for: distorted, but small. We might've been able to get the same thing from something like a small Pignose amp, thinking back on it, but we didn't have one at the time.

I think we used three different drum kits on the album because we were after different drum sounds. We set up one kit, got the sounds for the songs on that, tore that down, and put another one up. The thing with me is, because I'm such a creature of habit, I hardly had to change anything from kit to kit. I even used basically the same EQ, which I had to change very, very little for each kit. And as I always use the same frequencies it wasn't quite as much of a headache as one might have expected. I'm a firm believer that the sound comes from the studio, not from what I do.

In a departure, the band was there a lot for the mixes because they had a very strong handle on who they were and were very conscious of what they wanted to put across. At that point they didn't want to be commercial in any way, shape, or form. There were a couple songs that I would have loved to have recorded, but they felt were too commercial. Of course, the next album they did "Working in a Coal Mine," so go figure.

I have to give it to them; Devo were students though. Whereas a lot of artists get comfortable with a producer and like to keep going back to that same comfort zone, for these guys, each project was very much a learning experience. They wanted a different team every time so they could learn from them. Brian Eno produced their first album, then me, then Bob Margouleff (who had produced Stevie Wonder and Santana), then Roy Thomas Baker, yes Roy from Trident, but now a little cooler with the addition of his middle name. They liked to change and not get too comfortable.

KANSAS

I had been approached to work with the band Kansas several times very early on before they had their success, but what they did just didn't hit me for some reason. I know that if I don't get that feeling in my gut about a band, then it's not right for me, at least at the time. Eventually that feeling turned around though. I had just finished the first Missing Persons album (much more on them soon) and there was a lull before the second one, so I had a bit of time. The band approached me again, so I thought, "Yeah, why not. Let me give it a try."

Of course Murphy and his damn law got involved, and about two weeks before we went into the studio, lead singer Steve Walsh decided to quit the band. It was too late to stop the upcoming sessions, so we went ahead into the studio to record since we already had most of the material ready. The problem was, we didn't know who was going to sing it. We just recorded it in hopes that we would eventually not only find a singer, but one who sang in the right key too.

Picture this scenario. While we were recording tracks for the album, we were auditioning singers at the same time. Recording is already a very intense process, and so is auditioning players, but put the two together and it borders on crazy. The interesting thing is that we actually had some fairly successful people try out for the band. We had an ex-Eagle and someone who had played the role of Jesus in the popular *Jesus Christ Superstar* musical, but we finished up with the relatively unknown John Elefante, who fitted in perfectly since everything was in the right key for him. He also had some of his own material that we could record, and his spiritual leanings were completely in sync with most of the band.

THE CHRISTIAN SIDE OF THINGS

We did have a number of interesting things happen during the recording. One day Kerry Livgren, the guitarist and writer and recent born-again Christian, came in with a videotape of a Christian broadcast talking about backwards masking on songs. One of the things that they were talking about was a Pink Floyd song that at some point made reference to Syd Barrett as "the silly bugger." The Christians on this program were hitting on the dictionary meaning of "bugger," but in England "bugger" is slang for a silly person. It doesn't mean much and certainly isn't meant in the literal sense of a sexual deviant. In my mind, they had gotten it completely wrong.

Another thing was the Led Zeppelin track "Stairway to Heaven," which supposedly had a lot of backwards satanic sayings in it. That one fascinated me and, ever trying to keep an open mind, the next day I bought a copy of the record (music was still on vinyl records back then), and transferred it to tape. After we finished the session at about 1 o'clock in the morning, I said to Kerry, "OK, now let's listen to it properly." We turned the tape backwards and started to go through it, and I have to admit that I began to hear the same things too. We were there until about 5 o'clock in the morning going through this and I was absolutely blown away by what I heard. I was hearing all the same things that the people on the program heard and I was hearing them loud and clear. I know that it's just one of those freaky things and there was no way it could have been planned, but Kerry, being the born-again Christian that he is, just said, "But of course it is." We only did this in-depth analysis the one night, then

I veered away from the whole subject, lest we get carried away in a direction that wasn't conducive to making the record.

IT PAYS TO HAVE A LAWYER

Another topic of conversation that came up during my time with Kansas is something that maybe should be talked about as a warning to new acts reading this book. Musicians signing record deals these days have a lot more knowledge about the business than they used to, but this story is still worth bringing up, just in case. Kerry and I were talking one day and he was telling me about when they signed their recording contract. It came up in the conversation that they had signed away their publishing, then he told me the story about how it actually happened.

It seems that the band was playing at a small club in Georgia somewhere and the contract from Kirshner Records was delivered there for them to sign. As all bands who are signing their first record deal do, they wanted to immediately get their John Hancocks on there, lest it disappear and they be relegated to playing clubs forever. Every place that had a "Sign Here" clip, they signed. Finally they came to a bit at the back of the agreement that they hadn't seen before that had all these clips on it, and they thought, "Oh, I guess we have to sign these as well," and they all signed it and immediately sent everything back the next day. It turns out that the little bit at the end that they hadn't seen before was all about their publishing.

I said to Kerry, "Did you go over it with an attorney?" "Of course not. We were in a club," came his reply. "In which case, the contract is illegal," I told him. "What do you mean?" he asked. "You'll find in modern-day contracts there's a clause that states that if you haven't gone through it with an attorney, the contract means nothing."

"Yeah, come on. You've got to be joking," he replied. "I'm deadly serious," I said. "Well, you're wrong. If that had been the case we would've been told about that ages ago," he adamantly replied. "I can only tell you what I know," I told him, not willing to argue. He stuck to his guns, "I'm sorry, but you're wrong." "Fine," I said,

ABBEY ROAD TO ZIGGY STARDUST

"but do me one favour. Next time you see your attorney, ask him about it." The subject was then dropped and we went back to work.

It turns out that a couple of days later the band had a big meeting with their attorney on some other business. When they returned to the studio, Kerry immediately came up to me and said, "I owe you an apology. I asked our attorney, and he said that you were absolutely correct. We could have gotten all of our publishing back."

"Could" was the operative word here. It turns out that when the band became successful, they renegotiated their record deal using their attorney. As they didn't know about the law, they didn't tell the lawyer about how they came to sign the original contract, so he never acted on it. Since the attorney was now involved, they couldn't go back on something from the previous contract. They wound up losing millions of dollars as a result.

This is one of the things that happens when people get into the business and have absolutely no idea what it's all about. There are all of these legal loopholes that not many people know about, and they end up losing a lot of money because of it. On the other hand, there are those people that make money from those same loopholes as well.

THE SINGLE

After finishing the record that became *Vinyl Confessions*, we knew we had a problem: we didn't have a single. I will curse their manager Budd Carr forever because he put an ad in some music magazine looking for songs, and then sent all of the submissions over to me to listen to. Take the worst examples of the first two episodes of *American Idol* every year and that's what we received. It was nothing but people who thought they were outstanding singers and songwriters, but were the biggest heap of crap ever, and I had to wade through it all. Finally, we came up with a song from an established songwriting team, but we had to change the lyrics slightly so they worked with the Christian orientation of the band. "Play the Game Tonight" ended up doing quite well, but unless it hits number 1, one always wants it to do better.

I must at this point be totally honest. By the time of doing this record I was firmly ensconced in managing Missing Persons and so even though it was a relatively calm period with the album completed and the band not touring, I still had to deal with various business matters, so there were times when my mind wouldn't be 100% present on the Kansas sessions. Nevertheless, after the album was out for a while, the band asked me if I'd do their next album, but with one stipulation: I could have nothing to do with Missing Persons the entire time we were recording. I told them I couldn't commit to that, so I never worked with them again as a result. Of course, as it turned out, by the time we would have been recording I was no longer working with Missing Persons either.

CHAPTER 23

All That Jazz Again

Even after I moved to Los Angeles, my dealings with the worlds of jazz and fusion continued, much to my surprise. It was great to be working with what were now old friends, and still better reconnecting with even much older friends.

SCHOOL DAYS

Stanley Clarke's *School Days* was once again mostly tracked at what seemed to have become yet another home away from home: New York studio Electric Lady. As with all of Stan's albums, it featured a revolving cast of musicians, including one Gerry Brown on drums.

While most drummers I worked with were more than willing to work with me on the sound of their drums, Gerry, who played on "School Days" and "The Dancer," just hated the time it took. Although he wasn't particularly what you'd call a pure straight-ahead jazz drummer, he did come with that kind of purist mentality that went "just set up and play." I was taking my time doing what I do, and the longer it took, the more he got upset with me. What we got was really good, but Gerry did not like the process involved one little bit, and was the complete opposite of Tony Williams, the consummate jazz drummer, who gladly went along with everything

I proposed. In fact, Gerry was the only jazz drummer that I ever had anything that even resembled a problem with. All it takes is just one musician in the studio to get edgy about things and before you know it, it spreads to everyone else, so any musician out of sorts with what I'm doing is a concern. Hey, I was there doing my thing because Stan already knew what I was going after and capable of, so he was always there to calm down anyone who began to get a little anxious about things. Stan and I had been together for a couple of albums by this time, and he knew what it was going to be like. Different strokes for different folks, I guess.

BILL AND STAN

Having worked with Stan on a couple of albums and with Bill Cobham on four by that time, the one thing I really wanted was for them to play together. I just knew it would be an astounding combination. Finally it happened one day at A&M Studio D and I couldn't wait to hear what they would come up with. Oh, what a let down. I was crestfallen when they began to play and a major problem appeared: they were both trying to outshine each other and so were completely overplaying. It was a musical tug-of-war amongst giants, one trying to outdo the other with every lick. Finally, I called them into the control room and casually said, "Guys, you don't have to show off. You're both great. Just cool it a little." "OK, Ken. Right. We know. We'll cool it down a little," they both agreed.

So of course on the next take they both did exactly the same thing anyway. "Guys, please. Ease up a little." "OK, Ken," came the reply. Finally they eventually sorted everything out, but it took ages to get them both to settle down and realise that they didn't have to compete with each other. When we got the take it was amazing, just as I had hoped.

I remember that long piece that took us forever. Billy was playing everything he could and I was playing everything I could. When I went in to listen to a playback you [Ken] had a funny look on your face. I had worked enough with you to know that something was wrong. You just said, "I think we have to do that one again." After that we both calmed down after we ran out of stuff to play.

We were both trying to outplay each other. I was trying to murder him. Now when we play together we have to try to get each other to play more [laughs].

Stanley Clarke

AND A FEW OTHER THINGS

I didn't find out about this until years later, and it's probably a good thing. After we'd finished each day's session at A&M in Studio D, Billy would then go into one of the other studios in the building to work on an album with producer Quincy Jones. Quincy was the hottest producer in the world after his success with Michael Jackson so I don't begrudge Bill for wanting to do the sessions, but he was literally working around the clock. I had no idea about it until way after the fact, but I would have been really pissed off had I known. Bill kept it together on our session though, which was amazing. Even Stan did a late-night session with Q, and I was never the wiser.

We finished up running two multitrack tape machines in sync on a couple of songs because Stan wanted to overdub brass and strings and we ran out of tracks on the first 24-track. I edited a couple of takes together on "Life Is Just a Game" to make one good one, which caused a problem when it came to mix. There was a dropout of the time code used to sync up the two machines at the point of the edit, which caused the slave machine to lose its lock for a bit. It just so happened that there was enough time code left for the synchroniser to figure it out before the strings came in again, but we were panicking the entire time. The tape would hit the edit and we'd hear, "Eww, hrrrr, whooorrr, esss," and then it would go back to normal. Sometimes it would still be going like that when the strings came in, which ruined the mix, but we lucked out in that it was OK when it really counted.

It was the first time that we used a BTX synchronizer to link two 24-tracks together. It kind of worked, but it was a bitch. You had to get both machines spinning and hope that one would catch up. I just remember a lot of techs hanging out for those sessions. It was a little tougher to do 8-bar mixes at a time on that one.

Ed Thacker

WE MIX IN QUAD

The predecessor to the current 5.1 surround sound that we enjoy today was a format called "quadraphonic sound," which utilised another set of stereo speakers behind you in addition to the pair in front. This meant that the record had four channels instead of the normal two. As these things historically have gone, there were two competing methods of encoding the quad signal onto a vinyl record, and this led to its downfall, since consumers didn't know which one to choose. As a result, they didn't choose either. Well, that and the quality of most quad mixes.

As an example, A&M approached me to do a quad mix of *Crime*, and I immediately said, "That would be great. I'd love to do it." When they asked how long it would take, I told them, "Probably about the same time it took to mix the original—about two weeks." With typical record label logic, they came back with, "We've got a guy here that will do it in two afternoons!" I said, "I can't compete with that, so I don't want to do it." I don't think they ever did mix the album in quad, but that was basically the attitude of record labels at the time. The idea was, "Let's throw some stuff out there as cheaply as possible so we can make our quarterly bonus," a line of thinking that has never gone away and has helped put the major labels into the sorry situation they're in today.

Since quad was getting a lot of press at the time and was being pushed very hard by the consumer electronics powers that be, I had a talk with Stan and we approached Atlantic with a proposition. "Let us record this album specifically for quad," we suggested. "That would be great. No one has done that yet. Incredible idea. Yes, absolutely," came the reply. As a result, the entire recording was done with quad in mind. As an example, on the song with Stan and Bill, since Bill had a huge drum kit with a lot of toms, it was very easy to pan them all around the four speakers. Whenever he did one of his massive fills it went all the way around your head and sounded amazing. That was the kind of thing that we were thinking about all through the recording process.

When it came time to mix the record, we didn't even bother with a stereo mix. "It's going to come out in quad, why go to the extra trouble?" we both thought. The mix turned out just great and everyone was happy with what they heard, so we headed off to see mastering engineer Bernie Grundman, who at that time still worked for A&M and had his mastering studio on the lot. We were just about to start when I received a call from an executive at Atlantic. "Ken, we've been talking and we think we'd prefer to go with the stereo first. We'll come out with the quad version later," he said. "You gotta be fucking joking. We've only done it in quad," I hotly told him. "I'm sure you'll figure out something," he confidently, but sternly, replied.

We took the quad mix and blended it together in such a way as to make it into the normal everyday stereo that everyone is so used to, and that's the version you still hear today. The quad mix never did come out, which is such a shame because it's so easy for them to do, since it's all mixed and ready to go. With the surround sound capabilities that we have today on various delivery formats, Atlantic has a ready-to-go product on their hands that they're not even aware of, unfortunately, thanks to all the changes in personnel in the company over the years.

A&M was a quad room so we mixed it in quad. It's amazing that we'd even do that at the time. Cobham had about 15 toms and Ken had them panned all around, so all the fills would go around your head. No one ever got to hear that but me. It turned out amazing and the stereo even sounds great considering that it was just the front and back tracks blended together.

Ed Thacker

I always tell people about the song "School Days," which is pretty much a bass anthem right now. After we finished doing it, the second said to me, "Now that's a bass solo!" I went over to Ken and said, "What did you do, man?" He said, "I just turned it up. Let's move on now."

Stanley Clarke

JEFF BECK

My relationship with Jeff Beck had been rekindled, since he had played on a track on each of Stanley Clarke's albums, but we never worked with one another outside of that. That was to change soon enough though, because in the midst of recording an album with Jan Hammer producing, they had a huge falling out. The story I heard was that they were doing a live show together and Jan had recently got a keyboard that you could strap around your neck like a guitar. At one point during the show, he decided to do a Chuck Berry-like duck walk across the stage whilst Jeff was playing a solo. Jeff took offense to this and one thing led to another and Jan was out as producer. As a result, I got the phone call to come help finish the album that would become *There and Back* in Jan's stead.

Before we began, I took a leisurely drive down to Jeff's place in the English countryside for a discussion about the album. What fascinated me was that we went down to the local pub for a bite (where else?) and not only did no one take a blind bit of notice of Jeff, but a short time later Roger Daltrey walked in. It was his local too, and once again no one batted an eyelid. Try that in Los Angeles, why don't you. Anyway, it was decided that I would finish the album and there we were back at Abbey Road, once again in Number 2, both recording new material and doctoring some of the earlier recordings. Eventually we ran out of time, so we finished it with a single session in Number 1, then mixed it at Chateau in North Hollywood.

The thing I remember the most about that album was working with drummer Simon Phillips. I hadn't worked with Simon before, but I was very impressed with him right from the start even before he ever picked up a stick. His drums turned up before he did, so I went down to suspend the mic in the bass drum as I'd done with Tony Williams, only to find that it had already been done. He had checked up on how I recorded drums and had this apparatus premade so that we would both be ready to roll with the least amount of effort. What a guy! What a player!

I strive to get a feeling of depth, dimensionally not sonically, out of everything I record, and on most songs I hate it when everything seems right in your face. For me, there has to be some distinction between every part, so the bigger one thing is, the smaller everything else will have to sound. To illustrate this point, when we did the session in Number 1, which is the large orchestral studio, it just so happened that that Si was all alone in the studio for the recording. I decided to take advantage of the situation and take it to an extreme and set up a set of *very* distant microphones. The resulting drum sound was absolutely amazing. It was *huge*. As we overdubbed the other instruments it became very apparent that if this was Simon's record, I could maybe use about half the level of the distant mics. Since it wasn't, in the finished recording there is almost none of those wonderful distant mics. They just overpowered everything else. Unfortunately every time an additional part was recorded on top of his track I had to pull the distant mics back to enable the new part to be heard, and so finally the drum track finished up sounding about the same size as every other drum track on the album. Each time you add something, you have to lose something somewhere, and in this case it was all with the drum sound.

A NEW JEFF

By this time, I had been with Jeff through various stages of his career, and each one reflected a different state of his mind. On the first album (*Truth*), he was just a normal nice guy, but during my one and only session for the next album his ego was out the door and he was very much the arsehole. Then while working with Jeff on Stan's albums, he was back to being just a regular guy again. On *There and Back* he was completely different, and at the bottom of the cycle, if you like. He actually didn't feel he was good enough to play with the players he was playing with, and that made it really hard to pull things out of him. He genuinely didn't think he was capable of it. Fascinating, here was one of the greatest guitarists in the world and he didn't think he was good enough to be there.

I've been asked over and over again how I miked Jeff to get his sound, but all I can say is that it was exactly the same as I mic every other guitar player: a U 67 or U 87 a foot or two away from the speaker cabinet. I'm a creature of habit, and the way I always do it works. What more can I say? I did tend to ride the levels both on recording and mixing, and I would also have used some limiting/compression, probably an LA-3A, but that's just a guess.

The next question always is, "What kind of gear did he use?" Sorry, I never remember gear and there's nothing about his setup that even remotely sticks in my memory. For me it was work, work, work all the time in those days (or more aptly put, pleasure, pleasure, pleasure), and those details just seem to blur together. The only thing I can say for sure is that Jeff didn't play excessively loud in the studio, and was nowhere near the level of say, John McLaughlin, who always had a 100-watt Marshall stack cranked way up. With Jeff it was more of a combo amp vibe, if I remember correctly.

Being back at Abbey Road was amazing, and always is. I still wasn't enamoured with England at that point, but being back at the studio where I started was great and there were a lot of people I knew from when I worked there. Some of those people are still there some 40 years later. Astounding.

The most unusual aspect of *There and Back* was that very little was cut live; it was pretty much all overdubbed. Quite often Jeff didn't even play on the basics, and that was left to only the drums, bass, and keyboards, although there were times when we overdubbed the bass too.

Mixing *There and Back* went fairly quickly because there were already a few songs mixed with Jan, so I didn't have to mix the entire album. We did do one last-minute guitar part on "The Pump" back at Chateau in North Hollywood just before we mixed though. Nothing like waiting until the very last minute to get something.

A little after we completed the album I received one of those phone calls that you immediately think is someone pulling your leg. It was someone from the label saying they wanted to put one of the tracks out as a single, but they wanted it to have some vocals on it. Seriously? Now it just so happened that by this time I had already started working with Missing Persons, and since they needed some money in the early stages of the band, I asked them to come into the studio to sing "la, la, la" on the melody of a few sections. They sang on it and got a session fee, I mixed it, and sent it to the label. I have to admit that I don't know if it ever came out, but somehow I doubt it.

CHAPTER 24
The Unspecified Genre

By this time I had a great track record in the jazz-fusion genre, but I soon got involved with a couple of instrumental bands that didn't really fit that genre. One of the bands didn't truly fit any genre. They weren't jazz, they weren't rock, and they certainly weren't fusion, but they did play all of those styles along with some country and some funk, sometimes all in the same number. Nah, that's a little bit of an exaggeration, but they did manage to encompass all of those styles. And the other band might certainly be called progressive rock, or "prog-rock," as their influences were Yes and Gentle Giant but they certainly had their own personality, not clones of their idols. Regardless of where you put them, both bands were great. Although they never sold a lot, their music, in my humble opinion, still holds up very well today.

HAPPY THE MAN
I had first met and befriended Roger Birnbaum when he was an A&R guy at A&M, but when the company started to lose its family feel he moved to Arista. He called me one day and said, "I think I have a band that would be perfect for you." I trusted his judgement and so had the label fly me to a small town in Virginia to see a band play live at a hole-in-the-wall called The Cellar Door, and I fell in love with them. They were Happy the Man (see Insert Figure 24.1).

The band was fascinating in that they were American but had a very English sound. While Supertramp has sometimes been described as a "prog-rock" band (a tag that I've never quite understood), HTM was probably as prog-rock as they came. Their influences were all English bands, although they were all instrumental except for one vocal track, by no means my favourite track.

HTM's first drummer, Mike Beck, never thought of himself as a drummer but more of a percussionist. I don't think he felt totally comfortable behind a regular drum kit because he liked to make percussion sounds, sometimes from almost any household item laying around. He'd do things like get a hose like you'd find on a vacuum cleaner and swing it around his head and it would give out this great whistle that would change pitch as he changed the speed of the swing. You name it, he did it. On "New York Dream Suite," I remember slowly working through the song with him saying, "I hear this sound." He'd pick something up and "play" it, and we would find a place for it. "OK, Mike. Now what do you hear?" I'd ask. Sure enough, in ten seconds he'd have another sound that fitted another section. We kept layering the song with all these different "percussion items" that he used.

I only met one other percussionist anything like Mike, the famed Brazilian Airto Moreira, who Stanley Clarke brought in to play on a session on the first album I did with him. He came in and set up three tables with a variety of traditional percussion and non-percussion items on each table. He put items that were really loud like a school bell on one end and things that were quiet like a box of dried leaves on the other. I said to him before we began the overdub, "What will you be using?" to which he replied, "I don't know. I just feel it as it goes." I had to put up a series of mics in front of the tables and then played the recording side of things by ear just as he did. At one point he'd be throwing these leaves up in the air and I'd have to record that, then he'd suddenly dash down to the other end and play something ridiculously loud, and I'd have to immediately pull the faders down so it didn't distort. At least Mike was a little bit more controlled in that he told me what he was going to do beforehand so

I could get a level. He would have been really fun on *Crime of the Century*, thinking about it now.

Of course Arista had no idea how to market a band like HTM, so the first album (called *Happy the Man*) didn't sell very much. They liked what we did enough to take a chance on a second album though.

AM I A HYPOCRITE?

When it came time to cut the second album, HTM had a new drummer. The band was supposed to fly in from Virginia the day before we were to record at Chateau. Come the first day of recording, I was introduced to new drummer Ron Riddle and he just looked shattered. I asked him, "How come you look so tired when everyone else isn't?" It turns out that at the last minute he decided to drive cross-country instead of flying like everyone else. I knew this was bad right from the start, but decided to proceed as always anyway.

After getting the drum sound, we tried to get at least one basic track that night, but Ron's playing got progressively worse and worse, though interestingly, he seemed to be getting more alert and up instead of more tired. I finally discovered that to keep going he was dipping into the Columbian marching powder that was so common back then, so I stopped the session. "Let's go home and get a good night's sleep. We can start tomorrow at 4 o'clock as opposed to noon so you can be fresh," I said, "But I will not stand for anything like this for the rest of the recording." They had been warned.

All was going well and we were coming up to the end of recording as Christmas approached. We came to the last night and the band had planned to fly back to the East Coast the next day. We were out of studio time, and they were leaving, so we had to make sure everything was finished. We still had a lot to do, so it was obvious that it was going to be a long night.

One of the things left until the end was the one vocal track on the album to be sung by guitarist Stan Whitaker. When it was time for him to sing I started to look around for him, but he was nowhere to be found. "Does anyone know where Stan is?" I asked, and the ensuing conversation went something like this:

"He's gone outside to check the car," the band said as they all kind of looked down at the ground a bit.

Laughing a little at the absurdity of the response, I said, "What is it that he has to check all of a sudden?"

"We think he's gone out for some fresh air," came the reply.

This whole conversation felt strange, so I said, "I'll go get him."

"Oh, no. We'll get him," they all chimed in quickly.

I decided to go outside anyway and just like I had suspected, I found him inhaling the white powder. "That's it, guys. I'm off. You're on your own." I declared.

Since they were all leaving to go home, it was now up to them to sort out how they would come back to complete the album. I had made it perfectly clear that I wouldn't stand for any drug use, and now they suffered the consequences for doing it again. The band went home and we finished up *Crafty Hands* after Christmas.

I've only walked off two sessions because of drugs: this one with HTM and the one with John Lennon. I suppose I was lucky in that regard, but I always kept a very tight rein on that sort of thing. Well, almost always.

There was one time where I actually organised getting some drugs for a session. I was producing a band called Trans Lux, who eventually had to change their name to 3D because of a trademark violation. All power to them, I said "No drugs," so there were no drugs. We were having a lot of trouble getting keyboard parts though, so when I asked one of the guys in the band what was going on with the keyboard player, I was told, "He needs some smoke." "Tell him to go down to the store and buy a pack of cigarettes," I said, not realising what he was referring to. "No, not that type of smoke," came the confirmation. "No, we're not doing that," I said, and we carried on a bit longer.

After not getting anywhere, I decided that we had to try something, so I had my assistant call a friend to arrange for a weed purchase. Before you know it, the package was delivered, and after the keyboardist had his first joint, he started to play perfectly, and everything went smoothly from then on. I suppose it does have its uses for some people.

That includes The Tubes. Even though they consumed massive amounts of all kinds of illegal substances, it didn't cause any problems with the band's performance. It was such a part of their whole lifestyle that they seemed to have it completely under control, and even used it to improve their performances when needed. On the two occasions when I walked out, it was obvious that things were getting worse and worse because of the drug intake. I'm not going to sit there and waste my time with that going on. Because it had already gone downhill at one point with HTM, I said "no more," and when they went against that, I couldn't then back down. I had to stick to my word that there would be consequences. With The Tubes it was there right from the start, but it never caused any problems whatsoever. I'm a hypocrite, I guess.

The first time I ever walked into a control room with Ken was under a completely different set of circumstances. It was to deliver some pot to an artist he was working with. He was working at Chateau and he played about 5 seconds of something, and at that point in my life it was the loudest thing I ever heard.
Wyn Davis, owner of Total Access Recording

HTM and I did a couple of albums together and they unfortunately both died completely in the marketplace because, as previously stated, Arista just didn't know how to handle that type of music. Why they signed them in the first place, I'll never know, but they were an amazing band and it's just such a shame that most people have never heard of them.

DIXIE DREGS

Someone contacted my manager about me doing a record with the Dixie Dregs and sent their first album out for me to listen to. I really liked it, thought I could add something, so agreed to work with them. The first meeting was for some preproduction at SIR rehearsal studios in Hollywood, where I asked them to play me some material so we could sort out the arrangements. The first song they played was called "Take It Off the Top" and I had to stop them in the middle of it. The drummer, Rod Morgenstein, was overplaying so much that I just knew it would never work.

Just like with Bill Cobham and Stanley Clarke trying to outplay each other, here was an entire band trying to do the same thing. They were trying to throw everything they had into every bar, and Rod was by far the worst offender. We ended up cutting his part way back and at that moment in time, he absolutely hated me. That said, it made him change the way he looked at his playing. He now says it was the greatest learning experience of his life and he wouldn't be where he is today without that kind of tough love. I had to change his way of playing to look at the song first instead of his own performance, but that's exactly what's necessary when you're making a record.

I remember the very first song we played for Ken was "Take It Off the Top." So we're into it a little bit and I'm like all over the freakin' place, like any young drummer is, thinking you've got to fill in every available space. Plus, hey, we're an instrumental fusion band and you've got to show everybody everything you know in every song. Who cares about the song? So when we go to the section of the song where I was just filling everything in, Ken kinda stopped the band and that was the beginning of ... "simplify." I had no respect for simplicity and that's how it all ties in to that first experience. I felt a little defensive inside, like somebody was questioning my creative abilities. By the time he'd got finished with me I was hating his guts, thinking, "This is the stupidest thing anyone could do. What about my incredible chops?"

Through the process I came full circle and matured so much as a result of it and it's never left me. The bottom line is you have to play for the song. Think about the piece of music that you're trying to put your little piece of the puzzle to. Be a team player and play what works best, not thinking you have to shoot your whole wad at every turn. I mean it's a very important lesson for a young player to learn, but I think everybody goes through that when they're first starting out.
Rod Morgenstein, Dixie Dregs drummer

After the rough patch at rehearsal, we went into Chateau and recorded for about two or three weeks. Everything went great except for one thing. We put down all of the basic tracks and in almost all of the cases we only kept the drum tracks and overdubbed everything on top of it. The next thing we laid down was bass and we made sure that it was in tune with a tuner the entire time. What we didn't know was that there was a problem with the multitrack machine. We eventually discovered that there was something wrong with the tension of the take-up reel which led to the machine playing slower as it went through the reel of tape. Of course, someone spotted the problem with the tape machine and fixed it, which proved to not necessarily be a good thing. When we started to do other overdubs we found that depending upon where in the song we were, or how close to the end of the tape we were, the pitch of the bass was now wrong. Eventually we had to go back and redo all the bass parts at the correct speed, which, not surprisingly, slowed us up a bit.

> *The other thing I remember saying was, "Why can't my drums sound like this?" Ken said, "Here's the deal. The way you make drums sound good is by hitting them hard, and the fewer notes you play, the harder you can hit them." He illustrated it by playing me a Mahavishnu record, because Billy was my idol. He said "Listen to Billy's drums." Then he put on maybe a Bowie record or Supertramp and said, "Which drum sound do you like better?" and I went "That one." "Well, it's a different kind of playing and you have to simplify, then you can get that sound you're going for."*
> Rod Morgenstein

It was fascinating working with someone like Dregs guitarist Steve Morse, who has perfect pitch, because it showed me how one can train one's ear to be more aware of pitch. The next album I did after both Dregs albums, I had a hard time with players being out of tune. They were actually off so minutely, but I had become so accustomed to it being perfect while working with Steve, that the slightest inaccuracy leapt out at me. I had to actually make an effort to untrain my ear to get it back to that of a normal listener.

There's a track on *What If* called "Little Kids" that's almost classical in nature. It's just a nylon-string guitar and violin; I adore this piece of music. We actually recorded it the way I mix. We'd record on two tracks until a short section was perfect, then I'd play it back and they'd pick it up for another short section on two other tracks. Then we'd go back to the original tracks and carry on this way until the end of the song. I know how we recorded it, but when I listen to it today, it's seamless. I can't hear the section breaks at all. It was that striving for perfection, both in timing, pitch, and as far as we were concerned, feel, that caused us to try the process.

We were kinda disappointed from the first album we had done, and we had so many hopes for this one. I just remember the first song was "Take It Off the Top" and we were just hootin' and a hollerin'. Everybody just so ecstatic. It was just such a great great moment.
Rod Morgenstein

NIGHT OF THE LIVING DREGS

Speaking of feel, I've very often received comments about how my recordings lack feel because I try to get everything too perfect. In fact I remember that criticism reaching the point of absurdity when an A&R guy, now a *very* successful manager, told me that because of my strive for perfection, I was wholly responsible for the punk scene. I wish I had that much power. Anyway, I really do try to get as much feel as I can in my records but it still has to be played right. That said, I think what people term "feel" comes from the listener's perception as much as what's being played. In a live situation there's a built-in excitement for the audience, bolstered by others around also being excited, that leads to what they consider "feel."

I realise this is quite a generality, but I bring it up because on the second Dregs album, *Night of the Living Dregs*, Side 2 was recorded at the Montreux Jazz Festival. Unfortunately much of the recording that we got was unusable, so when we got back to Chateau, the only way we figured we could save it was to only keep the drums and overdub everything else. The recorded drums from Montreux were fine, but there was a hum or buzz in all of the electronic instruments that sounded awful. I recorded it, but because in a live situation you can't spend ages trying to find out what's causing the problem, you have to go with what you have. It's live and the show must go on.

Interestingly enough, there have been a number of people who have said how much better the feel of that part of the album was because it was cut live, but it really wasn't. It ended up being exactly the same process as we'd do on any studio recording; we laid down the drums first, then overdubbed everything else. It's the perception that matters.

In fact, it became even worse than a normal recording, in a way, because the band took it to the point where, because there was leakage coming through on the drum mics and the audience mics, they had to play all the mistakes they originally made as well. If anything, it should lack even more feel because in many respects it was even more precise as it had to match exactly what they had played.

There was another example of that kind of feel/perception thing. I was associated with a band called Christine in the Attic (more on them soon) who used a lot of programmed percussion effects that were additional bits to the basic rhythm. People would come and see the band live, and because they saw that the drummer wasn't actually playing these parts, they felt it was flat and mechanical. As opposed to either getting extra members to play the part or dropping the parts altogether, which to me were integral to the sound, I went out and bought two six-foot metal tubes. The next time they played live I set them up on mic stands on either side of the drums and taped two wires coming off the back end of each of one. I told the drummer, "When you're not actually playing the drum parts, make it seem like your playing the other parts on these." All of a sudden the comments we got were, "Now that he's playing those parts, it has so much more feeling." Purely perception. He was playing nothing more than he'd always played.

THE MULTITRACKS

On Side 1 of *Living Dregs*, which is the studio side, we ran two multitrack tape machines synced up to get more tracks to use. Eventually we ran out of time at Chateau so we went to a studio in Atlanta (where the band was from) to finish up the overdubs. The trouble was that the studio had only one machine, so we never heard what it sounded like with the two machines playing together. Let me briefly explain. Overdubbing using two machines could often become more than a little tiresome as you always had to wait for the slave machine to catch up with the master machine and so the normal way of working was to use only one machine as much as possible. To enable this I would put a rough mix of the basic track on to the second tape, the one that we were usually overdubbing on to. To keep a long story short, it finished up that as there was only the one machine in Atlanta, we only ever got to listen to one tape at a time and never heard what the entire song sounded like with all the parts. The band was answering each other in solos without ever hearing the other solos, which seemed like it should be impossibly hard. The keyboard and violin were on one tape while the guitar solos were on the other tape. Surprisingly enough, everything worked perfectly. I don't know how, but they did it. The first time I heard everything together back at Chateau, I was blown away—number one that we pulled it off, and number two at just how great it all sounded. Of course, the poor band never heard it until the record was completed, as they weren't around for the mixes, but luckily they trusted me.

AT THE MIXES

Speaking of the mixing, the Dregs and HTM were never there when I mixed. Devo, Kansas, and Missing Persons were. The Tubes were there when I needed them. They were going on tour, so they were on the A&M soundstage rehearsing. When I got close to finishing I'd send the second to get someone to come in and listen and pass their comments. That's always one of those things for me. I don't want them there all the time. I have them come in when I think I'm close so they can listen to what I've got so far. Under normal circumstances, once they're there they stay until the end of the mix, but give me six hours to get it close to what I'm going for first.

I can't stand it when someone from the band is there from the beginning. The conversation usually goes like this:

Artist: "Oh, I can't hear the bass."

Ken: "I'm not even listening to the bass. I'm listening to the drums."

Artist: "The guitar's not there."

Ken: "I'm not listening to the guitar yet."

Artist: "Can you boost the vocal a bit."

Ken: "I'm still listening to the drums."

I've got to get it nearly finished before the comments mean anything to me. I can keep my objectivity somehow, but the artists can't for some reason.

The Dregs started off on the Capricorn label and sold about 30,000 to 40,000 the first time out, but the second album sold about 200,000, which was a healthy increase. If the third one had been on Capricorn, it could have gone gold because the label learned how to promote the Dregs by that time. Unfortunately Phil Walden, the owner of Capricorn, was very into politics and the story I heard was that he gave way too much to Jimmy Carter for his second run at the presidency, and subsequently lost it all. That's apparently why the company folded. The Dregs were without a deal and for whatever reason, Arista signed them and it was downhill from there. Too bad—they were another great band that most of the music world would never hear.

CHAPTER 25

Missing Persons

Even though we lived across the street from one another, Frank Zappa and I got to know each other a little but we certainly never became close buddies, mostly because of our work schedules.

There was a mutual respect between the two of us, but that was about it. On occasion I'd visit him in the studio or go see him when he played a local gig around Los Angeles. It was at one of these shows that I first saw Terry Bozzio. Now, let's face it: Frank had a knack for finding good musicians, but a drummer like Bozzio? I was blown away by him and voiced my enthusiasm to Frank and his wife Gail after the show.

Cut to some time later and we'd bought a house in the same neighbourhood but down the street from Frank. One Saturday afternoon I'm hanging out at home and the phone rang. It was Gail Zappa, who politely said, "I've got Terry Bozzio here with his wife and one of Frank's guitarists, Warren Cuccurullo. They've formed a band and they'd like to play you some stuff. Would you take a listen to them?" Being a fan of Terry, it didn't take much arm-twisting for me to reply, "Sure, send them down."

Five minutes later this very strange woman with bleach-blonde hair accompanied by Terry and someone I assumed to be Warren banged on the door, tape in hand. They proceeded to play me what was probably one of the worst demo tapes I have ever heard in my life. "This is ridiculous," I thought to myself. "Terry is amazing, and Warren has to be good to have played with Frank, but this is awful. They just can't be this bad." I can only assume that my love of Terry's playing prompted me to take the next step and say, "Look, I don't like this, but let me come and see you play live." "Well, we don't play out yet. We're just rehearsing," was the sheepish reply. "OK, I'll come down and see you rehearse then," I answered.

So the next time they rehearsed, I'm there, but they still weren't that good. The whole thing seemed very un-together. There was certainly a hint of Terry and Warren's musical chops and the unusual vocal renderings of Dale Bozzio took a little getting used to, but while watching them I got this feeling in the pit of my stomach. Something grabbed me about them. Maybe it was because of the high level of the musicianship and the thought that they stood a chance of taking the audience to a whole new musical level. I really don't know exactly what it was, but I agreed to work with them. It didn't take long before everyone around me said I was nuts, insane, and out of my gourd, but I had to do it. Time to do some demos and see what they're really all about.

> *Frank got us his [Ken's] address and it was right down the street. I said, "Let's go! Let's go! We've got to go right now!" And we took this boombox and a cassette and we left like we were on a mission. So we drove over to Ken's in our tiny little car and I think I climbed over the fence and went up to the pool, and he [Ken] goes, "What are you doing here?" and I said, "Well, I've got this boombox and a cassette." He probably thought I was delirious. Ken was like, "OK, let me hear the tape." And we had this piece-of-junk boombox, in front of this multizillion dollar producer who'd just left David Bowie. We were so ragged, but he listened to it and said, "Oh, yeah, I think I like that." And that was it. He completely agreed and that one afternoon changed our lives.*
> Dale Bozzio, lead singer of Missing Persons

RECORDING AT ZAPPA'S HOUSE

It just so happened that Frank recently had a large studio built at his house whilst he was on the road. Typical of him he wanted to start recording the instant he got back, but knew that with a brand new studio there would be problems that he preferred not to have to deal with, so he told us we could use it to record our demos. Now he knew my reputation for finding every niggly little thing that is wrong in a studio and correctly figured that I would find every single one of them in his, so that when he got back everything would be working properly. We knew what the deal was, so we were fully prepared to be patient when things held us up a bit. That was just fine with everyone because we were getting the place for free.

> We're at the Zappa house and he said, "If you guys want to make a demo, my studio's almost done and I'm going on the road. If you got Ken Scott, I'll let you go in there because he's a great engineer and knows what he's doing. You can make a demo, get all the bugs out of my studio, and when I come home I'll know everything will be working and ready to fly." So I said "OK, we'll get him."
> Terry Bozzio, drummer for Missing Persons

Frank's studio, which, in typical Frank fashion, was strangely named the Utility Muffin Research Kitchen, was the equivalent of any commercial studio in Los Angeles at the time, with a large recording room with high ceilings, a fairly large drum booth, and a good-sized vocal booth. The only problem we had was mics. Even though Frank had an excellent complement of vintage Neumanns and Telefunkens, he took them all with him on the road. Frank recorded almost every show he ever did, and he had this huge library of all of his performances. He was notorious for taking bits from different songs from different shows and writing new songs around what was played live. As a result, we had to make do with the second-tier mics that he left behind. I don't remember exactly what we used, but I hadn't used any of them before so there was a certain amount of experimentation until we got things sounding right. Most of the demos that we finished at Frank's ended up being on the first album, and they matched perfectly with the songs we later did at a studio with the mics I prefer. It was at that point

I realised that up to a point, the mics don't make a blind bit of difference, because the sound we got with the lesser-grade mics was as good as the tracks we did later with the normal ones I use.

The band was in its formative stage and so for the demo, Terry, Warren, and Dale were augmented with two additional players, Gary Guttman on synth bass and Trantham Whitley on synthesisers. We recorded everything in a relatively quick three days, plus a couple days of mixing. I chose not to mix at Frank's though, because I was unsure of the monitors. I managed to get a couple of days at the studio where I normally worked at the time, Chateau Recorders, as I knew the room and I was more confident about what I was hearing there than at Frank's.

We ended up with five songs from those sessions, four which were totally finished and mixed: "Destination Unknown," "Mental Hopscotch," "I Like Boys," the obligatory cover song, The Doors' "Hello, I Love You," and "Action Reaction," and Frank got to effortlessly start work upon his return.

> *We went back and said, "Frank, we've got Ken. He's going to do it," and Frank said, "OK, fine. Here's your studio, I'll be gone three days. See you when I get back. I hope you make a good tape."*
> *I don't know what he thought, but he definitely had faith in us and knew we were capable of doing something, and he knew that probably the only person who could take us to another level would be Ken Scott.*
> Dale Bozzio

SHOPPING THE DEAL

With demo in hand, I immediately started to call around town to shop it. What an experience. Much to our surprise, everyone said, "No way, forget it." It seemed that it wasn't enough like what was number 1 on the charts at that particular time. In fact, it wasn't like anything that was on any chart at the time, so no one could "hear it" on the radio.

Three times around Los Angeles A&R departments, twice around New York A&R departments, once through London, and even a few in Sydney, Australia. Nada. For most A&R guys, it was the typical 20 seconds and onto the next song before passing. The A&M A&R guy's cassette machine ran at probably 75% of the correct speed, so he decided to pass after listening to a funeral dirge. And the one I loved the most came from one of the Scotti Brothers, a couple of independent promotion ghumbas who had been given their own label, who told me, "I can put you in touch with a great producer who might be able to make something of this." Thanks, pal.

> From our angle, Ken had done everybody, the greatest of the great, the best drummers in the world, The Beatles, Elton John, Supertramp, David Bowie, and on and on. I mean just the whole package was there, and we thought we were gonna have a record deal in a couple of phone calls. Ken takes the stuff to every major label in town and they all fucking pass. And within a month, John Kalodner [former A&R exec at Geffen Records] says in some music rag, "If this Missing Persons crap ever makes it, I'll quit the business." A year later he was eating his words.
>
> Terry Bozzio

Was everyone around me right? Had I gone off the deep end? Hey, in for a penny, in for a pound. Once no one wanted them, we thought, "OK, the only way we're going to do this is to put the record out ourselves." It was decided to put out four of the songs in a format straight out of 1960s England called an EP (Extended Play), which was a 7-inch 45 rpm record that was cut with shallower grooves (it wasn't as loud as most records as a result) in order to fit on the extra songs. The funding was provided by Warren's parents, a great couple who proved to be valuable on more than one occasion, and to save any messing around, we used my production company KoMoS as the "label." For the sleeve, we already had a great photo of Dale in this very strange swimsuit, which she had modelled for free on the condition that she could have the picture for any use she chose. Typical of Los Angeles, once the band became successful, they were sued over the use of that picture—not by the photographer, but the designer of the ridiculous costume she was wearing. Go figure.

*I did a session with Bobby [Colomby—A&R exec at Capitol
Records at the time, and former drummer with Blood, Sweat
& Tears], who was producing Henry Gross. At the end he says,
"Terry, I don't want to have to do this, but I'm gonna have to
let you go. I know you're a great drummer, but I don't want to
build the whole band around you. I'm just gonna try getting
another drummer to finish this up." So he drove me home that
night, and on the way I said, "I'm working on this thing if you'd
be interested in checking out the demo, Ken Scott and Missing
Persons" and so on. We give him the original five-song demo that
went on to sell 750,000 copies, and he sent a letter back that said,
"Boy, do I wish I loved this, but I don't. Please keep me in mind
for any future things," and "P.S. Dale is a credit to her gender."
Total fucking rejection from another drummer. I still have the
framed rejection letter* (see Figure 25.1).*

Terry Bozzio

*The underlying comment from most of the labels was, "We don't
hear this as the direction of music in the '80s."*

Warren Cuccurullo, guitarist for Missing Persons

While all this was happening, we were also trying to get the band
some attention. Through an acquaintance of an acquaintance, I was
approached with a request for the three band members to appear
in a movie. We all talked it over and the decision was made to do
it. Although there was very little money to be made, we thought
that since they also wanted to use two of the songs from the demo,
it might get us closer to a record deal. The filming took all of two
days and we didn't really think too much about it until we got to
see the finished film much later. If only we had known. It turned out
to be a really cheap and cheesy T&A movie called *Lunch Wagon*.
Oh well, you live and you learn, and that, we thought, was the end
of that. But things like this have a strange way of coming back out
of the woodwork, so as you'll see later, it really wasn't the end of
the story at all.

The band had appeared in *Lunch Wagon* using the name "U.S.
Drag," but we all felt that we needed something better. Here's where
our friend Mr. Zappa enters the story once again, this time with
an offhand comment about Terry and Warren being missing from

his band. Shortly afterwards, Warren coined the name "Missing Persons." The name stuck.

```
                    Capitol        Executive and General Offices
                    RECORDS
                    A CAPITOL INDUSTRIES-EMI Company




                                    July 15, 1980


           Terry Bozzio
           10989 Rochester
           Los Angeles, CA   90024

           Dear Terry,

           Boy, do I wish I loved this, but I don't...There is a lot of
           potential here; however, I believe that it's going to take more
           time to develop the material, and that's the name of the game.

           Please let me know when you are playing somewhere, so I can
           come to a live presentation where more material will be available
           for review.   Thanks.

           Sincerely,


           Bobby Colomby
           Vice President A&R,
           Pop Division

           BC/js
           enc.

           Dictated but not read

           P.S.  Dale is a credit to her gender.  All the best; sorry I
           can't be of more immediate help.
```

Figure 25.1: The rejection letter from Bobby Colomby.

Also by this time, the band had started to play live gigs around town, adding Chuck Wild to play keyboards and bass synth. The first gig at Club 88 in Hollywood in November of 1980 was a complete disaster. Amongst other things, as the audience was full of friends, came an unplanned encore. Of course, they'd already gone through all their material, so they played an instrumental, during which Dale rode through the audience on a kid's tricycle, which turned out to be the high point of that part of the catastrophe. Then, at a gig at the Florentine Gardens in Hollywood, the audience, who was there primarily to see Irish punk band Stiff Little Fingers, spat and threw coins at them. At other shows, people called out for Zappa numbers. But they learned from each show, so each one got a little better, a little tighter, and a little closer to the ultimate goal.

I'M A MANAGER

During this time, we contacted a bunch of managers and asked them to come to the shows. Just like the labels, most of them said they weren't the slightest bit interested. The only one who showed any enthusiasm at all, Roger Davies, Tina Turner's manager, only wanted Dale and none of the musicians. Needless to say, he was soon crossed off the list. As no manager of any note wanted to take on the band, I decided it was time to put up or shut up, so I went to the band and told them that I was willing, and eager, to continue looking after their interests on a day-to-day basis, *but* we had to enter into a management agreement. They agreed and soon all the financial and business stuff was discussed and agreed to. A contract was drawn up, but suddenly they got cold feet. For weeks they kept putting off the signing until the Cuccurullos, once again, stepped in and got them to sign what was a very fair and standard deal. Onward and upward (see Insert Figure 25.2).

By April of 1981, the time had come to get the record out. The EP included four of the songs that we cut at Frank's studio: "Destination Unknown," "I Like Boys," "Mental Hopscotch," and "Hello, I Love You." The first Sunday after we had the pressings in our hot little hands, Missing Persons went to a fledgling radio station in Los Angeles called KROQ. It was the night of the station's local music show, and they somehow schmoozed their way in to see the DJ and got him to play a song off the EP then and there, which was possible only because this was the time before jocks were told exactly what they had to play before preprogrammed shows dictated by conglomerates such as Clear Channel took over. Lo and behold, he liked it and not only decided to interview the band on-air, but to play some other tracks from the EP as well. Every time a song was played, the phones lit up, so they played it more and more. From this small start, "Mental Hopscotch" would go on to become the most requested record of the year, 1981, at the station.

We shopped it everywhere and we went everywhere. We tried to get whatever kind of deal we could. IRS Records offered us a little deal that was sort of like, "What's the point?" So what we decided to do was press a certain number of records on our own label. And we shopped that everywhere. We took it to KROQ. We took it to college radio stations. We had the problem where they wouldn't play it if they couldn't buy it, so we had to press some more to put in little local record shops. That's when little local record shops that did little off-the-wall private things were still around. So I would ask, "Would you please put 10 of these records in your store? We'll give them to you, and we'll give you T-shirts and we'll do whatever you want." And then KROQ liked it and started to play it and we started sending it to all the "power stations" who also started to play it. It was an interesting process because we were all learning how to promote a record and we were doing this nationwide. We started to get some national college radio play and on some local stations because our shows were doing really well. So with KROQ and the shows and the little bit of records here and there, it was starting to take off. We created demand in this city [Los Angeles] for product. We were doing bigger and bigger venues. The band was getting more and more popular. KROQ was getting a lot of airplay and a couple of other stations were picking it up. I had friends at KIIS-FM and once in a while they'd throw it on there. We had friends at KLOS that would play it. We all pulled in all of our favors from all of our friends. We were doing everything we could to get this thing signed, played, whatever. We did press interviews, we set up little radio interviews, and finally the record companies sat up and took notice.

Steve Brooks, Ken's assistant

OK, now we have a nice EP, but how to promote it? We couldn't afford independent promotion, which was really expensive, so I came up with an idea. At the time there was a radio tip sheet called the Album Network, which had a number of charts about what radio stations were playing in different cities and regions of the country. Why I subscribed to it I don't know, but I ended up making some connections with some of the people there and we arranged to take out a full-page ad with a bit of a twist. The magazine had various lists of people and companies they sent it to. The important radio and record company people were on the A-list, and so along with our ad, we got them to include a copy of the EP with the magazine sent to that list, about 750 copies in all. It was the perfect way of getting it to everyone we thought needed to hear it. Although the mailing gained us nothing record company-wise, it played very heavily into the airplay that we got nationally. The magazine even did us a deal on the full-page ad because they liked the idea of sending music out with their tip sheet. One of my better ideas, as it turned out.

As we were playing around town and doing better all the time, a few people from some record labels started to come out to see us. There was one person from Capitol, a young lady by the name of Nikki Randall, who got the bug for MP very early. She kept on egging Capitol execs to come down and check it out. Their reaction was usually, "Yeah, it's OK but ... " and they didn't want to know. But they all started to want to hear more material, so we went into Chateau Recorders and cut what would eventually be the band's biggest hit, "Words."

Slowly but surely, it all started to come together. We found an agent, Doug Isaac from the ICM agency, who was very important to our earliest success. He really believed in the band and managed to get deals that we could never have gotten ourselves. At that point, we started to play bigger and better gigs. In fact, we actually planned the build in such a way that the first gig we played in a larger venue we'd be the opening act, and then five or six weeks later we'd play the same place, but this time as the headliner.

We'd use guerrilla tactics to get the name out in front of as many people as possible, so we'd go out many nights at 2 A.M. and cover the town with posters for gigs. I had a blast, as this was an area of "the biz" that I had never dealt with before. We covered telephone poles in the canyons of Los Angeles with posters, the first of which was "We found Missing Persons," the next was "Have you?" and then on every third one was "Find Missing Persons at ... " with the details of the next gig. We had bumper stickers made that said, "We found Missing Persons," and with one of these on the back of my car,

I was often asked if I was a private eye. Anything and everything we could come up with to help bolster the name.

We'd be hanging posters and signs and we'd see the guys from Mötley Crüe hanging their posters up at the same time. There were bands just hanging their posters around that would come to see us just because of the Zappa connection.
Warren Cuccurullo

We played the legendary Whisky a Go Go club on Sunset Boulevard in Hollywood where acts such as The Doors and The Byrds had gotten their start in the '60s. The first time we played there it was half-full, but the second time we played it was a sell-out with a line around the block. We ended up playing three shows that night, the last two completely unplanned, to take advantage of the demand. That same night Duran Duran was playing at the Roxy just a little way up the street. It was easy to spot which kid was going to which show. Durannies were in the full New Romantic get-up and the MP people were very punkish, which was a very interesting sight. So we had to move up to a larger venue, and once again, first time half-full, next time sold out. And that kept on happening. We were always getting advances that we should never have gotten, considering we didn't have a label deal yet.

Then suddenly we had some airplay on the East Coast, so we decided to do some shows there, once again, funded by Warren's parents. It was great. We went up and down the East Coast being driven around in a limo, all set up by his parents. It was the strangest thing. I've often wondered if they were "connected." There was one time much later when Warren's parents had come out from New York. It was about halfway through the set and I was going to go and deal with the money with the agent and the promoter, and as I'm walking back Warren's father is on the end of the row and he says "Do you need any help?" and I say, "No, it's fine." And he pulls his trouser leg up and there's a piece in a leg holster, and he says, "Are you sure you don't want any help?" I said, "No, it's really fine. Thank you!"

On that same East Cost tour, I remember discovering that a New York venue had videoed our show to use whenever and however they wanted. I literally had to threaten to burn the place down in order to get the video from them. Wow, little old me, a mini-Peter Grant.

Oh yes, there was one very memorable show at the Country Club in Reseda, California. We had by this time realised that there was money to be made from merchandising and so we used to sell T-shirts inside the entrance to the clubs. I got word that there were some scam artists outside selling el-cheapo rip-offs of our shirts and after going outside to have a little talk with them, I found myself chasing after them instead, probably faster than I'd ever run before, two blocks away. The other thing that happened that night was that Dale managed to let two kids walk off with her wireless microphone. For insurance purposes we had to report the incident to the police and within half an hour we had the mic back. The stupid little buggers hadn't turned it off and the police heard every word they were saying and quickly managed to nab them.

Missing Persons kept getting bigger and bigger, but still no record deal, even though we were building this huge following. Labels would come down to a show and say, "No thank you," but the people from Capitol kept coming around more and more and suddenly, they weren't saying no anymore. It seems that our friend at Capitol, Nikki Randall, kept on pushing, and at some point, the powers that be all changed their minds. Lo and behold, they offered us a deal.

CHAPTER 26
Finally, a Record Deal

Once we had that offer from Capitol, suddenly other labels started to prick up their ears and say they were interested. The woman in charge of A&R for Geffen Records contacted me and wanted to start talking a deal, but the stipulation was that she and everyone else from Geffen had to come down and see the band first before they would make a definite offer. Since we were in the middle of signing to Capitol already, I didn't feel that we should do a showcase just for them and neither did the band, so we just told them, "Sorry, we're signing with Capitol." And sign we did on March the 14th, 1982.

Although Nikki Randall and another Capitol A&R exec Bruce Ravid were instrumental in our coming to Capitol, it was the head of A&R, Rupert Perry, who finally signed us. Having him behind us gave the project a lot of clout at the label, which was golden in terms of label priorities. He was one of the two A&R guys who I have really had any respect for over the years.

Ken came in to see us and he had this new project and there was a real buzz. You know A&R people by nature are jaded, but there was something about Ken Scott and everything that he had done. Everybody likes to get into business with people that have been successful, although it doesn't mean the band automatically gets signed. Ken came in with the project and we didn't immediately

315

go for it. We loved the band—loved the band—but I know it was my feeling that they were a couple of songs short at that point. "Mental Hopscotch" was getting played out here [in Los Angeles] on KROQ and it was a big local hit, but that just didn't sound like a career-breaking song. It didn't sound like something that would become a hit in Milwaukee.

I remember going to see them play at various clubs like the Whisky, and they were amazing. What a great band! Getting by Dale was a little hard, but I think I underestimated her eventual appeal a little bit. That wasn't a deal breaker in my mind. I mostly just wanted to hear more material that I thought was radio worthy. Then they came up with some new songs and in this batch was "Words," the career breaker, and "Walking in L.A." They already had "Destination Unknown," which I think was on their original EP with "Mental Hopscotch," but those two songs; that's when I changed my mind and really thought we had something we could go with.

Bruce Ravid, Capitol Records A&R

The day after we were offered our deal with Capitol, KROQ announced that "Mental Hopscotch" was the number 1 most requested record of the year. It was amazing. As they were counting down, they already had two of MP's songs on the list, but we were all thinking, "What about 'Mental Hopscotch?' " When they got down to 4, then 3, we thought, "Uh, it couldn't have made it." Then 2, and then suddenly, much to our unabashed and total delight, "Mental Hopscotch" was crowned number 1. What a great couple of days.

The culmination of this period of good fortune came on April the 9th, 1982 when we played a sold-out show at the 2500-seat Santa Monica Civic Auditorium. Even though we had just signed with Capitol, the fact that we'd managed to quickly sell out a venue of this size without their help was both pretty amazing and significant, which was not lost on the brass at the label one bit. On the night of the show, all the execs from Capitol were there (see Insert Figure 26.1), including label president Don Zimmerman and head of A&R Rupert Perry, and a sold-out show of screaming fans only reinforced their belief that they'd made a wise decision to sign the band.

The show was sold out. Weird Al Yankovic threw watermelons all over the stage before we went on, and there were watermelon seeds everywhere, and I said to Thomas, our roadie, "Get those watermelon seeds off the stage. I'm going to fall and kill myself!"
I had clear stiletto plexiglass shoes on with a candy kiss outfit wrapped up and tied around my waist with tubing, so I looked like a piece of candy. We invited the president of Capitol Records, Don Zimmerman and his wife Sharon, because I was convinced that we were the next biggest best thing ever in the '80s. I convinced Terry and Warren of that too, but Ken believed it when he saw me and that's why I believed in Ken, because he believed in me. What else is there in life? If you believe in someone, you're home free.

Dale Bozzio

But the most memorable night, performance wise and party wise, was when we actually sold out the Santa Monica Civic. Everyone who had passed on us were coming down to see us. We'd sold out a 2500-seat venue and I think we sold it out quite quickly as well. So we do the gig, and Rupert Perry was there from Capitol Records. So that was like a big night. A really big night.

Warren Cuccurullo

After a big event at the Santa Monica Civic Auditorium, a very interesting party ensued afterward. That hit the press bigger than anything else we'd ever done. It was amazing—all this national press for this little party

Steve Brooks

THE PARTY

As the Capitol deal had just gone through, I decided a big celebratory party should be held at my house after the gig and it had to be a big event. Invites went out to most of the Capitol Los Angeles employees, DJs, and the hierarchy of radio stations, press, and friends who had helped our rise to success. As the party was to start after the gig, I knew no one would arrive before 1 A.M., so I thought it might be a good idea to notify all the neighbours and anyone else within hearing range so they knew what was happening and, if they so chose, they could spend the night away from home. Everyone was grateful for the notification, or so I thought.

Everything had been dealt with in advance: two security guards, one big one that wouldn't harm a fly and one small and slight Asian that could do you major damage at the slightest provocation; bar staff; wait staff; a dance floor out back (this was Southern California, after all) ... so let the fun begin. We never did know exactly how many people walked through the doors but estimates ran to 250 during the night. After a few hours, I'm confronted at the front door by two police officers. "Good morning, sir. Is this your property?" "Yes officers, it is." "Well I'm sorry sir, but we've had a complaint from a neighbour about the noise. May we come in and have a look for ourselves?"

I used to have a very strict rule about the non-use of drugs in my house. On this one occasion, I just knew that the rule wouldn't stick and realised there were many illegal substances that might be seen by the cops. I remember slowing them up as much as I could whilst various people were running around trying to sanitise the place. We went through the house to the back yard (the dance floor) and they told me I'd have to turn it down. I, of course, immediately obeyed, and then a few minutes after their departure, turned it back up again. Let the fun continue.

Sometime later, they're back. "We're sorry sir, but there's been another complaint. May we come in and check it again?" On the way out back they asked me what the party was in aid of, and after telling them, I took great joy in their response. "Oh, yes. Missing Persons. That's the girl who dances around wearing fish bowls on her tits, isn't it?" They knew alright (see Insert Figure 26.2).

On reaching the dance floor, they told me it wouldn't do. "But officers, you saw me turn it down." "No sir. What we meant was, it won't do because it's too quiet. Turn it up. Oh and by the way, would it be possible to meet the singer of the band and maybe get a couple of autographs?" They walked out this time with posters, shirts, copies of the record, and, of course, the autographs. L.A. cops aren't always pains.

By this time, the sun was getting high in the sky, most of the business people had left, and many people had been in the pool, some voluntarily and some not. Time for the Jacuzzi (see Figure 26.3). There were maybe six or seven of us in there and at some point we happened to notice this kid, probably age 18 or 19, looking at us from the side of the pool. He had his chin resting on his hands and he had this strange grin on his face. We all eventually got out and there he is still in the same position, but the grin had now disappeared. What a strange person. We go in, get dressed, and when I come out to turn everything off, he's still there, but now looking slightly pained. I told him the party's over, get out and please leave. "I can't," was the reply. "What do you mean, you can't?" "My balls are stuck in the suction pipe."

Figure 26.3: The infamous pool.

Needless to say, I started to laugh and ran into the house to tell all who were left. Out we all march and one person who hadn't got changed yet jumped in the pool, determined to prove this person a liar. With hands around his shoulders and feet on the side of the pool he pushed off. I don't think I have ever heard such a pained scream in my life. He was very securely attached to the side of the pool thanks to the suction created by the pool filtering system. What the hell does one do next?

Dial 911, that's what one does. After getting through to the paramedics, I started to give them all the information, but as soon as I said, "His testicles are stuck in the extraction pipe," they hung up. Again, dial 911, and again when I reached the pertinent point, I hear nothing but a dial tone.

OK, I need a second opinion. I went outside and relayed the story and the next thing I know my wife is heading off to place a call herself. Well, the conversation was heading in the same direction, except this time there was added a "don't fucking hang up" and "fucking balls" and "fucking swimming pool." I have to admit it's quite amazing what the word "fucking" can sometimes achieve when used as an adverb. Ten minutes later there's a knock on the door, and upon opening it, I'm facing three giant firefighters in their full regalia. "What's this we're being told about someone being stuck in the pool?"

So out we trot. They look and they assess. They talk amongst themselves and give instructions to turn everything off. My first thought was, "What kind of a dumb sod would not have thought to do that in the first place?" but I just told them as nicely as I could that everything was indeed off and it hadn't helped. "OK. There's no choice. We have to break the concrete." Instantly, at the top of her voice, my wife went off. "You can break his fucking balls before you break my fucking concrete. There must be another fucking way." They all looked sheepishly at one another and the one who seemed to be in charge said, "Do you have any Vaseline?"

I couldn't move fast enough. Into the house, into the medicine chest, and back out with the requested item. I have had a good long life and I don't think I've ever had to work as hard as I had to that morning in my attempts to stifle the laughter whilst watching this 6 foot, 5 inch firefighter, in all his firefighting garb, on one knee, applying Vaseline to this young man's family jewels.

Anyway, all's well that ends well. Or so I thought. Just as the fire truck pulled away, a police car containing the earlier two officers pulled up outside. My immediate reaction was, "The music's been off for ages. What's up now?" "Relax," they said. "We were having breakfast and we heard this call to the paramedics about someone stuck in the pool and recognised your address. We had to come and see if it was true." After telling them the whole story, they drove off laughing, "Wait 'til they hear this at the station!"

The finale to the whole story was that this event got more notoriety than we could ever have imagined. A radio personality from the top L.A. morning radio show took the kid, who was a gatecrasher from up the street as it turned out, home to care for, and she finished up giving on-air daily updates on his bruising for the next week. As a bonus, Moon Zappa was there through all of this and relayed the story to her father, Frank, who just happened to be doing an interview with KROQ later that day. Of course, in his inimitable manner, he managed to spend the vast majority of the interview talking about the pool incident with a DJ who had been at the party but had left before the happening. And we also made several U.S. newspapers and one Brit paper. What a great party! And the best thing is, I actually remember it.

THE CAPITOL ERA BEGINS

The contract with Capitol wasn't what you'd call a "good deal" for us at all, but it was the only one around and as a result went fairly quickly because there wasn't much to really negotiate. It was a typical deal for the time with three albums guaranteed and an option for two more if the label so chose. In talking it over with them it was decided that we already had the buzz going so let's push it as fast as we can, so it was decided that Capitol would reissue our EP with two changes. We had put it out as a 7-inch EP, pretty much based around the format that I was used to whilst growing up in England. Capitol decided to put it out as a 12-inch, which allowed it to be louder since there was more space for deeper grooves. Secondly, we dumped "Hello, I Love You" and put on "Words" in its place, which finished up getting a huge amount of airplay. When we originally put together the demo, we had erroneously thought that we should do a cover, thinking it was going to get a lot of play. No one touched it.

Warren called me one time when he was stuck at Newark airport. Any time there was an announcement over the intercom, he realized that people weren't listening and said, "What are words for? No one listens any more." That was his hook line and I just thought, "OK, why would you say that then?" You've got to go work in reverse and say a bunch of things that make that conclusion. You know, pay off, so that's what I did.

Terry Bozzio

The EP came out and finished up selling about 800,000 units, which at the time was the biggest selling 12-inch ever. Most of the sales came from California, which was certainly our biggest market in the beginning. More than that, it started to penetrate into places that we couldn't get to before, thanks to Capitol's marketing muscle.

In those days it was all about seeding the market. You could be a reasonably well-known band in L.A., but how do you get it in front of the rest of the country? That's why we reissued the EP, because it was something different and we thought people would take notice, and there was an appetite at Alternative Album Radio for these types of things at the time.

Rupert Perry, former head of Capitol Records A&R

RECORDING THE ALBUM

Once the 12-inch EP had been put out, it was time to finish the album, so we headed back to Chateau Recorders in North Hollywood. It didn't take us much time to record the rest of the album since we'd already gone through the songs in preproduction for the live show. In the end, it took us about three weeks of recording and another couple of weeks mixing.

Recording was unusual because more often than not, Terry played the track by himself and then we'd start overdubbing from there. As he was co-writer for most of the songs, he knew exactly what he wanted to play without any help from the other band members playing along. Then we would add the bass, then guitars or keyboards, depending on which was most predominant in the song, then it would be Dale, and then backing vocals.

Terry played all the drum tracks first. The arrangements were all laid out because we had played these songs for months in our little incubator. No click. Nothing. Then we just started layering on top. We'd do a synth bass or guitar as overdubs, but it was like one bit at a time.

Warren Cuccurullo

Since I had co-written the music and I knew it all by heart, I could hear it in my head as I was playing. I'd go in there and play it all by myself, sometimes with a click track, sometimes just by myself. And then we would listen and if the drums were grooving by themselves, we knew we had a good bed to start overdubbing on. Then Warren would put down the guitar or somebody would put down the bass synth. If it sounded like it was rushing or dragging they had to do it again, so that's how we would get the grooves. We would just make sure it was perfect.

Terry Bozzio

By this time, Patrick O'Hearn, another from the Zappa flock, had joined the band on bass and bass synth. Even though he was a great player, Terry would consistently tell him, "No, lay it back a bit. I want everyone to think the drums are pushing. Lay it back. Lay it back." It was horrendous for Patrick, but he was certainly up to the task.

I always wanted the guitar or the bass to pull a little bit behind the drums to make it sound like the drums were pushing and were on top of the beat. That's where the aggression was coming from.

Terry Bozzio

A perfect example of Pat's ability was when we were overdubbing bass on "U.S. Drag." He first laid down a Moog synthesiser bass, which didn't quite do it for everyone. OK, let's try bass guitar then. Not just any bass guitar, he chose to use a fretless. Still wasn't right. Someone suggested listening to both basses together. Crazy. How could fretless and synth basses ever sound in tune, even if he'd heard the synth when overdubbing the bass? What we heard is what ended up on the final product, perfectly in tune and they fit the track amazingly.

He [Ken] was a caring nurturer. The reason why he's a great producer is because he's true to what the band is. I always expected him to start co-writing with us, but he told me, "No, that's not what it's about." Creatively he'd say, "Let's try this up an octave," or "Let's double this." Things that would make it sound better, or make it cut through the track better. Whenever anyone proposed something he'd always say, "Let's try it with the track." He'd never say, "No," or "That's not going to work". He was flexible and solution oriented. He made our ideas come alive and he did it in a way that made some really screwed up personalities at the time forget that stuff and do what we had to do.

Terry Bozzio

At some point, we decided to utilise my internal bass drum mic trick that I first used back with Tony Williams, which Terry took to immediately. Still, one track, "Windows," had a straight four-on-the-floor bass drum pattern that even Bozzio couldn't keep consistent for the entire song. So we recorded a short piece of the bass drum at the correct tempo, made up a tape loop, and he played along with that.

I'd run outside sneakily smoking pot, because I was a pothead and no one wanted me to smoke. Everybody would get mad at me. So Warren and I came in laughing one day and we laughed so hard our heads crashed together and he knocked out my front tooth, right in the middle of me singing "Windows" or one of those famous tunes. It was crazy.

Dale Bozzio

Another remembrance is a track called "Noticeable Ones." Warren was having difficulty playing the solo because something on the track seemed to be throwing him. We tried and tried, and finally Warren said, "When we get to the solo section, kill the track." I said, "What?" "When we get to the solo, turn off the volume of the track and let me try it without any music going on." First take, he nailed it.

Ken had worked with, you know, some of the greatest singers ever and now he's working with a singer who is more of a sound than a technician. She wasn't really a singer. He managed to get the best vocal performances out of Dale that anybody's ever gotten. Other producers who we've worked with subsequently to that didn't get such good performances because, in their defense, the melodies we

*wrote were beyond her abilities. The earlier stuff was right in the
pocket for her. But we made a lot of mistakes after we moved on to
our next record.*

Warren Cuccurullo

*Dale was not that strong of a singer but she pulled the best stuff out
of herself that she could. Ken would have five tracks and he would
have to construct a compilation from those five tracks, sometimes
pulling the best syllables or words or half a sentence from each one
to make one that sounded right. You know, nobody's perfect live
and the audience understands that, but in the studio it's more of an
art form where you're making something that's going to be heard
over and over again so you have to make it right.*

Terry Bozzio

*I think he [Ken] recognized my qualities even through the tug of
war that Terry Bozzio gave us when I started to squeak. I'd do these
little squeaks, and Terry would go, "No, don't do that. That's not
in the melody." And Ken would go, "Why don't we do this?" He is
very much a diplomat.*

Dale Bozzio

Finally, we finished the record, but a funny thing happened. This was
the time of cassettes as a means for checking your work away from
the studio, and for some reason, all the cassettes that we got from
Chateau were running slightly fast, so all of our songs were sped up.
After listening to them that way for three or four months, when we
came to mastering, everything felt slow when we now heard it at the
proper speed. We had to adjust the speed of the master so it ran faster
because we were so used to everything playing that way.

When we had finished the album, it was time to let the record company
hear it. My assistant, Steve Brooks, and I went to Capitol and were taken
to the boardroom. A large array of Chinese food was laid out and we
were joined by Don Zimmerman and the heads of all the departments.
After what to me was a long and very drawn out lunch over which they
talked about sports that I had no idea about, it was time to play the
acetate. God, I hate playing stuff for labels. As it turned out, they loved
it. In general anyway. One of the A&R guys, Bobby Colomby (the
same Capitol A&R exec who had unceremoniously passed on us after

firing Terry), wasn't happy with two of the mixes. The first one I was in complete agreement with. I had already wanted to remix it but, due to time restraints, had held back. The second, "Walking in L.A.," he felt needed more bass synth. Now, this was a time before computerised desks where you could easily recall everything, thus enabling you to change the most minute parameter. Doing a new mix and having it sound the same as the previous one back then was not easy. Knowing the inherent difficulty of redoing a perfectly good mix (especially for a reason I didn't agree with), I told him, "Of course I'll promptly remix it," then forgot all about it. When next he heard the album, with just the *one* new mix, he was pleased with me for the way the new mix turned out, and especially pleased with himself about how much better "Walking in L.A." was with the extra bass synth. It's enough to give the A&R profession a bad name.

THE ALBUM DROPS

The first album was entitled *Spring Session M*, an anagram of Missing Persons. One element of the album artwork was the band's name written in Morse code. I will never forget the first phone call I received from a fan asking if we were aware that the Morse code spelt Missing "Wersons," and if so, why? "Congratulations," was the reply. "You are the first person to spot the intentional error and you win the prize." Of course, everyone that later called (I seem to remember only about four) were all instant winners and they all received gift packages of merchandise and autographs.

Spring Session M was released and soon went gold. A celebratory bash was planned by Capitol at what was then The Palace (a very nice club across the street from the Capitol building), where the gold records were to be presented to the band. Unfortunately, by that time the egos had started to emerge and I received a phone call from Terry the day of the bash telling me that they didn't think Capitol had done anything for them. He said that they felt crippled by the label and therefore they were going to arrive at the event in wheelchairs. *What?!* "It will show everyone how we feel," he so matter-of-factly stated. I suggested the band have a rethink of this option, then immediately called Capitol to notify them that the event might have to be postponed. "What's going on?" they asked. "I will try and sort it out, but I may not be able to, so I just wanted to give you the heads up," I cautiously warned.

Needless to say, after several later phone conversations, the band backed down and showed up in the correct fashion. The worst thing about the whole event was that two of our closest allies at Capitol, Don Zimmerman, the president, and Rupert Perry, the head of A&R, were not present because they no longer held their positions at the label. The presentation was made by the new president, Jim Mazza, who had had absolutely nothing whatsoever to do with the band's success.

Soon afterwards I received a call from Geffen's much acclaimed A&R exec John Kalodner, the other A&R person besides Rupert Perry that I have a huge amount of respect for. When we were originally shopping the deal I had gone to see him because I knew him quite well. Kalodner knew his particular niche and we weren't in it, so he passed on the project. However, he was the only A&R guy that called me up after we were successful and said, "I was wrong. Congratulations." That meant so much to me then and still does now.

In the end, Capitol was amazing. Yes, it was a lousy deal, but thanks to sales of the 12-inch the band were only in the red for one week. After that there was always money coming in, which was very, very unusual. If we had been with Columbia, we probably would have sold two or three times what we ended up selling, but they could never have broken the band in the first place. It was widely known that Columbia couldn't break an act at the time, but when they had a band which had broken already, they could sell many, many more records than anyone else. But Capitol was one of the hottest new wave labels around at that time. They had Duran Duran, Thomas Dolby, The Knack, and, of course, Missing Persons.

But fate helped the cause as well. Sometime before the recording of the album, we did a gig at the Magic Mountain amusement park which I recorded for the *King Biscuit Flower Hour* radio show. It just so happened that the week the album hit the stores was the week that the radio show was aired, and as fate would have it, the awful movie *Lunch Wagon* was first broadcast, every bloody night it turned out, on one of the cable channels on TV. I can't tell you how many people asked how we managed to synchronise all of that. My answer then, "Just good planning." My answer now, the more honest, "Just good luck."

CHAPTER 27
Missing Persons: The Downfall

What a great band and what a great concept. Some of the greatest musicians around and a lead singer who oozed sex appeal. How could it fail? Well, until it became successful, it couldn't. Ain't egos great?

Missing Persons was now riding high, the gigs were getting bigger, the band was touring a lot more, but that's when the problems started to show up. We began to have problems with our great agent Doug, who was unfortunately spending our advances on some illegal white powdered substances that makes people crazy. He managed to keep things going until he had to cancel some dates because Dale got sick, and suddenly the promoters were asking for their deposits back, but he'd spent it all. That created some major problems and unfortunately we had to get rid of him because of it.

Then, unknown to me up until that point, Dale had started to get a habit of her own and this started to screw up her marriage to Terry, affect the egos of everyone, and certainly screw up the band direction. But up until that it point, it was, to say the least, one hell of a journey.

One of the greatest rock 'n' roll movies of all time is *Spinal Tap*, and what really scared me was when I started to live so many of the moments in that movie with MP, not least of which was us

329

getting lost when trying to get to the stage from the dressing room. Luckily, they never wanted Stonehenge on stage and Terry never spontaneously combusted.

As one example, we were doing a small promotional tour in Europe and the band was booked to do an English TV show being shot up in northern England. Unfortunately, the tour manager, who happened to stay back in London, got two of the flight cases mixed up so Dale's costumes went to the cleaners and her dirty laundry finished up with us. Luckily Dale happened to have two of the plexiglass bowls that she used to make a bra, but nothing else. I finished up dashing around looking for anything close to the materials she normally used and I struck gold. With just enough time to spare, we had everything that was needed—the only thing left to do was piece everything together. So there's me, on the ground with soldering iron in hand, making holes in two plastic bowls ready for plastic tubing to be threaded through so that Dale could have a bra for the show. That was when I discovered what it really meant to be a manager.

> The one thing that's always kinda stood out for me was I was sitting in Ken's office and he got a call from Elton John. Apparently they had been trying to reach each other for a couple of weeks. I couldn't hear Elton on the other end, but I heard Ken saying, "I would love to, except I've decided to stop producing because I really want to manage Missing Persons. There's something here and, you know, I haven't done this before and really want to go for it." So in my mind I'm thinking, "OK, he's turning down Elton John," and it always kinda stuck with me. It was amazing to me to hear that conversation.
> Scott Martin, Capitol VP of Marketing

Missing Persons were out on tour and the tour manager, Peter Scher, had gotten to Dale, and she had gotten to him. They couldn't stand each other anymore so we had to fire him. The problem was that we couldn't leave MP out on the road on their own and the next tour manager that we had found couldn't start for a few days, so I went down to San Antonio, Texas to look after them until he could get there. As I was standing on the side of the stage watching the show, Dale reached down and took what looked to be a joint from one of the audience members, took a few hits, and gave it back. We'd already discussed this kind of thing with Dale, telling her it was bad because A) it didn't look good, B) there might be police there, and most of all, C) who the hell knew what was in those things. Anyway she had sworn she would never do it again but there she was, doing it yet again.

When I saw what was going on I lost it and went storming down to the dressing room to wait for her after the show. Now this was at a college, and the dressing rooms were set up for jocks, so there was one large long changing room as opposed to the normal individual rooms. I sat there stewing and waited for them to finish the show.

At the end of the set, the first down was Terry, who sees that I'm obviously not my normal self. "What's up?'" he says. "She fucking did it again!" said I. "What do you mean?" was Terry's response. "Didn't you see?" I said. "No, you know me when I'm into playing. What did she do this time?" "She reached down into the audience and took a joint." At that point, he became equally inflamed.

Dale eventually came down and we both started into her, which caused her to fly into a screaming rage where she started to smash everything in sight. Luckily she didn't smash any of the mirrors, but any bottles, be they drink, be they perfume, be they makeup, whatever, she managed to smash them all. Then it was over and a few days later, Steve, my assistant, came down with the next tour manager and that worked out, barely, until the demise of all of us.

I remember the first tour manager we had just giving up and saying, "I can't deal with this woman anymore." We were in San Antonio, Texas and I had to find a new tour manager immediately. We found a guy who had done quite a few stadium acts and so he did pretty good with them for a while, but he said there were times he wanted to bail as well. But yeah, she got to be a little impossible. Ken was usually pretty good at calming her.

Steve Brooks

A FILM EDUCATION

Through managing MP, I got to actually find out a little more about the film business. Dale was offered a movie which turned out to be

Flashdance. I read the script, but couldn't see it being as big as it ended up becoming. That was OK because Dale couldn't do it for two reasons: first, she couldn't dance, at least not the way that was needed for that movie, and second, there was a scene where she had to undress. There was no way that Dale, who had done plenty of that in the past, was going to bare her flesh now that she had some success.

I turned the part down and it was only later that I found out that the actress they chose, Jennifer Beals, couldn't dance either and they used a stand-in, so Dale could have done it on that front. And the nude scene was taken out of the movie and she just took her bra off underneath her sweatshirt. Dale could have done that easily. One lives and learns, but let's be honest, Dale was no Jennifer Beals.

The band was also offered a horrendous comedy movie based on *The Phantom of the Opera* that took place in San Francisco, but it was all rock music. There's a classic scene where the lead in the movie, who was of course a rock 'n' roll singer, goes to the bathroom and actually has a conversation with his penis. After *Lunch Wagon*, I somehow couldn't see the band being in that, and unlike *Flashdance*, it was a complete flop.

THE VIDEOS

The band ended up doing a number of videos that always seemed to verge on the precipice of disaster during production, but ended up receiving a lot of MTV play. Maybe that was the reason. You've got to live dangerously to get people to notice.

The first video was "Mental Hopscotch." I was approached by a couple of people who saw how music videos were going to evolve as a tool for selling records and making money, and they wanted to do a video with MP. They took the band to a small studio, shot for a day, and after they edited it we got a copy that was an absolute disaster. We got permission from them to try to re-edit it, which the band did, and that's what finally went out as the first video. That one didn't cost anything as a result.

The second video, which was a live version of "Words," was done for a TV show that was being filmed on the A&M lot in Hollywood. A bunch of doctors had pooled their money together and decided that they wanted to do a rock 'n' roll series on TV, much like the old show *The Midnight Special*. They must have spent a fortune because they had every band in L.A. on it, some that eventually made it, and a lot that didn't. The TV show fell through so as sort of a payment, we got the video of the performance. Again, it didn't cost us anything.

The third one was "Destination Unknown," which was done in England. This was the idea of the record company and was before the advent of recouping video costs from the act, so once again they paid for everything and it cost us nothing.

Oh God, that was a nightmare. These guys at the record company just didn't know anything, so they hired any idiot who had what they thought were "artistic sensibilities." No one listened to the band about our ideas. It was just some director's little dream to make some art.

The building we shot in was so dilapidated that there was moss about two inches thick on it, a wooden floor that had holes, and piles of debris everywhere. Rats were swimming down the flooded subterranean chambers. It was a dangerous place. It was really like something out of a movie.

I remember when we were there scouting the location the day before we actually shot. We were standing under this old vaulted glass panel ceiling and suddenly you hear this "thunk," and there's a piece of glass that fell from hundreds of feet above just sticking like a knife in the wood floor, and we were like, "Let's go make a movie."

Everything started off pretty good. We had Dale looking beautiful and Warren and I were looking good. We had great makeup and clothes. Simon [the director] had us doing some things that were pretty right for our personality, except that Patrick and Chuck were in some limo running around doing something that was supposed to mean something, but none of us understood just what. Then it got a little more out there.

In one scene he had Dale running. It was like a Peter Sellers movie. "What am I running from?" "Well, you're running from yourself." Ha ha. So there was lots of running and the whole thing made no sense. It's late at night and Dale is running through standing water on the ground, she had been drinking, and she was in serious high heels. She was running in and out of the light of these weird spotlights when she slips and falls and bashes her face on some rusty pipe. Her face became absolutely distorted. She lost any sense of the bridge of her nose, and she had this massive cut, so we rushed her to the hospital and they stitched her up.

The next morning she had this massive bandage and her face was all swollen and black and blue and we thought, "That's the end of shooting." But everything just has to be done now or it's not going to get done because it costs too much money, so they took the bandage off and stuck a piece of broken mirror in her face, did some great makeup on her, and actually made it look OK. Then they shot her reflection in some mirrors that was semi-distorted, then shot her from behind with her reflection in the mirror. The next day we shot in this artist's studio with Dale sitting on some piece of furniture that had broken pieces of mirror on it. It all seemed to tie together. Simon whatever-his-name-was said he was cutting corners furiously, but you know, we made a good video at the end of the day.

Terry Bozzio

The fourth video was "Noticeable Ones," which was once again a live performance, and shot in San Francisco. Up until this point MTV had only been on the East Coast, so they had planned this huge opening for a nationwide broadcast which was due to happen on a Saturday. Because of our success on MTV, they wanted to use MP not only as the opening but they also wanted us to put on our live show. Of course we jumped at it because it put us in MTV's good books, and it would mean more promotion for the band.

We were filming it at a sold-out show at The Warfield in San Francisco and all was great, but at the rehearsal they only used the house lights so the stage lighting hadn't actually been turned on yet. The show's director was going through everything and said, "Yeah, this is going to be great." "Ah, it's not going to be this bright when we shoot," I told him. "Yes, yes, it'll be just fine," he replied. OK, he's the director and he knows what he's doing.

Of course, when the show starts it isn't anywhere near bright enough and the director starts calling, "We've got to get more light. Turn the lights up. We can't see anything." Ah, told you so. And he keeps yelling, "Hey, gotta get more light. Tell the lighting guys to start making it brighter."

The one thing that no one had quite realised was that the instruments and the lighting were on the same electrical circuit, so what happened was as the lights were made brighter, the circuit pulled much more power. As a result, it was lowering the voltage and having an effect on all of the synths, pulling them down in pitch. As soon as the lights were brought up, everything started to go out of tune on stage. Dale was singing terribly, and the guitar and the bass didn't match the synth. It was just plain awful.

It finished up being a total write-off. There was nothing that could be used. The only number that was any good musically was the first song, but that video was atrocious because there wasn't enough light. What did happen was one of those freaky type of things that sometimes occur. Terry, being as good as he is, played "Noticeable Ones" at almost the identical tempo to the record. This enabled us to take the original album recording and sync it up with the live recording so that we could still use the audience and a little of what was coming from the PA in the theatre. Then, the band went in and edited the video to that and it worked out great. As far as I'm concerned, it was the best video they ever made. Unfortunately, we'd had to cancel the MTV thing because the show was ruined, so they were really pissed as they'd already been doing a lot of promotion for it, and as a penance, never played the video that came from that.

THE PLAYGIRL INCIDENT

Prior to MP, Dale had done various photo spreads for those wonderful examples of fine American literature: *Penthouse* and *Hustler*. We realised that this was going to start coming up in interviews at some point, so we wanted to get ahead of the game rather than be asked a question about it and come out defensively. Knowing full well of Warren's, shall we say, sexual proclivities, we decided it might be a good idea to get him to do something like a spread in *Playgirl* magazine, so if it ever came up in any interview we could say, "Dale did *Hustler*, Warren did *Playgirl*, and Terry did *Architectural Digest*. So what?" I phoned them up, and before you knew it, arranged for a photo shoot with Warren in his total and complete birthday suit (see Insert Figure 27.1). What we didn't bargain on was that Warren would later go on to do nude spreads in other magazines and include assorted "adult material" on his fan club site. He generally blamed me for opening the door to that side of him, but all I wanted to do was soothe the blow of any potential negative press.

He fucked me up forever because of this [laughs]. When we did interviews the interviewers didn't really care about how good musicians we were or that we worked with Frank Zappa or we sold out the Santa Monica Civic. All they cared about was, "Why is your hair pink and blue?" when talking to me or Terry, and "You're wearing plastic fishbowls on your breasts?" or "Why did you pose nude in Hustler *magazine?" when talking to Dale. They never asked about how we wrote a song, it was always asking Dale about the naked this and the fishbowls on her tits that. Ken had been out with me a few times to the clubs and I was always pretty crazy and didn't mind dropping my pants and doing those kinds of silly things. I never put my things into a filter in a pool, but I've been known to expose myself just about any time. Anyway, Ken said, "Why doesn't Warren do* Playgirl *so when you do interviews and they ask Dale, 'Why did you do* Hustler *magazine?' she can say, 'Oh, talk to Warren. He just did* Playgirl,' *just to kind of deflect it, and then we could get back to talking about the music. Ken gets in touch with them, and* Playgirl's *way into it. So there I am doing a nude shoot for* Playgirl *magazine in 1982. Yes it did work. It deflected the attention from Dale and it brought even more humor in. It's all entertainment and it's all Ken's fault.*

Warren Cuccurullo

THE BREAKUP

I started to get funny feelings about my status with the band after we'd done the massive US Festival, which was the last time I'd seen them for a while. The US Festival was a Steve Wozniak (of Apple Computer fame) creation which featured three days of major acts such as U2, David Bowie, and Stevie Nicks, and held out in the hinterlands on the way from L.A. to Las Vegas. MP was lucky enough to be invited to play, and the show was videoed and recorded since the organisers were going to put a video together of it. I remember trying to reach the band to go over details about the upcoming album, and when I finally did, I found that they were working on the editing and the sound of their US Festival performance without ever letting me know. Funny the way it took that to get me started wondering what was going on.

A little while later I told the band up front because I didn't want it to be misconstrued, "I'm going to do some press, so be prepared. I'm doing it so that I can push your name out there in one form or another while things are slow." We were getting ready to begin recording the second album and we couldn't get much publicity on the band by just using the band's name at that point. They'd been written about and written about and written about. They were still hot, and I wanted to keep it that way, so we had to find a way to keep the publicity going. They said they were fine with it. It turns out that, at least in one of the interviews that I did, I said something that Terry didn't like, and as far as he was concerned, that was it. It was all over for me.

> *He talked in an interview about the "nurturing" of Missing Persons, which is exactly what he did, but at the time I took that as a serious ego blow. In the sickness of all of our personalities and our insecurities at that time, that's where everything went wrong. It was totally just my fucking ego and man, it was stupid.*
> Terry Bozzio

Another thing that occurred was because there was very little going on with MP at the time and we'd gotten the organisational side of the business sorted out, I was looking to find another act to look after. There was one day when an artist came by that I had actually tried very hard to organise producing before MP were ever on the scene. Her name was Shandi Sinnamon and she was the hottest thing in town. Every label and every producer was going to see her, and she was getting multiple offers.

I put in an offer for production, but was turned down as she signed with Mike Chapman's label, and he, of course, produced. The album died a death. She did the rounds for a bit, signed with Freddy DeMann (Michael Jackson's manager at the time), and finally wrote and performed one of the songs from *Flashdance*. She came around to see me not for production, but for management, which really got to me because she was still signed with someone I knew and who had no idea she was meeting with other people behind his back. There I am talking with her, Steve was in the room as well, and in the middle of our conversation the phone rang. Steve picked it up and it turned out it was Dale. Steve said, "Dale's on the phone," to which I said, "I'll call her back." Steve relayed the message, then covered over the mouthpiece. "Ken, she says she wants to talk with you now." I said, "Tell her I will call her back." It took 20 minutes before I called her back after seeing Shandi off, and Dale wasn't the slightest bit pleased. "How dare I not speak with her immediately," and all that junk. That occasion certainly didn't help my situation any.

Then of course there was the discussion of Terry's drums. He wanted to use Simmons electronic drums on the next album, which were all the rage at that point as they were on almost every record that was being done around that time. He wanted to be hip and happening and wanted to use them, but my argument was, "Terry, you're one of the greatest drummers in the world. Why do you want to sound like a second rate programmer?" "Because they're the 'in' thing. Everyone's doing it," and so on, and so on. He had to use them and I said, "No, you'll play normal drums like you did on the first album. We'll take it one step at a time, and no one will be using those drums by the time the album comes out. You'll sound old-fashioned if you use them." I could never get him to agree with me; that was probably another reason for the split. Egos like mad.

At that point we were so hung up in keeping up with the Joneses. The whole electronic thing had blossomed and Phil Collins had come out with that wonderful acoustic drum sound that everyone

thought was Simmons drums on "In the Air Tonight." Even the
Simmons guy said, "Yeah, you can get that Phil Collins sound
with these." The trouble was that the Simmons drums never made
that sound. It was an AMS gated reverb for God's sake, with
room mics and all that. At any rate, we were swept away by all
this and I was convinced we had to be as sophisticated as Bowie
was at the US Festival. He was a consummate artist. There wasn't
a wrong note the whole damn night and here we were too afraid
to do Saturday Night Live *because we were afraid if Dale sung*
poorly, or something would happen, we would blow it.

Terry Bozzio

They never actually confronted me about my not working with them anymore. My attorney, Stan Diamond, got a phone call from their attorney, Owen Sloane, and it was just passed through that way. They didn't even have the decency to tell me.

It turned out that they thought they'd done everything themselves and no one else had had anything to do with their success. Then they got rid of everyone on the team. They couldn't get rid of Capitol, but as happens all too frequently, Capitol had already undergone a lot of restructuring at that point and a new head of the company and head of A&R had come in. Because of the success of the first album, they became sycophants to the band. "Yes, you're right." "Yes, everything's great," and consequently the band ended up going into massive debt. That was during the second and third albums. It was obvious that the second album wasn't happening, but Jim Mazza, who was the president then, kept on going, "Oh, this is great," and they'd say, "We need more money to finish it off." "Yes, OK."

Label people don't want to deal with the artist directly because
they can't tell you to fuck off, which is something we learned later
on, and we learned again with Duran Duran. They can tell your
manager that and then go have a Scotch and Coke with them. They
can say "Ken, fuck off. You're not getting this," but they won't say
that to the lead singer. But we didn't know that, but Ken knew that.
He knew what we were getting into. We were stupid.

Warren Cuccurullo

They were great, but it takes more than being great. It takes that
machine to push the album and we were that machine. Ken pulled

ABBEY ROAD TO ZIGGY STARDUST

out every favor in the book that he had. We tried to make it easy for them. We tried to let them go in the studio, go in rehearsal, do what they had to do, and just think about being on stage, and that's why I think the next album should have been giant.
Steve Brooks

His [Ken's] idea was to go back and do some of the other tunes that we used to play live for the second album. He wanted to keep it more in the same bag because in a business like this, you repeat a successful formula. I did the stupid thing of not repeating a successful formula. I wanted to break with that and do something more, you know, bite off more than I could chew. And we did that and it was sterile. We lost the audience. The more sophisticated music and melodies that we wrote for the second album were beyond Dale's ability to sell as a singer. She just couldn't cut it and to me that was heartbreaking. That's why I can hardly listen to the second record because it gives me a pain in my stomach. It just wasn't the right thing. So yeah, I was wrong there and I've told him this and I admit it now. I couldn't see the forest for the trees.
Terry Bozzio

Even though I had a contract with them, they found a way around it in a way that could only happen in California or New York. There's a very strong law in this state whereby a manager cannot "procure employment" for an act, only a licensed talent agent can. It's an arcane law more designed to protect the movie agents of the 1930s than a music artist of today, but it is a law. Well, early on I got them an appearance on *Solid Gold*, which was a TV show that helped them sell a load of records. Because of the Musicians' Union rules they had to get paid scale for it, that meant I, the manager, had gotten them employment. As a result, they threatened to take me in front of the California labour board, which could have ended up turning out very badly for me. If you go in front of the labour board as a manager and it's found that you did indeed procure employment, then the labour board can determine that the contract you have with the band is null and void and never existed, thus any monies you had received because of that contract have to be paid back to the band. That's what happened with the band Weezer, and I have been led to understand that both Ke$ha and Lady Gaga are bringing the same action against their former managers right now so they don't have to pay them commission.

Oh my God, we were devastated. We had done nothing else but think about this band, and this is what happened. I think Ken took it pretty hard, and after that, everything fell apart for everybody.
Steve Brooks

A lot of my peers, friends and relations said, "Why on earth would you give up a good production career and get into management?" Firstly and most importantly, because I believed in the band. Secondly, because I did, and still do believe, that good management is as much about artistry as good playing, good production, and good engineering. I would manage again at the drop of a hat if I found the right act under the right situation. It was the most amazing learning experience, especially about the way laws are stacked against managers in California.

I eventually ran into Terry again at a time and place where the egos and petty squabbles were put aside and he said to me, "You know, you made it look too easy. We had absolutely no idea how much you actually did." Fine. Next time I'll make it look a lot harder!

The worst thing we did was we fired Ken. OK, let's get rid of the guy who is looking after our career, who has recorded some of the greatest records of all time, who we sold almost a million records with. Let's have the greatest drummer in the world not play drums. I can't even listen to the [second] record now. Well, one of the things that screams to me is the sound of the drums, which aren't drums. They sound like little tiny toys playing parts. It should have been recorded by Ken on a big drum kit in a big room. It was as bad as it could get. We were stupid.
Warren Cuccurullo

CHAPTER 28

The Downsides of the Business

As well as Devo, Missing Persons *et al.*, I did a few albums at Chateau that did absolutely nothing—albums by such household names as Jamie Sheriff, Tim Moore, and Michalski & Oosterveen, a duo managed by Jon Peters, who happened to be Barbra Streisand's beau at the time (I think the order was hairdresser, lover, manager). The one thing of any consequence that came out of that particular project was that a recording was used in the film *Eyes of Laura Mars*. For anyone interested, it's called "Burn" and was played behind the car crash photo shoot. The fact that so little happened with these acts is normal, since you win some and lose some in this business. Still, I only work with an artist because I believe in them and so it's always a disappointment when a record doesn't take off.

HELLION

My wife Patience was trying to manage a metal band called Hellion that I was going to produce. If I'm completely honest, I really didn't think she'd be able to do it, and figured that at some point I'd probably have to take over. We recorded what eventually came out as an EP and it was during that time that our marital relationship fell on hard times, which caused me to immediately end my association with the band because I just didn't want anything to do with anything that Patience was connected with anymore.

I remember when Ken was working with the singer from Hellion. She had a candle pentagram on the studio floor that she had to sing in the middle of. It wasn't even an issue for Ken. It was more like, "Today's business will be to set up a pentagram with candles for the singer. OK." Nobody questioned it.

Wyn Davis, owner of Total Access Recording

A little while later I returned from a project with a band called Rubber Rodeo that we did up in Canada. When I got back, Patience confessed about her ongoing cocaine habit and then told me that she was now going to Alcoholics Anonymous. While on the surface this seemed like a good thing, I didn't realise the effect that it would have on not only our marriage, but any marriage. What tends to happen is that after meetings you'll go hang out with other AA people at a restaurant or coffee shop. Patience wasn't coming home directly after the meetings and I didn't exactly understand what was going on, which lead to a number of rows between us.

Finally I learned about Al-Anon, an organisation that helps family members of people in AA understand what they're going through, and went to a meeting. As luck would have it, the very first face I saw as I walked in was Terry Bozzio's. We hadn't seen each other for several years, since the Persons travesty, but it took about a second to put everything behind us. In every respect, it was a fascinating event.

Patience lived up to the AA rule that when you start sobriety, you make no major changes for a year. If you're in a relationship you stay in it; if you're not in one, you don't start one until the end of that first year because you change so much in the meantime. Either way it's the wrong time for a major decision. On her first AA birthday she announced that she wanted a divorce. I was thunderstruck, and immediately grabbed a bottle of Scotch with the intention of downing every last drop. Then it hit me that if I took that first drink, I was not going to stop. I put the bottle down, and decided it was time that I switched from Al-Anon meetings to straight AA meetings.

I went to AA for over a year, but shortly after my first birthday I felt I had enough. Interestingly enough, I did have a problem with alcohol, but it wasn't so much about alcoholism as it was about me dealing with groups of people. It was more about the insecurity within myself. Today I can give one of my talks in front of a room full of people and I'm fine, but back then I was a total wreck. I remember I was on a panel at a conference with Ray Manzarek of The Doors and a couple of other people where I had to get completely blotto before I could even set foot on that stage. Going to a party, I had to get drunk first so I could deal with the people. Funny enough, I could deal with a group of people in the studio, but outside of that I was very insecure. Once I came to grips with that, I was fine thereafter.

In my day I loved to party with the best of them, but I could always stop. We had some incredible parties along the way as you've previously read, but I would always reach a point where I felt I had enough, then I'd go make a cup of tea. There were a couple of occasions where I kept drinking longer than I should have, but the general norm was that I'd stop at some point during the evening and then it would be tea time. It never had the control of me like that, but I did enjoy drinking.

I didn't drink again for many, many years after that, but always felt that it really wasn't an issue. When my second wife Cheryl and I took a trip to Italy for a vacation, I suddenly felt, "Oh, I've got to try some wine while I'm here." I had some and was fine with it and have been fine ever since.

LEVEL 42

The album I did with Level 42, *True Colours*, was one of the harder albums for me. First and foremost, they were huge in England and Europe, but had done nothing in the States to that point. Their previous album before I worked with them was released by A&M there in a one-off deal, but didn't make a dent in the U.S. charts. It was one of those typical things that happened in the U.S.; they were a white band that sounded black so no record company or radio station knew how to handle them. As a result, the band was without a label in the States at the time we decided to work together.

We set up recording dates in England and unusually, I didn't hear any of their material beforehand. When we went into preproduction I came to learn why: they didn't have any material. The way the band had chosen to work was to go into the studio and groove. When they found something they liked, that would become the basis of a song. This proved to be very difficult for me because I didn't know where to take anything. Normally there's at the very least a demo of a song so you can get an idea of what the final version might sound like, but when you start with nothing, I just had no idea where to go with it. There were also major tensions within the band, which didn't help things either. It was a very strange situation.

> *I feel bad that we couldn't present you [Ken] with any songs. We didn't know how to write them at that point and we were struggling as a band. There was a moment when Mark [bassist and vocalist Mark King] didn't know if he wanted to continue with the band, and the band was becoming a bit unglued. We had tried to do some writing early in the year but we just didn't come up with anything half-decent. I wish we could have done a better job of it.*
>
> Phil Gould, drummer for Level 42

Doing this album was also interesting for me on a purely technical basis. There were things going on in England that I hadn't yet been exposed to in the States, like the way you could sample a part in an AMS (see the sidebar "The AMS") and fly it into the track wherever you wanted. I'd never seen that in L.A., but when I got to England it was, "Well, we can always throw that in there with the AMS." I was like, "What the hell are you talking about?" but I started to learn it very quickly as it was used a lot on this project.

Figure 28.1: An AMS DMX-15-80 digital delay

The first studio we worked in was Genetic Sound, which was owned by Human League producer Martin Rushent, then we completed and mixed the album at Parkgate Studios, which was located on the south coast of England in a town called Hastings. While there we stayed in a hotel that had to be the closest thing to a real-life version of the *Fawlty Towers* television show ever. It was hysterical in all the same ways as the show. They did do us a few "favours" though. They were required by law to close up the bar way before we were finished recording, but would leave us the key so we could open it ourselves when we got in at around 2 A.M. That continued the entire time we were there. Boy, did we get a surprise when we were about to leave and we got this *huge* bill for the booze, which, of course, we couldn't pass off to the record label. Sometimes a favour isn't what it seems.

The AMS

Unlike today where it's so easy to just cut, copy, or paste a part in a digital audio workstation, the process of "sampling" was relegated to an outboard processor in the '80s. The first device to do this was the AMS (Advanced Music Systems) DMX 15-80 (see Figure 28.1), which was the world's first microprocessor-controlled, 15-bit digital delay unit. Included on the DMX was a function called "loop triggering," which launched the use of digital sampling on records. Subsequent versions of the DMX included pitch changing and up to 32 seconds of delay.

Everything on this piece of equipment was done manually. You'd press a button to record the part, then you had to press another one to play it back and record it on the multitrack at just the right time. It took a bit of experimentation to fly the part in at just the right place.

That was a strange hotel. It was something out of Fawlty Towers. *The eggs in the morning came out looking like some strange creature. The whole family was extremely odd. It's all a blur, apart from the memory of how weird it was.*
Phil Gould

It wasn't residential [Parkgate]; we stayed at the "lovely" Moor Hall Hotel nearby. That smell as you walked in, as if years of food had been impregnated into the carpet. And their favourite dessert— melon balls in Sambuca—yeuchh!
Mike Lindup, keyboard player for Level 42

Bassist and vocalist Mark King, who took the slapping funk bass style to another level (see Insert Figure 28.2), was interested in working with me because of my work with Stanley Clark, and I ended up recording him in a similar way. Where with Stan I took the high and low feeds directly from his Alembic bass, with Mark I took the outputs from his Trace Elliot amp, which gave me the same kind of control as with Stan, only later in the signal chain.

Sometimes we would find a part in a jam that we could edit together, while other times it was more of a "we like that part, now let's record it properly" kind of thing. We would generally record the bass and the drums and overdub on top of that. Once we got the form of the song together, Mark would record a phonetic vocal performance with a melody and no words, but sung in a way that he wanted the words to sound. Drummer Phil Gould would then go away and come up with the lyrics. The only problem was that Phil was being very slow, so there was constant pressure on him from everyone else to keep writing. That was hard on everyone.

Lyrics have never been one of my things, since I usually concentrate on melody. In fact, half the time I don't even listen to the lyrics. I've got to get the musical side of it more than the lyrical side, which probably didn't help in the situation with Level 42. It's not an area I could give advice on, although I have got better at it over the years.

Between Genetic and Parkgate, Phil and I went back to Total Access in California to record percussion with Paulinho Da Costa, one of the top percussionists during that era and someone the band had worked with before and loved. Unfortunately Paulinho couldn't be credited on the album because if you used an American union musician, a certain percentage of the album royalties had to be paid to the musicians union, the AF of M. The English record label didn't want anything to do with that (less profit for them) so we had to use the guy without anyone knowing.

There was a green, red, and amber light in the speakers that would come on to warn you that you were getting close to blowing a [speaker] driver. Ken used to have them lit up like a stop light. After he started working here [Total Access Recording] we found out really quickly that we needed to have another set of drivers always standing by. I remember standing in the control room back in the day when I and everyone else was still smoking cigarettes, exhaling some smoke, and watching the smoke actually move in the room from the volume from the speakers. I remember thinking, "Oh my God. That's really loud. Maybe I should put on some ear plugs." Terry Bozzio once told me that Ken would monitor so loud that he would grit his teeth every time the snare hit, and by the end of the session he would have this splitting headache.

Wyn Davis

There was a song called "Hot Water," which ended up being the single, that proved to be a problem because of the way the song was created from a jam. Twelve-inch vinyl remixes were very big at the time. Trevor Horn had just come out with some ridiculous number of different remixes of Frankie Goes to Hollywood's "Two Tribes," which were released at a rate of one a week, so the whole remix thing was very big. We did the 12-inch mix of "Hot Water" first, and then edited it into the single mix, the opposite way of how it was usually done. Because it was a straight groove jam and wasn't played to a click, it sped up as it went along. When we started to edit it for the single, there were some very strange tempo changes that still bother me to this day, but the 12-inch works great.

Hot water was laid down as a 10- to 15-minute jam (probably as long as the 2- inch reel had, timewise), without a click track. The track was eventually chopped around and down to just under 6 minutes (shorter for the single), and it gave us the hit single off the album. I remember a dance magazine review for the 12-inch pointing out a 5 BPM variation during the track—didn't stop people dancing to it though!

Mike Lindup

To me "Hot Water" is the best sounding track we ever did. I just love the drum sound on it and the way it just pumps along. It's the one studio track that reflected the energy of the band live more than any other track. By the time we did that track and the 12-inch, we kind of worked out where we needed to be as a band, but it was too late in the album to be able to go back and recut the other songs.

*The band sounded a bit heavy to me and was going in a direction
that I didn't like, but "Hot Water" was very Level 42 and we got
some of the best reviews we ever had on the back of that, and we
were generally hated by the press.*

Phil Gould

In the end, we were at Genetic for about a week, then in Hastings for
about three more to complete the album. After we finished, I came
back to L.A. for a week and then went straight onto another project,
which I heard pissed off Mark since he decided that he wanted to
remix a few of the songs. Unfortunately that couldn't happen because
I was unavailable. Sorry about that, Mark.

AUSTRALIA

I returned to L.A. right in the middle of the 1984 Olympics.
Everyone in the city was so scared that traffic would be unbearable
that it prompted many people to leave. As a result it was easier to
get around the city than ever before, or since. There was absolutely
no traffic even during rush hour on a Friday. Bliss! And then as
my plane took off for the next project in Australia, on the day of
the closing ceremony, they let off an enormous fireworks display
that was absolutely amazing to view from this highly unusual
perspective.

I went down under to produce a band called The Radiators. As
soon as I got there, I went around to check out a few studios and
wound up using the studios at EMI. Equipment was the same almost
everywhere by this time and all studios were very similar. Ironically,
Richard Lush, who had been a second for me at Abbey Road, was
managing one of the studios that I went to check out, and another
former Abbey Road engineer, Martin Benge, was working for EMI,
so I had some compatriots in town.

This became one of those projects where you're caught in the middle
and no matter what you do, someone is going to be unhappy.
The band used to do a Pink Floyd number in their show (I can't
remember the name) and I was given explicit instructions by EMI
America to record it. Unfortunately I received explicit instructions

by EMI Australia *not* to record it. Rock—Ken—hard place. EMI Australia was actually paying for the album, but since my contract was with EMI America, I followed their orders and suffered the wrath of EMI Australia as a result. It's always the producer who bears the brunt, isn't it?

I was down in Aussieland for a bit over a month recording, then I came back to the States to mix the album at Total Access with their manager present. I haven't heard that album (called *Life's a Gamble*) in donkey's years so I don't even remember if it was any good. I do remember that it went gold down there, but didn't really do too much otherwise. When the record was released in the States, there was already a Radiators based in New Orleans, so they changed their name to The Rads, but just for the States. Oh yes, the Floyd number wasn't used on either the Australia or the U.S. release.

KAJA

Somehow I got to know the agent for Kajagoogoo, and soon afterwards he contacted me to see if I might be interested in producing them. By this time the lead singer had quit the band and they decided to go forward with the bass player, Nick Beggs, singing, but they didn't want to go under the exact same name so they just cut it short to Kaja.

We recorded at Sarm East (Trevor Horn's original studio), where we had a blast. We mixed a 12-inch of the single at Sarm, then headed back to Total Access to do the rest. I was doing my normal thing of setting up a mix on the first day, then coming back the next day to complete it. On that first day most of the band was there except for Nick and the manager. On the second day I was close to completing the first mix, but still no bass player or manager.

Several hours into the mix the manager entered with a whole stack of albums with him. "What do you have those for?" I innocently asked him. "I'm going to spend today listening to the monitors so I can get used to them," he replied. "I beg your pardon?" said I. "Yeah, I need to know what the monitors sound like here for us to mix here."

"Fuck you," was my answer to that. That wasn't his job and we'd only be wasting time, time that was being charged to a budget that I was responsible for.

As you can imagine, it ended up that I didn't mix the album, which came out as *Crazy Peoples Right to Speak*. I immediately called up the A&R guy in England and we sorted it out to where I politely pulled out of the project. There was no way I was going to work under those circumstances. It was weird; everything had been fine up to that point.

What made it that much worse was that he came in two days after we'd already started to mix. Maybe *if* he had come in with his albums on the first day when we were setting up and said, "Would you mind if I listen to a couple of things so I can get an idea of how the monitors sound?" I would have been fine with it. But letting us get started, then bringing in this huge pile of albums, there was no way any work would have been done that day. Since I was responsible for the budget, it was my duty to say, "Sorry, mate. No way." Here was someone who had read too many mixing stories in the trade magazines. Unfortunately, a little knowledge can be a dangerous thing.

MORE MANAGEMENT

I really enjoyed management during my time working with Missing Persons. Management can be just as artistic as record production or singing or playing guitar, as long as you don't look at it strictly from the monetary aspect, which I think is what most managers do. Dealing with the artist and the label is so much like production and I really wanted to continue doing it even after how horribly my association with Persons ended.

As luck would have it, I met up with an L.A.-based band called Cock Robin that had two lead singers, a male and female. I produced some of their songs, and soon it progressed into another management deal. Unfortunately, the day we were going to sign the management contract they pulled out because some of members wanted to sign and others didn't. The drummer was so upset over the impasse that he put his fist through the bathroom door in my office, and that hole was there for some time. I never did discover why they decided against it, although I was told some time later that it might have had something to do with my wife Patience (that again).

We did two lots of demos at Total Access. The first batch were my typical "demo masters," the first songs that made the rounds to the record companies. We got a couple of bites but typically the labels wanted to hear more, so I went into Total Access one night and set the band up live and cut another eight or nine songs. They ended up being just as good as the songs that we spent ages on. We just went straight to stereo and avoided the multitrack altogether.

The phase of that project that I remember the most about is when they recorded live in the studio straight to 2-track. They recorded a lot of songs that came out really well. I think that recording was some of the best stuff they ever did, at least here. It still holds up pretty well.

Wyn Davis

Soon I had them play a showcase at The Palace in Hollywood and every label turned up. This wasn't too long after Persons so I had a bit of a reputation for finding talent at this point. Once again, Rupert Perry came by, but by this time he was head of EMI America. He brought A&R head Gary Gersh and a couple of other execs with him. After the show Rupert was very much to the point. "I want them, and I want to work with you again," he said. He turned to Gary and said, "I want this band. Meet with Ken next week." "Nice one, Scott," I thought, but of course I had no idea of the internal politics at EMI at this point. The bottom line was that Gary very much disliked that Rupert had come in as head of the label, and, it was safe to say, had his own agenda.

True to his word, Gary set up a meeting. The problem was that the entire audience with him consisted of, "I wish it were that easy, Ken, but it's not. Now you must hear my new signing," and he'd play me a new act he just signed. This went on for the entire meeting. The only thing he said about Cock Robin was, "I wish it were that easy." CBS had no such internal politics however, and wanted to begin negotiations to sign the band immediately. I didn't pursue

EMI any longer because I began to hear the rumblings about their internal strife and realised that it wasn't worth the effort. It was just one of those things: bad timing on my part, and theirs too, since I believe they could have made some money on the band.

The sad part was that I had gotten the band a deal with CBS/Sony, and after they dumped me, they continued on with the negotiations and signed the deal. Cock Robin ended up not doing much in the States, but were very successful in Europe for a time. Peter Kingsbery, the male lead singer, eventually went solo, and we found ourselves recording in the same facility in France some time later. I don't know who felt more awkward, him or me. We were pleasant enough to each other, but you could tell that there was a wall between us.

CHRISTINE IN THE ATTIC

You'd think that between Persons and Cock Robin I'd be soured on management, but what can I say other than I'm a glutton for punishment.

So we're now at around 1990 and my best friend at this time was a sax player named Michael Barbera. Mike had been with a few bands and at this particular time was playing with Mary's Danish, a band I really enjoyed live. One day Mike invited me to go see a band along with a keyboard player, Scott, he had once been in a band with. Scott showed up with a young lady and we all went to dinner beforehand, Thai food if I remember correctly. Yummy. During the course of the meal it came out that Scott and Christine, the young lady, had been writing and doing demos together and, of course, I asked to hear them. Now, being totally honest, I have to admit that I really was intrigued by the girl. OK, I fancied her, alright? As Mike and I were driving home after the gig I remarked to him just how smitten I was and he said, "Don't even bother. She's gay." OK, fine. I left it at that.

When I heard the demos from the two of them, later to become Christine in the Attic (or "CIA" as we used to call the band), I loved them, so we went right into Total Access to record some demos. I shopped it around but no one seemed interested, so we decided to try the same thing that we did with Missing Persons and put an EP out ourselves. I got them a deal with Almo/Irving publishing, which funded the EP, and it started to do really well on college radio when it was released. It was the same story as with MP: hanging fliers for live gigs and trying to up the ante for every gig, and it was working.

I managed to get a song played on a local L.A. radio station, thanks to radio personality Uncle Joe Benson, and the next day got a phone call from an ex-Capitol promotion exec. "Ken, I'm now working for a new label called Morgan Creek, which is being run by David Kirshenbaum and Jim Mazza [who took over at Capitol from Don Zimmerman]. We heard Christine in the Attic on the radio and would love to talk to you about it."

I suppose I should mention one little thing that happened after recording the initial demos. It was a situation that one hears about all too often and seems to happen to record producers over and over: an affair. I soon moved in with Christine, who decided she was actaully bisexual and had kicked her girlfriend out so we could be together. I suppose it's just like the male and female leads of a movie hooking up. You're so close for a period of time that things occur that you don't expect. It's all-encompassing because it's work and pleasure and everything else all rolled up into one. Thinking back on it, it was obvious that it had to end very quickly. There's so much fire in such a short period of time that it just has to burn out.

Back to the band. We played Hollywood's Club Lingerie and finally the whole Morgan Creek label came down and told us for sure that they "had to have us." The band and I were ecstatic and planned to meet up at a restaurant afterwards to celebrate, and as I was driving there I found myself just muttering away (whether it was to myself or another entity, I'll leave you to decide), "God, this feels so damn good that you can take everything away tomorrow and it will have been worth it."

A couple of days later I was surprisingly and unceremoniously told that the band was not signing the management agreement with me, that I was also fired as their producer, and that Christine, whom I was living with, had found someone else and I had to remove myself from our apartment. Basically I lost everything almost overnight. The old adage had happened to me: "Be careful what you wish for—you just might get it."

The band went on to sign the deal with Morgan Creek and do a CD, but it was never issued. Morgan Creek Records signed several acts whose work was never released, had one huge hit with Bryan Adams, and then folded, as did CIA.

Just to show you the influence that a record deal can have, Mike, the sax player for CIA, and I were best friends, but I was pushed to one side because the Morgan Creek deal became more important. It's frightening the control that a label deal can have over people, as suddenly nothing and no one else matters. It took a while, but Mike and I eventually did become friends again.

The whole thing had such an effect on me that I wanted to have nothing to do with music for a time. I couldn't even listen to it for two or three months. For some very obscure reason, the thing that brought me out of it was a compilation album that came out called *Red Hot & Blue*, which had various popular artists covering the songs of Cole Porter. I listen to it now and can't in any way understand why, but that opened me back up to music.

dada

Mike was in Mary's Danish and when I went to see them, they had a band called dada opening for them. Through my association with Danish I got to know dada and we decided to work together, so once again I went into Total Access to cut some demos. Wouldn't you know, they got a deal with IRS Records and now it was time to record the real thing. On the penultimate day of preproduction, they came in saying, "We wrote a new song last night. You've got to hear it." They played a song that I immediately loved, "Dizz Knee Land." It fitted them perfectly and was certainly catchy enough to be a hit.

The next day the label's A&R guy came in to hear the material, and after he heard "Dizz Knee Land" for the first time he told us that it was awful and we weren't to even consider recording it. Of course, I always listen to the bloody record company; that's why I've done so well in my professional life (a very big tongue in cheek here, just in case you were wondering), so of course we recorded it. I have to admit that I did bow to his whims a little as there were a couple of songs he wanted to record that I didn't like, but I thought it best to give in, at least a little. When the A&R guy found out that we had gone ahead and recorded the song he forbade, he hit the roof, but that seemed to pass quickly enough.

The album was completed and sent to IRS, which is where the trouble really started. Miles Copeland, the owner/CEO, liked some of the album but certainly not all of it, and especially not "Dizz Knee Land." He sent the band back into the studio to record a bit more, but because I'd gone against the wishes of the A&R guy, I was not asked to be involved.

It was a while later that I learned they went back into the studio to record some songs to replace "Dizz Knee Land" and the couple of other songs that the A&R guy had insisted on, those ones that we felt didn't work but he wanted anyway. Of course, I was the one in the wrong for recording the ones we did record, according to the label. They did three new songs and, for some strange reason, did a couple of additional overdubs and remixed "Dizz Knee Land," the song no one liked. It appears there then came a major row within the company over the song. Copeland said, "I'm not going to issue the record if that song 'Dizz Knee Land' is on it," while Jay Boberg, the IRS president, said, "We're not issuing that record unless 'Dizz Knee Land' *is* on it."

Apparently there was this major internal battle and Jay Boberg finally won. The CD came out with "Dizz Knee Land," and it became the band's one and only hit. It got stacks of airplay and sold very well, then came the follow-up CD and their career died. I'd gone against the record company and recorded the big hit and yet I finished up being the bad guy. Oh well.

The next thing I know Joie Calio, the bassist/vocalist of dada, is knocking me for being too much of a perfectionist in *Music Connection* magazine. I was dumbfounded and regrettably jumped into the situation with both feet and railed, in not too nice a manner, against Joie soon afterwards. In retrospect, I wish I would've just taken the high road and simply brushed it off.

We got a copy of Music Connection *some time after the record had been released, and in it they had an interview with Joie, and his tone was a little bit annoying to begin with as he was talking about the record. Then he got to the end of it and they asked him how it was working with Ken. His response was, "If you look up anal in the dictionary, you'll see a picture of Ken." That just sent me over the edge. I sent back a scathing letter about the fact that Ken took this band under his wing, chose the only song that got any airplay, and in my view, it would probably be the last anyone would ever hear of them, which turned out to be true.*

Wyn Davis

Do I feel the band deserved more commercial success? Yes, and no. They had all the potential to become a big-selling act, in my opinion anyway. They had the breaks but fell foul of the record company and their "We know better than everyone what direction you should go in" attitude. That's the biggest downfall of so many potential stars. Any artist worth their salt needs to follow their gut and win or lose on their own terms, not pander to the ever-changing staff and whims of "the label."

Some people don't understand where the seeds of their success are actually sown, and they usually don't go very far. They're their own worst enemy. I'd been around for the beginning, middle, and ending of the project and those guys were really super lucky to have worked with Ken and they had a lot to thank him for. They had a lot of nerve in putting that down when he did his best to make their marginal performances actually work on a record.

Wyn Davis

CHAPTER 29

Duran Duran

My association with Duran Duran came through my daughter Kim, who was living with me for a time after moving back to the U.S. from England. I was pretty much over the whole Persons situation, and by this time had rebuilt the bridges with Terry and Dale, so now it was time for Warren. After Persons ended, Warren had joined Duran Duran, and after a brief time as a sideman, soon became an integral member of the band.

Kim was heavily involved with the Renaissance Pleasure Faire and one of her associates there called her to work security on a special Arsenio Hall television show that was being broadcast from the Hollywood Bowl. As it turned out, Duran were going to be performing.

When I found this out I wrote a short note for Kim to get to Warren if the opportunity arose. When she got home that night she said, "I didn't see Warren but I gave the note to someone to pass to him." My immediate thought was that it would never reach him and it would be dropped in the trash. The next morning I was woken by the phone ringing and, totally unexpectedly, it was a call from Warren. The band was rehearsing down near the Santa Monica Airport. Would I care to go down and see him?

I took a trip down and, just as I had hoped, we got on great and all the fences were mended. A short time after I got a call from him to mix an MTV *Unplugged* that Duran had done. I went into Enterprise Studios in Burbank to mix and whilst there the news came out that Frank Zappa had died, which prompted a lot more communication with Warren for a time, as he was so close to Frank. The mixes I did for the show sounded great in the studio, but unfortunately, sounded like crap over the TV when the compressors kicked in, though luckily the band didn't hold that against me.

THANK YOU

Not too long after that, the band started recording what was eventually called the *Thank You* album. This album was meant to be a quick stopgap as their previous album, *The Wedding Album*, had featured two huge hits that had resurrected their career and they were on a massive tour in support of the record. *Thank You* was to be all covers of songs that had been important to them, and would be recorded while they were on tour.

We wanted to do a quick album of covers like Bowie's Pinups *while we were on the road. Who recorded Bowie? Ken Scott. We thought, "Why don't we get him to come out on the road and record us?" That was the first time we worked together in ages.*
Warren Cuccurullo, guitarist for Duran Duran

I was hired just as an engineer, but Warren and I knew each other enough that ideas would go back and forth between us. At least when working with Warren, it wasn't just sitting there twiddling knobs, unlike most of my participation with the others.

Strange as it may seem, it wasn't until working on this album that I discovered just how cosseted some top bands could be. With The Beatles, Bowie, and Elton I had seen a certain amount of it, but not that much. Elton was still staying in Holiday Inns when on tour when I worked with him. With Duran it was insane. No matter what city they were in, they would stay at the absolute best hotel. It was extravagance all around and while doing this album, a certain amount rubbed off on me. When they had three days off in a city, I would fly in, we'd go into whatever studio was available there, then I'd fly home. Always first class, of course.

Because Warren had his own recording setup at home, they had already laid down most of the basic tracks so we were just recording overdubs. The whole thing was very scattered. On some songs they wanted real drums, so we went into a studio in the San Fernando Valley and recorded Bozzio, then to another studio with Steve Ferrone (now the drummer with Tom Petty's Heartbreakers) on a few more of the tracks. I'd go into the studio in L.A. with Duran bass player John Taylor and record some things, then I'd fly off to Paris to do keyboards with Nick Rhodes or vocals with Simon Le Bon, who were both doing a tax exile thing and couldn't go back to England without being hit with a huge tax bill. That's where things got a little silly. If they didn't like Warren or John's parts, they wouldn't say, "We just won't use them in the mix," it was, "You've got to erase them," and they would actually sit there and watch me to make sure that I erased them. There was a lot of weird stuff like that going on.

This is how stupid we were. Nick and Simon wanted to do their bits in France, so Ken went to Paris, which turned into the South of France, where a studio had to be built. So the budget kept going up and the time kept getting longer and longer. Ken witnessed this and got to see the waste on a monumental level. The album wound up costing something like a million quid [about $1.5 million], where it should have cost like half a million dollars.
Warren Cuccurullo

They had this no-expense-spared lifestyle that was easy to get used to. In one case, I had to do an acoustic guitar track. I was home in L.A. while Warren was at home in London. They said to me, "We'll fly you over there. Where would you like to work?" so I jokingly replied, "How about Number 2 Abbey Road?" Much to my surprise, they said, "OK," and booked it for a Saturday. They flew me over, first class, put me up in one of the top hotels in London, and the overdub at Abbey Road took all of 15 minutes. Two days later I flew back.

That short session however turned out to be extremely important for me. The maintenance engineer working that day, Brian Gibson, was someone who started at Abbey Road around the same time as I did. When he saw that I was coming in, he specifically requested to work that day so we could talk. We were having a chat after the session when he said to me, "Do you remember when we first started to work here and all the old-timers told us their amazing stories about the beginning of the record business?" "Yeah, that was amazing," I replied. "Well, we're now them," he said. "What do you mean?" I asked, not getting the significance of his statement. "We're now the old-timers. The young ones now want to hear our stories."

That really resonated with me. It made me think about that whole generation of engineers who were there at the beginning of the recording business that Brian and I grew up with and that the world knows very little about today. They had the most amazing stories but no one was interested in documenting any of it at the time. As a result, those stories are now lost forever. It struck me that we couldn't let that happen again. Things move so fast that we have to try to document some of the stories of the second generation, my generation, before they're lost too. That started me on the road of doing my talks at schools, and started me thinking about doing this book. Up until that time I hadn't particularly liked talking about my past because I was always looking towards the next thing. Hearing what Brian had to say made me start to think that maybe there was some importance to my past.

CHARLIE

The first time I met Simon Le Bon in the studio, almost the first thing he said to me was "By the way, I like to be called Charlie when I'm in the studio." I sort of looked at him a bit funny and confusedly said, "I beg your pardon?" "Yeah, I like everyone to call me Charlie in the studio, so please call me Charlie," he replied. I don't know if anyone knew why, and if they did they never told me, but that was what he wanted to be called. That went for the entire band as well—they all called him Charlie in the studio. So strange.

Although not producing, I did manage to throw a few things into the project. Charlie's vocal on the single "Perfect Day" for instance. I recorded him my normal way, which meant five or six takes, and then I had them leave me alone to put together the best performance. I guess it worked as Charlie said that he felt it was the best thing he'd ever done. Of course it helped that he'd just spent a great day with his wife, the gorgeous Yasmin, and daughters, so he was in really good spirits, good voice, and the lyrics fitted perfectly with his mood. Despite all the strangeness, there were a lot of good times whilst making that record.

When it came to mixing, Duran were, shall we say, different. They had apparently made a pact way before this album that if they couldn't all be at the mix, then no one should be, which is fine since most engineers and producers prefer it that way. What I didn't understand was that they never wanted to hear it the same way as they'd heard it at the completion of recording. I kept creating these, what I considered, great-sounding mixes and they kept rejecting them because they'd heard it that way before and they didn't want to hear it that way again.

I thought the album was going to be amazing. One of the songs they covered was the influential rap masterpiece "White Lines," and they actually brought in Melle Mel and Grandmaster Flash to work on it. I have to admit, I'd never thought much of scratching to that point until Flash brought in his gear and played to the track. What he did was just stunning. At the same time, the band was working with a film company that was the competitor to IMAX. They filmed one of the Duran concerts whilst I recorded it and the song that they wanted to use to show off their product was "White Lines." The performance was OK, but I thought it could be made into something better. Knowing that everything was done to a click and always at the same tempo, I put the live and studio performance together, which really turned out better than I ever expected. I did rough mixes of this and some of the other songs and played them to some people when I got home and the general reaction was, "Who the hell is this? This is great!" No one would believe that it was Duran because it was so unlike them. It was more hard edged, more rock 'n' roll.

That was the problem. Both the management and record company suddenly said, "Hang on. You've just been successful again with *The Wedding Album*. You can't go off on such a curve. You need to make this record sound more like Duran." As a result, they went back to working with someone that they worked with before who liked to use lots of synths and tried to turn the record into more of a "Duran" thing. With that kind of thinking, it's no surprise that *Thank You* ended up being called "The Worst Record Ever" according to a *Q* magazine poll. Yes, very proudly I can say I've got some in the top 10 greatest records in the world, but I also happen to have the "worst record ever" on my résumé too. There aren't too many others that can boast of that.

DURAN REDUX: *POP TRASH*

Duran went on to do another record after *Thank You* that did very little, then I got the call from Warren to again come and help. *Pop Trash* was a little more settled in that it was all being done in England in just one studio. They had started off at Warren's place again, so it was just doing overdubs like before.

By this time Duran was down to just three members: Warren, Charlie (Simon), and Nick, and there was obviously a bit of animosity that had built up between them. Bassist John Taylor had quit the band and they hadn't had a drummer for some time, so recording consisted primarily of the three of them and me.

> *Nick and I wanted him [Ken] because we had a great batch of songs and he was a song guy. When we got Ken over to do the drum tracks and vocals and additional overdubs, we just had the greatest time.*
> Warren Cuccurullo

Charlie was having a lot of problems coming up with lyrics and Warren and Nick kept on pushing him, but it just wasn't happening. It finished up that Nick wrote a lot of the lyrics for the album, which really pissed Charlie off. This, plus a lot of stuff I'm sure I wasn't aware of, led to a lot of disrespect amongst them. There was one Saturday when we were supposed to be doing vocals with Charlie and we had agreed to start work at 2 P.M. When we got to the studio, no Charlie. We waited and waited, and gave it until maybe 5 o'clock before Nick and Warren started to make phone calls. It turned out that he had suddenly decided to fly out to supermodel Naomi Campbell's birthday party on an island somewhere. He left to party for the weekend without telling any of us, knowing full well that he was supposed to have been working. He just could give two shits, and jet-setting with Ms. Campbell held a higher priority for him. We carried on working with some other things that needed to be done, but that was what their relationship had become.

It was a difficult album to make on the lyric end because over the last few years Simon had a difficult time coming up with lyrics. He just dried up. Nick started writing lyrics and there was a sharing of the writing that had never happened before on a Duran record. It took a lot of the burden off him but also a lot of the creativity as well. He was having problems in his personal life, so it was a really traumatic experience and Ken had to deal with those issues. But we had such a great time doing the guitars and I loved working with him. Even though the record didn't do the business that we hoped, I'm really glad that I got to work with my good friend again.
Warren Cuccurullo

Eventually we got the recording finished and began to mix. Duran was paying for everything themselves as they didn't have a record deal at that moment. Whilst we were working they were shopping things around and managed to get interest from Disney's Hollywood Records in the States. The head of A&R flew over to England to have a listen and at one point during mixing pulled me to one side and said, "Ken, it's great, but I think that you might be compressing the mixes a little too much." Now I'd heard some of the records that this particular person had been associated with in the past and he'd always sent his records to one of the three major engineers that seemed to mix everything at that time. They did nothing but compress the fucking shit out of their mixes. I took it as a personal insult that my 2 to 3 dB of compression was somehow "over-compressing" these mixes. He ended up signing the band, but he had them do more overdubs and had everything remixed by one of his pet guys. He did throw me a bone though. I went to Studio One in the Valley and engineered a string overdub session for them. Gee, thanks.

One of the business problems that came about was that we made the record before we were signed. We had this great vibe and we were really happy with it and we were on top of the world when Hollywood Records wanted us. They heard a couple of songs that Nick and I had written for Blondie and they wanted us to do one on the album. We decided that we'd do it, then we heard from Hollywood that they wanted someone else to mix the album. Ken was mixing the album already and we wanted Ken's sound. The label said, "No, they [the mixes] sound flat and it's not going to work at radio." I felt really uncomfortable because not only was our creative vision being taken away, then I had the personal thing with Ken once again.

Warren Cuccurullo

The album ended up being compressed to holy hell, sounded like shit, and did absolutely nothing. It didn't even warrant being included on the poll for worst album of the year, it was that bad. That was the end of my association with Duran, as soon after the original band reformed, Warren was out, and my connection to them was gone.

Ken hated it because it [the remixed album] was very undynamic. The irony is that it sounds like it's on the radio even when it's not on the radio. It's really, really compressed. There was one song that I absolutely refused to go with the other guy's mix, so we went with Ken's mix on "Starting to Remember" and it's beautiful.

With a guy like Ken there's a depth of experience and a reverence for what he's done. He's a guy that's done it long before we did it. We all learned how to make records, but we got him for a reason. I'm really glad of what he did for us on a performance level, but on a mix level I was so let down when we had to change to another mixer. What he [Ken] did was exactly our vision for the album.

Warren Cuccurullo

Never was there a place that felt less like a record company: seven giant dwarves hold up the building. You're listening to these people, and finally I had to say, "How funny that your corporate logo is a large pair of ears, yet not one of you in here happens to have any."

Nick Rhodes, keyboard player with Duran Duran, from "Still Pretty: After All These Years," Rolling Stone, 21 April, 2005

CHAPTER 30

George

I was cooking dinner one night, and while awaiting the mushrooms to finish steaming, the phone in the office rang. I wasn't going to answer it because it was after hours and I didn't want to hold up dinner, but, luckily as it turned out, I thought to myself, "What the hell. I should at least check who's leaving a message." As I walked into the room I could hear a voice on the answering machine. "Hi, I'm trying to reach Ken Scott." I vaguely recognised the speaker, but just couldn't quite put together who it was. Then I heard, "This is George. George Harrison. I really want to ... " and I immediately picked up the phone.

The last time I'd seen George was when he stopped by a Supertramp session at A&M Studios almost 30 years earlier. While this for me was a most welcome blast from the past, my wife Cheryl kept walking in every five minutes, fuming because I was on the phone chatting merrily away, whilst our dinner was going to rack and ruin. Of course, she was totally unaware of just who might be commanding so much of my attention during what was supposed to be dinnertime. Finally I put my hand over the receiver and quietly mouthed to her, "It's George Harrison." Interestingly, she didn't bother me again. George and I finished up having about an hour's talk on the phone, and Cheryl and I had a very dried-out dinner.

ABBEY ROAD TO ZIGGY STARDUST

George had a number of projects planned, from getting the reissue of *All Things Must Pass* together to doing a new album, and in-between all that, getting the entirety of the material from his Dark Horse record label sorted out. By this time he'd already gone through one bout with cancer, so I think he just wanted to get things in order, realising better than most people that we're not here forever. The fact that after all these years he was calling on me to do that for him was a very unexpected and extremely welcome surprise.

George called out of the blue one day. He said that he wanted to go back to some of the people he originally worked with and asked Ken if he'd be interested. Ken had always spoken so highly about George and what a good connection they had before, but he wanted to be sure that they could get along first before he decided to take the job, since he hadn't seen him in so long.
Cheryl Scott, Ken's wife

We met up at the Bel Air Hotel a few days after the call and once again talked for about an hour. It was so wonderful to reconnect, and it seemed like no time had gone by since the last time we saw each other. I agreed to exclusively work with him on his various projects, and he promised that arrangements would be made for me to come over to England in a couple of weeks.

Then Murphy reared his ugly head again. A short time later the news came that George had been attacked in his home in England, knifed in the chest by a young trespasser, and was in a very bad way. I immediately got on the phone to try and find out how George was actually doing, and eventually talked to our mutual acquaintance, drummer Jim Keltner. Jim said that what he'd heard was that it was touch and go for a while, but he was going to be fine. As I put down the phone, my immediate thought was, "He's not going to come out of that shell again." He had been hiding away for what seemed like ages, and what immediately happens the moment he peeks out? Bang, some loony sticks him with a knife.

Luckily I was wrong. As soon as he felt well enough, George sent for me to come to his Friar Park estate in Henley-on-Thames to begin the process of sorting out his vast library and to start to get things together for the *All Things Must Pass* reissue.

> *It's [Friar Park] so amazing to look at. When you come up the driveway and get your first glimpse of it, you just can't believe it. While I was there, Olivia [George's wife] took me on a tour of the whole house. Inside it's very warm and all the rooms are very comfortable and welcoming. I've read there's something like 137 rooms, but it didn't seem that vast when you were in it.*
> Cheryl Scott

THE LIBRARY

George actually wanted to re-release all his albums over time, so my first job was to try to sort out all the master tapes. I went into his existing tape library, and while everything was supposed to be there, trying to find anything was ridiculously difficult. The tapes were in no semblance of order, so the first thing that had to be done was reorganise the library itself. There was a catalogue, but if you wanted to collect the tapes from one album, they were all in different places instead of together. Knowing that there may be times, possibly in the middle of the night, when George might want to go down and retrieve a tape, that made absolutely no sense to me. I finished up pulling all of the tapes out from where they were stored, then putting them back one section at a time. For weeks it was, "OK, this is from *All Things Must Pass*, and this is from *Dark Horse*," and so on. George's studio had piles of tapes spread all over the floor for months. Then I had to set up a whole new system for finding the tapes, which entailed renumbering and computerising them. I must say that I've never worked so hard in my life, lugging heavy tape boxes all over the bloody place.

As I went through everything I realised that we actually didn't have all of the masters, and we had no idea where the missing ones might be. George thought he had all of them but there were tapes that were marked as masters that soon enough became obvious they were not. So where were the real masters? Strange though it may seem, tapes, even Beatles tapes, weren't looked after particularly well back in the day. No one ever realised that 30 or 40 years down the line they would achieve such importance. Finding the original tapes was crucial not only from the reissue standpoint, but also because George wanted to put some bonus material on the re-release of *ATMP*.

The other possibly scary thing on our minds was that there had been too many stories of someone playing their old tapes once and all the oxide coming off, rendering the tape completely useless. This is a problem called "shedding" whereby the oxide, the magnetic stuff that actually contains the audio signal, comes away from the plastic backing. The general way of protecting against this is to bake the tapes in a convection oven before playing them, based on some time formula, which somehow adheres the oxide back to its correct configuration. I don't know why—I'm a recording engineer, not a scientific wizard. Luckily we never had any problems like that whatsoever with George's tapes, because, at least with the earlier recordings, everything was recorded on EMI tape, which never suffered from this phenomenon.

In the end I was fairly successful in locating the tapes—there was just one that eluded me. It was a master reel of 8-track to 8-track bounces done at Abbey Road that had five songs on it, including the hit "My Sweet Lord." It wasn't absolutely necessary, as it was an intermediate copy that we could get by without. Still, we looked and looked and couldn't find it in George's library, EMI's, or anywhere else we thought it could possibly be. In the end, we decided that it really wasn't absolutely essential and proceeded with the reissue of *ATMP*.

THE MISSING TAPE

I had returned to the States and soon after received a phone call out of the blue from an associate who knew what I was doing with George. "Guess what's been just put on my desk," came the voice on the phone. "I have no idea," I said, hating to play these sort of guessing games when we both knew he was going to tell me in the next sentence anyway. "I have a tape box with an orange label on it from Trident Studios. The artist is George Harrison, and it's … " "It's a 1-inch 8-track and it has five titles on it … correct?" I said, cutting him off. "Yeah, how did you know that?" came the surprised reply. "We've been searching all over for that for a while now," I told him. "How the hell did you get it?"

He proceeded to tell me about a gentleman named Steven Short who'd been an engineer at Trident, and who had managed to pull together a bunch of investors to buy the studio when Norman Sheffield decided to sell. "I've got to speak with this guy," I said, and the agreement was made to put us in touch.

Steven Short and I met at a fairly well-known place, Jerry's Deli in Woodland Hills, California, and after the typical small talk he told me how he came into possession of the tape (which he didn't bring with him, by the way). The day before he took over ownership of Trident, he did a final walk-around amidst some construction that was taking place. Trident was located on a small alleyway, and at the end of the alley on Wardour Street the builders had thrown out a whole pile of "trash."

He said that he just happened to see that in amongst the rubble were some tape boxes. He pulled one out and it was marked Elton John, another was marked Queen, and yet another was the tape with George Harrison's name on it. "That was the one I had to take," he continued. "I've been trying to find the rightful owners of it ever since so I can give it back. I even contacted Apple in New York," he asserted.

That struck me as slightly strange, since Apple never had an office in New York, and someone who had owned Trident and been in the business for a while must surely be aware of their presence in London. "I've looked after it very carefully, and all I want to do is give it back to its rightful owners," he went on. By this time George had passed, but I told him that I could arrange for him to present it to Olivia and Dhani Harrison personally, if that was what he wanted. "The next time they're in L.A., I'll get you all together and you can give it to them," I offered. "Oh, that would be wonderful!" Steven exclaimed.

The next time Olivia and Dhani were due to be in town I arranged a meeting with Steven to exchange the tape, but a couple of days beforehand, he called on the phone. "You know what? I can't make it that day. Can we make it for another time?" he asked. OK, I set it up for another time. Once again, a couple of days before the arranged meeting I received another call. "You know, I've been thinking," Short went on. "In looking after this tape, I've spent a lot of money to make sure that it's been in top condition. I think I should get that money back." At that point, he had us over a barrel. We couldn't let the tape stay out there as bootleggers would pay a fortune for it. He had to be bought off.

The payment of what I consider to be blood money was organised with the GH estate and the final meeting took place at my friend Brian Kehew's studio, which had a 1-inch 8-track tape machine. There was no way on earth I was going to allow the cheque to leave my hands until I had fully checked that the tape was indeed original and contained what the tape box indicated. After the tape was verified, he was paid his money and one of the missing pieces of George's library returned to the house where it should have been all along.

The Studio at Friar Park

By the time I got to work at Friar Park, the studio was slightly out of date, but all in all, still pretty good. The board was an old Cadac that had been modified by engineer/studio designer Eddie Veale, the person who had set up the speakers at Ramport, and the tape machines were all Studers. The monitors were not as loud as I would have liked, but that's only me. That was a little hard because after all these years, I like to feel what I'm mixing as well as hear, so I like a lot of volume and big speakers. George was used to nearfields and a not-all-that-loud playback level, so that was an adjustment for me, but it seemed to work out fine.

One thing that fascinated me was that George wasn't particularly up on modern technology. I did a few things using Pro Tools but he didn't want to have anything to do with it. We got in Paul Hicks from Abbey Road for some DAW help (who later did the 5.1 mix of Ziggy with me). Paul was a school friend of George's son Dhani and also happened to be the son of Tony Hicks, guitar player from The Hollies (who lived just down the road from George).

The studio had a lot of old gear like an EMT plate, a couple of Fairchild limiters, and a general array of equipment we used to use. The only new thing I got in was an Eventide Harmonizer because a piece of gear we needed wasn't working and I had to cover it with something. For mics, he had all the regulars like the Neumann U 87s and KM 84s, but he hadn't felt the need to go back and get any tube mics. Since I'm an 87 freak, I was perfectly happy as long as a few of those were around.

In the end, the gear that he had was far beyond what they had when they were making The Beatles' records, so it was just fine. He was also from the old school, remember?

ALL THINGS MUST PASS

When we did the remake of "My Sweet Lord," which was later retitled "My Sweet Lord 2001," there was a mix that I thought had a better beginning, but George was fine with the one we were already using. I thought to myself, "Let me put the new one on so George can at least hear it," and proceeded to edit it in. Much to my surprise, George got quite upset when I played it back for him. Somehow I had spoiled it by doing an edit. He wanted it so *au naturel* that he didn't even want to edit it to make one a bit better than another. I found that fascinating, considering the lengths that people go through these days to try to make things as close to perfect as possible. Truly old school!

Originally *ATMP* was only meant to be a double album in its initial release. The third record that had the jams on it was supposed to be a freebie, but thanks to taxes and publishing royalties, it had to be paid for, so over the years it's become an integral part of a three-record set. When we were putting out the re-release we wanted to dump all the jams, as they weren't really part of the album as such, but EMI said, "If you don't put them on, all hell's going to break loose because people want the original." As it turns out, they were 50% correct. Half of the reviews stated, "It's great that they put out everything the way it was," while the other half said, "Why the hell did they put those jams on? They were bad then, and they're even worse now." You can't please everyone, I guess.

Now I must explain that the first time George and I sat behind his board and we started to listen to a song from the original album, we just turned to each other and burst out laughing. Here we were almost 40 years on, sitting in the same positions and listening to exactly the same recording. It was just so absolutely bizarre that it took a while for the laughter to subside, but once it did we were in complete agreement about one tiny little thing: what's with all the reverb? All that bloody echo, the by-product of Phil Spector's hand. That mush. Both George and I were in far different places now, and we didn't hear it in the same way as we did back then. If we had our druthers, we would have immediately remixed the entire album to try to clean it up, "de-Spectorize" it as it were. But just going by the response to the jams, if we'd remixed the entire album again, we certainly would have liked it more, but I can only guess about the fans.

GEORGE'S HUMOUR

As I've said previously, George was one of the funniest people I've ever known. He was very funny with off-the-cuff comments, but he just loved pranks and put-ons. He told me this story about when 5.1 surround mixes were being done for *Yellow Submarine*, and he and Ringo were invited to listen to them upstairs in the new mix room at Abbey Road. As it turned out, Mel Gibson was down in Number 1 recording music for his film *The Patriot* and heard that George and Ringo were upstairs. It doesn't matter how big the Hollywood star, they all want to meet The Beatles. Mel got a message passed along asking if it was possible for him to come and meet them, and of course, they said yes.

When Mel walked in the room he went to shake hands with George, but George looked at him with a slightly odd expression and said, "Oh, I thought they said Mel Brooks." Gibson's face dropped. After a short pause, George laughed and let him in on the joke. "I'm kidding. I'm only joking," he said to a much relieved movie star. That was George at his best.

Another example of his humour came at the expense of Genesis drummer/singer Phil Collins. Over the years Phil has said in many interviews how he managed to play on *ATMP*. According to Phil, as a very young man, he was at Abbey Road for some reason, and heard someone call out for a conga player, for which he immediately volunteered and then played on the session. Phil told this story for years, but no one who was there could remember it ever happening. That's not to say that it didn't happen, since as you've previously read, no one remembers many of the particulars from those sessions.

When we were doing the additional tracks for *ATMP*, percussionist extraordinaire Ray Cooper came in to do some overdubs and at some point George asked him to play some really bad congas on whatever the track was that Phil had claimed that he played on. "Don't make it ridiculously bad, just bad enough that you know it would never be kept," George instructed. Ray did his usual excellent job of following the artist's directions, then I did a mix and put it on a cassette. George had Ray, who was friends with Phil, pass it along to him and say, "This is a gift from George." Apparently, Phil took the "gift" with an "Oh, this is so great," then proceeded to play it only to become crestfallen to learn that he had played that badly, and had been boasting about it all these years. George let the gag run for a couple of weeks before phoning Phil to let him in on the joke.

Ken was living in the garden lodge, one of the cottages that were part of Friar Park. He was working most of the time so I was on my own in the cottage reading, waiting for him to come back after they'd finished. The phone rang and there was this really weird voice on the other end that I could hardly understand. It was George playing a prank on me while telling me that dinner was ready and to come up to the house. He kept me going for quite a while. It turned out that he did that a lot with guests.
Cheryl Scott

But, of course, George was also Mr. Nice Guy. There was a couple getting married who he had met somewhere along the way. They weren't famous or even in the music business, just an ordinary couple that George, the most ordinary superstar you'd ever hope to meet, happened to cross paths with. One evening he asked me to record a special message that he made for them, along with him playing them a song. We put it on a cassette and sent it to them so they could play it at their wedding. Who wouldn't love George?

Ken had been working there continuously for four months and he told me so much of what he was doing and what George and Olivia were like. When I first got there, he took me up to the studio where George and Dhani were in the tracking room playing the guitar. George immediately came out and introduced himself, like he even needed to. He and Olivia were very warm and welcoming. It wasn't anything like someone would perceive meeting a Beatle would be. It was just meeting my husband's workmates.
Cheryl Scott

George had ukuleles lying around everywhere as he absolutely adored the instrument. There was one day that we walked into the big hall at Friar Park and he picked up one of the ukuleles and sat down and started to play one of the songs from what turned out to be his posthumous album. As he was playing, all I could think was, "Why me?" as tears filled my eyes. Why have I been so blessed to have McCartney, Elton, and now George play their songs for me, just one on one, in about as intimate a concert as you could ever get. Why me, God? It's one of those strange questions that one has about one's life as we get older. The moment was unbelievable. The song and the way he played it was truly beautiful.

THE END

We had to do a vocal for "My Sweet Lord 2001," but George's voice wasn't what it was back in the day and he seemed to be uncomfortable doing vocals with anyone around. His health and the nutter had taken their toll on his voice. I'd set him up in the control room so he could operate the tape machine, then retire to the cottage while he tracked all the vocals himself. It was very much like the Jan Hammer/ Jerry Goodman session I did years previously.

I was there the day he left his precious Friar Park for the last time. We would very often have dinner together in the evening and towards the end he hadn't been eating much. It was blamed on some stomach bug that he'd got. I was told that he and Olivia were taking a trip for a bit, but it just didn't feel quite right. There was just something in his eyes, as he walked around everywhere, studying everything intensely as if he wanted to be sure to remember it all. I remember talking to him for a bit that day and it was obvious that he wasn't very happy. In hindsight, I'm sure he knew he was probably never coming back, but that was never spoken about. It was just a stomach bug.

I firmly believe that George was more than ready to move on. That quest for God had been such a big part of his life, and he was fully prepared for the next chapter. It's safe to say he's with him now.

I continued to work on George's library after he passed until the end of my contract. His library now in order, my work for George was finished.

EPILOGUE

There is just one other brief story to go along with all this and it has to do with my stepson. I have had numerous conversations over the years with divorced parents, some who were huge celebrities, about how the first family sees a totally different lifestyle compared to the second. My first life had recording artists hanging out with my family all the time, so my daughters were raised with very well-known people frequently about. My second family has lived a much more sedate life and that led to this.

Alex, my youngest son, always had a vivid imagination and loved to write stories, so it came as no surprise when Cheryl and I received an invitation from his school to attend the monthly "feel good" awards celebration during which he was to receive an award for his imagination. Cool. We were really proud of him.

There we were in the main hall surrounded by other parents and all the kids. A couple of awards are given out, and then Alex's English teacher walked to the podium. "This next award is being presented to Alex McMahon for his vivid imagination. He has written the most amazing essays, but as opposed to reading one of those I would like to use this story as a brief example of how his mind works. Just the other day in class he came running up to me and told me about a phone call his stepfather had received the night before. He told me that some guy named George Harrison had called the house and it seemed like quite a big deal. What an incredible imagination." I will just leave it at that.

CHAPTER 31

The EpiK Epic

One day in July '06, I spoke with a gentleman by the name of Doug Rogers, the founder of the EastWest sample library company and a lifelong Beatles fan. He had this idea of doing a library of Beatles sounds where he wanted to recreate many of the distinctive sounds from Beatles records as closely as possible. I'd never worked on anything quite like that before so I was interested, but when I discovered the level to which he was taking it, I became way more than "interested." He spent a small fortune to get it as close as possible, buying everything from two old EMI desks (a TG and a REDD) and a couple of Studer 4-track machines, to Altec compressors and AKG D 19C microphones. You name it, if it was used at Abbey Road, he bought it.

Then came the musicians. He brought in drummer Denny Seiwell, who had played with Paul in Wings and knew a lot about the kinds of things that went into the drum sounds back then, and Laurence Juber, another ex-member of Wings, who could get as close to the original guitar sounds as possible with his great collection of instruments. And last, but I hope not least, since I had spent a little time with The Beatles, I joined in to record it all.

THE IDEA

During the course of recording what became known as the *Fab Four Virtual Instrument*, it dawned on me how great of a tool this type of library could be. Over the years I've been constantly asked how I got various sounds on the records I produced, and in this day and age it's becoming harder and harder to get those sounds because the instruments, the mics, the boards, and even the studios are becoming few and far between. I thought this might be an ideal way to make available some of the sounds that we got back then, but getting it from a nice idea to reality turned into a very, very long slog.

With the *Fab Four VI* finally completed and due to be shown at an industry circus called the NAMM (National Association of Music Merchants) show, I decided to go to see how Doug was handling the product and to hear some of the demonstrations of it. Typically, I got bored quickly, but got a jolt of enthusiasm when I heard that Rod Morgenstein, the drummer for Dixie Dregs whom I hadn't seen in donkey's years, was due to play on one of the stages. I rushed over just in time to catch some of his performance and when it ended, I walked to the edge of the stage and called over to him. He immediately turned around, but had absolutely no idea who I was and so I took something from our past and said, "That would've been a lot better if you hadn't played quite as much!" He looked at me sort of strangely and didn't know quite how to take it, then it suddenly dawned on him who the one person was that had made that comment to him before. A broad grin appeared across his face and the conversation that had ended almost 40 years earlier continued as if no time had passed.

As we were talking, an idea crossed my mind and I asked him, "Would you be interested in doing a sample library session with me, getting as close to the old Dixie Dregs sound as we can?" "Absolutely. I'm with you all the way," he eagerly replied. I suppose one would have to say that the idea had hatched and it was now time for me to come up with a proper plan.

I began to refine the concept. I thought back to the odd occasion when I had used drum samples in my past and remembered how long it took going through all the different sounds. The problem, as I saw it, was that they weren't really based on anything in particular. You got things like "Fat Snare 1" or "Fat Snare 2" and of course one mustn't forget the quite thin-sounding "Fat Snare 3." I decided to pick very specific albums that have very identifiable sounds and, as I also wanted the package to contain real grooves, it had to be centred around some of the world-class drummers that I had worked with during my career—the real drummers, and not some stand-in that attempts to play like the originals.

Once I really started thinking about it, my choices were remarkably easy to make: Woody Woodmansey from the Spiders from Mars, Bob Siebenberg from Supertramp, Rod Morgenstein from Dixie Dregs, Bill Cobham from Mahavishnu Orchestra, and Terry Bozzio from Missing Persons. I'd done signature records with each of these drummers, and they each had totally different feels and completely different sounds. As a result, the sounds of this library could be categorised as just *Ziggy*, or *Mahavishnu Orchestra*, or *Dixie Dregs*, and anyone who knew those records would know exactly what to expect.

Having the musicians on board, the next thing was to find all the other connecting factors between the drummers and their records. At one point or another, I used a Trident A Range board to record each of them, so it made sense that everything be recorded through an A Range to get that same sound. There were only 13 of those ever made, so that meant tracking down the studios they were in, then trying to match up the acoustics of the studio to where the records were recorded. Both Woody on *Ziggy Stardust* and Bob on *Crime of the Century* were done in the drum booth at Trident, which was small and very dead, whereas Cobham on *Birds of Fire* was done in the main room of Trident, where the sound was much bigger, to match the size of his kit. Those were the sounds that we had to match up to.

We finished up using three studios: New Monkey in Van Nuys, California for Bob; Long View Farm in Massachusetts for Billy; and

Emblem in Calabasas, California for the other three. Emblem worked out for the three because the studio had a small drum booth that was perfect for Woody's sound, and while Rod and Terry were originally recorded in the main room of Chateau Recorders, Emblem's room was about the same size, so that worked for them. We had a bit of a close call when it came to Bill's recordings at Long View Farm though, as the studio was in the middle of selling its A Range and had to be talked into holding on to it until after our sessions were completed. The ironic thing is that they ended up selling it to Doug Rogers for his EastWest Studios in Hollywood.

We were inching towards having everything together, but next it was time to find the old vintage drums, which is where the Drum Doctor Ross Garfield became so important. The drummers all told him what they had played on the original recordings and he then had to find everything. Terry was easy (he still had most of his original Missing Persons kit) but we ran into a major problem with Bill. He originally used a Fibes kit made out of plexiglass, but I quickly discovered that Fibes was no longer in business, so a mad scramble was on to find something similar. What we finished up with was not exactly what he had used on the original recordings, but it was pretty damn close, thanks to Ross, who pulled a rabbit out of the hat and put it all together. The only problem was that it had to be shipped across the country to Massachusetts, which I think ended up costing more than the bloody sessions themselves, even including all the mics that had to be rented. Oh yes, I *had* to have those the same as well.

EPIC RECORDING

Before we began recording, I went onto eBay and found the best original vinyl records of each of the albums I could find. It was these that I had each drummer play along to so I could match the sound to the original as closely as possible. Once satisfied with the sound, I had them play along with the songs on the album and recorded it in order to get the same grooves as they played on the original recordings. Considering that the drummers were now 30 to 40 years older than when they originally did those records, it was a workout for them, both physically and mentally. They had to try to play the same way they did back in the day, and after all this time they had matured, some more than others, and their styles had changed. In the end that actually proved to be a huge benefit. They were out of their element and had to play everything with a fresh approach, putting them on edge and making it exciting for them, and me, again. They went for hours on end with very few breaks, with sweat pouring and a smile everywhere along the way. It was amazing.

After that was finished, we had each of them just jam for a bit so we had completely separate grooves that weren't connected to any of the records. After that, samples of the individual drums, cymbals, bells, and anything the drummer used during the album were recorded. In the end it had become quite an all-consuming project. What I didn't realise was how much more all-consuming it would become in putting the rest of it together.

I didn't have much to do with the individual drum samples; the guys at the music software company Sonic Reality had been doing that kind of thing for ages and so I was more than happy to leave it up to them. It was a different story when it came time for the grooves though, since I knew just how I wanted them to be, and this was where my perfectionism took over. I jumped in and decided to take over the editing of the loops. What had I let myself in for? Day after day after day listening only to drums. Finally they're finished. I'm done ... If only.

The way Sonic Reality was used to dealing with grooves for its libraries was to just keep them in the order they were recorded, but these were different because we were dealing with entire songs. The way their recording engineers generally worked with drummers was to just let them jam, and in so doing, one idea would lead to another idea and so on. The groupings would all work as they are basically a bunch of random patterns. That's not quite the same when working with a song pattern, because generally speaking each song will have three parts—the verse, the chorus, and the bridge—and a real drummer will change the feel slightly with every section of a song. The folks at Sonic Reality were categorising the sections so that the loops were in order of playing, which meant a bunch of the verse loops then chorus loops and back again to verse loops. That's not very helpful for the user, in my mind, so I took on the task to put all the verses of all the songs together, then all the choruses, and so forth, and we ended up with something that was much more logical. I'm done ... Ha ha ha.

THE ODD TIME THING

One of the things I strove for in making *EpiK DrumS* unique was the inclusion of some of the strange time signatures that Bozzio, Cobham, and Morgenstein play in their music. There were no other products available that had anything close to these odd time signatures, so, of course, I had to have them, and, of course, that caused a whole new set of problems. To get technical just for a moment, Sonic Reality translated everything into a Rex file format, which is a native file format for the Recycle app that splits the sound file up into minute sections so you can change the tempo of the groove without changing the tone. The only problem is that Rex doesn't work on many of the odd time signatures that we were dealing with. The answer? Simple: give the user the odd time signatures with the ability to change tempo via MIDI. Ah, why is nothing as easy as it sounds?

There are various programs that take a drum loop and MIDIfy it, but after trying them I quickly learned that they all totally lose the feel and fail to accurately capture the way it was played, which is obviously a really important part of the whole project. Some of the hits were slightly early for some reason, while some would be late, and some were dead on. If you get a number of drummers to play exactly the same part, because of where in the beat they hit the drums (and it only needs to be milliseconds off), that's what differentiates the feel of one drummer from another. If you have a piece of software that only captures here and there what they're playing, the end result could be the feel of any drummer, and not the legends on *EpiK DrumS*. I came up with only one answer. I decided that I had to programme by hand every bass drum, every cymbal crash, every bloody sixteenth note, everything the drummer played, matching up exactly where they hit. This proved to be an enormous task. It was so far beyond what I signed up for, but that's what you have to do if you are a perfectionist and a sometimes control freak who just happens to want it right.

Finally, after two years of development, the *EpiK DrumS* package with all five drummers came out in January of 2011 on a hard drive containing more than 130 GB of drums. Since a package that large can be daunting (hell, it's got my name on it and I can hardly use it to its full potential), we decided to provide smaller packages of just the individual drummers that contain everything from the original package, as well as more MIDI grooves. In the end, I am extremely proud of *EpiK DrumS* and I think it beats any other library out there because it really does have a human feel to it, in all areas, from the sounds to the playing to the MIDI, but of course I openly admit that I'm biased, just a little.

EPIK DRUMS EDU

The last part of the *EpiK DrumS* story is the idea that there's an educational side to it all. There are a lot of young people going through schools learning to become engineers, and many of them never get to deal with a live drum kit. I originally described *EpiK DrumS* as "real drums," but a lot of samples are real drums too, so that term doesn't seem apropos; it's really a "live drum kit" that we're talking about. When you're dealing with samples, recording can be very easy—time consuming, but easy. You just select single drum sounds and programme them into a part. The thing is, there's no interaction between any of those drum hits because everything is totally separated, unlike with a live drum kit where a snare hit will set off a tom, or you'll have a mic on a tom which is right by the cymbal, so when the drummer hits the cymbal you pick it up on the tom mic as well. There are many "interesting" problems that occur when you record a live drum kit that you'll never see or hear with samples.

With *EpiK DrumS EDU*, trainee engineers, or anyone else interested in what's involved in mixing a live drum kit, get multitrack grooves and can hear exactly what goes on within them, and can spend time learning what works for them and how one can deal with different audio problems that might arise. If one day they actually have to deal with a live drum kit, they'll have a better idea of what to listen for and won't have to waste studio time experimenting. The *EDU* package provides some of the best drummers in the world recorded by a guy who has a slight idea of what he's doing when it comes to recording drums. It's perfect for them.

At the moment people don't mind sampled drums, but going by past history, everything is cyclic in the music business and so the cycle will come around again where live drums will be all the rage. People had better learn how to deal with them for when that happens.

The *EpiK DrumS* project was a labour of love. It went on far longer and was way more complex than I ever imagined when I had that beginning idea. There were many times I'd be going through the drum tracks for some reason or another and I'd really wish I'd never started the whole thing, then I'd come across a tom fill or a groove that only that particular player could come up with, and with a huge grin on my face, I'd know exactly why I took on the project.

CHAPTER 32

A Look at the Big Picture

All through the book I've shared my experiences, my luck, my losses, and as much as can happen via the written page, my techniques. Now that we're at the end, I want to answer some questions, express some regrets, furnish my philosophy, and maybe even offer a little advice.

QUESTIONS ... MORE QUESTIONS

First, the questions. What do I love most about recording? Everything really, but the buzz of hearing good music more than anything. During the editing of *EpiK DrumS*, there came a few moments that were perfect examples of what I mean. Editing drums for 16 hours a day, 7 days a week can bring you down at times, since you can't see the light at the end of the tunnel. Then I'd come across a lick from one those amazing drummers that would take my breath away and I'd suddenly think, "That is just soooo amazing," and it made the past couple of weeks of tedium worthwhile. In the end, it's all about making a record that you enjoy listening to when it's finished. The added perk is later when you're walking down the street and you hear it blasting out of someone's house. I can't begin to tell you how great that feels.

What do I hate about recording? Nothing. There is absolutely nothing that I hate. I do dislike dealing with record companies, but that's something that's only fairly recent. Once upon a time there were A&R guys that I had so much respect for that were very easy to deal with. These days they have the same mentality as many producers, engineers, and artists: they won't make decisions. You hear, "The album has to sound like this," before you go into the studio, then halfway through when they hear it you get, "Now we have to change it to something else." They try to follow trends as opposed to setting trends. It used to be a lot easier.

Where do I see the industry going? I see the death of the major labels as we know them and the rise of artists and bands doing everything for themselves. That's the easy side of things and already happening everywhere today. The hard part is how to get the acts' recorded music in front of the public. That's the next big area in music and the place where someone will make a fortune. My thought is that we need to go back to where it's more like it was on the '60s and '70s radio stations. That's when you had DJs who picked their own music and you followed them because you trusted their taste. We'll have something like that in the future, and it won't be done by a computer. It will be personality driven, with personalisation and recommendation being the keys to the new business. It's already happening to some degree, but the big breakthrough is coming.

THE ONE THAT GOT AWAY

I've had very few regrets in my career, but there is one that very much disappoints me to this day. I was approached, probably in the late '70s, to do a reunion album of The Hollies with Graham Nash, which I leapt at, since I've always loved their sound. The band flew over from England and joined Graham in his studio in Hollywood. There they picked out a song and decided to try just vocals and piano to see if they still had any magic together. Even more importantly, they wanted to see if they could get along again, and if I would get along with them.

As everyone had hoped, it worked. It sounded wonderful and we all got along amazingly well, so plans were made to go ahead with the project. The first thing was to find material for them to do, so I went around to everyone I knew and came up with a number of songs that I thought were really good. Whenever I found something, I would send it over to them, and for the majority of songs, their response was, "Yes, yes, yes."

Everything was lined up. I booked studio time at Chateau and they all made plans to come over to the States (Graham already lived in Los Angeles), but a couple of weeks beforehand I got a call from their manager stating that they needed to postpone the recording. It seemed that the time we booked was in the middle of a school holiday and Allan (Clarke, the lead singer) was scheduled to go away with his family. "OK, how long is he going to be away for?" I asked. "He'll be away for two weeks," came the reply. "OK, we can make that work," I thought to myself, so I backed up our recording plans two weeks.

Two weeks later I once more received a call from their manager. "We've got to postpone again," he said. "What is it this time?" I asked, a bit peeved at the prospect. "It's the middle of the school holiday and Tony (Hicks, the lead guitar player) has to go on vacation with his family." Once again, this had come out of the blue after all the plans had been made to record. Were they trying to tell us something?

Shortly thereafter Graham, his manager, and myself had a meeting where we determined, "What's the point? They're really not that interested." The whole project was dropped, which really disappointed me. The funny thing is, since then I've worked with Paul Hicks on some things with George Harrison and the *Ziggy* 5.1 mix. He's the son of Tony Hicks and the alleged reason why they went on holiday and stopped the whole reunion project. When I told Paul the story, he was very upset as he would have loved to hear them back together. Too bad his dad didn't feel as strongly.

MY RECORDING PHILOSOPHY

I was lucky. I had the best training in the world at EMI as far as I'm concerned. I got to watch some of the greatest engineers of the time and was able to pick and choose from their techniques. That said, maybe my biggest learning tool was that I started from a 4-track background where you learned to make decisions right away because you had to. I can't emphasise enough that that's one of the things people need to do more of. It's ridiculous to keep putting things off until the end. Make decisions, then live or die by them.

I still think that the best way to learn how to record is to limit yourself to just four tracks, because then you have to learn how to balance everything together almost on the fly. We used to mix bass, the entire drum kit, guitar, and/or maybe piano all onto one track and it was no big deal. You had to determine right up front what the sound was going to be and then you went from there. Try suggesting that today and you'd get a look of horror from pros and apprentices alike. Working with only four tracks trains you to make decisions up front and learn to think about how you want it to sound in the end, only you're doing it as you record.

I wrote about working with Level 42 and how difficult that was for me, and that was mostly because I couldn't make any decisions up front. I didn't have any idea of what a song was going to be like in the end because there were no songs written to start with. It all came from a jam in the studio, which leaves things too open-ended, in my opinion. You can't conceive of what it might sound like in the end because there's nothing yet to work with.

I'm sure that there were points in the 4-track days when I regretted the balance that I committed to, but it didn't matter. There was no going back because you just couldn't change it. That said, I don't think a listener won't like a song because the high-hat is mixed 2 dB too low.

On Bowie's "Watch That Man" where the vocal was mixed way down in the mix, I'd dearly like to go back and remix that now with the vocal up front. On *All Things Must Pass*, George and I would have loved to remix it without all the reverb, but that's the way it was. It makes no difference what we'd like to do now. It makes no difference even two months after the mix is completed. As long as you stick with the initial intent and don't try to change everything mid stream, there's very little that you could go back and redo that would make someone either like it or not like it. It's all in the song. Performance wise, maybe you have a case, but purely from an engineering standpoint, it makes little difference.

MY PRODUCTION PHILOSOPHY

When it comes to production I have one rule: I do it for the band and myself. I don't do it for the record label, a philosophy that I'm sure has cost me some work along the way. As long as the band or artist is happy, then it's a great record. I've been lucky enough where the record label liked what we did and the public liked the album enough to buy it, but first and foremost for me is that both the band and I liked what we've done.

That said, I will always bend to the will of the band, but I will do my best to make sure that we're both happy in the end. If there's a point of contention, we'll go through all the reasons why they feel so strongly about it and see if there is some way of altering it slightly so we're both happy with the result. But ultimately, if there's no way around getting it so that we both like it, I will always bend to their way. After all, it's their record.

MY BUSINESS PHILOSOPHY

In the most simplistic terms, the music industry used to be run by music people, and now it's run by accountants and attorneys. Now all they care about is how much growth they're going to see at the end of the quarter. There is no such thing as developing an act because "maybe three or four albums down the line they're going to be huge" anymore. These days a record has to become an immediate hit or just forget it. That generates musical rubbish, as far as I'm concerned.

The job of the A&R person has completely changed. It used to be where there was no such thing as a producer; the A&R guy was the producer and went into the sessions and controlled what transpired. The A&R guy/producer back in the day was the person who found the act, signed the act, sorted out the material to record, picked the arranger, then oversaw the recording and mixing. Then he'd meet with the marketing and the sales departments and would guide them through the album's release. He had the vision, and he'd follow the entire project through to the end. These days you can be signed by an A&R person who's straight out of college and before you finish the album, that person has already moved on to another company. Then you have to deal with someone new who doesn't understand the music you're making and isn't willing to back you up because it's not "his project." Now A&R people are just pen pushers.

I believe that one of the worst things that ever happened to the music industry is when it stopped requiring artists do two albums a year. As soon as that requirement was lifted, artists started to drag things out, and with technology advancing the way it did, it gave them more opportunities to put decisions off. As a result, artists and bands soon began to go three or four years between albums, which is absurd. Although all artists are not worthy of two albums a year, I think they should be. Look at the talent and the classic records that came out of that two-albums-a-year era that still hold up today. You were forced into a situation where you had to come up with the goods, and only the really talented ones are going to be able to do that.

ADVICE? WHAT ADVICE?

I'm frequently asked to give advice to people about getting into the business. It's easy: become a doctor instead if you're concerned about money. Recording has to be a passion. You can't get into this business for the money because more than likely you're not going to make any. You have to get in because you're passionate about music or passionate about recording. As I said before, I make records for myself and the artist or band. If they sell, that's icing on the cake, but I'd still be working in a studio even if I was only paid five bucks an hour (although not if everyone else was making more; I like to get paid just like the next guy). I got into it in the first place because it was a calling for me, and that's the way it has to be for everyone. Unless you're passionate, find another job.

Be aware that when you do get into the business, you're going to be seeing a lot of the local Chinese restaurant or pizza joint while picking up someone's order from the studio. Or you might be required to do some good old-fashioned toilet-bowl cleaning. That could continue for a period of three months, six months, or more until you start to move up the ladder. Be prepared to use this period to your advantage and spend as much time in the control room listening to what's going on when you're not being a gofer. Always keep your mouth shut, and watch and listen and learn from how other people work.

Soak that experience up like a sponge. Don't talk too much and, especially, don't offer advice. Always be aware of what's going on so that you almost know what you're going to have to do next without being told. Don't do it until you're told though, because you might be wrong.

Sometimes I'm asked for specific advice by an engineer who wants to take their game to the next level. Sorry, I can't do that. My life and career has been so blessed in the way things have come together that I just don't have that kind of perspective. I've been in a unique position most of my life so I can't in good conscience offer advice on something that I haven't personally gone through.

For musicians, once again it's all about the passion, and once again, be prepared to make zero money. But most of all, have your own voice. Make the music yours and don't try to emulate anyone else because you'll always be too late. That's one of the mistakes that record companies make. When a new trend suddenly hits, they begin to sign acts that sound just like the latest thing. The problem is that those albums will come out in a year's time, but the public will have moved on by then. You're better off to start out with your own music and be happy with what you're doing. Hopefully you'll get something happening from there, rather than trying to copy someone else and riding the bandwagon.

MY FITTING END

We all have visions of how we'd like to die and I certainly know mine. It's at the conclusion of the perfect mix. I'm pulling the master fader down, and when I get to the bottom ... The end.

Until then, I'll still be in the studio, hopefully making music that both excites and pleases myself and the acts I'm working with. And maybe you too.

Glossary

78 12-inch vinyl records that spin at 78 revolutions per second (rpm). These predated the 33 rpm records still in use today.

Ambience The background noise of an environment.

Assistant engineer A junior engineer who assists the main recording engineer, mostly with setup and documentation of the session; in the early days of recording, the assistant would operate the tape machine.

Attack The first part of a sound. On a compressor/limiter, a control that affects how that device will respond to the attack of a sound.

Automation A system that memorises, then plays back, the position of all faders and mutes on a console, and just about every parameter in a digital audio workstation.

Bottom Bass frequencies, the lower end of the audio spectrum. See also Low-end.

Bottom-end See *Bottom*.

BPM Beats per minute, the measure of tempo.

Bus A signal pathway.

Chinagraph marker A white wax pencil, also known as a grease pencil or china marker, used to temporarily mark tape or indicate parameter positions.

Clean A signal with no distortion.

Colour To affect the timbral qualities of a sound.

Compression Signal processing that controls and evens out the dynamics of a sound.

Compressor A signal processing device used to control audio dynamics.

Control room The room that contains the audio recording console, any additional audio processors, and the recording medium (e.g., tape recorders or digital audio workstations). The control room is usually smaller than the tracking room and is acoustically optimised for audio playback.

Cut To decrease, attenuate, or make less.

Cutting The act of physically cutting the grooves in a record by a cutting or mastering engineer.

DAW Stands for Digital Audio Workstation, a computer loaded with a recording software application which is connected to an input/output interface box.

dB Stands for Decibel, a logarithmic unit used as a measurement of sound level or loudness. 1 dB is the smallest change in level that a human can hear, according to many textbooks.

Decay The time it takes for a signal to fall below audibility.

DI Direct Inject (sometimes called Direct Input), an impedance matching device for electric guitar or electric bass that eliminates the need for a microphone.

Double or double-track To play or sing a track a second time for the purpose of layering it on top of the first. The slight inconsistencies between the two tracks make the part sound bigger.

Direct To "go direct" means to bypass a microphone and connect the electric guitar, electric bass, or keyboard directly into a recording device.

Dynamics The sound level of the audio, whether it is soft or loud.

Echo chamber A large tile room fitted with a speaker on one end and a microphone, or microphones, on the other to simulate the sound of a larger space. Sometimes called a reverb chamber.

EQ Equalizer, or the process of adjusting the equalizers (tone controls) to affect the timbral balance of a sound.

Equalization Adjustment of the frequency spectrum to even out or alter tonal imbalances.

Equalizer A tone control that can vary in sophistication from very simple to very complex.

Fader A linear control found on a mixing console that slides vertically and usually controls the volume of a microphone input or the input from a recording device such as a tape machine or digital audio workstation.

Feel The groove of a song and how it feels to play or listen to it.

Flying The analog version of cut and paste in a DAW. The part to be flown in is recorded from the first tape machine on to a second one. The second tape machine is started at another place in the song and recorded back onto the first machine. Flying took a lot of trial and error since there was no way to automatically start the second machine at the right time, so it had to be started manually.

Groove The pulse of the song and how the instruments dynamically breathe with it. Or, the part of a vinyl record that contains the mechanical information that is transformed into an electronic signal by the stylus.

High-end The high frequency response of a device.

Hz An abbreviation for Hertz, the measurement of audio frequency. 1 Hz is equivalent to one cycle of a sound waveform per second. The higher the frequency of the signal, the higher the number of Hertz, and the higher the sound. Low numbers of Hertz represent low sounds.

ips Inches per second, the speed that the magnetic tape passes by the heads of a tape recorder.

Kepex The brand name of an audio processor known as an expander or noise gate, which keeps an audio track muted until the signal reaches a certain predetermined level.

kHz Kilohertz; 1 kHz equals 1000 Hz.

Leakage Sound from a distant instrument "bleeding" into a mic pointed at another instrument. Acoustic spill from a sound source other than the one intended for pickup.

Leslie speaker A wooden cabinet that contains a rotating speaker for the high frequencies and a rotating drum surrounding a woofer which together provide the modulation effect popular on Hammond organ sounds.

Limiter A signal-processing device used to constrict or reduce audio dynamics, reducing the loudest peaks in volume.

Low-end The lower end of the audio spectrum, or bass frequencies usually below 200 Hz.

Machine room A room specially designed to house the loud and hot tape machines. Keeping them out of the control room keeps the noise to a minimum.

Mastering The process of transferring the contents of a master tape or audio file to a different medium such as a vinyl record, CD, or MP3. In Europe it's considered the first stage of manufacturing while in the U.S. it's considered the last stage of the creative process.

Mastering engineer An engineer who transfers the contents of a master tape or audio file to a different medium such as a vinyl record, CD, or MP3.

Mid-range Middle frequencies between around 250 Hz up to 4000 Hz (or 4 kHz).

Mono Short for monaural, or single audio playback channel.

Monaural A term used to describe a mix that contains a single channel and usually comes from only one speaker.

MP3 The standard data compression format used to make digital audio files smaller in size.

Muddy Non-distinct because of excessive low frequencies.

Mute An on/off switch found on a mixing console. To mute the signal means to turn it off.

Out of phase A miswiring of the polarity of one of a set of speakers which makes one speaker push outwards while the other is pulling inwards when a signal is applied. This causes dips in the audio frequency spectrum and is very undesirable.

Pan Short for panorama, pan indicates the left or right position of an instrument within the stereo spectrum.

Panning Moving a sound across the stereo spectrum.

Parametric equalizer A tone control where the gain, frequency, and bandwidth are all variable.

Phase The relationship between two separate sound signals when combined into one.

Pilot tone A steady oscillator tone recorded onto a tape machine track that was used in the early days of recording for syncing multiple tape machines together.

Points Short for percentage points. Refers to the royalty rate an artist or producer gets on the sales of a record.

Presence Accentuated upper mid-range frequencies (anywhere from 5–10 kHz).

Producer The music equivalent of a movie director, the producer has the ability to craft the songs of an artist or band technically, sonically, and musically.

Pumping When the level of a mix increases, then decreases noticeably. Pumping is caused by the improper setting of the attack and release times on a compressor or limiter.

Record A generic term for the physical manifestation of a recording. Regardless of whether it's vinyl, a CD, or a digital file, it is still known as a record.

Recording desk A recording console, the main audio routing and processing device in a recording studio.

Return Inputs on a recording console specially dedicated for effects devices such as reverbs and delays. The return inputs are usually not as sophisticated as normal channel inputs on a console.

Score The paper that contains the musical notation for every musical instrument in a group; most commonly used for orchestral instruments.

Second engineer Another name for an assistant engineer.

Sel-sync Short for selective synchronisation, the process of using the record head to play back some tracks while simultaneously recording on others. This keeps the newly recorded material in sync with the previously recorded material.

Source An original master that is not a copy or a clone.

Stems A mix that's broken down into multiple elements to give the mastering engineer more control when mastering. Also used extensively in film mixing.

Sync The act of synchronising two tape machines together.

Tea towel A very thin dish towel.

Tempo The speed, or timing, of a piece of music.

Test tape A tape containing oscillator tones at standardised levels used to align the playback levels of a magnetic tape recorder.

Time code An audio code recorded onto a track of a tape recorder that provides a way to synchronise multiple tape recorders to the same location on the tape.

Top-end See *High-end*.

Tracking room The room or studio where the principal recording takes place.

Track A term sometimes used to mean a song. In recording, a track is a separate musical performance recorded onto a multitrack audio recorder.

Varispeed A control on later generation tape recorders that allowed the speed to be varied from the standard 7½, 15, or 30 ips for effects or to correct timing or pitch issues.

VSO Variable speed oscillator. In the early days of magnetic tape recorders, a VSO was used to vary the speed of a tape recorder from the preset speeds of 7½, 15, or 30 ips to create effects or to correct timing or pitch issues.

Photograph Credits

TEXT AND INSERT ILLUSTRATIONS

P1.1............. Andy Ameden

1.1............... Peter Kettwig

1.2............... EMI Archives

1.3............... EMI Archives

1.4............... EMI Archives

1.5............... EMI Archives

2.1............... EMI Archives

2.2............... EMI Archives

2.3............... Source Unknown

2.4............... Ken Scott

2.5............... Ken Scott

2.6............... Ken Scott

2.7............... Ken Scott

2.9............... Nick Mason

2.10............. EMI Archives

4.1............... Ken Scott

4.2............... Ken Scott

4.3............... Source Unknown

6.1............... Source Unknown

7.7............... Brian Gibson

9.1............... Source Unknown

9.2............... Source Unknown

9.3............... Source Unknown

9.4............... Photograph by Richard DiLello

9.5............... Photograph by Richard DiLello

9.6.............. Source Unknown

9.7.............. Gerry Beckley

9.8.............. Ken Scott

9.9.............. Ken Scott

9.10............. Source Unknown

10.1............. Source Unknown

11.1............. Source Unknown

13.1............. Source Unknown

15.1............. Joe Stevens

15.2............. Source Unknown

15.3............. Source Unknown

17.1............. Jasen Emmons @
Experience Music Project

18.1............. Redferns

20.1............. Source Unknown

21.1............. Source Unknown

24.1............. Source Unknown

25.1............. Terry Bozzio

25.2............. Ken Scott

26.1............. Source Unknown

26.2............. Source Unknown

26.3............. Ken Scott

27.1............. Playgirl

28.1............. Source Unknown

28.2............. Mike Lindup

ADDITIONAL IMAGES

A.............. Ken Scott

B .... Photographer: Linda McCartney, © Paul McCartney

C.............. Photographer: Linda McCartney, © Paul McCartney

D.............. Photographer: Linda McCartney, © Paul McCartney

E .... © Apple Corps Ltd.

F.............. Gilead Limor

G............. David Hodge

H .... Photo copyright Mick Rock 1973, 2012

I .... Source Unknown

J .... Mike Banks

Discography

Band/Artist	Title	Release Date	Produced (P) or Engineered (E)
America	*America*	1971	E
The Aynsley Dunbar Retaliation	*The Aynsley Dunbar Retaliation*	1969	E
David Batteau	*Happy in Hollywood*	1976	P&E
Beatles	*Magical Mystery Tour*	1967	E
Beatles	*The Beatles (White Album)*	1968	E
Jeff Beck	*Truth*	1968	E
Jeff Beck	*There and Back*	1980	P&E
The Big O	*"Monster Mash"*	1988	P&E
David Bowie	*Man of Words/Man of Music (Space Oddity)*	1969	E
David Bowie	*The Man Who Sold the World*	1970	E
David Bowie	*Hunky Dory*	1971	P&E
David Bowie	*The Rise and Fall of Ziggy Stardust and the Spiders from Mars*	1972	P&E
David Bowie	*Aladdin Sane*	1973	P&E

Band/Artist	Title	Release Date	Produced (P) or Engineered (E)
David Bowie	Ziggy Stardust and the Spiders from Mars (movie)	1973	E
David Bowie	Pinups	1973	P&E
Petula Clark	Now	1972	E
Stanley Clarke	Stanley Clarke	1974	P&E
Stanley Clarke	Journey to Love	1975	P&E
Stanley Clarke	School Days	1976	P&E
Billy Cobham	Spectrum	1973	P&E
Billy Cobham	Crosswinds	1974	P&E
Billy Cobham	Total Eclipse	1974	P&E
Billy Cobham	Shabazz	1975	P&E
dada	dada	1992	E
dada	Puzzle	1992	P&E
Devo	Duty Now for the Future	1979	P&E
Sacha Distel	[unknown]	ca. 1970	E
Dixie Dregs	What If	1978	P&E
Dixie Dregs	Night of the Living Dregs	1979	P&E
Duran Duran	Thank You	1995	E
Duran Duran	Pop Trash	2000	E
Gamma	Gamma 1	1979	P&E
Jan Hammer & Jerry Goodman	Like Children	1975	P&E
Happy the Man	Happy the Man	1977	P&E
Happy the Man	Crafty Hands	1978	P&E
Hard Meat	Hard Meat	1970	E
Don Harrison	Not Far from Free	1977	P&E
George Harrison	Wonderwall	1968	E
George Harrison	All Things Must Pass	1970	E
Hellion	The Witching Hour	1999	P&E
Mary Hopkin	Postcard	1969	E
Mary Hopkin	Earth Song/Ocean Song	1971	E

Band/Artist	Title	Release Date	Produced (P) or Engineered (E)
Elton John	Madman across the Water	1971	E
Elton John	Honky Château	1972	E
Elton John	Don't Shoot Me I'm Only the Piano Player	1973	E
Davey Johnstone	Smiling Face	1973	E
Kaja	Crazy Peoples Right to Speak	1985	P&E
Kansas	Vinyl Confessions	1982	P&E
Jonathan Kelly	Wait til They Change the Backdrop	1973	P&E
Al Kooper	New York City (You're a Woman)	1971	E
John Lennon	"Give Peace a Chance"	1969	E
John Lennon	"Cold Turkey"	1969	E
Level 42	True Colours	1983	P&E
Linda Lewis	Say No More...	1971	E
Lindisfarne	Fog on the Tyne	1971	E
Lord Sitar	Lord Sitar	1968	E
Mahavishnu Orchestra	Birds of Fire	1972	E
Mahavishnu Orchestra	The Lost Trident Sessions	1973	P&E
Mahavishnu Orchestra	Visions of the Emerald Beyond	1974	P&E
Michalski & Oosterveen	M & O	1979	P&E
Missing Persons	Missing Persons	1982	P&E
Missing Persons	Spring Session M	1982	P&E
Tim Moore	High Contrast	1979	P&E
The New Seekers	"I'd Like to Teach the World to Sing"	1971	E
Harry Nilsson	Son of Schmilsson	1972	E
Pilot	Pilot	1974	P&E

Band/Artist	Title	Release Date	Produced (P) or Engineered (E)
Pink Floyd	"Apples and Oranges"/"Paintbox"	1967	E
Pink Floyd	"A Saucerful of Secrets"	1968	E
Principal Edwards Magic Theatre	Soundtrack	1969	E
Procol Harum	A Salty Dog	1969	E
The RadhaKrsna Temple	RadhaKrsna Temple	1971	E
The Rads	Life's a Gamble	1984	P&E
Lou Reed	Transformer	1972	E
The Rolling Stones	Sticky Fingers	1971	E
Rubber Rodeo	Heartbreak Highway	1986	P&E
The Scaffold	L the P	1969	
The Shadows	"Slaughter on 10th Avenue"	1969	E
Jamie Sheriff	No Heroes	1980	P&E
Ringo Starr	"It Don't Come Easy"	1971	E
Supertramp	Crime of the Century	1974	P&E
Supertramp	Crisis? What Crisis?	1975	P&E
Patrick Swayze & Larry Gatlin	"Brothers"	1989	P&E
Third Ear Band	Alchemy	1969	E
3D	3D	1980	P&E
Doris Troy	"Ain't That Cute"	1970	E
The Tubes	Young and Rich	1976	P&E
Van der Graaf Generator	Pawn Hearts	1971	E
Rick Wakeman	The Six Wives of Henry VIII	1973	E
Whiteheart	Inside	1995	P&E

Index

Scaffold, The, 76

School Days, 283, 287

Scorpio Sound, 242

Scott, Cheryl, XII, 74, 113, 345, 367, 368, 369, 375, 377

Sears, Elliott, XII, 200, 201, 204, 205, 206, 210, 211, 212, 213, 214

Secret Agent Man, 276

Sgt. Pepper's, 27, 29, 30, 57, 63, 70, 71, 87, 118

Sheffield, Barry, 33, 100, 108, 111, 119, 134, 136, 145, 179, 196, 239, 241

Sheffield, Norman, XI, 95, 97, 118, 136, 179, 240, 241, 371

Short, Steven, 371

Siebenberg, Bob, XII, 69, 90, 228, 229, 230, 234, 235, 236, 246, 249. 251, 252, 255, 260, 262, 381

Sklar, Lee, XII, 207

Smith, John, XII, 39, 41, 42, 48, 51, 58, 59, 60, 63, 93, 125

Smith, Legs Larry, 151

Smith, Norman, XI, 13, 14, 20, 28, 71, 72, 73, 74, 75, 82

Soapbox Opera, 252, 257

Something, XVI, XVII, 48, 53

Sorrow, 180

Sound Techniques, 99, 104, 105, 126, 127, 140

Space Oddity, 134, 137

Spanish Phases, 224, 225

Spector, Phil, 4, 101, 102, 103, 108, 110, 111, 113, 114, 266, 373

Spector, Ronnie, 108, 110, 111

Spiders from Mars, 137, 162, 165, 169, 174, 177, 178, 184, 381

Spooner, Bill, XII, 266, 267, 268, 271, 272

Spring Session M, 326

Stage Fright, 112

Stagge, Alan, 91, 92, 93, 94

Stairway to Heaven, 278

Stanshall, Viv, 120

Starman, 159, 160, 162, 163

Starr, Ringo, 10, 14, 19, 31, 32, 33, 35, 42, 48, 49, 51, 52, 54, 55, 66, 68, 69, 89, 99, 102, 107, 108, 124, 214, 252, 263, 374

STC 4038, 35, 104, 140, 207, 270, 271

Stewart, Rod, 76, 77

Sticky Fingers, 129

Stranger in a Strange Land, 185, 186

Studer 4-Track, 20, 44, 61, 104, 379

Studer J 37, 61

Studio 1, 10, 30, 47, 48, 82, 86, 87, 121

Studio 2, 4, 5, 6, 7, 10, 20, 32, 34, 47, 48, 49, 50, 52, 76, 88, 89, 257, 288, 361

Studio 3, 10, 11, 13, 32, 127, 186

Studio D, 250, 252, 259, 263, 266, 284, 285

Styles, Re, 268

Wild, Chuck, 309

Williams, Tony, 207, 224, 283, 288, 324

Wilson, B.J., 89, 150

Winkler, Henry, 265

Wonderwall, 86, 87

Wood, Ron, 77

Woodmansey, Woody, XII, 134, 135, 137, 138, 141, 143, 158, 166, 176, 381

Words, 10, 34, 130, 134, 307, 312, 316, 321, 322, 325, 333, 348

Yer Blues, 10, 52, 53

Young and Rich, 266, 267, 271

Your Mother Should Know, 28, 29

Zappa, Frank, 260, 303, 336, 360

Zappa, Gail, 303

Zappa, Moon, 321

Ziggy Stardust, I, III, VIII, 153, 154, 161, 162, 177, 228, 381

Zimmerman, Don, 316, 317, 325, 327, 355